THE POLITICAL WRITINGS

OF SAMUEL PUFENDORF

The Political Writings
of Samuel Pufendorf

EDITED BY

Craig L. Carr

TRANSLATED BY

Michael J. Seidler

New York   Oxford
OXFORD UNIVERSITY PRESS
1994

Oxford University Press

Oxford New York Toronto
Delhi Bombay Calcutta Madras Karachi
Kuala Lumpur Singapore Hong Kong Tokyo
Nairobi Dar es Salaam Cape Town
Melbourne Auckland Madrid

and associated companies in
Berlin Ibadan

Library of Congress Cataloging-in-Publication Data
Pufendorf, Samuel, Freiherr von, 1632–1694.
[Selections. English]
The political writings of Samuel Pufendorf / Samuel Pufendorf :
edited by Craig L. Carr : translated by Michael J. Seidler.
p.   cm.   Translated from Latin.
Includes bibliographical references and index.
ISBN 0-19-506560-3
1. Natural law. 2. Political science—Philosophy. 3. State, The.
I. Carr, Craig, L., 1948– . II. Title.
K457.P8A2 1994   340'.112—dc20   93-10249

1 3 5 7 9 8 6 4 2

Printed in the United States of America
on acid-free paper

Contents

Elements of Universal Jurisprudence
in Two Books

BOOK II

On the Law of Nature and of Nations
in Eight Books

THE POLITICAL WRITINGS

OF SAMUEL PUFENDORF

Editor's Introduction

Samuel Pufendorf was one of the most prominent political and legal thinkers of the seventeenth century. His stature as an intellectual figure of some historical importance has long been understood by students of natural law, who remember him as the architect and systematizer of the modern natural law tradition begun by Grotius. His reputation has grown in recent times, however, as scholars in diverse fields have begun to explore his influence on the Enlightenment, classical liberalism, and modern jurisprudence. Yet, as the work of someone who labored to demonstrate how it is possible to live with political authority, and why it is not possible to live well without it, Pufendorf's political philosophy also remains most pertinent for anyone who wonders about the ethical legitimacy and practical necessity of the modern state. He intended his political thought to be, at least in part, a response and corrective to what he considered the cynicism and excesses of Thomas Hobbes. He strongly opposed the methodological individualism that he correctly understood to be a central feature of Hobbes's political thought, and he labored to developed an alternative view inspired, in large measure, by the Grotian notion of sociality. Contemporary students of politics can thus find in Pufendorf an alternative to Hobbesian and liberal individualism built upon a distinctive vision of human sociality.

Pufendorf was born in 1632 in a rural region of old Saxony. As a young man, he entertained thoughts of following his father and entering the Lutheran pastorate, but a taste of orthodox theology during his student years at Leipzig sent him in more philosophical directions. While this early experience left him with a desire to avoid the limitations of Lutheran orthodoxy, it did not alter the religious orientation of his thought. But it did leave him sufficiently dissatisfied with theological traditionalism to be receptive to new and emergent philosophical methods that would eventually guide his political theory.

By his own admission, Pufendorf was an eclectic thinker, both in terms of methodological style and field of interest.[1] His intellectual endeavors ranged beyond moral and political thought to theology, history, anthropology, law, and even political sociology. But eclecticism also aptly characterizes a lifetime of situation

---

[1] Pufendorf to Thomasius, June 19, 1688, in Konrad Varentrapp, ed., "Briefe von Pufendorf," *Historische Zeitschrift*, 70 (1893), p. 31.

and career changes that mirror his intellectual meanderings. Following six years of study at Leipzig, he left for Jena (1656) and there fell under the spell of the rationalist mathematician and philosopher Erhard Weigel. Under Weigel's influence, he developed his interest in moral and political thought and undertook the challenge of building a new natural law doctrine upon a rationalist foundation. He took as his first premise the idea that God has bestowed upon humankind a certain "light of the mind" in the form of sound reason (*sana ratio*) that allows humankind, if judiciously exercised and observed, to forge its own future and escape its own folly (DJN, I,1,2). Through the exercise of sound reason, humankind can gain insight into the law God has ordained to govern human affairs, an insight that permits human beings to appreciate the necessity—or rationality—of the social conventions that have emerged through time.

Upon leaving Jena (1658), Pufendorf took a position as tutor to the family of Baron Peter Julius Coyet, the Swedish minister in Denmark. He had no sooner arrived in Copenhagen when the already poor relations between Sweden and Denmark degenerated into war and Pufendorf was tossed into a Danish prison. He put this time to good use, however, writing from behind prison bars the text of his first major work in political theory, *Elementorum jurisprudentiae universalis* (*Elements of Universal Jurisprudence*), which he eventually published in 1660. Following his dreary experiences in Denmark and a brief stay in Holland, Pufendorf returned to Germany and took a position on the philosophy faculty at Heidelberg (1661). Nine years later he was off again, this time to Sweden where he had been offered a position on the faculty of the University of Lund. At Lund his thoughts were devoted exclusively to political thought, and he soon completed and published (1672) his most important work, *De jure naturae et gentium* (*On the Law of Nature and of Nations*), along with a short summary of this work designed to be used as a text, *De officio hominis et civis juxta legem naturalem* (*On the Duty of Man and Citizen According to Natural Law*), which appeared in 1673.[2] The latter work proved remarkably successful and served in its role as text on the fundamentals of natural law for over a century.

In 1676, Pufendorf's career, along with his intellectual focus, took a change of course. He managed to be appointed royal historiographer to the Swedish Court, and with this his scholarly concerns changed to history. He remained in this position for ten years—a long stay for him—before returning to Germany to assume similar duties at the court of The Great Elector of Brandenburg, Frederick William. In 1694, Pufendorf again ventured to Sweden to retrieve a manuscript confiscated by the Swedish crown upon his leaving for Germany. His success at prying the hostage manuscript loose proved a pyrrhic victory. He took ill as a consequence of the rigors of the journey and died in the fall of 1694.[3]

---

[2]For a new edition and English translation of this work, see Samuel Pufendorf, *On the Duty of Man and Citizen According to Natural Law*, ed. James Tully, trans. Michael Silverthorne (Cambridge: Cambridge University Press, 1991).

[3]For a more thorough biographical sketch of Pufendorf, see Michael Seidler's introduction to Seidler, ed., *Samuel Pufendorf's "On the Natural State of Men"* (Lewiston, NY: The Edwin Mellen Press, 1990); see also Horst Denzer, *Moralphilosophie und Naturrecht bei Samuel Pufendorf* (Munich: C. H. Beck, 1972).

The main corpus of Pufendorf's political thought is composed of eight works. Along with *Elementorum* (EJU), *De jure* (DJN), and *De officio* (DOH), this body of work includes *De statu imperii germanici* (*On the Constitution of the German Empire*), published in 1667 under the pseudonym Severinus de Monzambano; *Dissertationes academicae selectiores* (*Select Academic Dissertations*), published in 1675; *Specimen controversiarum* (*A Sample of Controversies*), published in 1677; *Eris Scandica* (*Scandinavian Polemics*), which appeared in 1686; and *Einleitung zu der Historie der vornehmsten Reiche und Staaten so itziger Zeit in Europa sich befinden* (*Introduction to the History of the Principal Empires and States Presently Existing in Europe*), published between 1682 and 1686. The present volume is limited to excerpts from his two most important and thorough contributions to political theory: EJU and DJN.

The extraordinary differences that separate these two works are (perhaps unhappily) minimized by the editing process. While EJU is a shorter piece, committed to a rationalist methodology, that moves along with a certain ease and flow of argument, DJN is a much longer, greatly labored, meticulously referenced, and exhaustively argued work. EJU begins with a conceptual analysis that yields a series of definitions (twenty-one in all) intended to serve as the foundation for two axioms, or basic principles, of morality. From these principles Pufendorf "derives" five observations, presented in propositional form, that state a set of conclusions about the nature of morality and political life. The work is faithful to Pufendorf's conviction that a natural law theory free from both religious orthodoxy and Aristotelian traditionalism was needed to meet the new challenges of political legitimacy. The challenges he had in mind came from skepticism on the one hand and the intolerance associated with religious orthodoxy on the other. In the absence of an objective theory of law and politics capable of legitimating the emergent state and justifying the presence of political authority, political association would almost invariably decay to a contest of belief and an accompanying struggle for power. As Pufendorf understood, such a condition would merely exacerbate the insecurity and conflict that the state system promised to transcend.

Yet the abstract, rationalist style of EJU proved unable to establish the solid foundation for the first principles of natural law that Pufendorf wished to defend. The assertion of these principles based solely upon sound, albeit abstract reason could only persuade those already dedicated to the superiority of the rational method over more theological, traditional, or historical modes of inquiry. Pufendorf took to heart the welter of criticisms his early work generated and set about, in response, to construct a methodological viewpoint that would remain faithful to the idea of sound reason and yet provide the systematic rigor required to achieve the desired synthesis between his rationalism, on the one hand, and religious orthodoxy and Aristotelian traditionalism, on the other.[4] His solution to these methodological difficulties—forthcoming in DJN—was to generate a dialogue between the demands of sound reason and the insights of ancient and contemporary authorities on moral

---

[4]Timothy Hochstrasser, "The Foundations of the History of Morality: Samuel von Pufendorf and the Invention of a Tradition," written for The Workshop on Modern Natural Law, convened by Istvan Hont and Hans Erich Bodeker, Max Planck Institute for History, Göttingen, Germany (June 26–30, 1989), pp. 26-28.

and political matters, as recognized by the traditions of theology, law, history, and philosophy. Classic and contemporary texts were culled with care to discover instances where they could be used to supplement, reinforce, or illustrate the requirements of sound reason, and in turn sound reason was used at times to expose and correct the errors, confusions, and contradictions on display in these texts.

The result is an exceptionally thorough and meticulously, if not always consistently, argued theory of political legitimacy. DJN contains both a defense of Pufendorf's version of modern natural law—a theory that develops the view that natural law is imposed by God upon human beings and is not built into them in the form of intrinsic dispositions—and an elaborate discussion of the logic of human development from a natural, or non-civil, condition to the emergence of the modern state. Throughout the text, Pufendorf labors to place the logic of political association within the larger context of humankind's social, economic, and legal development. This leads him to discuss and examine in tedious detail the emergence of the family, the rise of private ownership, and the nature of the socio-economic forces that inform the challenges of political association.

Much of this detail, most of the nearly 6,000 citations,[5] a great deal of Pufendorf's anthropology, and a large amount of the argument that had relevance only in the seventeenth century are the necessary casualties of editing. The editorial objective has been to provide the reader with a readable and comprehensive introduction to Pufendorf's moral and political thought by reducing both EJU and DJN to their basic points and fundamental arguments. The passages from EJU serve both as an introduction to Pufendorf's political project and as a supplement to the more laborious argument of DJN. Despite their methodological differences, the substantive elements of the two works are generally consistent. Readers should also be able to discern the moves Pufendorf makes to strengthen his overall argument in those rare cases where the argument of DJN diverges from his positions in EJU. To be sure, Pufendorf develops his basic political themes with greater precision, and with a stronger understanding of the complexity of the problems he is addressing, in his more mature work. In some areas, however, precision is achieved at the expense of increased confusion, and here the selections from EJU can guide the reader through the text of DJN.

Man, Politics, and Society

Pufendorf constructed his political theory at the dawn of the modern nation-state following the Peace of Westphalia in 1648. Like both Hobbes and Grotius, his more illustrious predecessors, he looked to the state as the primary vehicle of order and stability in social life. He shared their view that social prosperity and economic development could progress only in the presence of a state system capable of maintaining internal order and tranquillity and international peace and security. The defense of this point constitutes the first stage of his theory of political legitimacy.

[5]Horst Denzer, "Pufendorf," in Hans Maier, Heinz Rausch, and Horst Denzer, eds., *Klassiker des Politischen Denkens*, 2 vols. (Munich: C. H. Beck, 1968), vol. 1, p. 42.

Pufendorf took inspiration from Hobbes's effort to raise law and politics to a scientific level and establish with certainty the need for the state. But he rejected Hobbesian methodological individualism and cynicism, and in his own words, "fought against Hobbes at close quarters."[6] By way of refuting Hobbes, he endeavored to build a scientific—and hence objective—theory of politics upon the notion of human sociality. However, his convictions about the necessity of the state did not detract from his realization that the state itself posed a fundamental threat to the very order and security it was designed to promote. In fact, Pufendorf was one of the first to state the dilemma of modern politics:

> Here it is evident . . . that no form of commonwealth can be so precisely outfitted with laws that no disadvantage can, through the inattentiveness or wickedness of rulers, redound on the citizens from the very government established for their welfare. The reason for this is that supreme sovereignty was established in order to repel the evils threatening mortals from each other. But that very sovereignty had to be conferred on men, who are surely not immune from those vices which provoke men to molest one another. . . . (DJN, VII,5,22)

So, the second challenge of his theory of political legitimacy is to discuss whether it is possible to moderate the threat posed by sovereign authority and to examine whatever rights citizens hold against their sovereign that might conceivably justify resistance.

He achieves his first objective—the defense of civil association—by means of the systematic development of a natural law theory coupled with an anthropology (intended to replace Hobbes's reliance upon physiology and psychology) devoted to the historical manifestation of human sociality. While the appeal to natural law establishes that human beings must comprehend sociality as a fundamental law of nature binding on all persons at all times, his anthropology illustrates how this natural law requirement has come to be concretely implemented through the emergence of specific social conventions.[7] His second objective is achieved, on the other hand, by means of independent but reinforcing theories of limited sovereignty, civic responsibility, and civic education. Although Pufendorf is sufficiently realistic to recognize that there is no ultimate guarantee against possible sovereign tyranny, his argument advances the search for legitimacy by introducing the need for constitutional or structural limits upon sovereign authority, and by illustrating how an informed and astute citizenry can contribute to a just and stable polity.

Natural Law and Obligation

It is difficult to underestimate the importance of God in Pufendorf's political thought. He refused, for example, to countenance even for the sake of argument

---

[6]Samuel Pufendorf, *De jure naturae et gentium, libri octo, . . . accedit Eris Scandica*, ed. Gottfried Mascovius (Lausanne & Geneva: Marcus-Michael Bousquet, 1744), vol. 2, p. 341 (trans. by Michael J. Seidler).

[7]Cf. Stephen Buckle, *Natural Law and the Theory of Property: Grotius to Hume* (Oxford: The Clarendon Press, 1991), p. 67.

the possibility that God does not exist, and he went so far as to chide Grotius for his decision to entertain, albeit hypothetically, this very possibility (DJN, II,3,19). He understood that natural law argument slides easily toward secularism once it is divorced from Christian faith. If God becomes ancillary to reason as a lawgiver, then faith in reason and philosophy replace religion as the final source of epistemic certainty. But any such slide will inevitably erode natural law and consequently disrupt the ability to construct an objective science of law and politics.

No doubt this is a fitting attitude for the son of a Lutheran minister, but Pufendorf's insistence upon God's pivotal role in any conception of the natural law is not simply a matter of religious conviction. He embraces the traditional jurisprudential view that law is the command of a superior will; there can be no law without a sovereign legislator possessing the right to command (DJN, I,6,4). Law, in turn, is an institution used to order and coordinate the relations of objects and subjects; without law, and therefore without some sovereign to impose the law on its subjects, there is only chaos. So, if natural law exists—and reason informs us that it does—then there must also be a divine Legislator; for the legislator is conceptually prior to the law.

Pufendorf has still another use for God in his theory of natural law. Again following traditional jurisprudence, Pufendorf further understands law to constrain a rational being's will or to restrict freedom of choice. Subjection to law means standing under an obligation to obey. But his understanding of obligation is somewhat tighter than the one on display in contemporary moral and political discourse. He believed that two conditions must be met for someone to stand under an obligation: the requirement of obedience must be both rationally compelling and effective (EJU, I,df.XII,14; DJN, I,5,5 & 12). Law is compelling if it promotes the good; this supplies a reason for a rational being to subscribe to it. There is of course no question about whether the natural law promotes the good; the insights of sound reason remove all doubts on this score. The effectiveness of an obligation, on the other hand, resides in the power of a superior to enforce compliance with some obligatory act; consequently the command of someone who lacks the power to coerce others into obedience fails to qualify as law even if the commanded action has moral value (EJU, I,df.XII,16). The natural law qualifies as law, then, because God does double duty as the divine Legislator and Executor of the law.

It is perhaps understandable that Pufendorf should model his vision of the natural law after domestic legal systems. The terms we use to conceptualize a legal system fix what it is possible to understand a legal system to be, regardless of whether we imagine it in a civil or natural context. Yet there is a limit to the extent the analogy can be pressed. While civil laws are made known through statutes, Pufendorf subscribes to the standard natural law view that God's law cannot be known—or cannot be known in its entirety—in this fashion. Instead, he imagines that insight into the natural law is achieved by rationally reflecting upon the human condition. Pufendorf wants us to understand the resultant insights of reason as natural laws, for only if we do so can we establish a science of politics capable of objectivity. Only the commands of a superior sovereign can obligate. If the insights of reason are advanced as merely prudent ideas, they cannot obligate; and they are therefore subject to rejection by those whose beliefs or traditions carry them in alternative directions.

This point has considerable importance for Pufendorf's political thought. One way to theorize in the face of contesting traditions and belief systems (a way imagined by Hobbes) is to identify a basic ground or Archimedean point epistemologically prior to whatever convictions might accompany any given belief system. Epistemic primacy presumably guarantees universal acceptance of the Archimedean point and so the next task is to rationally deduce or infer certain conclusions from the Archimedean point which must then also seem rationally compelling. Pufendorf was wary of this—now rather popular—method of theorizing. Any effort to identify such an Archimedean point will seem arbitrary and unpersuasive to a group whose belief system or traditions counsel in favor of something else. Instead of establishing neutral ground, the identification of an Archimedean point will likely only generate a new belief system and thus succeed only in adding another voice to the squabble.

A second way to theorize is to look for some universal agreement or common base shared by all contending belief systems and traditions. This leaves tradition and customary belief in place and does not require that they be bracketed off. The idea of God as the Supreme Being fulfills this latter objective for Pufendorf. By linking the insights of reason to God's law, Pufendorf is able to achieve the common ground that would be lacking in any theory that simply claims its conclusions to be objective because "rational." Since there can be no such common ground without God, faith must be prior to theory. But faith also gives a point and purpose to theory. The basic belief in a loving God directs the student of philosophy to inquire into those fundamental laws God has ordained to govern humankind; for this is a job for human reason.

Pufendorf's most important theoretical task is to establish his notion of human sociality as the first principle of the law God has imposed upon humankind. To avoid the pitfalls of orthodoxy, this principle must be deduced from the human condition using reason alone. In EJU, he introduces two basic observations about the human condition (II,obs.IV,4). First and following Hobbes, he claims that humans are motivated by a self-love that inclines them toward self-preservation and the promotion of their well-being. Second—and now following Grotius—he insists that humans need the society of others in order to sustain themselves and to enhance their well-being. The complementarity of these two insights is clear: if humans need others to sustain themselves and flourish, then associating with others is the obvious thing to do. In DJN, the requirement of sociality is directly inferred from the apparent paradox of humankind's social dependency coupled with its asocial tendencies:

> Man, it is clearly apparent, is an animal most eager to preserve himself, essentially in need, ill-equipped to maintain himself without the aid of those who are like him, and very well suited for the mutual promotion of advantages. All the same, he is often malicious, insolent, easily annoyed, and both ready and able to inflict harm. For this kind of animal to be safe and enjoy the goods that befall his worldly condition, it is necessary that he be sociable. (DJN, II,3,15)

The rational acknowledgment of each person's inescapable need for the society of others is put forward as the basic principle of natural law; "Any man must, inasmuch as he can, cultivate and maintain toward others a peaceable sociality that is consistent with the native character and end of humankind in general" (DJN, II,3,15). By drawing such a tight association between individualist and societal visions of humankind, Pufendorf constructs an alternative to methods of theorizing that see pre-civil humans in an isolated and largely independent condition. To consider our own self-preservation requires us also to appreciate the degree to which it is linked to our association with others. As individuals we naturally desire to preserve ourselves, but self-preservation is possible only through our association with others. Therefore, human beings must be regarded as social creatures.

The point expressed in Pufendorf's basic principle of natural law is undoubtedly a good idea. But the strength of his argument depends upon his ability to convince his readers that this is also a command of God; for only if it is recognized as such can it qualify as an obligatory natural law. By refusing to allow reason to carry independent normative force, he commits himself to a theory that demands a theological presence. But in the absence of such a commitment, Pufendorf offers no reason to think that it is possible to construct a viable natural law theory. There can be no natural law without a natural lawgiver.

Pufendorf's Anthropology and Humankind's Natural State

To establish the legitimacy of the emergent state system, Pufendorf needs to demonstrate that the civil state is required by natural law or that the move to civil association is necessary in order to promote the ends of sociality for some group of individuals. His own theory of sociality complicates this since he cannot simply imagine that social life is the proper remedy for certain defects of the human character and then insist, as Hobbes had done, that civil association is the necessary condition for bringing social life into being. If humans need society in order to preserve themselves, then society must be a constant feature of human history since humans have managed to preserve themselves. Social life must therefore be prior to the emergence of political units, and if social life is possible without political association, one wonders why the move to a state system has become necessary in the strong fashion required by natural law.

To make his case, Pufendorf adopts a two-pronged strategy. First he imagines a hypothetical natural condition—a condition typified by the absence of any artificial or conventional authority relations—that enables him to identify the basic moral relations that hold naturally among human beings. This imagined natural state provides Pufendorf with an analytical device with which to display the fundamental moral rghts and obligations individuals enjoy under natural law. But he develops alongside this analytical device an anthropological account of humankind's social development. His account, culminating in the need for civil association, characterizes the way the ideals of natural law come to exemplify themselves in human history. The Hegelian sound of this is not misleading; Pufendorf's argument is a justification of social and political developments based upon the belief that they advance the end of human sociality.

The fit between the moral vision that emerges from Pufendorf's hypothetical natural state and his anthropology is not always comfortable. While he employs many of the traditional tools of the social contract tradition, his use of such notions as consent and natural freedom is frequently tortured. Because human beings are subject to the will of God, natural freedom is circumscribed by the law of nature. So, humankind's hypothetical natural condition is typified by the absence of any *earthly* or secular authority. The only rule governing the relationships among persons, in this imagined state, is the natural law requirement of sociality. But Pufendorf's natural law does not tell us exactly how to be social; it only commands that we be sociable. The emergence of conventional relations that give substance to the notion of sociality is thus entirely consonant with natural law, but in accordance with natural freedom, they can have currency only if they are consented to by all participating parties.

Pufendorf follows legal tradition in identifying two methods for expressing the consent necessary for the establishment of a conventional relationship between persons: pacts and contracts. He reserves the notion of a contract for commercial agreements and transactions only and uses the term 'pact' to describe all other types of voluntary agreements and arrangements. But the claim that all conventional arrangements and practices must be the product of some anterior pact or contract gives rise to an obvious problem that typically plagues consent theory. The customs and conventions in which we participate are, for the most part, simply present for us; as we grow from childhood to adulthood we are socialized into them and we almost invariably come to take them for granted. Rarely, if ever, does one ponder their social viability, moral validity, or logical necessity and render an official decision to consent to them. This problem is particularly troubling for Pufendorf, who wants both to explain and to justify existing social arrangements by reconciling them with natural law.

His remedy for this problem makes it necessary to qualify severely his standing as a consent theorist. He approaches the question of consent occasionally in historical and occasionally in analytic terms. This mixture of strategy suggests that he believed only those social arrangements and conventions logically and practically necessary for the pursuit and development of social life actually come into being. For Pufendorf, social customs are composed of shared and necessarily learned rules that structure and organize social life, rules that are explicable in terms of the rights and obligations they bring into being. Rules of this sort can exist of course only if they are recognized, understood, and accepted by those subject to them. Because human beings need one another to sustain themselves and because this need can be met only through the acceptance of customary rules that constitute and coordinate social life, Pufendorf concludes that people have embraced rule-based associations from the earliest times forward. Such rules are thus understandable as a conscious effort to implement the natural law requirement of sociality and construct coordinated systems of association or societies.

Seen historically, the social customs that emerge simply implement a division of labor and role differentiation, considered necessary and logical at some given historical moment, in order to promote sociality and human flourishing. The need for such divisions gives rise to customary practices and authority relations to which people are presumed to consent (tacitly or otherwise) in the face of this need. Seen analytically, however, the enhancement of sociality and flourishing that is realized by social custom and convention continues to provide reason for new generations to accept these practices. This reduces the question of consent to a matter of historical fact. For Pufendorf, existing social conventions must have emerged from general consent and acceptance; otherwise they could not have endured and gained their present status, that is, a mutually recognized, understood, and accepted system of rights and obligations. The apparent weakness of this argument could hardly have escaped Pufendorf's notice, but it does not particularly seem to bother him. In more candid moments he insists that if a given social arrangement promotes human sociality one should consent to it, and this is all that is required to establish an obligation to adhere to its rules.

So at best, consent serves only to legitimate the origin of social conventions and customary practices. Once in place, their continued legitimacy and obligatory character follow from their supposed contribution to sociality. Thus, the artificial authority relationships that come into being through consent do not require the express consent of future generations in order to be binding upon them, provided their continuation still contributes to human sociality. Pufendorf does not worry to any great degree, for example, about the need for future generations to consent expressly to sovereign authority before they can be said to have an obligation to obey the law. Because new-born members of the state benefit immediately from the presence of sovereign authority, their consent to this authority is simply assumed. (DJN, VII,2,20).

This is, to be sure, an odd-sounding consent argument. Pufendorf's attempt to situate consent historically is weak and unpersuasive. But this is disappointing only if one privileges Pufendorf's view of natural freedom and human equality over his anthropology, something Pufendorf himself does not do. When the inevitable tensions between these two elements of his theory become extreme, consent gives way to utility as the chief mechanism of defense and legitimacy, though he struggles, awkwardly at times, to have these two reinforce one another.

While this argument seems awkward by contemporary standards, it is not entirely without merit, and if it fails, its failure is instructive. Pufendorf wants to reconcile two separate ways of appreciating the human condition, both of which carry a considerable amount of moral importance. Since he is committed to the basic moral equality and natural freedom of persons, consent is a necessary component of his theory if he is to explain the emergence of social conventions and justify human authority relationships. But since he also sees humans as social beings whose social life is as old as humankind, he must also emphasize our socially situated existence. The integrity and necessity of at least some of these conventions—and here Pufendorf emphasizes property relationships, the family, and civil association—are fundamental aspects of human sociality to be supported, rather than challenged, by a theory of consent. Because we are social beings, and no longer creatures enjoying an initial condition of natural freedom, the role consent can and should play in our lives is severely mitigated and circumscribed by our social reality. Thus Pufendorf preserves a place for consent in his theory without also moving toward a position of social atomism. His dependency upon consent tends to be overwhelmed by the role that the socio-historical reality of our situatedness plays in his thought. But if we are to escape atomism and build a sense of ourselves as situated creatures into a theory of civil association, it is difficult to imagine how this could be otherwise.

Pufendorf completes his anthropology with a meticulous discussion of the emergence and development of property relationships and the family unit. The family unit is typified by the woman's acceptance of, and the child's recognition of, the authority of the male (DJN, VI,1,9; VI,2,4). As a basic social unit, the extended family is capable, in Pufendorf's view, of providing all the social assistance necessary for self-preservation; therefore, if all other things stand equal, the natural law requirement can be fulfilled by committing oneself to the health of the family. But things have not stood equal according to Pufendorf's anthropology. The emergence and growth of economic relations have brought with them a force that encourages humankind's propensity toward evil and exacerbates the natural human inclination toward ambition, vengeance, and "raging against" others (DJN, VII,1,4).

Pufendorf viewed the new economic order of his day as the ideal environment for these defects of the human character to grow and flourish; therefore, he believed it necessary to take appropriate precautions against them. Quite predictably, he imagines the proper precaution here to involve the move to civil society:

> Although the race of mortals is molested by various evils, its cleverness has devised a remedy against each one. Against the power of illnesses the arts of physicians have been invented; the harshness of climate and weather is resisted by means of dwellings, clothes, and fire; hunger is driven off by men's industrious cultivation of the earth; the ferocity of beasts is restrained by weapons and traps. But against those evils which humans, on account of their depraved character, enjoy directing against one another, the most effective remedy had to be sought from man himself, from men joined together into states and from the establishment of sovereignty. . . . And after men were so organized that they could be secure from mutual injuries, it easily followed that they had that much richer an enjoyment of the advantages that can come to men specifically from men. (DJN, VII,1,7)

Civil Society and Sovereign Authority

The socio-economic development characterized in Pufendorf's anthropology situates the problem of politics for Pufendorf and establishes the necessity of the state according to the principle of sociality. The problem a science of politics must now address involves demonstrating how the state can deliver on its promise to protect humans from themselves and cure the inclination toward evil. Pufendorf thinks the challenge here is primarily educational; it falls to political theory to enlighten us first on the character of civil association, and second on the nature and role of sovereign authority. If we are to believe Pufendorf, the necessary conditions for a just state depend upon the emergence of a citizenry and a sovereign who understand, according to the strictures of sound reason, the importance of civil association and the roles and responsibilities appropriate for each.

The move to civil society is an act of both unification and subjection. Because human beings are not fundamentally political animals in Pufendorf's estimation (DJN, VII,1,4), they must learn to appreciate the nature and consequences of their commitment to civil association. Entrance into civil society constitutes the formation of a body politic enjoying the status of a moral person and possessing one will in the form of sovereign authority. The newly constituted citizens stand in relation to one another as part to whole; yet to assure that each remains faithful to his commitment to all, a sovereign authority capable of enforcing each citizen's commitment is necessary. By conceptualizing the new state as a moral person, Pufendorf wants to demonstrate how it is possible to get the new associates on the same side, so to speak, and to identify their personal interests with the interests of the new community. Through unification, the variety of differences that otherwise separate persons from one another are transcended, and a sense of mutual identification valuable for political stability is generated (DJN, VII,2,5).

Pufendorf uses the familiar device of the social contract to illustrate the move from family units existing in a pre-civil condition to civil society. He uses it, moreover, both as a heuristic device and as a historical artifact. It facilitates his educational objectives by detailing the moral nature of civil association. He imagines a two-stage process involving the formation of two separate pacts (EJU, II,obs.V,2; DJN, VII,2,7–8). (In DJN he adds to the process an intervening decree allowing for a moment of constitutional design.) With the first pact, the future citizens come together and unite themselves into a single group for purposes of achieving security and promoting their collective welfare. The second pact completes the process through an act of subjection and a corresponding act of sovereign empowerment. With the introduction of the sovereign, a new authority relation emerges with the sovereign pledging to promote the security and welfare of the new state and the people, for their part, pledging obedience to the sovereign. Interestingly, Pufendorf also locates in this pact the moment of unification at which point the people become one moral person. So it is something more than a pact detailing the dual responsibilities of sovereign and citizen; it is also a constitutive moment that bonds previously disparate family units into a singular moral entity. From a moral perspective, of course, the two-stage contract is necessary to account for the surrender of natural freedom and the assumption of the duties of sovereign and/or subject—depending upon the form of government adopted by the community—associated with the transition to civil society. But as Pufendorf well knew, the historical need for such a justificatory claim is somewhat beside the point; given the presence and moral necessity of civil association, it matters only that the citizenry understand that the obligations of citizenship have replaced the opportunities of natural freedom.

Pufendorf's second educational task is rather more taxing, and yet here the merit and originality of his political thought are most on display. In order to mollify the potential dangers imaginable from the presence of sovereign authority, he needs to show how it is possible to blend the dual roles of citizen and sovereign together into a just and secure state. This requires considerable educating on the roles and responsibilities of both parties. He first examines the possibility of adopting structural safeguards against potential sovereign abuse. Next, he discusses the importance of political obligation and the required limits upon permissible citizen opposition to sovereign authority. Finally, he turns to the job of the sovereign whose responsibilities to maintain the state and secure its welfare require the cultivation of good (i.e., obedient and faithful) citizens.

Pufendorf's political realism is evident, in part, in his appreciation of the fact that sovereign authority must be supreme. A sovereign is by definition not rightly answerable to anyone or subject to any earthly political authority (EJU, II,obs.V,16; DJN, VII,6,1). Yet the rather crude description of sovereign authority he offers in EJU is subtly amended and qualified in DJN. In the latter work he emphasizes that sovereign authority need not be absolute, although it must be supreme within its proper sphere. It is possible, he insists, and desirable to place legal limits upon the reach of sovereign authority by carefully delimiting its desired jurisdiction.

The argument for the importance of limitations upon sovereign authority is a quiet testimony to Pufendorf's political cautiousness.[8] At best the argument is elliptical; nowhere does he advocate the adoption of a constitutional structure that limits sovereign authority. Instead, he advises that the people contracting to establish a state can, at the time they vote to decree a particular form of government, choose either to institute a general pact with the sovereign that empowers him to do as he wishes and obligates only his (or its—in case sovereignty is lodged in a council) conscience, or to construct a specific pact that identifies and enumerates certain limitations upon the reach of sovereign authority (DJN, VII,6,10). In the event anyone is worried about the potential abuses that might result from an unlimited sovereignty—and Pufendorf's general pessimism about man's propensity for evil indicates that everyone should be so worried—then it would be wise to opt for a specific pact, though Pufendorf leaves this inference to his readers.

Although limited sovereignty might be a reasonable guard against an abusive sovereign, it has its risks. A government needs the authority to govern and Pufendorf was a sufficiently perceptive politician to understand that a people who so limits sovereign authority from fear of sovereign tyranny that it renders its government ineffectual has done little to promote its own welfare. So he offers a second defense against an abusive sovereign designed to permit sufficient political flexibility to allow government to respond to political necessity without leaving the citizenry vulnerable to the excesses of sovereign authority. He advises, in effect, that a system of checks be implemented where the sovereign (Pufendorf seems to have in mind a monarch here) is required to refer matters of policy "over whose disposal he has not been left absolute authority to a council of the people or leading men," whose agreement is required before policy can become law (DJN, VII,6,10). Rather uncharacteristically, Pufendorf candidly endorses this proposal as a matter of political prudence and insists that a "people is not sufficiently watching out for itself" if it does not adopt this plan.

[8]For a comprehensive analysis of Pufendorf's political thought that works from the idea that Pufendorf was generally careful not to upset those political actors who were in a position to benefit his career, see Leonard Krieger, *The Politics of Discretion* (Chicago: University of Chicago Press, 1965).

Constitutional architecture, to be sure, offers only a modest relief from the potential dangers of an abusive sovereign. Pufendorf thinks the sovereign abuses its authority when it ignores the fundamental laws adopted to limit its authority or when it violates the natural law. Following the traditional view, Pufendorf is willing to state that there is no obligation to obey a sovereign's command if doing so results in a violation of natural law, and he even permits a right of self-defense against the sovereign in the event the latter threatens one's life (EJU, II,obs.V,17; DJN, VII,8,6). But he does not countenance a general right of rebellion against the sovereign. Only those directly subject to the sovereign's injustice are allowed to defend against this abuse and to flee the state if possible. The people more generally are never justified in rebelling against their sovereign since it is wrong to take back by might the authority that the sovereign has received by the consent of the people and is therefore allowed to exercise by right (DJN, VII,8,6).

In place of a theory of justified rebellion, Pufendorf advances a lecture on the responsibilities of citizenship as a defense against the tendency toward political instability that might result from an unappreciative or uninformed citizenry. He allows citizens to emigrate in the face of oppression, but he also insists that the general public should tolerate rather than oppose an abusive sovereign. Not only would a right of rebellion render pointless the people's contract with the sovereign, since the people could void the contract whenever they wish, but it would also leave the people as the judge of proper or improper sovereign behavior. In Pufendorf's judgment, this is unacceptable because the people are ill-placed and too poorly informed to judge the community good for themselves.

To reinforce this argument, Pufendorf advances a limited theory of political neutrality. He thinks the sovereign is the only one properly situated to judge the true interests of the state free from personal bias; the people themselves are unlikely to distinguish between their own particular interests and the general interests of the community (DJN, VII,8,6). This argument offers appropriate testimony to Pufendorf's own beliefs about the realities of pluralism and the evils of faction in the state. It is this very disparity of interests and ideas that serves as the cause of domestic unrest and necessitates the state in the first place, and regardless of his characterization of the state as a unified moral person, he understands that ideological, theological, and personal interests will continue to divide the body politic. So it is dangerous to worry about sovereign authority in a manner that pits the sovereign against the people, for the people are not easily assimilated into a singular entity. Instead, distinct factions that believe the sovereign is acting against their interests may likely rush to sound the alarm of sovereign abuse, and Pufendorf's refusal to countenance a right of rebellion seems a sober precaution against this potential source of political instability. Once again Pufendorf's political savvy is on display in his theorizing; for he reminds us that the commitment to sovereign authority should be made in sight of the realization that political unrest and social injustice can be catalyzed as easily by an uninformed, unaware, or impassioned public as it can be by the abuse of political authority.

Perhaps then it should not come as a surprise that Pufendorf would insist upon the cultivation of good habits in the citizenry as the surest way to insure a just and stable political system. For civil association is not only a mechanism for insuring sociality by establishing peace and security; it is also a most effective instrument for teaching the virtues and values capable of sustaining and promoting the spirit of sociality. The task of proper habituation falls to the sovereign. The sovereign must promote religion; establish public schools and see to the general level of education; set a proper example of exemplary behavior for the citizenry; make only clear and simple laws; increase the well-being throughout the state; and encourage industry while guarding against laziness in the citizenry and a tendency toward materialism or consumerism (DJN, VII,9).

Pufendorf was hardly the first theorist to offer the sovereign instruction on the responsibilities of political office, but he is one of the first to entrust the sovereign with the affirmative responsibility both for maintaining a degree of economic and social welfare and for overseeing the social and moral development of the citizenry. This latter responsibility, in particular, is indicative of Pufendorf's general view that human beings are not by nature fit for civil society and can only become so through careful nurturing and cultivation. In his more pessimistic moments he seems to think that most human beings will fail to develop a proper political consciousness and will continuously require the threat of punishment to bend them to political obedience (DJN, VII,1,4). Yet he does not permit this pessimism to stifle his own theoretical convictions that civil association can work and that a state system can breathe a much needed stability and security—and even a modicum of justice—into human life.

The proof of the matter likely lies with the success of the sovereign in encouraging good citizenship, however. For the sovereign can control those who remain bad citizens only with the aid and cooperation of good citizens (DJN, VII,2,5). Yet a lingering doubt surfaces at this point. If humankind is as prone to wickedness as Pufendorf suggests, how is it possible to cultivate good citizens? This can be partially answered by indicating that the human character is not a fixed thing for Pufendorf; it is capable of growth and maturation. While we learn from his anthropology that an unfettered social and economic growth has generated an atmosphere where humankind's wicked inclinations can work toward destructive ends, we also learn from his theory of political legitimacy that it is possible to develop methods for instilling and cultivating in people a sense of responsibility and beneficence. But of course it remains incumbent upon humankind to develop and socialize its own character, and this is the rub that only the exercise of sound reason can match. Yet if sound reason provides the guidance and inspiration Pufendorf requires here, political association becomes the vehicle he thinks necessary for the proper cultivation of the human spirit.

Pufendorf and Political Theory

Pufendorf's political thought seems an ambiguous moment in the narrative of western political ideas. There is, to be sure, ample evidence that he deserves to be recognized as one of the initial architects of modern liberalism. Not only does he insist that man's natural state is governed by a moral law discoverable through reason; he also derives from this standard natural law posture a theory of human equality premised upon a rudimentary, but not insignificant, theory of individual rights. While Pufendorf's list of natural rights is not as robust as Locke's, it does nevertheless cover the individual right of self-preservation and self-determination so central to the liberal creed (DJN, II,2,3). Moreover, Pufendorf's derivation of his natural rights is both more simple and in certain ways more convincing than Locke's maker's rights thesis. Since natural law does not reveal any natural earthly superiors among humankind, all persons stand equal under natural law, and all persons are responsible for judging and pursuing their own well-being under this law.

But Pufendorf does not press his natural rights thesis beyond a crude ethical individualism. Instead his anthropology situates humankind within the conventions and traditions he concludes are necessary for the human end of sociality. The natural freedom of individuals thus fades into historical myth, and the social roles that have emerged to give exact expression to sociality determine and obligate us as social beings. With the notable exception of a citizen's right to preserve himself against a life-threatening attack from his sovereign, a person's social role as citizen, as family-father or wife, and/or as master or slave fixes one's social being and cements one's social commitments. The rich individualism of the liberal tradition that seeks to unmask as arbitrary and morally questionable the social conventions that configure social life is thus completely missing in Pufendorf's thought. Nor is its absence mitigated significantly by Pufendorf's generally unbelievable effort to reconcile social being with natural freedom by insisting that social roles must necessarily be understood as the result of voluntary expressions of (tacit) consent authored and offered by naturally free persons.

There are also methodological reasons to distinguish Pufendorf from the liberal tradition. Limited though his ethical individualism is, there is more to it than there is to his methodological individualism. He does of course rely upon some basic biological and psychological characteristics of human beings. But these are intended primarily to illustrate the degree to which humans are tied to one another and in need of human companionship and the governance of law. By comparing humans with brute animals, he details human frailty and dependency on others. And by exploring the psychological propensity toward evil, he displays the importance of law and the cultivation of goodness through education for a sociable life. While humans in a natural state are not the sorry creatures Hobbes imagined, they are also neither particularly noteworthy nor noble. Without the society of others they simply cannot endure, and if they are not careful, even in the company of others they might behave in a fashion that jeopardizes sociality. But if humans are not naturally noble, if they do not naturally possess a particularly strong sense of justice or empathy, they can at least ennoble themselves by dedicating themselves to the leadership of sound reason. In many respects then, Pufendorf is the antithesis of Rousseau, who also emphasized human sociality but who was perhaps more pessimistic than Pufendorf on the ability of education and law to check the corrosive elements of the human psyche.

Ambiguity aside, there is much to dislike in Pufendorf's thought. His anthropology—his science of man's social evolution—is poor social history. In spite of his awareness that states emerge mainly from the violence of the conqueror and the horrors of war, he insists on maintaining the fiction that social and political conventions are the product of voluntary consent and mutual agreement. Yet he can perhaps be forgiven for bad social history; after all, this detracts only from his *science* of politics and not from his moral characterization of human sociality. But of greater concern is the fact that his own use of social utility seems inconsistent with his ethical individualism. There are clear limitations upon the ability to invoke arguments appealing to the collective good built into any theory that takes individual rights seriously, and Pufendorf's argument is no exception. No matter how extensively some social conventions might aid human sociality, they are surely objectionable if those subject to them do not accept them voluntarily. Pufendorf wants finally to avoid the need for actual consent by claiming that enduring social conventions continue to commend themselves to sound reason by facilitating sociality. But the argument is unduly conservative; even if a given social convention really was instrumental for the promotion of sociality at some historical moment, it is not clear that it remains so, or that it could not—and should not—be replaced by another convention that might serve sociality just as well and more closely approximate the social manifestation of the ideal of equality. In effect, he makes no effort to reconcile his own moral egalitarianism with his natural law commitment to sociality, and the resultant tension between the two erodes the success of his social theory.

Poor social history and bad social theory are probably reason enough to account for the withering of Pufendorf's intellectual influence on the development of political ideas. If they are not enough, the conservatism of his thought must also be acknowledged as a contributing factor. In his day of course he was a radical thinker; his natural law theory set a new standard that helped wash away the vestiges of traditionalism and orthodoxy. But he was not radical enough; his ethical individualism was too underdeveloped and his theory of political legitimacy too steeped in traditionalism and too wedded to the need for political stability to withstand the scientifically and politically radical days of the Enlightenment that followed him.

Yet it is a mistake to be unduly negative here; for there is also much in Pufendorf—in the often challenging ambiguity of his thought—that contemporary students of politics will find both likeable and edifying. Just as it did in his own day, Pufendorf's thought continues to offer a possible source of relief for those who think that much of the theorizing about politics that remains in the shadow of Hobbes is premised upon an excessive or unnecessarily abstract individualism. The remedy Pufendorf offers, however, does not involve resorting to a reworked Aristotelianism or a reconstituted communitarianism. His effort to reconcile his ethical individualism with his anthropology is itself an attempt to build a theory of politics that gives proper weight to the integrity of the individual within the larger moral context of human sociality.

Pufendorf's egalitarianism is central to his individualism. Although some persons deserve greater esteem than others by virtue of the lives they have led, there are no natural superiors among humankind (DJN, II,2,3). Yet this egalitarianism also informs his "socialism." As social beings, the well-being of each is a part of— or perhaps more precisely a product of—social well-being. Therefore, we are charged by natural law to promote sociality, that is, to live for others rather than—and (although it will likely sound odd) in order—to live for ourselves.

It is important to understand that Pufendorf does not regard this insight as a precept of rational prudence. He is not saying that rational and self-interested beings should embrace sociality because it is in their best interest to do so. To read him this way is to place his work in the shadow of Hobbes—his self-declared primary antagonist. While human beings are free and equal under the natural law, they are also fundamentally sociable. This means for him that humans are social by nature; they live in and depend upon the association of others. The realization and appreciation of this fact about human beings lead to the natural law mandate to promote this sociality. As an insight of reason, all rational beings are capable of drawing this inference from the fact of human sociality and of appreciating the demands of natural law (EJU, II,obs.IV,1; DJN, II,3,13).

Social life, in short, is not an artifact of human choice in Pufendorf's judgment; it is a necessary feature of the human condition. As such, it is natural to facilitate it, but the precise form or structure such facilitation should take remains up to human ingenuity and judgment. Pufendorf was convinced that civil association has become a necessary response to humankind's socio-economic development. But once again, it is important to see that he is not making a Hobbesian point here; a decision to enter civil society does not involve the prudential acceptance of a *modus vivendi*. Instead, the movement to civil society is a mandate of natural law; only by entering civil society can sociality be insured and promoted. The acceptance of civil society is thus mandated by sound reason as a moral requirement. And the challenge of political thought, as he understood it, is to explain how civil society can effectivly promote sociality and avoid becoming another source of social antagonism. This, of course, is the traditional problem of political legitimacy.

By insisting upon humankind's basic sociality, Pufendorf blocks the reduction to methodological individualism. And by fashioning human sociality in moral terms, he blocks the inclination to divorce civil association from its larger moral context. Yet in a sense his theory also minimizes the overall moral importance of civil association. He does not think that civil association provides the glue that binds human beings to one another and fixes the associative enterprise. And while he emphasizes the importance of cultivating good citizens, he does not wish to make good citizenship the defining feature of human life. Important though it surely is, citizenship remains one feature of human association among others. It does not replace these others; nor, for that matter, is it necessarily ethically prior to these others, particularly the family unit. Civil association is thus characterized as a social system composed of important but attenuated social relationships that bind more basic social groups together and allow for the emergence of other, more intimate associations that inevitably build diversity into the body politic. Civil unity, for Pufendorf, must be built upon social diversity; it is, after all, a way to manage this diversity.[9]

It follows that Pufendorf's thought is compatible with a liberal desire to defend diversity and difference within the body politic and at least partly with the com-

---

[9]For more on Pufendorf's theory of tolerance, see Krieger, pp. 240–46. But see also, EJU, II,obs.I,2.

munitarian desire to appreciate the situatedness and fundamentally social feature of human life. This compatibility, however, depends upon Pufendorf's success in reconciling his own ethical individualism with his anthropology, and as noted previously, these two rest uncomfortably beside one another. The resultant tension emerges, in his theory, in terms of a question about how civil association is best able to promote sociality. How, that is, can it promote an ethically defensible sociality and not simply reinforce those unsociable and ethically indefensible, but conventionally established, power relationships that might have emerged through time?

Some of Pufendorf's ruminations on this problem can be read as quite radical, for example, his incipient theory of social justice (DJN, I,7,9), and his theory of sovereign responsibility. Others seem horribly conservative, for example, his apology for private property relations (DJN, IV,9), and his defense of paternal authority in the family. Had he chosen to insist that sociality requires the political revision of certain social conventions based upon unacceptable power relations, or that sociality requires a particular pattern of resource distribution, he could have written a more radical politics. Instead he chose, for the most part, to allow his anthropology to swallow his ethical individualism and to accept as useful those social conventions he identifies with man's socio-economic development. Yet conservative as this may seem by today's standards, it does not render Pufendorf's thought uninteresting; for his theory also offers a justification for the continued inquiry into the requirements of sociality. If civil association results from the exercise of human ingenuity reflecting upon the most appropriate way to fulfill the natural law requirement of sociality, it seems reasonable to suppose that human ingenuity should continuously re-examine this question. And if this is correct, the question of political legitimacy that Pufendorf introduces remains constantly before us, as does the cognate question about how we can, as a polity, best promote sociality.

Translator's Introduction

The following translation of Pufendorf's *Elementorum jurisprudentiae universalis* (EJU) is based on the 1672 edition of this work which was photographically reproduced in 1931 as part of the Carnegie Classics of International Law Series.[1] This reprint was accompanied by a new English translation prepared by the classicist William Abbott Oldfather.[2] Both volumes are now out of print. The selections from Pufendorf's *De jure naturae et gentium* (DJN) are based on another Carnegie series reprint, the one-volume edition of Pufendorf's great work published in 1688 in Amsterdam.[3] This edition follows Pufendorf's second edition of DJN, published in 1684, in which he enlarged the original work by a fourth, partly by incorporating discussions of Spinoza and Cumberland into the text. Oldfather (with the collaboration of C. H. Oldfather) translated this work as well, and again, both volumes are out of print.[4]

I have compared the text of the 1688 edition of DJN with Gottfried Mascovius's 1759 edition, which has recently been reprinted.[5] The relatively few differences between the two editions are due primarily to the influence of Pufendorf's eighteenth-century French translator, Jean Barbeyrac, who had in his own editions occasionally emended or completed passages he deemed deficient or obscure by drawing on Pufendorf's pedagogical summary of DJN, the *De officio hominis et*

---

[1]Samuel Pufendorf, *Elementorum jurisprudentiae universalis libri duo*, vol. 1: The Photographic Reproduction of the Edition of 1672 (Oxford: Clarendon Press, 1931). The original title page reads: Samuelis Pufendorf[ii], *Elementorum jurisprudentiae universalis libri II. Una cum appendice de sphaera morali et indicibus, editio novissima et emendatissima* (Cantabrigiae: Joann. Hayes, 1672).

[2]Samuel Pufendorf, *Elementorum jurisprudentiae universalis libri duo*, vol. 2: The Translation, by William Abbott Oldfather (Oxford: Clarendon Press, 1931).

[3]Samuel Pufendorf, *De jure naturae et gentium libri octo*, vol. 1: The Photographic Reproduction of the Edition of 1688 (Oxford: Clarendon Press, 1934). The original title page reads: Samuelis Pufendorfii *De jure naturae et gentium libri octo*. Editio ultima, auctior multo, et emendatior (Amsterdam: Andreas Hoogenhuysen, 1688).

[4]Samuel Pufendorf, *De jure naturae et gentium libri octo*, vol. 2: The Translation of the Edition of 1688, by C. H. Oldfather and W. A. Oldfather (Oxford: Clarendon Press, 1934).

[5]Sam. L. B. Pufendorf, *De iure naturae et gentium libri octo*, 2 vols., edited by Gottfried Mascovius (Frankfurt & Leipzig: Knoch-Eslinger, 1759; photographic reprint at Frankfurt/M: Minerva, 1967). This edition is itself a reprint of Mascovius's 1744 edition, and its second volume consists of Pufendorf's *Eris Scandica*, which was not included in the 1967 reproduction.

civis. My policy has been to follow the 1688 edition in the case of all longer discrepancies, but to accept silently any obvious corrections and a few word substitutions where it makes little or no difference to the meaning. On the other hand, since the punctuation of the 1759 edition seems generally more careful, I have more frequently relied on it to determine Pufendorf's meaning.

The DJN was first translated into English in 1703, by Basil Kennet, with the assistance of "the Reverend Mr. Percivale, and the Reverend Mr. Itchiner," who respectively rendered books five and eight. Later editions came to include Barbeyrac's notes and famous "prefatory discourse," and like the original were reissued many times during the eighteenth century.[6] Kennet's translation is generally reliable and reads extremely well for an eighteenth-century rendition. Though somewhat rich and florid by our standards, it is sometimes still preferred to that of Oldfather, who sought intentionally "to preserve not only the thought, but, to a certain degree, also the style of Pufendorf, which, for all its intricacies and obscurities, has a certain flavor of the author's personality and age that ought not to be entirely lost, as is frequently the case in the extremely free paraphrases of which Barbeyrac and Kennet generally avail themselves."[7] Kennet's version is sometimes so general and circuitous that it fails to translate certain Latin phrases at all. Yet it is extremely smooth and readable, and its frequent use of multiple expressions for simple Latin terms or phrases is sometimes more successful in capturing the full meaning of the text than Oldfather's more literal and far leaner version, which often challenges even interested readers. Suffice it to say that both translations have their merits, and if my new rendition offers any improvement it is partly due to the fact that I was able to consult and compare them.

My own translation imitates neither the rococo style of Kennet nor the overall literalness of Oldfather, but seeks instead to find a middle way. Its general goals are well expressed by the comment of Edwin Curley in the preface to his edition of Spinoza:

> By a good translation I understand one which is accurate wherever it is a question of simple accuracy, shows good judgment where the situation calls for something more than accuracy, maintains as much consistency as possible in the treatment of technical terms, leaves interpretation to the commentators, so far as this is possible, and, finally, is as clear and readable as fidelity to the text will allow.[8]

To this I would add one other feature which is, perhaps, but a combination of those already mentioned, namely transparency. A translation that aims to be both faithful to the original and helpful to those at one remove from it must be transparent in the sense that it not only reveals the text's meaning but also gives some indica-

---

[6]Samuel Pufendorf, *Of the Law of Nature and Nations. Eight Books*, translated into English from the best edition, by Basil Kennet (Oxford: Lichfield et al., 1703). Kennet identifies his helpers in the Preface to his translation. I have consulted the text of the 1717 (or 3rd) edition of Kennet, published in London by R. Sare, during the course of my work.

[7]Translator's Preface to Oldfather's translation of DJN, p. 63a. Richard Tuck thinks, in his *Natural Rights Theories* (Cambridge: Cambridge University Press, 1979), p. 160, note 12, that "Basil Kennet's translation . . . [is] much to be preferred to any subsequent version."

[8]Edwin Curley, in the General Preface to his *The Collected Works of Spinoza*, vol. 1, edited and translated by Edwin Curley (Princeton, NJ: Princeton University Press, 1988), p. ix.

tion of how that meaning is linguistically constructed. This requires a certain literalness, to be sure, though not one as far-reaching and complete as Oldfather's. That is, the translation need not correspond exactly with the original in terms of word order, sentence structure and length, and so on. Instead, what is required is that the function of every component of the original text be somehow reproduced in the translation. This goal allows and even demands some rearrangement of the text, guided by the need to respect the individual parts of the text and their role within the original semantic and rhetorical whole. Transparency requires a creative moment between the two wholes, that of the original author and that of the translator, yet one that is always guided by the text itself.

Pufendorf was committed to Latin as a universal language of the learned and had his doubts about Christian Thomasius's advocacy of the use of the vernacular for this purpose. His style is powerful, rich, and complex, and his vocabulary diverse, both in its use of descriptive terms and in the search for suitable neologisms and expressions. Despite Kennet's characterization of it as "difficult and discouraging" to most, and Oldfather's mention of "intricacies and obscurities," the former, at least, also allowed that it is "expressive."[9] This must refer in part to its ability to communicate complex ideas and arguments clearly, to its revelation of Pufendorf's combative personality, and to its capacity to accommodate Pufendorf's striving for explicitness and explanatory completeness.

We have omitted the subtitles for the numbered sections in Pufendorf's chapters or their equivalent (that is, definitions, axioms, and observations), particularly in view of their number and also the length of some of the selections translated here. Moreover, since these sections are not subdivided in the Latin text, all paragraph divisions below this level are my own. I have sought by means of them not only to break up long passages that would tax the patience of most contemporary readers, but also to emphasize distinctions that might otherwise not emerge as clearly. Moreover, I have occasionally broken up Pufendorf's longer sentences, combined shorter sentences, reordered clauses and other elements within sentences, interchanged active and passive voices, and employed parentheses and the dash to tuck away subsidiary or tangential comments that might otherwise interrupt the flow of the text or even occlude its meaning. I have tried harder, however, to respect Pufendorf's moods and tenses, not only because he tends to employ these correctly but also because they have a greater interpretive value, being relevant among other things to the question (discussed in the editor's introduction) whether Pufendorf is providing an analytic or a historical account.

It should also be noted that whereas the names of authors cited or quoted by Pufendorf are italicized in the Latin text, I have not followed this practice in the translation. In addition, since nothing seems to ride on this either, I have taken the liberty of standardizing the capitalization of some of Pufendorf's terms and expressions.

Given the nature of our project, the extensive use of ellipses throughout the translation was unavoidable. Ellipses always indicate omissions within Pufendorf's numbered chapter sections, but not the omission of whole sections or chapters,

---

[9]Kennet, Preface. Oldfather, Translator's Preface, p. 63a.

whose absence is clearly visible in the interrupted enumerations—both in the Contents and in the text itself. Moreover, they almost always begin or end with complete Latin sentences, except when indicating the omission of Pufendorf's in-text references. Brackets, on the other hand, which are always a temptation for translators, have been used far more sparingly; they either enclose Pufendorf's untranslated (into Latin) Greek terms, supply occasional Latin equivalents for key English terms in some contexts, or identify modest clarificatory and stylistic additions that cannot easily be said to be already implicit in the Latin.

The Latin text signals quotations by means of emphasis, that is, italics. This creates some ambiguities since expressions that are not direct quotations are emphasized as well. I have used quotation marks for what I take to be direct quotations and have reserved italics for ordinary emphasis. Also, as Oldfather notes, "[i]n the matter of quotations from other works Pufendorf often took considerable liberties with the text, in omitting words and phrases at will, and sometimes whole sentences, as well as changing the word order. But he was apparently most scrupulous in not modifying the actual views expressed by his authorities."[10] Oldfather actually corrects some of Pufendorf's loose quotations (where he is probably paraphrasing from memory) and uses standard translations of other authors where they are available. My own practice has been to translate Pufendorf's text as it stands, leaving judgments about his memory to others.

Furthermore, I have used cognates whenever possible and have sought to have the translation mirror the diversity of Pufendorf's terminology and idiom, as well as the tone and flavor of his language. Hence I have preserved most of his concrete analogies and colloquialisms, even when attracted by more abstract expressions. Also, where Pufendorf employs two similar yet distinct expressions that appear for some purpose to be synonymous, I try to reflect this difference in English instead of suggesting identity by using the same word. This is particularly important in the case of technical terms, where earlier translators were sometimes too lax or even inconsistent.[11]

While I have made some effort to employ gender-neutral language where possible (for example, the use of 'one,' 'someone,' or 'a person' in association with verbs lacking explicit subjects), complete concealment of Pufendorf's use of gender terms would falsify the translation and make it useless for anyone interested in studying this aspect of early modern contract theory. It should also be noted that Pufendorf borrowed extensively from EJU when he wrote DJN, linguistically as well as conceptually, thereby justifying Kennet's description of the former work as a "first Draught" of the latter.[12] Numerous EJU passages are reproduced almost verbatim in DJN. I have tried to have the respective translations reflect this continuity, wherever I have noticed it.

[10]Oldfather, Translator's Preface, p. 63a.

[11]Kennet has, in general, a better understanding than Oldfather of what is going on in the text philosophically speaking. Silverthorne's recent translation, in Samuel Pufendorf, *On the Duty of Man and Citizen According to Natural Law*, edited by James Tully and translated by Michael Silverthorne (Cambridge: Cambridge University Press, 1991), is even better in its attention to Pufendorf's terminology and meaning, though my own rendition of technical terms differs from it in certain respects.

[12]Kennet, Preface.

Finally, the following equivalents should be kept in mind, since they both distinguish this translation from others and also allow comparisons between them. Though it is almost impossible to render a term or expression by means of a single equivalent that is used in each instance, it is possible to establish some general patterns. Thus, the first translation for each of the terms below is the main and most frequently used rendition, even though others have been used as needed in particular contexts.

AUCTORITAS: authority. (This term, which is relatively infrequent in Pufendorf, refers to the personal influence which one has on account of age, eminence, achievement, and so forth. 'Authority' is also used to translate POTESTAS, a far more frequent and important term, but it is fairly easy to guess from the context which term is being rendered.)

CIVITAS: the state, or, the civil state.

COMMUNIS: common, communal, ordinary.

CONTRACTUS: contract.

CONVENTIO: agreement, convention.

DOMINIUM: dominion, ownership. (I have retained the English cognate wherever possible. DOMINIUM is sometimes equivalent to PROPRIETAS, but the two terms are distinct and the translation should reflect this.)

EXISTIMATIO: esteem, reputation, measure.

GENTES: nations, tribes.

IMPERIUM: sovereignty.

INIURIA: injury. (INIURIA, like DAMNUM [damage, harm, loss], refers to the violation of a perfect right, but DAMNUM [DJN III, 1, 3] is also used more broadly, like the non-technical NOXA [hurt, harm] and LAESIO [hurt, harm].)

IUS: right, law. (The particular meaning intended depends upon context.)

LEX: law (that is, divine or human positive law), condition.

PACTUM: pact.

POTENTIA: power, potency.

POTESTAS: authority, power (in very few instances). (Oldfather translated POTESTAS as 'authority' in the EJU but then switched to 'power' in DJN. Yet the latter rendition loses almost entirely the clear normative dimensions of the term, which implies having a right (IUS) to something. There are other terms for 'power,' such as POTENTIA and VIS, and a translation's inability to distinguish between them and POTESTAS constitutes a serious loss. As is clear from the philosophical dictionaries of both Micraelius [1662] and Goclenius [1613], POTENTIA and POTESTAS were seen as equivalents in metaphysical discussions where they meant 'power' in the sense of 'potency' [as opposed to 'act'], but they were clearly distinguished in political contexts).[13]

---

[13]Johannes Micraelius, *Lexicon philosophicum terminorum philosophis usitatorum*, 2nd ed. (Stettin, 1662; photomechanically reproduced at Düsseldorf: Stern-Verlag Janssen & Co., 1966), pp. 1079-80; and Rudolph. Goclenius, *Lexicon philosophicum quo tanquam clave philosophiae fores aperiuntur* (Frankfurt: Matthias Becker, 1613; photomechanically reproduced at Hildesheim: Georg Olms, 1964), p. 844.

PRETIUM: price, worth.

PROPRIETAS: ownership. (Since PROPRIETAS is a relation between persons and things I have avoided the now too reified term 'property,' even though it is the most obvious descendant of PROPRIETAS. One can see the evolution of the term in Locke, who finally settled on 'property.')[14]

RECTE: rightly, correctly.

REGIMEN: government, rule, control.

RES (pl.): things, affairs. (I have remained literal here, avoiding the more interpretive 'property.' After all, whether or not things are property is often the issue.)

RESPUBLICA: commonwealth. (Though other translators have sometimes rendered RESPUBLICA as 'the state,' this sacrifices the linguistic distinction between it and CIVITAS, which may be important. In any case, nothing is lost by this translation, which also serves to bring out the contrast between RES PUBLICA [public affairs or 'wealth'] and RES PRIVATA [private affairs or 'wealth'].)

SALUS: welfare, safety.

SERVUS: slave, servant.

SOCIETAS: society, fellowship, company, partnership.

SOCIALITAS: sociality. (Pufendorf also uses the term SOCIABILIS, but not nearly as often. The noun SOCIABILITAS is rare and occurs only once in the passages translated.)

STATUS: state, condition, status. (The use of 'state' for both STATUS and CIVITAS is unavoidable, since 'condidition' or 'status' would often be awkward or misleading. Context usually suffices to indicate which term is being translated, though I have sometimes used 'civil state' for CIVITAS in order to avoid ambiguity. It seems that Pufendorf does not use STATUS, like CIVITAS, for 'the state' as a political entity— though some occurrences are ambiguous.)

SUMMUM IMPERIUM: supreme sovereignty.

VALOR: value.

VIS/VIRES: force, power/strength.

---

[14]Stephen Buckle, *The Natural History of Property: Grotius to Hume* (Oxford: Clarendon Press, 1991), pp. 169–74, associates Locke's notion of 'property' in one's person with Grotius's notion of *suum* (that which is one's own) and notes both that 'propriety' and 'property' were generally interchangeable in the seventeenth century, and that Locke initially preferred the first term and decided on the second only in later versions of his works. 'Propriety' is indeed closer to 'ownership' than 'property,' but it has lost the relevant meaning in current usage.

Elements of
Universal Jurisprudence
in Two Books

Preface

... And now, as for the book's method, reason itself sufficiently shows that one about to propound some discipline must first explain what may be understood through the things with which it will deal and look about for certain principles from which he may deduce necessarily true statements concerning them. Hence any discipline should be divided into three parts, the first of which contains definitions, the second principles, and the third propositions or conclusions derived from the principles. To these, if it seems needed, must be added a fourth into which those matters whose certitude is not clearly apparent are to be thrown. For the things ordinarily maintained about the difference between the analytic and synthetic methods are without substance. Indeed, it has seemed appropriate to us not to devote a special book to propositions but to subjoin each of them immediately to the definitions or principles on which they chiefly depend, since it seems that this discipline would be deformed by I know not what sort of aridity if it were set forth torn into minute parts, as it were, in the manner of the mathematical sciences. ...

BOOK I

Definition 1

HUMAN ACTIONS ARE SAID [TO BE] THE VOLUNTARY ACTIONS OF MAN IN COMMUNAL LIFE, REGARDED WITH THE IMPUTATION OF THEIR EFFECTS

1. We call voluntary those actions placed in the power of man which so depend on the will as on a free cause that they would not occur without its determination by acts elicited by a previous cognition of the understanding; and indeed, inasmuch as they are regarded not according to their natural aspect but as occurring by a decision of the will. For a voluntary action involves two things. One is as it were material, being the performance regarded in itself; the other is formal, that is, the performance's dependence on a decision of the will, and the rational choice, so to speak, by which the action is conceived as decreed by the will.

The performance—regarded, for the sake of distinction, separately and in itself—is said to be an action of the will, or to come from the will, rather than to be voluntary. For an action of the will is further considered either in itself and absolutely (insofar as it is a certain physical motion undertaken by a previous decision of the will), or reflexively (insofar as its effect is imputed to man). Voluntary actions which include this reflexivity are, in a special manner of speaking, said to be *human*. And because imputation looks chiefly at the mental inclinations and habits of life which are properly called *mores*, it has come about that human actions themselves are by reason of synecdoche called *moral*.

2. The essence of a human or moral action therefore consists in these three principles, one of which is as it were material, another fundamental, and the third formal. The material principle is some physical motion of a physical power such

as locomotion, the sensitive appetite, the external or internal senses, and the understanding *qua* exercise of apprehension (for judgment necessarily depends on the quality of an object in such a way that there is no room for the will to direct it). Indeed, it is even the act of the will itself considered in its own natural being— that is, inasmuch as it is regarded, in short, as an effect produced through a power that has, as such, been instilled by nature—as well as the privation of some physical motion which a man could have produced either in itself or in its cause. Likewise, it is the inclinations of natural powers toward certain objects which have been produced through preceding voluntary actions, as also those acts or practices consisting in certain rituals introduced by the human will, which by the mere decision of men signify some moral effect.

Nor is it only my own actions which are of this sort, that can be the material of my moral actions, but also the similar actions and privations of other men who can be directed by my will; indeed, even the actions of brutes, plants, and inanimate things that are capable of a direction proceeding from my will. Thus in the divine law itself the damage done by a goring ox which an owner knew to be such is imputed to him. Likewise, a vinedresser is himself held responsible when a vine has through his neglect poured its entire fecundity into the branches. And one who has set a fire pays for its voracity. Yet it is necessary in all these cases, before the actions of others can be considered as ours, that there have been on our part either the omission of some required action, or any kind of action apart from which another action could not have occurred. Indeed, permissions or allowances of someone else's actions can also be the material of moral actions. These are "passions" when considered in their own natural being, yet they are regarded as actions when imputativity is added—something which arises from the fact that they could have been prohibited or prevented.

3. The fundamental principle of a moral action is rational choice, by which physical motion is understood as produced by a decree of the will. This rational choice presupposes or includes the faculty of man in which the production or omission of those motions lies.

4. The formal principle of a moral action consists in imputation, or rather in imputativity, by which the effect of a voluntary action can be imputed to an agent, whether he himself has physically produced the effect or has caused it to be produced by others. By this formality of an action the agent himself also participates in the denomination of morality and is called a *moral cause*. Hence it is easily understood that, properly and strictly speaking, the formal principle of a moral action consists in imputation (regarded in a final sense, however), and that it is nothing other than a voluntary agent to whom an effect either is or is to be imputed because he was either the total or partial cause (more precisely in German, the *Ursache*) of its occurrence, and its author. And so if anything good occurs it must be credited to him, and anything evil ascribed to him, and he himself as agent is bound to stand for the effect, at it were, and to answer for it.

5. Furthermore, the formal principle of a human action, that is imputativity, has the character of a positive form from which those characteristics, properties, and consequences to be treated here radically spring. Hence a moral action can be said to be a positive entity (in the category of moral, not natural, things), whether its

material principle is a physical motion or the privation of such a motion. For it suffices for the being of positive entities in the category of moral things if they posit something from which true characteristics in the same category may spring, since just as there are no characteristics of a non-entity, that to which certain positive characteristics belong can by no means simply be said to be a non-entity. What these characteristics are will be made known below.

6. Now moral actions are chiefly distinguished here, (1) by reason of their cause, into *immediate* (which someone has produced through himself) and *mediate* (which he has made to be produced through another); and, (2) by reason of the act itself, into *pure* and *mixed*. Pure moral actions are those completed by the motion of some power directed toward an object in a certain manner. Such are the acknowledgment and celebration of God, the exhibition of honor and respect, obedience, love, aversion, consolation, praise, criticism, and so forth, whose effect consists in the object's being affected by the action in a certain manner, or understood to be moved to pleasure or displeasure. Other actions, however, which bring some real advantage or disadvantage upon a person or things, are as it were mixed. Such are, for example, gift-giving, lending, theft, murder, and so forth, whose effect consists chiefly in some operation that really helps or hurts another's person or things. The various distinctions of moral actions (3) by reason of their object are treated below.

Definition 3

A 'STATE' IS A SUPPOSITIVE MORAL ENTITY IN WHICH POSITIVE MORAL OBJECTS, AND ESPECIALLY PERSONS, ARE SAID TO BE

1. A 'state' is said to be a suppositive entity because it is, as it were, spread out beneath positive moral things, so that they rest what moral existence they have upon it and exert from there their actions and effects. And thus it is somewhat analogous to space, which is as it were placed beneath natural things in the same way, so that they set what natural existence they have, and exercise their physical motions, within it. It differs from space, however, in that space is a certain kind of immovable and extended (originally and through itself) substance that exists even when natural things themselves have been removed, while a state (like all moral entities considered formally and as such) has the character of a quality and an attribute only, so that it can by no means maintain its existence when physical things have been removed.

2. Now state can be divided upon the analogy of space into *locational* and *temporal*. The former involves regard to some moral 'where' and can be considered either *indeterminately* or *determinately*. Considered indeterminately it is either *natural* or *adventitious*. Man's natural state, since it lacks a special term, we will for the time being call humanity, or human life, which is the condition in which any man whatever is constituted simply by virtue of being a man. And it involves an obligation to observe the law of nature toward both oneself and other men, and to live with them in a social manner; the right to enjoy from any man whatsoever the duties owed by virtue of the law of nature, and to assume the remaining privileges that universally accompany human life; as also the capacity to acquire special rights for oneself among men. Contrasted to it is the state or life of brutes, which are tied to one another by no bond of right, so that they may without injury inflict on one another, even through force, whatever things they can or wish.

3. Now since that obligation of which we have spoken, as also the rights, accompanies the natural state of man, it is not inappropriate at this place to inquire into the limits of this state, namely when it has its beginning and its end. The former seems correctly to be fixed when someone can truly be said to be a man, even if those perfections which accompany a man only after some extent of time are still lacking; when he begins to live and feel, therefore, even though he has not yet come out of his mother's womb. Now since obligation requires for its fulfillment an understanding of oneself and of what is done, it exerts its efficacy only when a man knows how to direct his actions to some norm and to distinguish them from one another. Rights, on the other hand, which impose on others who already enjoy the use of reason a certain obligation to furnish something, and can benefit even those who are ignorant of what is being done, bring their force to bear as soon as someone begins to be a man.

Hence one who takes from someone who is still in the womb something left him by a will, or bestowed by some other title, without doubt does him an injury— even if that right may have accrued to him within the first days after conception; and so the latter can thereafter, as an adult, rightly vindicate it. And it suffices that he then testify, when he is able on account of his age to indicate this adequately, that it was done to him against his will, especially since his disagreement should always have been presumed. In the same manner one who has carried off or destroyed a thing of mine during my absence has directly done me an injury, even though I may find out about the damage only upon returning after an interval.

An injury cannot be inflicted on the body of an infant, however, unless it already actually has a body, or a material disposed in such a way that if it is hurt harm will arise for the body to be formed from it. Hence if anyone has unjustly done violence to a mother so that an infant impaired in some member is born from her, we think that the latter can as an adult bring action against him for these injuries, unless he can prove effective ignorance. But indeed, since an unformed seed cannot properly be said to be either a man or a human body during the first days after conception, we think that if anyone should cause it to be damaged and aborted he cannot be said to injure it, even if he is in fact sinning against the law of nature by cutting off a member of human society and doing an injury to the state and the parents, whom he deprives of a citizen and a hoped-for offspring.

5. Subordinate to the natural state of man, and immediately flowing from it, is *peace*. This everyone, by virtue of the fact that he is a man, is obligated to cultivate with anyone whatever, so long as care for his own welfare does not persuade him to break it off on account of others' injuries. Now peace is either *universal* or *particular*. The former extends itself to any men whatever who observe the law of nature toward us, and it consists chiefly in this: that one does not unjustly hurt another, and that if perchance any controversies occur he will see to it that they are settled either through a mutual arrangement or through arbiters. This peace rests solely on the obligation of the law of nature, and it is useless to fortify it by means of a pact or treaties unless those who are contracting come together into one body or society for that purpose.... Particular peace is either *internal* or *external*. The former exists among those who have come together into one body or society, when they furnish that for the sake of which society was established and do not resist by force the authority which society by right exercises over them....

6. But since the obligation to observe the law of nature toward another ceases when the other does not observe the same toward me (about which we will treat in more detail in Book II), *war* emerges as a sort of subsidiary state of man when our welfare cannot be furthered except through force. Even if it is occasionally necessary to enter into this state, such as when, on account of the perversity of men who spurn peaceful reasons, we cannot defend or obtain our right except through arms, it can nonetheless not properly be said to be a natural manner of attaining one's right, because nature has not directly destined men to make use of it but only allowed them to resort to it for lack of a better means.

Now war can be divided according to the manner of peace into *universal* and *particular*. The former is an immediate consequence of the state of beasts, where no one observes any law toward another and all conduct their affairs by means of force alone. Such would have been the state of men if they had not been obligated through the law of nature to cultivate society toward one another. Particular war is either *internal* or *external*. The former exists among those who have come together into one particular society where, after the bond of society has been ruptured, they rise up against one another with arms. Such a war, when it burns during its first effervescence, as it were, and without elaborate preparation on both sides, is said to be *sedition*; when arms are unjustly taken up against a prince it is *rebellion*. In democracies, however, and aristocracies, when the people and the leading men split into parts that act in a hostile fashion toward one another, it has customarily and properly been called *civil war*....

7. Now the Roman lawyers made *freedom* and *slavery* the widest and most general states of men (regarded, of course, as they were in the Roman republic or one similar to it). In order that their nature may be more accurately known, it must be understood that freedom is commonly conceived as a state in which there is a faculty of doing something from one's own choice, slavery on the other hand as a state in which it is necessary to conduct one's affairs according to another's will; and that there are two categories of impediments constraining the faculty of acting: physical (such as bonds, fetters, prison, guards) and moral (such as obligation, law, sovereignty, authority).

Supposing these things, it is apparent that freedom is either *of every sort* or *lim-*

ited. The former is that circumscribed by neither natural nor moral impediments. We believe that no one enjoys such freedom absolutely besides God. Among men, however, the highest degree of freedom is possessed by those who are exempt from civil laws, that is, those who enjoy the highest authority in civil states. For these, even though they are subject to the divine sovereignty and the law of nature, nonetheless acknowledge no man's sovereignty and cannot, so long as they are such, be coerced by anyone by way of penalties.

There are several kinds and degrees of limited freedom. The word 'freedom' is attributed in a special sense to those who live in an aristocracy and, above all, in a democracy. Ordinarily, however, freedom denotes the state of those who serve only the civil state, not also a fellow citizen, and who are permitted to direct as they choose any actions of theirs concerning which nothing has been ordained by the common laws. This freedom is the more restricted as someone is bound by further, particular obligations. Thus one who is under his own jurisdiction in a state, and has not made over a determinate part of his own services to another, surely enjoys a less restricted freedom than one who is under the authority of a father or of guardians, or has leased his services (whether more honorable or more vile, that is intellectual or physical—with hirelings and servants coming, among us, under the latter of these categories) to a fellow citizen.

Slavery, however, commonly exists when someone is bound to direct those of his actions concerning which nothing has been ordained by the common laws not only as another decides, but also entirely to the other's benefit, so that no external utility redounds on him directly from his own actions except insofar as the other gratuitously wills. In addition to this, slaves are understood to have no standing in the state and are classed as things, not persons. Those captured in war in the past ordinarily were, and among some nations are even today, reduced to such slavery by a certain mixture of humanity and cruelty, so that those who could by right have been killed might render perpetual services to their captors in return for the use of their life. A number of states have left masters the right of life and death over these slaves, because it did not seem unfair for the life which had once been under their power to be so thereafter as well. Those born from them enter into the same state, as do those who descend to it of their own accord. Some people even have slavery imposed on them in place of punishment. However, the ultimate degree of slavery is experienced by those who are also restrained by means of physical bonds, such as those consigned to workhouses, to prisons, and to galleys, who are compelled to work while encumbered by fetters or enclosed by a barrier of walls.

Furthermore, that which the lawyers say, that all men were by natural law born free from the beginning, is to be understood negatively [*apophatikōs*], not privatively [*sterētikōs*], as some put it. That is, freedom has through a precept of the natural law not been taken away from anyone absolutely, and without a preceding deed of his. Still, the same law has by no means prevented the possibility that a person may be carried off into slavery for a certain reason. For the state of slavery and its conditions were, by men's choice, introduced by the same act. The fact that philosophers ordinarily call some men slaves by nature—those, namely, who are of a somewhat slower disposition and not at all fit to rule themselves—is not to be understood as if men of this sort were by nature constituted in a state of slavery, or had necessarily to be carried off into it, so that it would be against nature if they remained free; but that their dispositions have been formed in such a way by nature that they are able to bear slavery with equanimity and neither comprehend nor know how to make appropriate use of the goods of freedom.

Definition 4

A MORAL PERSON IS A PERSON REGARDED WITH THE STATUS WHICH HE HAS IN COMMUNAL LIFE

1. This is the most general definition of a moral person. Otherwise, among the lawyers mainly, a person is said to be someone who has civil standing, that is, personal freedom—by which token slaves are classified as things. Moreover, moral persons can be considered either *separately* or *conjointly*. Considered separately, according to their different statuses, they are either *public* or *private*, depending on whether the status they occupy is public or private. . . .

2. The distinctions among private persons are drawn from the following sources. (1) *Gender*, whence are male, female, and hermaphrodite. Although these have their proper place among physical things, they are nonetheless pertinent here on account of some moral respect, insofar as they are treated differently in civil life. For we not only consider most women beneath the dignity of male anger but also make less of their reproaches than those of men; nor do we value their judgments and testimonies that highly, or ordinarily admit them to public offices, capable though they are in other respects. From a hermaphrodite, however, we turn as from a monstrosity of nature.

(2) *Moral status in time*, whence a youth is dealt with in one way and an old man in another, and something that does not befit a youth befits an old man, and vice versa. So, too, the authority of an old man differs from that of a youth.

(3) *Moral position in the civil state*, whence one man is a citizen, another a resident alien, another an inhabitant, and another a foreigner. These, just as they are obligated to the state in a different manner, are also not valued in the same manner in the distribution of goods and the imposition of burdens.

(4) *Moral position in the family*, whence are husband, wife, father, children, master, and servant. These are as it were the ordinary members, to whom a guest is occasionally added in unusual circumstances.

(5) *Lineage*, whence are noblemen sprung either from an illustrious or a less

illustrious family, and commoners who are variously distinguished in different civil states.

(6) *The trade* to which someone applies his effort in a special manner, and which is either noble or ignoble. Here belong the merchants, who make their living by exchanging wares—a group whose rear is brought up by peddlers—as well as those who have the care of fields and of plants or animals, such as peasants, vinedressers, gardeners, herdsmen, and so on.

3. Considered conjointly, persons make up a *society* or a council when several of them are so united among themselves that both their will and their action counts as a single action or will, and not as several. And this is understood to happen when single individuals coming together into a society so subject their own wills to the will of some one person who is head of the society, or to a whole council, that they are willing to acknowledge and have regarded as their own will and action whatever he or the major part of the society has decreed or done in seeing to the society's affairs. Hence it is that although before, whatever several persons willed or did was considered as so many wills and actions as the number of physical persons there, a single will is attributed to those who have been conjoined into a society, and whatever action proceeds from them as such is deemed the action not of many persons but of one, even if many physical individuals have concurred in it. Hence a society of this kind also obtains special rights and goods which individuals as such can by no means claim for themselves. It must also be observed here that just as single persons remain the same even though their bodies undergo significant changes in the course of time through various additions and losses of particles, so a society is not made other through the particular succession of individuals. Rather it remains the same, unless there falls upon it at one time a kind of change that utterly destroys the former body's or society's principle.

Definition 5

A MORAL THING IS A THING REGARDED WITH
RESPECT TO ITS PERTINENCE TO PERSONS

2. Dominion is commonly divided into three kinds, which you may call modes of having, namely *eminent, ordinary*—which may be direct—and *useful*. The first denotes the authority belonging to a state or its head over citizens' things for the sake of public utility. Its effect is this, that it can effectively restrict the power of ordinary dominion as seems advisable from the public good. Ordinary dominion is that by which private individuals possess goods of their own over which they have

the full faculty of disposing, except insofar as this is restricted by eminent authority. Here, if the usufruct is under another's control, the sort of dominion which the owner of a field given over to tenancy has is called direct. Finally, we are said to have useful dominion over those goods whose usufruct only is under our control, such as those we possess as tenants, the direct dominion being under the control of others.

4. And so the things that belong to us as *our own* in an ordinary or even an eminent manner (the way in which states or their heads possess their goods), we can enjoy as we decide and keep any others whatsoever away from them, unless they have acquired a special, overriding right through agreed-upon pacts; nor can they, while they are ours, be fully another's in the same manner. *In the same manner*, I say, for nothing prevents—what is also very common—the same thing from belonging to different individuals according to different modes of having. Thus the state has an eminent, a field's owner a direct, and a tenant useful dominion over the same field. . . .

11. Now the final complement of ownership, as it were, and that by which, when given, it begins actually to exert its full effects, is *possession*. By it someone actually apprehends and occupies some thing, either through himself or through another acting in his name, as the nature of the thing allows, and has it under his authority in such a way that he can actually exert the power of ownership and dispose of it. Possession begins from bodily apprehension, but for this to produce some effect there not only should be in the one apprehending an intention to take possession of the thing by that act, but it must also be undertaken in such a way that the rest can presume it to have been undertaken for that end. Apprehension is understood to occur, however, not only when the body is brought into contact with a thing, but often also through some sign intended for this, such as the receipt of keys when, for example, someone buys a house or merchandise stored in a warehouse, and similar things. . . .

12. The next thing, therefore, is that we examine the origin of ownership and the more common ways of acquiring. Here we suppose, at the beginning at any rate, what the Sacred Scriptures say: that it was by the concession and will of the Deity that man asserted ownership and dominion for himself, not only over inanimate but also over animate things. For we read that the things springing from the earth were expressly assigned to man for food—which cannot happen without their consumption. Nor did God grant man a lesser sovereignty over animate things living in the air, the land, or the waters. This grant, as we have already implied above, has no prescriptive force but is merely a gracious privilege which man can use to the extent he pleases, without being bound to exercise it in all respects. For he would otherwise sin against the divine law if he set some animal (for instance, a bird, a fish, or a wild beast) free or neglected an opportunity to bring it under his power—something which no sane person would say.

13. Now whether this grant of dominion over animate things bestows on man a boundless authority, so that he can kill them even for unnecessary uses, is not sufficiently apparent from the nature of dominion itself. For this does not involve a license to kill with impunity and as one pleases; nor could men have complained that the divine bounty toward them had been meager or insufficiently attentive to

their necessities, even if authority over the life of animals had been denied them. For their service in cultivating the earth, and those fruits of theirs which are otherwise not useful to themselves, such as milk, a portion of their eggs, wool, and so forth, could have sufficed for men to maintain their lives. Nor did man receive the authority to turn animals into food as he pleases directly from the fact that God commanded him to sacrifice them as a sign of divine worship. For something can be permitted to man by virtue of a special command of God which would otherwise by no means have been permitted him. But because we find that God has nowhere disapproved of that slaughter of animals for man's food, but has rather enacted certain laws concerning it, we correctly conclude that it is not opposed to His will.

15. Moreover, just as the law of nature has granted man the authority to claim and take for himself the things necessary for life (an authority which extends also to those things which somehow furnish some use, provided some right existing in the thing to be used or in some third party is not opposed), so it has left the measure of authority, and its degree and extent, to the will and disposition of men. That is, it was left up to them [to decide] whether to confine it within certain limits or none; so too, whether they wanted anyone to have authority over anything or only over a certain part of things; or, indeed, whether to assign everyone his own portion so that, content therewith, he could attribute to himself no right to the things that remained.

Even so, the peace and tranquillity of humankind, which the law of nature intends before all else, do not at all obscurely suggest what it is most agreeable to nature for men to establish here. For that an equal authority over anything should lie open to anyone, that is, that anything should be set out for anyone to use and dispose of, or—what comes to the same thing—that all things should be common to all, this the peace of humankind, at least now that it has multiplied, does not admit. Indeed, the conflicting appetite or neediness of two or more persons with regard to the same thing is the readiest opportunity for war, and no one would be willing to put up with another's desire to assert for himself as much of a right to a thing produced by the former's care as the former himself. Hence I shall pass over the remaining disadvantages with dry feet.

Nature therefore urged that for the sake of preserving peace in regard to those things from whose indiscriminate use quarrels would probably arise, each person be assigned some certain thing over which another could claim no right for himself. The rest, whose use is inexhaustible, were left by nature to the bare choice of men, to dispose of as they might please. Nor, indeed, was there ever such a state— at least after men had dispersed into several families—where all things were common. For the things which poets fabricate about a golden age are either distortions of man's state in Paradise or hint at the liberality and humanity of ancient men, by which they generously allowed the use of their own things to anyone who needed them. In this way we say even today that all things of friends are common. Nor was it necessary to mark a field so anxiously with a boundary when its expanse amply sufficed for a few men.

The sum of what has been said comes down at last to this: The first man claimed things for himself, with God's leave and no countervailing obstacle in their nature, and at the urging of necessity, as they presented themselves [to him], as it were. After men had multiplied, nature recommended that these things be possessed separately by individuals in shares, to the exclusion of the rest, so that the disadvantages that would arise from communion be avoided. Their actual division, which confers dominion over a certain portion of things on individuals, has been confirmed by the tacit or express pacts of men. And so ownership, insofar as it implies a division of things among many owners exclusive of others, was recommended by nature; actually, however, it was established by men's pacts.

16. It appears from what has been said, if we regard the pure law of nature, that *occupation* alone sufficed for the first owners of things. For since no right prevented man from designating both animate and inanimate things for his own uses, nothing remained but to assert his title to them by an act. This method has a place even today in the case of things which are considered abandoned, that is, those which no one has ever wished to claim for himself, or those which a former owner has thrown away or by some accident lost without the intention of recovering them.

This intention is presumed from words and from deeds: when a thing is thrown away, for instance—unless it was done because of the times, and in order that the thing might be reclaimed again; or when someone knowingly makes with another (as with its owner) a contract about a thing that was formerly his own, but which the other now has in his possession. It is also understood from deeds not done, that is, when someone, for no plausible reason, omits that which he could easily have done to recover that thing.

Now the reason that other men cannot also lay claim to these kinds of things, as to a common inheritance, is that a right to things which will pass to another by way of inheritance is transmitted hand to hand, as it were, without interruption, from a former owner at his express or presumed will; but in the case of these things there either was no actual right of anyone at all, or it has completely expired without passing from a former owner to another, so that no one can lay special claim to that right for himself except one who has specially acquired it anew. For when those who came after them took possession of the inheritance left by the first men, they should also be thought to have entered—besides the original pact whereby any of the heirs, upon having received his portion, renounced his claim to the rest—into another, tacit pact to the effect that since they themselves had entered upon the entire inheritance of the globe, as it were, whatever had at that point not been expressly assigned to someone, at least in a general manner, would in the future be left to the one who first occupied it. This sort of pact must necessarily be understood [to have occurred], in order to avoid the quarrels that would otherwise have arisen thereafter. Even so, any one person can by no means claim, through occupation, things that have by the tacit consent of nations been regarded as derelict in such way that no one can attribute them to himself as his own without their indulgence; . . .

If you were to remove God's grant, therefore, the first man received authority over all things by title of occupation alone, and there was no need for any other besides, since no one existed whose right could be an impediment to him. Nor did he acquire any less dominion over all things because he could not actually take possession of them all and direct them to his own use. For it sufficed that while he apprehended some portion of things with his body, he embraced the rest with his mind, intending to apprehend them as well when the occasion allowed. Just as someone who has entered only one room of a palace is judged to have occupied the whole, and in the case of things that have devolved on someone in their entirety, one who has apprehended only some parts is judged to have taken possession of all. And the same right would have sufficed even if God had created several men at the same time. For the pact concerning the division of things which they would have considered it necessary to enter then, in order to preserve concord, would not have given them a new title or right, but would only have circumscribed a common right by means of certain boundaries and assigned to each a proportionate share; inasmuch as such a pact concerning things altogether presupposes some right to them.

Definition 7

AUTHORITY IS AN ACTIVE MORAL POWER BY WHICH A PERSON CAN PERFORM A VOLUNTARY ACTION LEGITIMATELY AND WITH A MORAL EFFECT

1. Authority, as it comes into consideration here, is either *perfect* or *imperfect*. The former is that in which someone who forcibly and illegitimately impedes its exercise (which happens when that authority does not depend on his own will) does an injury. This gives the injured party an action against him in a human court, an action replaced by war among those not subject to a common judge, unless one of them happens to be subject to the other as to a supreme judge. The latter is that in which someone who has been illegitimately and forcibly kept from exercising it, is treated inhumanely, to be sure, but in such a way that he does not have an action in a human court, unless perhaps the occurrence of necessity supplies what is lacking in right. Thus, for example, someone who forcibly prevents me from entering my own field does an injury, which gives me an action against him. But someone who denies me a harmless passage through his field, which I can find elsewhere only through troublesome meanderings, acts inhumanely, to be sure, yet I am by no means able to bring an action against him in a human court for that reason. Except that, for example, if an enemy sets upon me from the rear I am permitted to pass through in order to save my life, even by destroying one who stands in the way. The former authority can also be called a right to act, the latter an aptitude.

3. Furthermore, most instances of authority may by reason of their object be reduced chiefly to four kinds. For they concern either *persons* or *things* and, in each case, either *one's own* or *those of others*. Authority over our own persons and actions is said to be *freedom*, which can be understood from the things said above, where we dealt with states. Authority over one's own things is called *dominion*, which has likewise been explained above. Authority over other persons is called *sovereignty*. By means of it another can be legitimately and effectively enjoined to furnish something; that is, he has an obligation not to resist the command, or not to refuse it.

Now sovereignty is either *absolute* or *restricted*. The former is that whose acts can neither be rendered void by some third, superior party, nor refused by those over whom it is wielded, on account of some right acquired or retained through a pact entered into in the conferral of sovereignty. The latter is that where either or both of these things can happen.

For someone's sovereignty admits of restriction in a twofold manner: either when a sovereign's power is restricted by one who has a superior sovereignty, or those who obey are absolved from their obligation to carry out certain commands; or when those who have given someone sovereignty over themselves have, by means of a pact, done so with the express reservation that they do not wish to be obligated by his commands in certain matters. This kind of restriction is by no means repugnant to nature. For since he to whom the sovereignty is given otherwise has no right against me, and therefore has whatever authority he holds over me by my mere will, it is no doubt apparent that the extent to which I am willing to admit his sovereignty over me has been left up to me—though these restrictions should by no means be such that they overturn the end of sovereignty and reduce it altogether to nothing, or render the pact between sovereign and subject useless. But subjects are not understood to have the authority to refuse certain commands of a sovereign unless they are permitted either to appeal to arbiters or a judge, or to come together with one another into a council where they have the right to examine the sovereign's deeds. . . .

4. Finally, by authority over others' things we mean those rights over another's things which have been acquired either from the owner's grant or from some pact, with the ownership of the thing remaining under the owner's control. Here usufruct is pertinent, as it is the right or authority to use and enjoy another's things while their substance remains unimpaired. It is a matter of custom that this can be established in the case of any useful things whatever, except those which are consumed by that very use, or those whose use consists in abuse. . . .

5. The effect of authority is the conveyance to another of an obligation to do something, and to allow or not impede the actions performed by virtue of that authority, as well as the ability to confer on another a faculty to do or have something which he previously lacked.

Definition 8

A RIGHT IS AN ACTIVE MORAL POWER,

BELONGING TO A PERSON, TO HAVE

SOMETHING FROM ANOTHER BY NECESSITY

1. Besides those meanings whereby the word 'right' is used for law and for a complex or system of homogeneous laws, as well as for a judicial or legal opinion applied to deeds (when we say, for example, that a judge pronounces law or that a lawyer gives an opinion about law), it is most frequently used for that moral quality by which we either rightly command persons or possess things, or by which things are owed us. Thus the authority over both persons and things, our own or those of others, commonly comes with the name of 'right,' and the authority which regards things is specifically said to be a 'right in the thing.'

Yet the following distinction seems to be observed concerning these terms. 'Authority' better conveys the actual presence of the said quality over things or persons, but connotes more obscurely, and leaves almost undecided, the manner in which anyone has acquired it. The term 'right,' however, gives clear and proper indication that the quality has been correctly acquired and is now also correctly possessed. But because most kinds of the quality of which we have just spoken enjoy special names, which that quality whereby some thing is owed us lacks, we have decided to distinguish it here with the word 'right,' yet in such a way that we by no means wish to be bound always to accept this term within these narrow confines.

2. Now a right is either *perfect* or *imperfect*. One who infringes the former does an injury, which gives the hurt party an action in a human court against the one who hurt him. To it there corresponds, on the other side, a perfect obligation in the one from whom that which is owed us will come. I can for this reason compel him when he refuses to pay the debt of his own accord, either by threatening action before a judge or, where there is no place for this, by means of force. Rights of this kind, when they have not yet been clearly enough deduced, or are called into doubt by the one whom they regard, are ordinarily called pretensions.

5. An imperfect right, however, which some call an aptitude, is when someone owes something to another in such a way that if he should refuse it he would, indeed, act unfairly; yet the hurt party would by no means receive an injury giving him an action against the one who hurt him. Nor could he claim that right for himself by force, except where necessity does not admit another way of promoting his welfare. Now we have only an aptitude in regard to all those things which others owe us from some imperfect obligation—concerning which we will have to treat in greater detail below. Thus I can neither compel another to give benefits nor bring an action against him for ingratitude, even though one who neglects an

opportunity to benefit others, or fails to return the gratitude he readily could for benefits received, does sin.

It often happens as well, however, that someone can rightly accept something bestowed by another, yet in such a way that the latter does not have an obligation to bestow it, nor the former a perfect right to have it, but only the bare ability. Thus, for example, when several equally qualified persons seek to obtain a post to which none of them has some special right before the other, the one who has the authority to confer it can at his pleasure select whom he wishes, leaving those who have been rejected no cause for complaint.

Definition 10

PRICE IS THE MORAL QUANTITY OR VALUE OF MERCHANDISE OR THINGS, AND OF ACTIONS THAT ARE GOOD FOR MAN IN COMMUNAL LIFE, IN ACCORDANCE WITH WHICH THEY ARE FIT TO BE COMPARED WITH ONE ANOTHER

1. The most natural foundation of price in things is their ability to furnish some use in communal life. Hence we are ordinarily accustomed to say that things which are altogether useless have no price. However, a thing's use is determined not only from the fact that it really contributes to the preservation and enjoyment of our life, but also from the fact that it affords, even in certain men's sole opinion, some pleasure or ornament—which kinds of things have often had an inordinate price placed on them by men's luxury and craving.

Now there are various factors which are commonly considered in the comparison of things with one another by reason of their price. For here a thing's necessity, and the nobility of its use, are so far from being always the primary considerations that, instead, those things which our life cannot do without are by a particular providence of nature, which pours forth an abundant supply of them, quite cheap. That which above all contributes to this is rarity, which is none too little commended when things toward which men's passion is frequently and vehemently drawn are brought from far removed places. For most men value mainly things that they will have in common with a few; on the other hand, whatever is seen among anyone's household belongings is cheap.

Now price is ordinarily determined on the basis of usage or custom; that is, things are ordinarily valued at the amount that tends commonly to be offered or given for them. This hardly prevents it from having some latitude within which more or less can be demanded, except where the law has established a thing's price at a precise point. However, the common price usually takes account of the labors and expenses incurred by merchants. There can also be certain estimable accidents of a thing on account of which it may be lawfully bought or sold above or below the common price: a consequent loss, for example, deferred profit, a special feeling, or if something otherwise not to be bought or sold is bought or sold in order to please another. . . .

2. It is not only corporeal things that have prices of their own, but also incorporeal ones; even men's actions themselves, insofar as they are able to afford others some advantage or delight. It must nonetheless be noted concerning these that some of them have through divine or human laws been placed outside [the sphere] of human commerce, so that men should not establish a price for them, or exhibit and perform them toward one another for a price. Of this sort are those sacred actions to which the divine will and institution has assigned some supernatural effect: the remission of sins, for instance, and of the punishment owed for sins, through priestly absolution; the application of spiritual benefits through the performance of sacraments; and similar actions which, if someone does them for another for a price, he is said to commit simony. Similarly, a judge cannot rightly sell for a price the justice which he should administer without charge. . . .

3. Now price can be divided into *vulgar* price and *eminent* price. The former is that contained in anything whatever which enters into commerce, on the grounds we have just spoken of. Men did not know another price besides this before the use of money was introduced, and some barbarians still do not know of one. Hence the commerce of such men consisted in the simple exchange of things, and they could not offer or obtain one another's labors for hire except in return for a thing. But this method of carrying out contracts among men was not convenient enough. For it is not easy for just anyone whatsoever to possess the sort of things which another may wish to exchange for his own, or which are equivalent to the other's thing. And in states, where citizens are distinguished by various ranks, it is necessary that there be many kinds of men who can either not maintain their lives at all by means of that exchange, or at least only with difficulty. Hence civil life was uncultivated and simple so long as only that simple exchange of things obtained, and those who make use of it even today are far beneath the customs of the more cultivated nations.

Therefore, most nations agreed among themselves, upon considering the disadvantages of [such] exchanges, to impose some eminent price, as it were, upon a certain thing, by reference to which the prices of the remaining things might be measured, and in which they would be eminently contained, as it were, so that it could be exchanged for any thing whatsoever and easily used to execute commercial transactions and carry out whatever contracts they wished. The nobler metals—gold, silver, and bronze—were deemed most apt for this thing, inasmuch as their material is not too frequently encountered, durable, and not hard to handle on account of its bulk; though a state could also designate other materials for this use, to be employed by the citizens in place of money. . . .

Definition 11

PRINCIPLES OF HUMAN ACTION ARE [THINGS]

FROM WHICH HUMAN ACTION ARISES,

ON WHICH IT DEPENDS,

AND BY WHICH IT IS COMPLETED

1. Principles of action are either *dispositive*, by which a human action is only begun, or *efficacious* and *determinative*, by which it is reduced to act.

Dispositive principles include (1) *principles that move*, both *indirectly* and *directly*. This they do, in the former case, either naturally, as an *end*, or morally, as an *occasion*; and likewise in the latter case, either naturally, as a *feeling*, or morally, where they do so either externally, as *persuasion*, *command*, or *incitation*, or internally, as *obligation*. (2) *Principles that direct*, either morally, as a *law*, or naturally, as the *understanding*. (3) *Principles that assist*, such as *means*, which are either natural, such as a natural power and the *locomotive force* that especially exerts itself here, or moral, such as *authority*. Efficacious or determinative principles are the proximate causes from which human action has its being; and they are such either simply, like the *will*, whose regard for a directive moral principle is called *obedience*, or together with inclination, like a *habit*.

2. An end is some good that is sought for its own sake, or that has in itself something for whose attainment the action may be undertaken. It is either *ultimate* or *intermediate*, with the latter revealing the greatest variety. The former is called the highest good, which is either *imaginary*, that is, something which seems such to the corrupt judgment of men, such as bodily pleasure, riches, honor, power, fame, and so forth; or *true* and congruent with reason, such as the pleasure and repose of the mind that results from the exercise of the virtues and the contemplation of things. Opposed to it is the highest evil, which is, again, either *imaginary*, such as poverty, diseases, servitude, contempt, and so forth; or *true*, such as the unrest and anxiety of the mind that springs from the exercise of vices and the ignorance of things. Now the end has assigned to it the chief place among principles because it is necessary for it to be known and evaluated before a rational agent, whose nature abhors proceeding into a vacuum, as it were (that is, undertaking something without a predetermined end), moves himself to perform an action.

5. An agent employs a means in order to obtain some end when the will cannot immediately bring it about by its own motion that some end approaches the agent, as it were, or the agent an end. The following rule must be observed concerning this: One who grants a right to the end is deemed also to grant a right to those means without which the end cannot be obtained; for otherwise nothing would be done. From this it follows that if the means are illicit or impossible, I am not bound to an end which cannot, and insofar as it cannot, be obtained without them.

Hence evils are not to be done in order that goods may come from them, because no one is thought to be obligated to a good which he is given no way of reaching without sin. . . .

6. . . . Here we must note, concerning the will, only that it may be called a habit insofar as it has been strengthened and readied to deal expeditiously, in regard to a moral object, with the difficulty of abstaining from or the vehement inclination toward it. A will disposed in such a way is carried toward the object, the moment it presents itself, with so great an impetus that it can hardly restrain itself. And this habit is directed mostly toward moral actions, whatever they may be, because an action's good and evil is measured chiefly by the agent's choice, a choice that is commonly thought to have been hardly complete unless a person has acted from habit. Hence, also, only a person who acts well out of habit is assigned the name of a good man, and one who acts badly out of habit the name of a bad man; not one who has done something good once or twice by a chance impulse or because he could not easily do otherwise, or done something bad through thoughtlessness or the violence of the passions.

Those habits, however, by which the mind is so composed that it conducts itself according to the prescription of right reason in regard to the objects by which it is moved, come with the special name of virtues. For what reason prescribes is this: that the appearance of either good or evil, when presented to the mind, not perturb and shake it out of its tranquillity. Just as we say, on the other hand, that someone labors under vice if his mind is so moved by the appearance of a harsh or pleasant object that his tranquillity is interrupted by the agitation of violent waves, as it were. . . .

Definition 12

OBLIGATION IS AN OPERATIVE MORAL QUALITY BY WHICH SOMEONE IS BOUND EITHER TO FURNISH, OR TO ADMIT OR SUFFER SOMETHING

1. This definition agrees with that common definition of the lawyers which defines obligation as a bond of law by which we are constrained by necessity to furnish some thing. For obligation throws a kind of moral bridle over our freedom of action, as it were, so that we cannot rightly proceed in any other direction than the one in which it leads; although the natural efficacy of no obligation so constrains the natural freedom of our will that it cannot in fact turn toward other things.

Now obligation can, by reason of its origin, be divided into *connate* and *adventitious*. The former belongs to all men immediately upon birth by virtue of the fact that they are such, fully exerting itself as soon as they have begun to be able, on account of their age, to understand its force and to regulate their actions through reason. This class contains that obligation of all men toward God as supreme Master of this universe, by force of which we are bound to acknowledge and venerate His sovereignty and to observe the laws He has given us; and likewise the obligation of all men toward any men as such, through which they should carry out the natural law toward one another and live a social life. Adventitious obligations are those voluntarily assumed by those who have already been born, or those enjoined by the command of a superior or by law.

2. Next, obligation is, by reason of its subjects, either *equal* or *unequal*. We call an unequal obligation that which constitutes him to whom we owe something as our superior, and which confers authority or some kind of sovereignty over us. Such is subjection or the obligation by which someone is bound to do the things enjoined by another by virtue of his sovereignty. This can be divided into universal subjection, by which anyone whosoever is bound to render obedience to God, and particular subjection, by which certain men are subject to certain men.

The latter, in turn, is either public, by which someone is subject to the public sovereignty of another, or private, by which we are placed under someone's private sovereignty. Each is either limited, such as the subjection of a wife, a son, a ward, an employee, and so on; or unlimited, such as the subjection by which citizens are bound to the state, and the complete personal servitude by which someone is bound to direct his own useful actions entirely to the use and according to the discretion of another. Yet each of them gives way to the obligation toward God, and the latter also to the obligation toward the state, when it is not possible to satisfy both at the same time.

4. Next, as to duration, some obligations are *permanent*, some *temporary*. The former cannot be removed so long as the persons in whom they inhere exist. Such is the connate obligation toward God and any men as such, which a man cannot put off so long as he is a man. For even if I myself am not bound to perform the law of nature toward another when he does not perform it toward me, but can deal with him by force and, indeed, by right of war—and this, because that obligation is a mutual one, so that when it is broken off on one side it no longer binds the other, which is why its performance is suspended, at least as concerns most precepts of the law of nature prescribing the duties to be performed toward the other, . . . it nonetheless always remains the case that as soon as the consideration of our own safety permits, we should be prepared again to deal with him according to the law of nature and to cultivate peace. Such is the nature of all obligations resulting from affirmative precepts or laws: They order us to be always prepared to perform their acts whenever an opportunity to perform them is supplied, and to cease from actually performing them when there is no object to receive them, when the object labors under an evil disposition, or when a stricter obligation leaves no place for a looser one—just as, here, the care for my own safety in no way permits me to take into consideration the safety of one who proceeds unjustly to attack it.

Now the debt of honor and gratitude which children owe their parents can be listed here among adventitious obligations insofar as it ordinarily does not cease so long as these are among the living. Even so, it seems that cases can be given in which that obligation would altogether expire: namely, when parents, without the urging of any necessity, throw aside the care of a newborn infant and expose it, deprived of all human assistance; or when, thereafter, they shamefully neglect its education or otherwise proceed with a hostile intent to subvert its welfare. For that obligation of children flows chiefly from the law of gratitude, which looks back upon preceding benefits. Parents can certainly not impute to their offspring that bare act of generation in which, indeed, they seek little else than their own pleasure; nor can a mother, though exhausted by great discomforts during gestation and birth, be regarded as having given a benefit if she has brought her offspring into the light in order to reject it, or if by neglecting its education she allows it to contract shameful mores. And I am thought to be remitting the debt of gratitude which someone is to return if I myself strive to destroy his gratitude for my benefits by the harshness of my injuries. . . .

5. As for that way of looking at obligations by which they correspond to one another, obligation is either *mutual* or *non-mutual*. The latter is the case when one person is, indeed, bound to furnish something to another, yet in such a way that there is in that other to whom something is owed no corresponding obligation which binds him to furnish something equivalent. Such is men's obligation toward God, through which they, indeed, owe Him absolute obedience, while He, on the other hand, is in no way bound, as by the force of an externally derived obligation, to furnish them something for that obedience. For whatever things He furnishes to men proceed from His own gratuitous benevolence.

Of the obligations involving men on both sides, however, none seems to be of this sort. This is because it is repugnant to the natural equality of men among themselves for one to be so obligated to another that the latter is in turn obligated to him in no way at all. Of course, nature in no way intends that all men be actually equal, as far as their adventitious states and authority are concerned, in that it destines man to a social life, which can by no means continue to exist with that complete sort of equality. Yet because the actual inequality of men among themselves—that Gaius is superior, for instance, and Titus inferior, that Sejus is prince and Sempronius subject—is from men's mutual agreement and from positive laws, it cannot be presumed that one person wished to bind himself to another in such a way that the other would be in no way bound to himself in turn, at least by another kind of obligation. Add to this that society could not exist unless each and all were connected with one another by a mutual bond.

6. A mutual obligation is one to which there corresponds another obligation in the person to whom something is owed on account of it. This is, in turn, either *imperfectly mutual* or *perfectly mutual*. The former is one to which there is, indeed, a corresponding obligation in the other, but of a different sort; such as when a perfect obligation has referred to it one that is only imperfect. This happens chiefly for two reasons: Either an adventitious inequality is so great that one person has supreme sovereignty over the other, or one person does not himself wish to bind

the other with an obligation equal to his own. The former occurs in the case of obligations that intervene between an absolute prince and his subjects, and between a state and a citizen. The nature of these is such that there indeed is a perfect obligation in the citizen or the subject, but only an imperfect one in the prince or the state.

There are those, of course, who say that an absolute prince cannot be obligated to a subject at all, or a state to a citizen, the reason being that subjects or citizens do, by virtue of the fact that they are such, resolve their will into the will of the prince or the state in such a way that it is comprehended in and therefore identical with it. But now, they say, no one can be obligated to himself, because this would be in vain. For since the one obligated and the one obligating are the same, and the latter can release the former, one could release oneself by one's own decision, and whoever can do this is already actually free.

Yet this reasoning, though no doubt acute in other respects, leads to no other conclusion than that an absolute prince cannot as such (that is, while remaining an absolute prince) contract with his subjects an obligation that is effective in a human court concerning the mode of sovereignty. It by no means concludes, however, that he cannot be bound in any way, either to administer the sovereignty well or, if he has perchance agreed, to something else besides.

To grasp this more clearly, we must observe that one who subjects himself to a prince or a state in such a way that it has supreme sovereignty over him, thereby acknowledges in it the authority to make determinations about the public welfare (in which the welfare of individuals is also contained) as it chooses, so that he does not reserve to himself any authority concerning this. Hence a case cannot be given where a prince can contract some special obligation with a subject about those things which properly concern the supreme sovereignty or its exercise. For to have supreme and absolute sovereignty, and to enter with one's subjects into a special obligation giving grounds for action among men concerning the manner of exercising the supreme sovereignty, implies a contradiction. For if an obligation of this kind were laid upon any prince, with the effect that an action could be brought against him by the citizens, or coercion brought to bear, it is apparent that he would not have supreme sovereignty at all.

Therefore, the obligation that exists between a prince and his subjects concerning things which pertain to the supreme sovereignty is such that there is, indeed, in the subjects, a perfect obligation to carry out the prince's orders, with the prince having grounds for action against those who refuse, and the authority to bring them back into line. In the prince, however, by virtue of his conducting himself as such, there is an obligation to care for the public welfare in the manner that he has promised, though only an imperfect one. This binds only by force of the divine and the natural law, of course, and not as if by force of some civil law; for there is no forum among men where an action of this kind can be brought against a prince, and subjects themselves do not have the authority to examine and judge a prince's acts. And so a prince is obligated to his subjects concerning the exercise of supreme sovereignty, but in such a way that if he uses it in a manner that is less than correct he sins against God as vindicator of the natural law. Because of the lack of a human forum and the inability of his acts to be judged, his subjects can have no action against him, no matter how much he has also pledged his faith by means of an oath. . . .

7. The other way in which an imperfectly mutual obligation arises is when someone, in obligating himself to furnish something to another, does not demand that the latter be in turn obligated to himself in the same way. This happens chiefly in the case of gratuitous promises. For in promising something to another I myself contract an obligation to furnish it, and this gives the other an action against me, even before a judge, when such arrangements have been sanctioned by the civil law. . . .

12. A *perfectly mutual* obligation is one which arises from an agreement of two or more persons concerning certain things or actions that are to be furnished to one another in such a way that there is, on each side, the same sort of obligation with respect to one another. Obligations of this kind commonly come with the name of 'pacts' or 'contracts,' even though the latter term mostly signifies those involving things or actions entering into commerce. Moreover, since these obligations regard things that have been agreed to on both sides, and presuppose a reciprocal promise, it is readily apparent that if one party has violated his given promise the other is also no longer bound, and therefore, that someone who does not stand by pacts already violated by another is not breaking a promise. . . .

14. Now the force of obligations arises either from the law of nature or from civil law. And concerning the latter kind of obligations, at least, it is beyond controversy that the effectiveness with which they bring their necessity to bear, so that what has been agreed to is furnished on both sides, ultimately resolves itself into the power or faculty to compel, which inheres in the one who wields the supreme sovereignty in a state. Hence the ultimate reason, in this category of obligations, why things owed from obligations legitimated by civil law should necessarily be furnished, is that if men do not wish to do so they are compelled to it by the civil authority.

States have for this very reason sanctioned most agreements, which otherwise contained obligatory force by virtue of the law of nature, by means of their own laws as well, and have on the basis of these given those entering into agreements a cause for action, so that if someone were unwilling to furnish what he should out of respect for the law of nature, he could be compelled by the power and might of the magistrate. For unless those agreements were recognized as inviolable, business transactions among citizens and a peaceful society could not continue to exist. Nor did it seem that peace had been sufficiently provided for by leaving each person to his own conscience here, especially the common crowd in which there is a feeble sense of morality, but of which a great part of the citizens consists.

Now although there is in almost all agreements which have been confirmed by the civil law an obligatory force from the divine law as well, so that even if someone cannot obtain his own right through the assistance of a judge—either because a slip has through imprudence been made in the customary pronouncement of formulas, or because the judge has rendered an unfair sentence on account of a bad grasp of the case, or his feelings, or has altogether failed to investigate the case—there still remains for the other, on the basis of the law of nature, the obligation to furnish the things concerning which there was an agreement; the former, to whom the injury was done, by no means retains the faculty to obtain the things owed him on account of the law of nature through the means otherwise granted him by that same law, namely through private force or through war. The reason for this is that individuals have through civil subjection renounced the authority to exact from the unwilling, in any other way than through the aid of the magistrate, that which their fellow citizens, at least, owe them. . . .

15. Now there is controversy among the learned about the strength of obligation in pacts which have been formed by the law of nature alone, such as exist among those who acknowledge no common judge in a human forum, or about which the civil law makes no disposition. For some have maintained that the efficacy of such pacts consists in a bond of shame and modesty alone, especially where no agreement [*sunallagma*] has as yet interceded and nothing has been furnished by either side, while the rest harshly criticize this opinion as weakening the trustworthiness of all treaties.

To us it seems that the matter is not so difficult if it is initially supposed that men have been fashioned by nature to cultivate society among themselves, and that no one should inflict on another that which can furnish a cause for discords and wars—something that happens chiefly when a person who has acquired no special right through pacts does not allow another to enjoy the same right with himself, and by his own effort makes the latter's condition worse. However, since society cannot be cultivated or preserved without mutual agreements—and the greatest cause that irritates men and throws them into discord, and without a doubt makes another's condition worse, is if someone is tricked by someone else whose trustworthiness, as expressed in a pact, he had relied on—it is quite apparent that men are altogether obligated by the law of nature to observe their pacts and that those who violate them sin against it. . . .

16. But the honor alone of having kept faith, the shame of having violated it, and concern about ruining one's reputation, even though they have no little importance, seem by no means to be effective enough to prevent a man from neglecting an obligation which he has contracted, if perchance his will has been altered by a regard for advantage or through desire. This is evident from the same reasons by which we will show below that the law of nature alone is not at all sufficient to preserve peace among men. It is necessary, therefore, that there be something which brings it about that a man does not easily dare to change his will once it has been expressed and bound fast, and that he judges it better to preserve it than to violate it, even if perchance a present advantage seems to urge the contrary.

Now we find that nothing has such an effect besides the fear of some evil which is to be inflicted by someone stronger on account of the violation of a pact, so that therefore the efficacy of obligations is ultimately derived from force. This force is either in the person himself, to whom the injury is done; in other men with whom the one breaking faith may perhaps have some business, or whom his faithlessness concerns on account of its common example, at least; or, finally, in the supreme governor of the universe, God. The force in the one with whom a pact was entered tends usually to be most immediately effective in constraining men not to depart from it. For most mortals are of such a disposition that given a just cause for exerting violence (such as the violation of pacts provides), they rarely restrain themselves, so as not to exact without delay the gravest penalties from the faithless one. . . .

But when someone's affairs are placed in such a state that, in his own judgment, he need not greatly fear any other man—a conviction that tends, for various reasons, to steal up even on those who are not exceedingly powerful—there remains the fear of God, the supreme vindicator of justice, Who does not allow violators of the law of nature to go away unpunished. This divine retribution often walks with a slow step, and others cannot always discover the manner in which it has revealed itself. Nonetheless, because there are frequent examples, and illustrious ones at that, of faithless persons afflicted by the greatest miseries, which all non-atheists commonly refer back to God as the avenger of faithlessness, it turns out that fear of the Deity adds ultimate strength to human trustworthiness.

It also appears from this, incidentally, how greatly it matters to human affairs that atheism not grow strong. For if you remove God from the function of administering justice, the entire efficacy of pacts which one of the contracting parties cannot by force compel the other to observe will immediately expire, and each person will measure justice by his own advantage. And, we may be sure (if we are willing to admit the truth), once the fear of divine retribution has been removed no sufficient reason appears why I should be bound at all, after the nature of my advantage has changed, to furnish that which I obligated myself to furnish another while my affairs so indicated, at least if there is no real evil for me to fear from any man on account of that [act].

26. Now it must be observed that so long as a number of persons have not come together into a composite moral person, they do whatever they do, and contract whatever obligations they contract, as individuals, so that there are as many actions and obligations as there are persons. Hence even if someone has existed in some multitude with which he himself has not coalesced into one moral body, and in which most or all the rest do or contract something that he himself has nonetheless not consented to or otherwise participated in, he must be thought not to have done it. And so a foreigner is not bound by the acts or obligations of the state in which he is staying, which have been contracted by it as such at the time he was there, unless he himself has specially concurred with them.

Yet when a number of persons enter as individuals with [other] individuals a kind of pact to the effect that they wish a certain category of their affairs to be cared for in common with them, and if, indeed, they have consented to some one form of accomplishing these things and, once some form has been commonly approved, have contracted with certain persons concerning the administration of that care for the common interest, these pacts are like a bond by which all those who have thus contracted have the character of one moral person, be it a family, an association, a state, or whatever name they may come with. From this it happens that all who are included in that society are understood to have consented to whatever is done or contracted by those to whom the care of the common interest has been entrusted, and to have contracted an obligation therefrom; in such a way, however, that all are bound by one (not each by some special) obligation, which has the same characteristics as the obligations contracted among individuals, except where the consensus of nations has introduced special observances concerning them.

27. Two pacts concur, therefore, in the establishment of society, especially civil society: one of them a pact of individuals with individuals, to the effect that they wish their mutually conjoined affairs to be administered by a common counsel; the other that which is entered into with those to whom the care for the common welfare is entrusted. The former necessarily requires the consent of each and all, and whoever does not express it is in no way bound by the plurality of votes to join himself to that group, but remains outside that society. Moreover, this pact is either absolute, by which someone binds himself absolutely to adhere to that group, whatever form of administration ultimately pleases the majority, or one supposing as a condition that a form of government approved by oneself is introduced.

In the latter case, also, the consent of individuals is required, and whoever does not signify it is not regarded as a member of society. In the former case, however, the consent of the majority is accepted as that of all, and so even a person who is not pleased by the form of government will be obligated through a plurality of votes by force of the prior pact. For since one who obligates himself to a group in such an absolute fashion cannot demand that all the rest follow his opinion, he is thought to have obligated himself to ratify that which the greatest part has approved, since no way of dealing with the matter could otherwise be found, and without this most pacts of this sort would come to nothing. Hence, in almost all societies which are administered by more than one person, it is accepted that the votes of the majority have the force of all, even if it happens now and then that the opinion of the minority is more conducive and becoming to the common interest. For in the case of general arrangements of this kind, since one can find almost no means for dealing with such matters that is without all disadvantage, that which is most expedient is to be followed....

49. Non-perpetual obligations are most naturally removed by the fulfillment of that which is owed, for if this is done, the obligation has fully and directly achieved its effect.... An obligation is also removed by being forgiven, when the one to whom something is owed himself releases us from the burden of furnishing it. This is because the right that was transferred to the other from the obligation is understood to return to us through his donation; just as, also, an obligation is not contracted from the beginning if the other, to whom something is offered, has refused it.... An obligation also expires when a person has altered the status on which the obligation was solely based—something which holds as much of the person in whom the obligation inheres as it does of the person in whom it terminates. Thus a magistrate who promises to defend his subjects is no longer bound if he has resigned his office. Similarly, someone who has promised obedience to a magistrate is no longer bound when he himself has ceased to be a subject, or the latter a magistrate.

Yet the kind of change in a subject which, though it would perhaps have impeded the obligation if it had been present at the time when it was being contracted, and little agrees with the subject at present, does not despite this render the subject unable to fulfill the obligation; [this kind of change] does not have the power to remove an obligation. For my right against another, which I have legitimately acquired, can by no means pass away, even if it may afterward seem less advantageous to him, unless this was expressly inserted into the pact from the beginning as a condition. Thus a people that subjects itself absolutely to a king is by no means freed from its obligation toward him even if another form of commonwealth should afterward, when its character has changed, be more advantageous to it. On the other hand, also, many obligations can be dissolved by the consent of the contractors, especially if a thing is still whole, that is, if nothing has by force of the pact been furnished on either side. . . .

Definition 13

A LAW IS A DECREE BY WHICH A SUPERIOR OBLIGATES SOMEONE SUBJECT TO HIMSELF TO DIRECT HIS ACTIONS ACCORDING TO WHAT THE SUPERIOR PRESCRIBES

1. To begin, law must be accurately distinguished from other things such as *advice*, *pact*, and *right*, which seem to have a certain kinship with it and are therefore confused with it by certain people.

Law differs from advice in that a person tries, through advice, to get someone over whom he has no authority (at least as far as the present matter is concerned) to do or omit something by means of reasons drawn from the thing itself, without bringing an obligation to bear on him, so that it is left up to him to decide whether he wishes to heed the advice or not. Even though it is true that law should not be without its own reasons, these are nonetheless not the proper cause why obligation is shown toward it. This lies, rather, in the authority of the one prescribing, who in signifying his will obligates a subject to act entirely according to his prescription, even if the reasons for the precept are perhaps not so clearly apparent to the subject.

2. Those who refer to laws as common agreements of some sort (or *koinas sunthēkas*) are not sufficiently accurate either, since they confuse laws with pacts by speaking in this manner. For certainly neither divine positive laws nor natural laws can be said to have arisen from the agreement or consent of men. Nor are civil laws pacts in a proper sense, even if they have originated from a pact. For even if some multitude not connected among themselves by supreme sovereignty mutually consented, to the highest degree, to certain rules of living, this would

nonetheless be in vain if a supreme sovereignty by whose force those going against the rules could be coerced by means of punishments had not yet been established. For that agreement would have no other force than that contained in pacts by virtue of the law of nature. But the end of civil laws is to bind men to the performance of something by a tighter bond than natural obligation; namely, by the addition of penalties which are to be inflicted in a human court by men who have some kind of authority over us.

What of the fact that it does not seem possible at all to enter an agreement of this kind without the establishment of supreme sovereignty? For where no one has a right to compel me by means of force to furnish that which was agreed upon, if I should be unwilling to do so of my own accord, nothing has been done between us.

Now if the authority to coerce reluctant individuals by means of force, and to bring them back into line, is given to the rest as a whole, something like a democracy is created. Still, civil laws derive their origin from a pact, because this is what establishes the supreme sovereignty to which the authority to enact laws in a group subject to it belongs. And this is not opposed by the fact that, in democracies, at least the major part of the citizens must consent in order for a law to be enacted. For that consent is the manner in which the force of the supreme sovereignty (conferred on the group as a whole on the basis of the pact, so that all of them together could by virtue of their sovereignty enjoin on individuals what the major part had approved) reveals itself.

In addition, since pacts depend upon our choice for their origin, what is to be done in them should be determined before we are obligated to do it. In the case of a law, however, which presupposes another's authority over us, we are first obligated to do something, while what is to be done, on the other hand, is determined afterward.

4. Now it is above all required, in a person who is going to enact a law for another, that he have such authority over the one on whom the law is to be enjoined that he can compel him to observe it by proposing a penalty. For it is vain to prescribe something that can be neglected with impunity. Hence no one is obligated by the laws of a person or group which has no authority over him. And the faculty of enjoining something in the manner of a law or precept implies superiority, just as the obligation to obey proves that we are inferior to one who is able to prescribe to us, at least where his sovereignty extends itself.

No one can, for this same reason, be directly and irrevocably obligated by his own decrees. For the fact that I am on account of my own consent so obligated in pacts or promises that I can either not be freed therefrom at all, or only by leave of the one toward whom my consent was directed, comes from the law which prohibits my withdrawing from that consent by which some right was once given to another. Where such a law (whether natural or civil) is lacking, nothing prevents me from being able to change the determination of my will, once it has been made by me, as I choose.

It must also be observed, however, that it makes no difference who draws up the formulas of the laws when they are being enacted, provided that the one to whom the legislative faculty belongs acknowledges and promulgates them as his own. Thus, in a monarchy, whatever is propounded by the authority of a prince has the validity of law, whoever has, in the end, drawn up the words of the law. So too, in a democracy, it can happen that a people enjoins the task of writing down the laws on one or more persons; yet the force of these laws is not from those writers but from the people, and so the legislative power does not inhere in them but in the people.

6. Now since God is as much the author of natural laws as of His own positive laws, and it would be impious to think that He establishes contradictories, it is no doubt obvious that divine positive laws can by no means be opposed to natural laws. There are those, on the other hand, who deny that even civil laws can be opposed to natural laws (unless, perchance, they have been enacted as an insult to God), arguing that those who come together into a state obligate themselves by means of a pact to the effect that they are willing to obey the mandates of the one who has supreme sovereignty, that is the civil laws, and that the law of nature orders them to observe that pact. But since that pact, and therefore the obligation to observe civil laws, is older than the promulgation of the laws themselves, we are commanded by force of that same natural law about the non-violation of pacts to observe all civil laws. For where we are obligated to obedience before we know what will be commanded, there we are obligated to obey in general and in all things. In addition, they say, even though theft, homicide, adultery, and so forth are prohibited by the law of nature, it is nonetheless up to the civil law to define what is another's and what one's own, what force it is licit to inflict upon a man, and what sort of lying together is adultery. . . .

But because these things flow from a hypothesis concerning the natural state of man, whose disadvantages we will indicate in their proper place, they cannot be admitted in so crude a form. For, to begin, as far as we who venerate the Sacred Scriptures are concerned, in the case of many crimes prohibited by the law of nature it can be determined from the very laws which were divinely promulgated to the Jews, and from the extraordinary revelations by means of which God has declared His will to men, in what way God, the author of nature, wishes them to be defined; so that although a state may in fact have excepted certain actions from being designated as criminal, they may all the same be opposed to the divine law. This is especially so since one cannot point to a sufficient reason God has assigned to those things, in the laws given to the Jewish people, definitions which need not have an equal place in the case of the remaining nations. . . .

7. Still, however this may be, the entire matter can be clearly settled if it is carefully observed that permission is one thing, a precept another; that is, it is one thing for civil laws to prescribe something, and another for them to permit or not prohibit it. For these are not opposed to one another: to be forbidden by the law of nature, and to be permitted by the civil laws. The permission of the civil law does not bring it about that some act is not contrary to the law of nature, or that someone can allow it without sinning against God; but only declares that someone who wishes to do it is not prevented by the civil authority or afflicted with a [civil] punishment, and that those acts are granted the same effects in a human court as those which follow upon acts that are also licit and legitimate according to the law of nature. . . .

But can a magistrate rightly permit such acts? This is a different question which depends on the following: Is a civil magistrate bound to punish any transgressions whatsoever that have been committed against the law of nature? This I would not dare to affirm in general, inasmuch as it may be necessary for one man to punish another on account of a violation of the law of nature or the divine law, not because it is necessary to assert the authority of the Legislator which has been infringed by men through sin (since He has His own special tribunal), but insofar as a moral society and peace cannot be preserved among men apart from this kind of punishment. If, therefore, the supreme civil authority has judged that the society of which I have spoken can be easily enough preserved even if the force of civil law is not assigned to some precept of the law of nature, it hardly seems bound to exact penalties from those who violate it, at least where it seems that on account of the peculiar character of the citizens, or for other reasons, greater disadvantages would follow from the civil prohibition of that thing than from its permission.

But if a state should enjoin upon its subjects, in the manner of a precept and with the threat of punishment, the performance or omission of something which the law of nature forbids or prescribes, we strongly oppose the notion that obedience is owed to it here. From this it appears that the pact by which someone obligates himself to obey the supreme sovereignty is not so absolute that it does not involve at least this limitation: "insofar as the things prescribed are not opposed to divine and natural laws."

9. Now the nature of a law consists chiefly in this, that it is a conceptual norm of actions insofar as these should be formed according to the will of some superior. I say a *conceptual norm*, because it confronts actions only conceptually, in representing to the intellect a superior's will about something to be done or omitted. For when it has become known, there immediately arises in a subject an obligation to act according to that law. This is because he understands that the one who enjoins that law on him has the authority to compel anyone who refuses by imposing some evil, and that he will certainly exert this authority in act, because it is presumed that no one wishes his action to have no effect.

10. ... Now civil laws become known through promulgation, where one should be certain about two things. One is that the laws proceed from the one who has the supreme sovereignty, the other what the meaning of the law is.... Nor is it plausible that any minister would publicize as the will of a prince something that is really not such, or would assume this kind of office without the prince's orders, since someone who attempts such things has no hope of hiding or of eluding the punishments for such brazen daring. In order that the meaning of a law may be grasped correctly, it is incumbent on those who promulgate it to do so as clearly as possible. If anything about the laws should seem obscure, one must request an explanation of it from the legislator, or from those who have been publicly appointed to render judicial decisions according to the laws. For it is the proper function of these persons to apply the laws to individual cases by interpreting them, that is, to declare, when particular deeds have been proposed, what the legislators have ordained concerning them.

14. What the law of nature properly is, from what spring it gushes forth, as it were, and by what sign something may be recognized as belonging to the law of nature, [on this] the learned are not well agreed. The Roman lawyers commonly

define the law of nature as that which nature has taught all animals. Those who refer to it as the order implanted in things by the Creator, by which each thing acts in accordance with its own nature and is carried toward the end that has been destined for it, do not differ much from them. But we are looking for a law of nature that directs the actions of a rational man. Even though this can be elucidated by contemplating the remaining creatures and their customary manner of acting, nonetheless, since we see that most things which are done by them do indeed agree with their nature but are abhorrent to man's, and do not find one animal in which all man's functions appear but different animals doing different things, from which the rest recoil, that law is to be derived from man's own nature alone and not drawn from brutes or inanimate things.

Nor have those who have deemed it sufficient to say that the law of nature is that which is universal in regard to time, place, and men left its essence any less obscure. Most of them have thought it appropriate to seek the idea and, as it were, the prototype of the law of nature in God Himself. Still, they are divided into two parties. Some of them derive it from the divine will, and since this is free they conclude therefrom that God can alter the law of nature; indeed, that He can command its contrary, just as commonly happens in positive laws. Others, however, assert that it is founded on the essential sanctity and justice of God, and since this is immutable they conclude that the law of nature is also immutable.

Now even though it has always seemed profane to us for a mortal to wish to probe divine matters more carefully than we are led by God Himself [to do], it nonetheless seems appropriate to note in a few words, concerning the former opinion, that it undoubtedly depended on God's will to assign man a nature with which that law would necessarily accord. For there appears to be no necessity which compelled God either to create man at all, or to create him different from brutes, with an obligation toward the law of nature. But, indeed, since God formed man's nature thus in order that His splendor might, as it were, be preserved by the complete observance of the law of nature, it is by no means right to believe that He wishes to eliminate or to alter this law, at least so long as He does not bring about a change in human nature. And so, given the constancy of human nature—even though it has been fashioned in this way by the divine will—the law of nature admits no change in contrast to those laws which depend on the divine will in such a way that they do not seem necessarily required by the human condition.

As for the latter opinion, even if no one would be so absurd as to dare to assert that the law of nature contains in itself something repugnant to the divine sanctity and justice, it will nonetheless be very difficult to prove that it is so modelled on the divine sanctity and justice, as on a prototype, that the manner in which God conducts Himself toward creatures, and especially toward men, is also how men should by force of that law conduct themselves toward one another. For the things which can be adduced from Sacred Scripture—that man has been fashioned in God's image—contribute nothing to this, since even those who admit that that image has been lost acknowledge that a sense of the law of nature has remained in man's reason. Among men, we commonly call holy someone who holds himself back from the crasser vices and observes his duty, [but] it would be extremely indiscreet to conceive God's holiness in this manner. Justice among men is almost completely summed up by these principles: "Hurt no one," and "Give to each his own." Yet it is not permissible to doubt that God can inflict something painful on a certain creature, in fact reduce it entirely to nothing, even without regarding its antecedent merit. Nor, indeed, can God owe anything to any man, so that He can be said to have done an injury if it is denied. The rules commonly observed by God's punitive justice are above our grasp, [though] it is certain, at least, that it does not always follow in the footsteps of a human court.

Finally, those who say that the law of nature is a dictate of right reason which indicates, on the basis of a certain act's agreement or disagreement with rational nature itself, that it contains moral turpitude or necessity and is, as such, consequently either forbidden or prescribed by God—the author of rational nature—speak well enough in other respects; except that they do not describe what the foundation of those acts' congruence and incongruence with rational nature is. We maintain, however, that it is the fact that man has been made a social animal by the Creator, and will set forth at greater length in Book II that this is properly the reason why things said to belong to the law of nature are so congruent with man's nature that if the contrary were done, it would seem as if violence had been inflicted on it.

16. The laws of nature are commonly divided into *principles*, which we will speak of below as fundamental laws of nature, whose truth and necessity follow directly from the character of human nature itself; and *conclusions*, which are deduced from these principles by necessary consequence or subsumption. Some of these can be more clearly deduced from principles and others less so, and some are also nearer to them and others farther.

Next, among the precepts of the law of nature some are *absolute* and obligate any men in whatever state; others are *hypothetical* and presuppose a certain state or act that depends on men's choice; that is, they deal with things that follow upon man's will. For there are many things which are arbitrary as far as the performance of some act goes, or where it is left up to men to choose whether they wish to undertake the act or not. But once that act has been undertaken it is followed by a moral necessity or obligation from some precept of the law of nature, or its manner and circumstances are determined thereby. . . .

17. Furthermore, just as the law of nature has its effect of obligating from the supreme legislator, God, so that anyone who has violated it must be thought to have gone against the will of God Himself; so there is no doubt about the fact that it rests with God to punish the violation of the law of nature as such. Yet because few have so modest a disposition that they are willing to do what nature commands solely out of reverence toward God, and since divine retribution often unfolds itself in hidden ways, so that it is spurned by most because they are unable to detect it anywhere, the law of nature alone did not suffice to preserve peace and fellowship among men. Rather it was necessary besides that men select from among themselves, through a pact with other men, those who would administer the execution of justice in a human court. For since the law of nature does not specifically determine who should command another or who obey, nor delineate the amount of punishment to be exacted among men, the latter obviously had to settle among themselves, by entering a pact, who would have sovereignty over the rest, by force of which they could prescribe rules of acting to others and exact punishments from

those who transgressed them, according as they judged it conducive to the public good.

18. Therefore, whatever laws the supreme civil sovereignty enjoins subjects to observe, under threat of a punishment that is to be exacted in a human court from those who violate them, are said to be *civil* laws. Whether these are taken from the law of nature or from positive law, or whether they proceed from the mere will of sovereigns, they obtain the entire effect which they exert in a civil court from the force of the supreme power that lends them its authority.

Most provisions of the law of nature, at least those without which peace cannot be maintained in society as such, do indeed have the force of civil law in all commonwealths; that is, they have been carried over into the body of civil laws. . . . Natural laws reinforce the civil law in all states, so that when the latter is lacking with respect to some case which absolutely demands a decision in a human court, recourse is had to the laws of nature and to an analogy resulting from a comparison with them, and that which is borrowed, as it were, by virtue of this from the law of nature acquires the force of civil law. . . . Yet it by no means follows from what has been said that human laws can make any modifications to the divine law, or that the extent to which it is necessary to observe divine laws depends on human authority. . . .

And so it is true to say that utility is the mother of law, that is, of the civil law as such (but not of the natural law), or that it has given the reason for its establishment. For it is by no other thing than utility or the public good that it is decided to which natural laws the effect of civil law is to be assigned in this or that commonwealth, and to which it is not; which legislative enactments are to be superadded to the natural law; and how punishments are to be inflicted and remitted—into which headings the civil law is almost completely resolved. . . .

24. We must also add something now *about the law of nations*, which is to some nothing other than the law of nature, insofar as it is observed among nations not connected with one another by supreme sovereignty, who must in their own manner perform toward one another the same duties that the law of nature prescribes to individuals. There is no reason for us to deal specifically with this here, since the things we are saying about the law of nature and the duties of individuals can easily be applied to whole states and nations that have also coalesced into one moral person. We do not think there is a law of nations in addition to this law, at least one which can be properly designated by such a name. For most of the things which are referred to the law of nations by the Roman lawyers and others—for example, certain matters concerning modes of acquisition, contracts, and other things—pertain either to the law of nature or to the civil law of individual nations, which coincides in these matters with the civil laws of most peoples. It is not correct to make a special kind of law out of these, however, inasmuch as those laws are common among nations not from some mutual agreement or obligation, but because they have been established by a special resolution of individual legislators in individual states, so that they can therefore be changed by one people without consulting others, and are often found to have been changed.

Definition 14

AUTHORITY IS AN ACTIVE MORAL POWER
BY WHICH A PERSON CAN PERFORM
AN ACTION LEGITIMATELY AND
WITH A DIRECT MORAL EFFECT

1. There are two powers of acting in man. One is the *natural* power by which he can perform some action through his natural strength, or omit it, without considering whether it is rightly done or not. Thus men can in fact do things that have been forbidden by the laws and omit those prescribed by them. The *moral* power in man, however, is that by which he can perform a voluntary action legitimately and with a moral effect, so that, in other words, the action agrees with or at least is not repugnant to the laws, and can produce moral effects in others.

Now man is deemed to have the authority to do all that can be done by him through his natural power—whatever is not forbidden by the laws, whether it is also prescribed by them or left indifferent. Indeed, his authority is often greater than his natural strength. But he has been deprived of the authority to do those things which have been legitimately forbidden him, either by some universal legislator or by someone else who has a special sovereignty over his actions.

Definition 16

A GOOD ACTION IS ONE THAT AGREES
WITH THE LAW, AN EVIL ACTION
ONE THAT DISAGREES WITH IT

1. The formal principle of goodness and badness consists in a bearing or determinative relation to a directive norm which we call a law. (This we always understand here as necessitating, not permissive, and if human, as not contrary to divine law.) For an intentional action is said to be good insofar as it proceeds from and is undertaken in accordance with what a norm prescribes, so that it agrees exactly

with the norm. It is called evil or, in a word, a sin insofar as it is undertaken against what the norm prescribes or is discrepant with it.

Now just as any directive norm, such as a nautical compass, for example, is said to be the cause of a journey's rectitude and a ship's arrival in port, not so much because the ship cuts a course that coincides exactly with the direction in which it points as because the captain steers the course prescribed by it, so a law is said to be the cause of rectitude in an action not so much because the action— for whatever reason it was undertaken—squares with it, but mainly because the action proceeds from the dictate of and in dependence on the law, that is, with the intention of rendering obedience to it. Hence if anyone by chance, or induced by a reason other than that of making himself compliant with the law, does what the law prescribes, he can indeed be said to have acted correctly (more in a negative than in an affirmative sense: that is, not badly), but not morally well; just as some- one who has downed a bird with a chance discharge of a gun cannot be said to have fired in an expert and skillful manner.

2. Moreover, since a law determines the quality or disposition of the agent, or the object, or the end, or, finally, certain circumstances of the action, an action is morally good or evil either because the agent is or is not disposed as the law requires, or because it is or is not directed toward the object, with that end, and in those circumstances ordained by the law. It must be noted here, however, that for some action to be good, it is necessary both that it agree with the law in regard to all its, so to speak, material requisites, and that as far as its formal aspect is con- cerned it be performed not out of ignorance or from some other cause, but in order to render to the law the obedience which it is owed. Hence an action that is other- wise materially good, as it were, is imputed to an agent as evil on account of his evil intention. Thus a person who helps while intending to harm deserves no reward. Similarly, one who uses his legitimate authority toward an evil end (for instance, a judge who uses his authority to exact punishments from those who are guilty in order to satisfy his private desire) sins.

And yet an action that is otherwise materially evil, as it were, by no means becomes good on account of an agent's good intention. This is why no one can use his own sins as means for the attainment of a good end, as it were, and why evils are not to be done in order that goods may come of them. For it is sufficient to render an action evil if even a single material or formal requisite thereof does not agree with the law. Hence an action immediately becomes evil if either the quality of the agent, or the object, or the end, or some circumstance, or the inten- tion should differ from the law. And furthermore, it is not only a completed mis- deed, or one that has obtained its end, that is reckoned as a crime, but even one only contemplated and begun, which even civil laws now and then afflict with the same penalty as (or one not much lighter than) a consummated misdeed, inasmuch as they judge it to be expedient that some crime be repressed even in its first impulses.

Definition 19

THAT WHICH IS PRODUCED BY A MORAL ACTION
IS SAID TO BE ITS EFFECT

1. Our chief focus here is the effect of good and evil actions as such, which is either *formal* or *material*, the former in turn being either *internal* or *external*. The internal effect of a good action is the approbation of a consequent conscience that sweetly delights itself in the recollection of that act. The internal effect of an evil action is the condemnation of a consequent conscience, and the disturbance of a mind that anxiously lingers in the contemplation of its misdeed and turns away with shame from those who also know of it. The external effect of a good action is its approval by upright men, especially by the one who prescribed it, as well as a good reputation and honor. The external effect of an evil action is its disapproval by the one who forbade it and by other good men, as well as a bad reputation and ignominy.

2. The material effect of a good, beneficial and, indeed, unowed action is *merit*; that of a bad action *demerit*. The former of these is compensated by *payment* and *reward*; the latter is followed by *punishment*.

BOOK II

Axiom 1

ANY ACTION WHATSOEVER THAT CAN BE DIRECTED
TO A MORAL NORM, AND WHOSE PERFORMANCE
OR NON-PERFORMANCE IS UNDER A PERSON'S
CONTROL, CAN BE IMPUTED TO HIM. *AND,*
ON THE CONTRARY, AN ACTION THAT WAS NOT
UNDER A PERSON'S CONTROL, EITHER IN ITSELF
OR IN ITS CAUSE, CANNOT BE IMPUTED TO HIM
(*AS A DEBT, THAT IS; THOUGH IF SOME GOOD*
HAS BEEN [PROVIDED] IT IS WELL FOR SOMEONE
TO IMPUTE IT OUT OF GRATITUDE)

1. Now that we have, in accordance with the plan of our undertaking, elucidated in the previous book the definitions of the things contained in Universal
Jurisprudence, it follows that in this book we should examine the *principles* to which
one ultimately ascends in juridical demonstrations. Accordingly we find, besides
the common axioms derived from first philosophy occurring here and there throughout this work, two kinds of principles which are proper to this discipline, namely
rational and *experimental*. The former's truth, certitude, and necessity flow from
reason itself without the perception of particulars and without engaging in discussion, merely by the bare intuition of the mind. The latter's certitude, however, is
understood from the perception and comparison of particulars which are in constant agreement with one another. We call them *observations*, just as we call the
former *axioms*.

Moreover, since man is in this world more for the sake of acting than of contemplating, and it is therefore more necessary for him to act rightly than to engage in the subtle contemplation of things which he may encounter only with the gaze of the mind, [the world was so] made (not without the special providence of the Creator) that the certitude of theoretical truths would for the most part have to be laboriously derived from first principles, and through an extended series of consequences, as it were, while the certitude of practical matters would be very easily based on the fewest foundations, and those as clear as possible, from which most of them can be deduced by an easy process. This was, of course, so that someone—even one with slight intellectual powers—could not allege as an excuse for his sins that because of the obscurity of things, as it were, he was not permitted to understand what had to be done.

Hence it seems to us that no more than two rational principles of this discipline need to be established; namely, that "A man must render an account concerning those actions whose performance or non-performance are under his control," and that "An obligation to act can be enjoined on us through the authority of another." If anyone should add to these the following, which are most manifest through common sense and experience, namely that "Man, whom nature has given the ability to understand things and to move himself to act by means of an internal movement of the will, has been enjoined by God, to Whose sovereignty he is absolutely subject, to live a social life, and to observe those things which, according to the dictate of right reason, make for its preservation," it will be easy for anyone whatsoever to find out what he should do or omit, especially now that civil sovereignties, "whose establishment was required by the necessity of social life," have also sanctioned most of those things by means of civil laws.

2. Imputation, therefore, occurs when the moral effects of an action that proceeds immediately or mediately from some person, or is performed toward him by another, are declared actually to inhere and to exert their force in him by the one whom that action regards. For people commonly suppose two kinds of imputation: *that from gratitude* and *that from debt*. The former occurs when someone derives upon another, from benevolence, the effects of some third party's action which the other could otherwise not claim for himself by right. This kind of imputation has place only in the case of things regarded with favor, not likewise in the case of those which are odious. For just as the nature of goods is such that they can be rightly furnished to another even for free, and without a reason, while evils cannot be inflicted without a preceding demerit, so if someone should be unwilling to confer some good upon another under the name of a pure benefit, he will be permitted to do it under the title of an imputed action which the other could otherwise not claim for himself. Yet it is by no means permitted to impute some evil to another unless he has by his own deed made himself a party to the offense. Thus, for example, a prince can rightly impute paternal benefactions to a son who is not conspicuous for any merits and, in view of these, confer on him honors which are otherwise not owed to him, but an innocent son should by no means pay for his father's failings in this way. For it does not properly have the rationale of a punishment when children are compelled to do without their feudal privileges upon

the occasion of a felony committed by their parents. For they do not have a right to these except after they have been handed down to them unimpaired. Our discussion here is chiefly about the latter kind of imputation, however, where the reason for the imputation inheres in the one to whom something is imputed.

6. Now the foundation of imputability, that is, an action's ability to be imputed to an agent, is that its occurrence or non-occurrence was under the agent's control. For since man was to live in such a way that he was not permitted to do whatever he pleased without having any regard for anyone, it followed that an account could be demanded of him concerning those actions which he himself had the faculty to do or omit.

It is evident from this that the following cannot be imputed to anyone: (1) Things which come about on account of physical necessity, or on account of natural causes, except insofar as someone has perchance applied active to passive things in order to produce that effect, or in some way moved the cause directing those things to determine that effect—as if, for example, someone should entreat God by means of prayers that rain may fall during a drought.

(2) The actions of our vegetative faculties in themselves, except insofar as someone has suggested an object to them. Thus, no one can demand that something be directly imputed to himself from the fact that he has been endowed by nature with a body that is robust, vigorous, tall, and so forth. And, on the contrary, no one can be rightly faulted for a body that is weak, fragile, and small, at least if no fault of his has intervened here. Also pertinent to this are those other things which are present from nature without our effort: for instance, the fact that someone enjoys a livelier or slower intellect, and sharper or duller senses, and so forth.

(3) Compelled actions, that is, those by which a person is compelled to lend or apply his members through the unavoidable power of someone stronger, and where it was not his own fault that this force could be brought to bear on him. For just as no one can by his command or sovereignty, or in another way, obligate another to do something contrary to the laws on his own, so if he has through force applied the latter's limbs to some act that is otherwise illicit, he cannot cause it to be rightly imputed to him. Hence no one can be compelled by another to sin, provided he himself does not wish to sin. Thus, for example, even if a virgin should be compelled through force to lend her limbs to the lustful action of a stronger person whose violence she is unable to ward off from herself, nothing can be imputed to her for that reason, unless perchance she has by her own fault placed herself into a situation where she had foreseen that force would probably be brought to bear on her.

(4) Things that can be neither prevented, nor promoted or accomplished, through our strength—if, indeed, that impotence was not contracted through our own fault. Hence the common saying: "There is no obligation to do things that are impossible," that is, "No one is bound to do the impossible." And just as nothing can be imputed to a person because he does not furnish things which were impossible for him (if, indeed, it was not his fault that they were such), or because he does not grasp things which are superior to his intellect, and punishment consequently finds no place in him for this reason (whence it also comes that the matter of the laws

should be possible for those for whom they are enacted); so no sane person is thought to have prescribed impossible things to someone. Hence in human laws, in wills, and in contracts, one departs from the proper meaning of the letter if it involves something impossible. Thus, also, complete misfortunes are not imputed, except if someone has specially obligated himself to be responsible for them.

(5) The actions of those who do not enjoy the continuous use of reason, unless they have corrupted it by their own fault. Such are madmen, whose acts are considered morally null, and likewise infants, before reason begins to exert itself more brightly.

(6) Things which were committed out of a concomitant or effective ignorance that is invincible in itself and in its cause.

Axiom 2

ANYONE CAN EFFECTIVELY (OR WITH THE OBLIGATION TO FURNISH THEM) ENJOIN ON SOMEONE SUBJECT TO HIMSELF THOSE THINGS TO WHICH HIS AUTHORITY OVER THE OTHER EXTENDS ITSELF

1. That man can arrange his actions according to a certain norm comes from the fact that nature allotted him a mind that would not necessarily act always in one manner but could be turned toward either side of a contradiction. But that he also should do so is from the fact that the condition of human nature also commanded men to establish over one another, besides the general dominion of God, sovereignties that can bring to bear on those whom they embrace the necessity of determining their actions in a certain manner.

Now a certain action becomes necessary for a man as a result of the authority of a superior who, when he has declared what he wishes to be done or not done by another, has the strength to compel him by fear of some evil, if perhaps he shrinks from the things which are to be done, or certainly to afflict him with an evil if he violates the commands. For otherwise no obligation can dispose a man in such a way that he is altogether unwilling or unable to do a certain thing, that is, that he no longer enjoys the natural freedom of contrariety or contradiction; rather this freedom, at least, is always left him, that he can choose either obedience or the danger of undergoing punishment.

2. Moreover, the effectiveness of the authority from which obligations are capable of being generated ultimately resolves itself, in fact, into nothing but the power or faculty to inflict punishment. All remaining things bind the will with a bond too weak to be able to reduce it to a stable harmony of its own actions. A person's own decisions bind no one any longer than it pleases him. The hope of future goods moves most people too languidly for them to be willing to undertake present labors or to neglect present advantages. And you will find rather few who are willing to act continuously in a uniform fashion—and mostly against the desire of the will at that—solely for the reason that they may be said to have constantly obeyed another, when doing so is followed by nothing but praise for obedience and neglecting to do so by no evil besides a reputation for disobedience. Finally, the force of all commands is precarious unless the commander has such strength that he can bring upon another who does not obey an evil that is deemed graver than the trouble of necessarily undertaking to carry out his orders.

3. It is necessary, however, that that authority also be legitimate, that is, that it be derived and constituted from the express or reasonably presumed will of the one who is being commanded, lest someone be able to complain that he has been done an injury when he is compelled to conform himself to another man's will. For on account of the natural equality of men among themselves, concerning which we shall say more later on, one person's authority over another cannot possibly arise except from the other's consent, which is either expressly signified in a pact, as in civil subjection, or presumed from a tacit pact, as it were, as happens in the servitude following a state of war and in filial subjection. Yet once another's authority has been constituted by our consent, it can no longer be refused, even if it should afterwards begin to displease, because the other has now acquired a right which the law of nature by no means allows to be taken away from him against his will.

4. Now as for the rest, no one can effectively enjoin something, in the manner of a precept, upon another over whom he has no legitimate authority. For however and whenever one may for a time hold him bound by force alone, entirely without his consent, when a favorable occasion has smiled upon him, he will nonetheless be able rightly to shake off the yoke and to claim his freedom (which is something by no means permitted to those who have consented to their own subjection). Furthermore, the axiom of which we have spoken gives rise to these conclusions, which diffuse themselves throughout the entire matter of the law: "Whatever the law commands is to be done." "Whatever the law prohibits is to be omitted." "Anyone at all is bound to carry out the commands of one who has authority over him, to whatever point that authority extends itself."

Observation 1

MAN CAN JUDGE CORRECTLY CONCERNING THINGS
APPREHENDED BY THE POWER
OF THE UNDERSTANDING

1. There are in man two faculties of the understanding, as it were, which he exerts in the case of voluntary actions, namely the *representative* and the *judicative*. The former places an object before the will as in a mirror and shows what kind of goodness there is in it. Since this faculty is assigned to the class of those things which we commonly call natural, in contradistinction to those which are free, and it is therefore not in man's power to apprehend things otherwise than as their images offer themselves to the understanding, it readily appears that no place has been left for laws to dispose of it, and that someone's inability to apprehend some thing, or to apprehend it in another way, cannot be imputed. Hence, inasmuch as assent or belief cannot but respond to the appearance apprehended by the understanding, it is extremely unfair to wish to compel someone by means of a proposed penalty to believe that some thing is other than the way he knows it to be.

This must nonetheless be restricted in this manner: unless a kind of lazy negligence was involved, in that a person was careless in attending to the thing, whose true appearance he would otherwise have apprehended by applying to it the study required. And so there can be a place for laws and obligation in regard to someone's conceiving some thing rightly with the mind only insofar as he receives information about it and makes an effort at diligent reflection. But it can also happen, and often does so, that although one may with impunity favor a particular opinion concerning any thing with the mind, a penalty is established for anyone who openly expresses it or labors to spread it among the common crowd.

2. One must judge from these things how far it is appropriate for a magistrate to apply force in enjoining a religion upon men. To be sure, since a conviction about divine matters is formed from the apprehension of the understanding, whose mode of operation is by no means subject to man's choice, it easily appears that a person cannot be compelled to give assent to some thing in any other way than it offers itself to his understanding. Therefore, nothing but calm means of persuasion has a place toward this end; tortures and force, by which a pretended confession can perhaps be extorted, but by no means true assent, are in vain. (Though someone can be compelled by penalties to receive information, and to employ means that otherwise tend generally to be followed by assent to those things.) Where those means are of no avail, however, it is fruitless to bring civil sovereignty to bear, especially since a special, divinely granted grace is required in order that someone give assent to the Christian religion.

Yet because it makes no little difference to a commonwealth by which formulas a religion is publicly propounded, and it is extremely conducive to the tranquillity of a state if all the citizens openly profess the same opinion about religion, which has great power to excite or mollify minds, a magistrate can rightly prohibit all who are subject to his jurisdiction, even by threatening a penalty to be exacted in a civil court, from propounding in their public or private teaching anything opposed to that formula which he has promulgated for the citizens to follow as being congruent with the principle of faith. For this end it is even accepted in a number of regions that those who are to be promoted to public offices be compelled to a certain confession about religion by means of an oath, by which they are obligated, so long as they remain members of that commonwealth, not to teach or display publicly anything which may be opposed to that confession.

3. Through the judicative faculty, the understanding discerns and dictates what is to be done, as well as when and how, and deliberates about the means which are most accommodated to the end. This faculty is otherwise called practical reason and practical judgment (for it is not our business now to inquire what force of understanding there is in the bare contemplation of things). Since this faculty is, as it were, the torch of human actions, whose failure to shine forth in the proper manner makes it necessary for man to falter, and indeed, since it can be molded into rectitude by diligent cultivation and meditation, so that no cause of erring arises from it, a man must certainly take great care to form that judgment in such a way that it corresponds exactly to the thinking and intention of the one to whom he is bound to make his actions acceptable.

4. Furthermore, although we have proposed to deal here mostly with good and evil, just and unjust, and have referred the investigation concerning the useful and the useless to another discipline, it will nonetheless not be beside the point to touch also in a few words on what rules the judgment of the understanding should heed in its deliberation concerning the useful. This is because a person often has enjoined on him an obligation to act in the manner he himself judges to be most expedient, in which case he without doubt does badly if through imprudence he undertakes that which is less useful. Therefore, in deliberations that are commonly undertaken about things to which we are not bound by necessity or a definite obligation (for necessity excludes deliberation, and a definite obligation leaves the execution alone to the agent), it is supposed as a foundation, as it were, that nothing be undertaken from which it seems in one's moral estimation that as much evil as good, or even more evil than good, will arise. The reason for this is obvious. For each thing loses so much of its goodness as it has evil adjoined to it, and so if the evil is equal it lays aside the character of a good.

But the kinds of things about which we are now speaking are undertaken in order that we may acquire some advantage for ourselves from them. From this, in turn, flow the following consequences: (1) If the thing concerning which there is deliberation should seem in one's moral estimation to have an equal efficacy toward good and evil, it is to be chosen only if the good is somewhat more good than the evil is evil. (2) If it should seem that the good and the evil that can come from the thing in question are equal, the thing is to be chosen only if its efficacy for the good is greater than that for the evil. (3) If it should seem that both the good and the evil are unequal, and the efficacy of things no less so, a thing is to be chosen only if its efficacy for the good is greater, in comparison to its efficacy for the evil, than the evil itself in comparison to the good, or if the good is greater in comparison to the evil than the efficacy for the evil in comparison to the efficacy for the good. (4) If the good of each thing, as much as the evil, as well as the efficacy toward each, is not evident, one should refrain from both, if it can be done. (5) Even things that seem capable of being added to our plan by accident are to be attended to, unless the good to which our action tends is that much greater than the evil which is feared or, in the case of equal good and evil, the hope of good is much greater than the fear of evil.

5. Now the judgment of the understanding concerning morally necessary actions, insofar as it is imbued with a knowledge of the laws, is specially referred to as *conscience*; although this name also designates the reflexive judgment, as it were, of the understanding concerning acts, which approves those done well and condemns those done badly, and is accompanied by a tranquillity or disquiet of the mind, in accordance with the testimony it renders on behalf of each act. We can, for the sake of distinction, call the latter a *consequent conscience*, because it follows men's deeds and summons them to be examined; the other, however, we can call an *antecedent conscience*, as it precedes deeds and dictates what is good and what is bad, and for that reason to be done or omitted.

6. Now conscience is either correct or not correct. That which is correct either knows itself to be such for certain, or it only thinks so. The former is called a *correct conscience*, the latter a *probable conscience*. A correct conscience is one that dictates the performance or omission of what is absolutely to be done or omitted, that is, one which knows itself to be in agreement with certain and indubitable divine and human law. A probable conscience is based on an opinion constructed out of reasons that are not thought to be evidently infallible but only probable, so that it is not deemed impossible that the opposite side can be true, even though this is not apparent from the present reasons. About a correct conscience one must know that every spontaneous action which is contrary to it, and every omission of an action which it dictates to be necessary, is a sin. This is because a correct conscience and the meaning of the law intended by a legislator correspond to one another, and so things which are done in opposition to the former are also discrepant with the latter.

The same judgment is to be made about a probable conscience, which coincides with a correct conscience as far as its rectitude is concerned and differs only in regard to the evident and steadfast knowledge of its own rectitude. For the sake of informing this conscience, it is appropriate to note the following: (1) In a probable conscience, in the case of things which are to be deduced from laws (especially the law of nature) through a process that is somewhat obscure, when one of two opinions which have been proposed rests on firmer reasons while the other seems to be safer, although neither of them is contrary to the law, either can be undertaken. (2) When two opinions have been proposed, one of which is based on reasons that are rather weak while the other seems to be safer, the safer one is rightly preferred to the other. (3) In a probable conscience a learned man can follow that opinion which seems to him most probable, even if it may perhaps not seem so to others. (4) An unlearned man most safely follows the opinion of those who are wiser. (5) Someone constrained by another's sovereignty can, at the command of his superiors, rightly do what he does not know for certain to be illicit, even if it may not seem so probable to himself. (6) In things of little importance, if there are probable arguments on both sides one can choose whichever one pleases. (7) In things of great importance, if probable arguments should reveal themselves on both sides, the safer side is to be preferred. And so if the proof of a crime is unclear, and an inconclusive verdict does not suffice, it is better to absolve than to condemn.

Observation 2

MAN CAN MOVE HIMSELF FROM
AN INTERNAL PRINCIPLE EITHER TO UNDERTAKE
OR TO OMIT A CERTAIN ACTION

1. Since man was to be formed by the Creator as an animal to be governed through laws, he had to have a will as the internal directress of his actions, so that when objects were placed before and known by him he would move himself toward them from an intrinsic principle, without any physical necessity, and could select what seemed most suited for himself. This will is conceived to exert itself through two faculties, as it were, through one of which it acts *spontaneously* and through the other *freely.*

Spontaneity commonly has attributed to it certain actions or motions, some of which are interior and are called *elicited,* while others are exterior and are called *commanded.* Elicited acts are those that are immediately produced by and received in the will. Some of them, such as volition, intention, and fruition, concern ends; others, such as consent, election, and use, concern means.

Volition is said to be the act of the will whereby it is carried directly toward an end without any regard to whether it is present or absent, that is, the act whereby it simply approves the end. *Intention* or choice is an effective desire to obtain the end; that is, the act of the will whereby it is effectively carried toward, and strives to reach, an absent end. Although intention has several degrees, it is nonetheless commonly divided only into full and half-full. They call it full when the will is carried toward something after having sufficiently weighed it, and is not swept away by the vehemence of the passions; and half-full when there has not been sufficient deliberation, or when reason has been shaken by the whirlwind of the passions. . . .

5. *Freedom* is a faculty of the will that can, when all the requisites for acting are given, select one or more of a number of proposed objectives and reject the rest, or when one objective is proposed, can either accept or not accept it, and do it or not do it. [More] specifically, however, the faculty of selecting one or more of a number of objectives is called "freedom of specification or variety," and the faculty concerned with the selection or rejection of only a single objective "freedom of contradiction or exercise." Therefore, freedom superadds to spontaneity an indifference concerning the exercise of its own acts (namely, those of willing and not willing) so that the will does not necessarily elicit one or the other but can, in the case of a particular proposed objective, elicit whichever it pleases, even if it perhaps inclines more toward the one than toward the other. It also adds a free determination, so that the will may here and now elicit either one of its acts, that of willing or that of not willing, out of an intrinsic impulse.

6. Now it is taken for granted that the will wields sovereignty, as it were, among man's faculties, at least those which are capable of that direction. For there are those, such as the powers of the vegetative soul, that altogether spurn that free regimen of the will and preserve a natural mode of acting which it is not granted man to alter, and whose active exercise he cannot suspend once all the requisites for action are given. [Here] only the carrying out of the objective has been left to him, and although this occurs with the mediation of the locomotive faculty, it is up to the will to direct the latter to the service of those powers either more or less quickly; in such a way, however, that the times when nature desires the objective to be carried out do not depend on the will's decision. . . . The internal and external senses cannot, when an organ is rightly disposed, fail to perceive an object that has been brought before them, and to judge it as it appears to them, even if the will can with the intervention of the locomotive faculty move objects closer or farther away from them.

All of this may be applied to the understanding. Indeed, the will exercises an absolute sovereignty over the locomotive faculty not only when this has been left to itself but also when it is impelled by the sensitive appetite. For the will has sovereignty over this as well, although not one so quiet, in that passions repeatedly surge up in it in tumults whose repression requires a great effort. Yet the will must never despair of victory when it has rightly applied its own powers, even when the passions have grown strong through lapse of time or by habit. But there is no longer any place for reason in those whose mind has been disturbed by disease, and the actions of such persons are not regarded as human.

7. But this, too, is obvious: The will cannot be compelled, by either an extrinsic or an intrinsic principle, to turn away from something that agrees with it, or to seek after something that does not, so that absolutely no freedom (of exercise, at least) is left to it. For the proper effect of an external force is not that we are carried toward something abhorrent to our will, but either that a lesser evil is rendered desirable and thus agreeable to the will by the proposition of a greater evil (just as it is profitable to be freed from an entire debt by paying only a part), or that we are persuaded to disguise our desire for or aversion to some thing by means of external signs. All other things which attempt to mollify the will by means of flattering enticements, or to frighten it through asperity, cannot bring any necessity

of obedience to bear. Indeed, the will always seeks the good in general and turns away from evil. But there is no particular good, even one commended by the judgment of the understanding, which it cannot still neglect, just as it can desire even that which reason has judged to be a moral evil, when the appearance of the good which has been adjoined to that evil, and is commended by the judgment of the senses, prevails. Thus, whatever the obligation with which the mind may be indued, its only effect is that reason judges that you are to act in accordance with it, not that you are in fact altogether unable to tend in the opposite direction.

8. It also readily appears from these things that man has been allowed to direct the actions that depend immediately on the will, or that are subject to its sovereignty, according to a conceptual norm. For since the will is a free faculty whose acts are not bound by natural necessity in regard to either specification or exercise, and which is not determined to one mode of acting that is always similar to itself but moves itself to act by an intrinsic impulse, as it were, and itself designs its own mode of action; it is surely manifest that if some rule indicating a certain mode of acting should become known (for a preceding cognition of the intellect is always required, and someone cannot conform his actions to a norm of which he is ignorant), the will itself can if it pleases elicit its own acts, and direct the other faculties subject to itself according to what that rule prescribes. Yet it is presupposed about this rule that it should not conflict with the universal inclination of the will. That is, it should not prescribe to it that it should seek what is opposed to its own nature, or turn away from that toward which it is naturally carried; in other words, it should not order it to turn away from the good as such or to seek the evil as such. For one can in no way get the will to do this, even if external acts are able to simulate what is contrary to its inclination.

9. It follows from this that man's will is capable of receiving an obligation from an extrinsic principle, so that it determines the specification and exercise of its own acts, and its mode of acting, from its prescription. For obligation certainly presupposes a natural faculty of acting and not acting, and if someone should determine this in such a way, through some physical necessity, that it was in the manner of natural causes utterly unable to strive toward diverse things, he would extinguish the entire morality of his actions; just as also, someone who restrained men by nothing but physical bonds would reduce them to the condition of brutes. But when moral bonds are laid upon the will, that is, when what is to be done—unless one is willing to expose oneself to the danger of undergoing some evil—is indicated by one who has the authority to impose that evil, then surely, although the natural faculty of tending toward contraries may remain, the will's freedom is nonetheless confined by a moral necessity, so that it seems according to the judgment of right reason that what has been prescribed, rather than its contrary, is always to be done.

10. But on the other hand, when an obligation is lacking the will is understood to be free and to have the authority to do all those things which can be brought about by it through its natural powers. And furthermore, once it has determined itself to something, its own decree by no means has such force (unless some law stands in the way) that it cannot rightly change or cancel it whenever it so pleases. . . .

Observation 3

MAN HAS BEEN DESTINED BY NATURE
TO LIVE A SOCIAL LIFE WITH MEN

1. Man has in common with all animate things to whom an awareness of their own existence has been given that he loves himself to the highest degree, studies to preserve himself in every manner, and strives to acquire the things that seem good to himself and to repel those that seem evil. And indeed, this love of any person toward himself is commonly so great that any inclination toward any other man yields to it.

To be sure, some seem now and then to embrace others with a more tender affection than themselves, to rejoice more in their goods than in their own, and to be pained more by their evils than by their own. Thus parents would often prefer that the pain which they see their children feeling be transferred to themselves. Similarly, it is well known that many have gone to their death with equanimity in order to save those who were tied to them by a special bond. However, they did this either because, on account of strict necessity, they considered others' goods or evils as their own, or because they were going to procure some special good for themselves by that display of affection or trust. Thus, some parents rejoice more effusively at their children's goods than at their own because they judge that a good which affects themselves and those born from them equally is doubled. Likewise, we would often be willing to purchase the pain of one whom we deeply love with our own pain, because a weapon seeking to reach us through so dear a body will wound more deeply, as it were. And one who does not refuse to die for someone else's sake either expects so much glory from that deed that he judges it cheap to purchase it with his life, or else he fears that such evil will redound on himself when the other has been extinguished that life will no longer be something to be greatly desired by him.

2. But man would have been but little removed from beasts, and would not lead a much more cultured and commodious life than they, if there were not also implanted in him by nature another inclination, so that he enjoyed living in the society of those similar to himself. This is too manifest to have to be demonstrated here by means of further evidence. Nothing is more miserable for man than perpetual solitude. He alone among living things has been given the ability to expound to others the perceptions of his mind by means of articulate sound, and there is no fitter instrument than this for contracting or preserving society. In no class of living things can the advantages of one be so greatly promoted by others as of men by one another. Such is the neediness of human life that it can be preserved only with difficulty if a number of persons do not conspire to be of service to one another. The weakness of newly born men is greater than that of any other living thing; and while a few days or months suffice for the rest to be able to look out for food,

several years are hardly sufficient for them. In addition, the earth has everywhere placed food in beasts' way, but the things which are suited for man mostly require diligence and cultivation. And yet the ability to supply food for the stomach is the least part of why one merits the dignity of the name 'human.' Why? Because if nature had not ordered us absolutely to come together into a peaceful society, we would not only be prey to beasts but would also, in the manner of beasts, set upon one another.

3. But lest someone perhaps be moved by the reasonings of those who take it upon themselves to deny these things, which are so clear, it must be known that: (1) These two inclinations, by which man loves himself and seeks society, should according to nature's intention be tempered in such a way that nothing is lost to the latter on account of the former. That is, nature has commended the love of himself to man, yet in such a way that he does not on account of it wrongly do anything that conflicts with the inclination toward society, or that damages the very nature of society. When he neglects this on account of the exorbitance of the passions, and seeks his own advantage together with an unfair hurt to others, there arise all the disturbances by means of which men are set at variance with one another. (2) When certain individuals come together into a certain kind of society this happens either on account of a particular congruence of dispositions or other qualities, or because they think they can attain some particular end more among these persons than among those. It is not at all necessary, however, that all men coalesce into one society in which all are equal among themselves; rather it suffices if they congregate themselves into several distinct groups. Yet these are by no means entirely unsociable among themselves but mutually refrain from unjust harms and, to the extent they can according to their stricter obligations, share advantages and goods with one another.

4. . . . Therefore, the meaning of that threadbare saying, "Man is by nature a social animal," is this: Man is destined by nature for the society of those similar to himself, and this society is to the highest degree congruent with and useful to him. He has also been endowed with such a disposition that he can through cultivation acquire the aptitude to conduct himself rightly in that society. Indeed, it is perhaps the chief fruit arising from societies that those recently born, into whom nature has not implanted an actual understanding of those things, are formed in them into suitable members of themselves. Nor is that aptitude confined to marriages or families, but it also extends itself to the states that are to be established, where several families come together for the sake of security and a richer life, and administer the society's affairs by a common counsel under certain laws of commanding and obeying. It was altogether nature's will that such societies exist among men, even though it was left up to men to decide, and is therefore to be determined through pacts, which individuals are to be joined to which society, or who is to be set over them in order to govern them. . . .

6. Now it is worthwhile to consider the condition in which men would live if they were left by nature without any obligation to cultivate society among themselves, or if they were not social animals. Here it is no doubt apparent that since no law would have come between them on either side, anyone would have had a right equal to the rest to anything whatsoever, and that anyone could have inflicted

on anyone else, without any injury, that which seemed to make for his own preservation—as much as each person's strength had admitted; and that from this there would have arisen a war of all against all—which is exactly what the life of beasts is. For just as anyone may when he pleases, to the extent his strength allows, kill any animal or compel it to render services to him, without inflicting injury upon the brute, because there is no community of right between man and brutes (here you should set aside that respect in which certain men have now acquired a right over brutes for themselves before others); so if I had no obligation toward any man (assuming a natural faculty to hurt or even kill another) I would surely be permitted to protect my life and limbs as much as I could and to apply all means conducive thereto, whose aptness for that end would be up to me alone to judge. And so I would not only be able to claim for myself those things which I had judged to be advantageous to myself, but also—if indeed it seemed to promote my own security—to kill, weaken, or in another way constrain any man, whom I could surely not watch out against in such a state (where no mutual obligation exists) except through force. And since the same thing would have been permitted to and against anyone whatsoever, what else would men have been except beasts preying on their own kind?

But since men never did and according to the Creator's intention never were to exist in such a state, it is completely incongruous and almost contradictory to call it a state of nature. Hence the disadvantages resulting from it should also not be directly laid down as foundations of the law of nature (even if the law of nature in fact brings it about that that state does not exist among men). What should rather be laid down is the fact that God has directly destined man to cultivate a social life. For if this had not been God's direct intention it would have been no more necessary for men to enter into pacts with one another on account of the disadvantages arising from a non-social life, than for other living things to do so with bears, wolves, or lions, for the sake of avoiding the disadvantages of the non-social life which they lead. Nor is it possible for you to retort that they lack the reason by which they may understand the force of pacts. For the Creator would not have given reason to men either unless he had wished to destine them to cultivate society.

Observation 4

RIGHT REASON DICTATES THAT MAN MUST CARE FOR HIMSELF IN SUCH A WAY THAT HUMAN SOCIETY IS NOT DISTURBED

1. Although the mind of man is not found to be imbued with a knowledge of things when he comes forth into the light, God has nonetheless formed his understanding with such a disposition that after his powers have with age begun to exert themselves, he conceives from the inspection of natural things certain notions that are useful for the richer knowledge that is later to be built thereon, and recognizes from the contemplation of himself which actions, as being in accord with his nature, the Creator has wished him to perform, and which, as being repugnant to it, He has wished him to avoid. It is the task of others to occupy themselves about the former matters; we must examine the latter a bit more carefully here.

Accordingly, it is well established through experience that when the light of reason emerges from infantile ignorance and reveals itself a little more clearly in man, and he turns himself to the contemplation of his own nature, a reason that has not been corrupted through passions or faulty habits should tell him that it is indeed appropriate that he care for and preserve himself as much as he can, but that it is nonetheless necessary, because he becomes aware that he has been destined by the Creator to cultivate society with other men, that he so temper his care for himself that he does not become unsociable with others or disturb society among men. This very thing is what we call the law of nature.

This law, as has been said, becomes known from the consideration of nature and the human condition, without any supernatural support. Nor does that nature cease to be known because many do not have the strength of intellect to be able to investigate it by their own reasoning, or because most acquire their knowledge of it through being informed by others. For it suffices that it may be found out by the perspicacity of even mediocre intellects, and that the rest, when they have compared the knowledge of it which they have acquired from the teaching of others with the condition of their own nature, are able to discern that this law is necessarily in accord with themselves. And just as human society is formed and preserved through the law of nature, so it is by no means the least fruit of already established societies that in them even those who are somewhat dull learn about the law of nature through the instruction of others and by its very exercise.

3. Now that dictate of reason, or the law of nature, obtains the power to obligate men from the authority of the Creator, Who wields supreme sovereignty over them, as it were. Since He formed man's nature in such a way that it is sufficiently apparent that he has been destined to cultivate society, and has for that reason made for him a mind that is capable of those notions, it is no doubt understood that He

also willed that man should adjust himself to the end which He has prescribed; and therefore, since that end may be obtained through the law of nature, that He has also obligated man to observe it, not as a means that was invented by men's will and is changeable according to their desire, but one that has been expressly established by God Himself for the sake of attaining this end. . . .

4. Now there are two fundamental laws of nature from which all the rest flow: (1) "That anyone whatsoever should protect his own life and limbs as much as he can, and preserve himself and his things." (2) "That he should not disturb human society," that is, "that he should not do anything whereby society among men may be less tranquil." These laws should agree with one another and, as it were, be so interwoven that they coalesce, as it were, into one law: namely, "That each person should study to preserve himself in such a way that society among men is not disturbed."

5. There are those, indeed, who quite cleverly deduce all the remaining laws from the former law alone. That is to say, since anyone would have an equal right to anything if all society among men had been removed, from which a war of all against all would have arisen (a state that is maximally opposed to men's preservation and security, however, and that brings infinite discomforts and miseries with itself), peace is to be sought insofar as there appears to be any hope of having it, and when it is not possible to have it one must seek the helps of war. And so the right to all things must not be retained, but society must for the sake of mutual assistance be established by means of pacts, by which one must altogether abide, and so on.

But since it has been shown above that nature has directly destined man to a social life, so that although he has bound himself to a particular society by a special bond he ought nonetheless to cultivate a universal peace with all men, even those who live outside that society, insofar as they allow, and to perform toward them the duties of humanity which he can easily perform; the preservation of social life is also deservedly laid down as a foundation for the laws of nature, and indeed, not secondarily assumed as something that men have been compelled to take up by accident. . . . It is firmly established, therefore, that just as the life of men would without society be similar to the life of beasts, so the law of nature is chiefly based on the principle that social life is to be preserved among men. And the condition of our nature is so far from being opposed to our assertion that, instead, it firmly supports it; since even if we were not bound by a law of nature to cultivate society it would urge us to establish it of ourselves, on account of the advantages that flow from it and in order to avoid the disadvantages that accompany a non-social life.

8. Now from the former fundamental law [of nature] flows this general law: "Anyone whatsoever should omit those things that either weaken the use of reason or inflict harm or ruin upon the body." Even though the exercise of this law terminates immediately in anyone's own person, it nonetheless also involves a general regard for the preservation of society and consequently redounds to its benefit, in that it commands the members of which society consists to preserve themselves, or to adjust themselves in such a way that they are not a burden to

themselves and to society alike. Indeed, it seems that this law was hardly needed, and nature could have left each person to his own instinct with respect to the care of himself, if it had not wished to destine man to cultivate a social life. . . .

11. Furthermore, just as the latter fundamental law obligates all men whatsoever to furnish one another voluntarily and amicably that which they owe, and its careful observance results in peace (which is the state that most of all agrees with human nature, and for whose establishment and preservation the law of nature has chiefly been implanted in man); so war may on the basis of the former law be licit and sometimes necessary, namely when another has violated the latter law of nature against me and refuses to make good the damage done thereby. For here the former law about preserving myself creates for me the authority to defend the welfare of myself or mine in any manner whatsoever (when there is no opportunity to appeal to a judge, of course) against one who unjustly violates it, notwithstanding the latter law, which otherwise prohibits the infliction of harm on another's body and things. For since the law of nature obligates all men equally to exercise toward one another the duties owed on account of the law of nature, it is no doubt obvious that as long as another exhibits toward me what the law of nature prescribes, I should furnish the same to him. But indeed, when another violates the law against me, then it will certainly be very impudent for him to demand of me that I should proceed to perform those duties toward him, unless he has repented and binds himself to take them up again. Otherwise all the goods that nature or industry has given us also would have been granted in vain, if it were not licit to oppose against another who unjustly violates them the force which nature has allowed us to employ, as the proper manner of acting in war, as it were, when my welfare cannot be furthered by peaceful means. But the exception made by the obligation of subjects toward those who have supreme sovereignty is explained elsewhere.

21. The second fundamental law of nature, we have said, is that "Men are to preserve a social life toward one another and not do anything that results in its being disturbed." This social life is almost entirely contained in these general duties: That no harm should be inflicted on anyone, in either his person or things, without some preceding deed of his through which we are afforded a license or necessity to harm him; and that anyone whatsoever should furnish to another, voluntarily and without the application of external force, both those things which are owed him on the basis of specially contracted obligations and those which common kinship demands. The latter sort are commonly considered as those by which we can benefit another without disadvantage to ourselves: For example, showing the way to someone who is lost or inquiring; allowing the use of flowing water as a watering place when our field is not made worse thereby; granting a harmless passage, and one that tends to no one's injury, through our lands on the public road, especially when adequate precautions are taken and there is no danger from contagion; not destroying that which neither hinders nor helps me but can be useful to another; granting the use of one's shore to someone who is shipwrecked; and the like. But it is also required by force of this precept that anyone join himself freely to those particular societies which necessity or a notable advantage of life has recommended be established.

22. Moreover, since that obligation to cultivate a social life accompanies human nature as such, it appears that it binds all men equally, and that all men are equal to the extent that no one, however great the goods of mind and body whereby he excels the rest, has more of a right than they to afflict others with injuries; just as also, on the contrary, the grudging liberality of nature or slender fortune does not in and through itself condemn anyone to a worse position than others in regard to the enjoyment of a common right among men. One who disdains this equality can no more present himself as a useful member of human society than one who desires to live in some particular society but is nonetheless not eager to adjust himself to its laws. Moreover, that obligation has the force of a mutual agreement which, when one person departs from it, no longer binds the other person either, and grants him in addition the right to compel the former by force to furnish the things agreed upon. For one who has not treated others according to a common obligation cannot object if his own examples are inflicted upon himself and he is, besides, brought back into line by the rest by means of force.

Yet this equality is to be understood apart from any preceding human deed by which it is restricted, either by consent or on account of a transgression, as far as concerns the action that arises for one who has been hurt against the one who has hurt him. For even if everyone who has not treated another according to the prescription of the law of nature violates this law equally, it was nonetheless expedient for humankind, on account of the necessity of supreme sovereignties, that those on whom sovereignties had been conferred should be a little better situated here, to the extent that others do not have the faculty to bring them back into line even if they have perhaps violated the law of nature in some matters. And this is not because they themselves do not in that matter sin equally with the others, but because the force of supreme sovereignty renders those subject to them unable to coerce them; since otherwise the entire efficacy of sovereignties would be overturned, if you wished to fashion among subjects and sovereigns some reciprocal authority to exact penalties from one another on account of violations of the law of nature. . . .

In other respects—so that we may also add this here in passing—it may be easily gathered from equality by what method things should be divided among several persons. Namely, when other things are equal, if the right of individuals is equal, things should be divided into equal parts. And those which cannot be divided are to be used in common, if it can be done—as much as each person wishes, if the quantity of the thing permits. But if a thing's quantity does not permit, then in a predetermined manner and in proportion to the number of users. If a thing can be neither divided nor held in common, however, let it either be used in turns or assigned by lot to one person only, for a more convenient means cannot be devised here.

This lot is either arbitrary, coming about by the consent of the contestants and at the direction of mere chance; or natural, such as first occupancy and primogeniture. The common practice with respect to these lots is that the arbitrary kind is employed when several compete with one another for some thing to which they have sought a right for themselves by some preceding act, and the natural kind when no one has sought a right thereto for himself by some preceding act of his.

Hence things which are considered abandoned are granted to the first occupant, and the indivisible hereditary dignity of a father to the firstborn, unless the matter has been disposed of in another way by an express statute.

Observation 5

THE LAW OF NATURE ALONE DOES NOT DIRECTLY SUFFICE TO PRESERVE THE SOCIAL LIFE OF MAN, BUT IT IS ALSO NECESSARY THAT SOVEREIGNTIES BE ESTABLISHED IN PARTICULAR SOCIETIES

1. Although all precepts of the law of nature which flow from the second fundamental law tend to this, that a peaceful society without the infliction of mutual injuries may be cultivated among men, we nonetheless find many reasons that those precepts are not immediately sufficient to produce this end. For even though conscience sufficiently inculcates into each person what ought to be done or omitted, few have so modest a disposition that they are constantly willing to follow this when no present punishment, and one that strikes terror into the senses, has been proposed for one who violates it. This is especially so when the sweetness of vices has through habit stolen over a person, and the mind, having ejected shame, has become addicted to the passions and deaf to the admonitions of reason.

Therefore, since the crop of men's injuries against others would be far more abundant if each person were left to his own conscience in regard to the observance of the law of nature, and the rest would also have to seek the protection of their own welfare by nothing but force, all places would as a result of this reverberate with wars between those who are inflicting and those who are repelling injuries. In addition, even though the law of nature commands that controversies be brought before arbiters, since these have as such no jurisdiction over the litigants through which the latter can be altogether compelled to follow the sentence, this remedy for keeping the peace will also come to nothing if either of the litigants rejects that judgment of an arbiter which displeases him. And what would happen if no one acknowledged the sovereignty of any man over himself, since so many wars are today waged in a nearly uninterrupted series among so few who have been released from human sovereignty over themselves, now that the size of humankind and the infinite multitude of affairs have not permitted all men to coalesce into one body; inasmuch as a man would in that vast number be threatened by the same and by nearly greater disadvantages from internal turmoils, than those which exercise humankind now, when it has been divided into many smaller sovereignties?

2. It was altogether necessary, therefore, in order to preserve peace and security among men, to establish something through which it might commonly be rendered more desirable to them to perform toward one another the duties they owe, than to arrange for their mutual destruction by means of injuries, as it were. But no better means (which is also intended by nature) could be found here than for men to join themselves together in order to render mutual assistance to one another; and indeed, not only some few, but as many as have on account of their number such strength that those who would assail them with injuries will gain nothing of any importance, for purposes of overpowering them, by the addition of a few more.

Here it is certain, however, that no matter how great the number of those may be who have come together for their mutual defense, if they do not agree among themselves about the best method by which that should be brought about but each one applies his strength according to his own judgment, the proposed end will by no means be attained. For unless they are restrained by some common bond by which each and all are so bound to follow one opinion about the common defense and welfare that they are not able to go off in any other direction—even if that opinion has displeased a certain few of them or does not seem very conducive to their own private interest—their discrepant opinions about the method of defense will either enervate their divided strength, or emulation will involve those who refuse to yield to one another in internal wars. But that restraint can be obtained in no more appropriate manner than if each one of them so subjects his own will to the will of a single other man or council, that whatever has seemed good to these concerning the public welfare is equivalent to the will of all, and he or it is able to use the strength and faculties of individuals for the common welfare.

For this end two pacts are needed. By one, individuals engage themselves with other individuals to subject themselves jointly to the sovereignty of some one; by the other, each and all bind themselves to that one, to the effect that they are willing to provide the use of their resources and strength for the public good as he decides, and not to resist his commands. By means of it individuals also renounce the right to proceed by war against one who hurts them, according to their own judgment, since they will expect the prosecution of their own injuries from the judgment of the sovereign, unless by chance a present necessity does not permit them to ask for his assistance. Hence it comes that because the right to use the strength and faculties of all in accordance with what he himself has judged to be expedient for the common interest has been transferred to him, he is possessed of that same strength and is able thereby to compose all of them into an internal harmony and peace—even if some may want very much, in view of a special advantage, to strive after different things—and also vigorously to repel the injuries of outsiders. Those, therefore, among whom such pacts intervene, have coalesced into one moral person or society that has its own will, interests, and proper rights which are distinct from the interests and rights of individuals as such, and which neither a few of the members nor even all of them together—if the one in whom the sovereignty inheres be excepted—can claim for themselves.

3. Furthermore, such pacts by which societies are generated come into existence either on the occasion of birth, on the occasion of a war in which in one side has succumbed, or in consideration of greater security. By the former methods *families* are constituted, through which the end we have spoken of cannot be so fully obtained; by the latter method the *state*, which attains the aforesaid end as perfectly as human affairs allow. Nuptial society or matrimony, however, even though it is the wellspring and, as it were, the seedbed of all societies, is not properly contracted for this end. For it also exists among persons who are too few to be able to provide mutual security by means of their joint strength (inasmuch as the conjunction with one woman or particular women furnishes one man little protection); and it neither has the security of humankind as its end, but its propagation, nor does it in itself establish any sovereignty. . . .

15. Therefore, in order that men's security might be fully provided for (as much, at least, as the condition of human affairs allows), and where one person's unjust hurting of another could not be altogether prevented, to bring it about that this could nonetheless not be done with impunity, it was necessary at last for several families to be joined together. When these families entered into a pact with one another concerning the procurement of their common welfare, and conferred on the person to whom its administration was committed the right to command those things which seemed conducive to this end, having at the same time contracted the obligation to carry out his commands, the state came into existence.

16. Now it is easy to gather from the end of the state of what sort and how great the sovereignty should be by which it is held together. For since, as was said above, it does not suffice for this that each of those about to coalesce into a state should promise to observe the laws of nature toward his fellow citizens, it is necessary that the one to whom the administration of the state as a whole is committed have the faculty to afflict with some evil or punishment anyone who refuses to do what he has ordained should be observed as being publicly expedient. For only when an equal or a graver evil awaits one who is about to afflict me with injury do I not have a probable cause to fear my fellow citizens.

But since those who are unable to protect themselves against outsiders cultivate peace among themselves in vain, and those whose strength has not been united cannot protect themselves against outsiders, it follows that in a state someone should necessarily have the authority to unite and arm as many citizens, in whatever danger or opportunity, as seem in view of the enemies' strength to be needed for the common defense, and again, to make peace with enemies as often as it is useful. This authority will also belong to the same person who has the authority to exact punishments, since no one can by right compel citizens to arms and to the expenses of war except one who is also able to punish those who refuse. No less will he have the faculty to pass judgment on the deeds of those about whom it is disputed whether they should be punished. . . . Finally, since mutual duties among citizens cannot be rightly performed or demanded unless the extent to which individual things are owed has been defined, it will be up to the same supreme authority to promulgate certain rules (called civil laws) by which it is declared what right or what obligation one citizen has toward another; what they should furnish one another, or what they can demand from others, and by virtue of what rationale; in a word, what they must through civil sovereignty necessarily do or omit with respect to one another.

18. Now just as this kind of supreme sovereignty is found in any state whatsoever, and a group in which it does not exist is not to be reckoned a state, so it is self-evident that it has no one on earth to whom it is accountable, or who can through a legitimate authority reduce it to order. Not in the state itself, for that implies a contradiction; nor outside of it, because no one can, on account of the natural equality of men, pretend any right of sovereignty over another unless he has acquired it by some antecedent act or consent of his—such as we suppose has not intervened here. From this it follows that it is also absolute, that is, that it can at its discretion exercise those acts which it has judged expedient for its own end, so that it is neither compelled to borrow the authority to exercise them from another, as it were, nor to accept another's rescinding of them. Much less can one who enjoys that sovereignty be prosecuted in a civil court or afflicted with a punishment on account of some deed of his. . . .

19. Just as this supreme authority of which we have spoken exists as in a common subject in any group that is not subject to another and, indeed, constitutes one moral body, so it inheres now in one person, now in a certain few, and now in a whole people, according as the special forms of the commonwealth vary. And so no one will easily call into doubt that in democracies, indeed, the supreme authority is in the manner we have described in the whole people, so that its acts cannot be rendered null by anyone else nor it itself be reduced to order or punished. For when assemblies or gatherings of the people have degenerated into a confused rabble of seditious men, the greater part of the people can by virtue of its own right restrain and punish those rabble-rousers; the reason being that in the form of such a commonwealth the greater part has the force of the whole, and those fewer seditious men do not have some special right before those more numerous good citizens to care for the commonwealth. . . .

Now such supreme authority is understood to be enjoyed by anyone on whom the people has conferred sovereignty over itself in such a way that it has not reserved to itself a right to conduct (through itself or its deputies) assemblies with the authority to inquire into and invalidate the sovereign's acts, and to reduce him to order; or where a prince is not bound from the beginning to request the express consent of the people regarding the exercise of acts of sovereignty which will be invalid without it.

Still, one must not think here that if certain princes are willing to have their acts be invalid if they are not approved by a certain council that has been constituted by themselves, it immediately has greater authority than they. For if any acts are rescinded here they should be understood to be rescinded by the will of the prince himself, who wished to look out for himself in this manner, both in order that he not decree anything with too little consideration and also to ward off the more conveniently the importunate solicitations of men, to whom he grants something which he knows will be disapproved by that council. In the same way, the ranks and classes in a pure kingdom also take nothing away from the supreme authority of a prince, inasmuch as they have the authority of counselors only, so that the necessities of the people may become that much better known. But if some disadvantages should seem to follow from that absolute authority which remains under the control of one person, they neither bring it about that someone cannot be constituted in such a way, nor indeed will they be more grievous than those that accompany the other forms of the commonwealth, since individuals must everywhere live under absolute authority, which not only monarchs but also nobles and a whole people can sometimes abuse.

20. Hence an extremely dangerous error is made by those who out of their own hatred against monarchs, or that drawn from a certain class of writers, contend that supreme authority necessarily and always belongs to the people (insofar as it is distinguished from its head), so that it can and should look into the deeds of kings and afflict them with punishment. Nor are they more sane who imagine some mutual subjection, to the effect that princes are indeed under no one so long as they rule according to the laws and in a civil fashion, but that they are subjected to the people's coercion when they abuse their authority and are, for this reason, to be deposed from office before being prosecuted. For what if a king should assert, and perhaps truly, that he has used his authority rightly and the people should deny this, who will be the arbiter? Especially since the obscurity of civil acts is on most occasions so great that the common people are rarely able, or often on account of emotional turmoils unwilling, to discern their equity or necessity, and it is to the highest degree expedient for the commonwealth that the reasons for its decisions not be open to the majority.

As confusion of this kind utterly subverts the end of sovereignties, so no people without exception, in handing over sovereignty to someone, is presumed to have wished to introduce it. For a people that has altogether willed to inquire into the acts of princes has expressly reserved to itself the authority to hold meetings concerning that thing by its own right, and prescribed certain standards according to which those acts are to be measured. But where there is such a prince, he does not have supreme sovereignty at all and only plays the role of a magistrate properly speaking, by whatever title he may shine; just as a magistrate also can decide nothing about public affairs, or at least the weightier ones, except with the express consent of the people or its deputies or estates, who sit in council by their own and not a borrowed right.

22. Lest someone believe, however, that we are giving an infinite license to princes and handing over subjects to their pleasure like cattle, bereft of every faculty to fight back, we are altogether of the opinion that if, indeed, even an absolute prince should assume a hostile attitude toward his subjects and openly seek their destruction, without the pretext of a cause that has at least the appearance of justice, his subjects can for the sake of defending their own welfare rightly procure against him as well the means customarily employed against an enemy. And this because he himself is thought on this occasion to have remitted the obligation by which they had been bound to him, since someone's wishing at the same time to be a prince, and to act as an enemy against all his subjects, implies a contradiction.

Yet it is scarcely possible for it to happen that a prince assumes such an attitude toward a whole people, unless he by chance has sovereignty over several peoples and brings about better conditions for one by destroying or oppressing another. It can more readily happen, however, that he is like this toward individuals or a certain few. Since he ejects these from the number of his subjects, they will in the same way be permitted to employ the defense that is otherwise licit against an enemy, observing, however, the things which we noted above in regard to this case.

Still, the rest of the subjects will not for this reason be permitted to put off their obedience, or to defend the innocent person by force, whether the prince offers some pretext or not. For besides the fact that they are not permitted to inquire into the deeds of a prince which he exercises by virtue of his judicial authority, as it were, and it often happens that an accused person falsely proclaims his innocence in order to stir up ill will against a prince, the rest are by no means absolved from their own obligation toward a prince by an injury that has been done against a fellow citizen. This is because each of the subjects negotiates on behalf of his own person for a prince's care and protection toward himself, and does not suppose as a condition that the prince will treat each and all of the citizens as his subjects. Nor does the fear that one may be treated in a similar fashion suffice to break off an obligation, inasmuch as it is uncertain, since it is possible that there may have been special causes of hatred in that case which are not found in mine. But while a subject's obligation toward a prince still stands, he will be permitted neither to inquire into the latter's acts, nor for any reason or on any pretext to set force against him.

On the Law of Nature

and of Nations

in Eight Books

[*Preface to the First Edition*]
To the Benevolent Reader
Many Greetings!

If I considered my native ability and diligence sufficient, it would be superfluous to inquire about all the reasons that I too have made some effort to cultivate
and illuminate a most noble and useful discipline (which after being long neglected
and almost ignored, has finally in this age begun to assert its own worth), since
the wish to deserve well of the public is sufficiently approved of among everyone.
But since the writers who first shed light upon this science are so widely famed, it
will not be beside the point to set forth the reasons for this undertaking, so that I
do not seem either to be doing what has been done, or to affect a poor comparison
against the monuments of such illustrious geniuses.

First of all, since formerly in my youthful years I had undertaken the publica-
tion of some *Elements* of this discipline (not so much out of boldness or disre-
spect for this most learned age, but so that those who then wished me well might
have some kind of sample which they could seize upon as an opportunity to recommend me) which [*Elements*] were excused by most good men on account of
the simplicity of my age and effort, it seemed entirely fitting to apologize publicly, as it were, by means of some more mature composition, for the former's
immaturity. . . .

But the following reason, too, was able to impel me to make some attempt in
this branch. Namely, when the Most Serene Elector of Palatine had most kindly
called me to teach this discipline at the University of Heidelberg and ordered me
to be the first to take from it the title of professor (because of which example others
seem, thereafter, to have received the same professorship of the Law of Nature
and of Nations into their own universities), I had at least to try to make some
contribution toward its development, since it had first taken its place upon the public
platform with me as its interpreter. It was certainly still capable of supplying
material which admitted no less of natural ability than of effort, and we are not
left here solely with the consolidation [*sōmatopoiein*] of a particular learned man's
views. . . .

To be sure, Hugo Grotius has not undeservedly been judged to have carried off
the palm thus far, not only because he is seen as the first to have called upon the
age to value that discipline, but also because he was so well versed in it that with
respect to a large part of it he has left the rest nothing but the labor of gleaning.
Yet no matter how dear this man's reputation may be to us, who are also bound to

him by the peculiar name of 'son,' it must be confessed that many things were entirely passed over by him, others only lightly treated, and finally, others admitted which prove that he too was a man.

No slight aspersion is cast on his most noble work by those especially for whom it diverges here and there from the received opinions of the orthodox church. This labor of great minds, to make innovations regarding divine matters, has always seemed to me most unhappy, since there remains such a great abundance of other matters in which a person may without harm "put out the eyes of crows" [that is, "deceive even the wary"]. Such endeavors detract from the authority of even true and useful statements and provoke the harshest censures from many people who are otherwise not worthy even to open their mouths against such great men. Some learned men have sought to remedy Grotius's book *On the Law of War and Peace* by publishing commentaries on it, and one or other of them has achieved something valuable that is not to be disdained. Others, however, have judged it far more useful to place that entire material upon the anvil once more and to refashion it into a new form.

Thus Thomas Hobbes, in his works devoted to civil science, also has many things that are of some value, and no one who understands things of this sort would deny that he has so deeply probed the structure of human and civil society that few of those before him can be compared with him here. And where he does stray from the truth he still supplies an opportunity for reflections that would otherwise perhaps not have come into anyone's mind. But because he too has devised doctrines in religion which are dreadful and peculiar to himself, he has, not without reason, aroused many people's aversion against himself. Although not rarely, you may also see it happen that he is most haughtily condemned by those who have read or understood him least. . . .

And so, moved by these considerations, I have set my hand to this task and arranged all this material in the order which seemed to me most appropriate, laboring to confirm all things so far as possible by means of solid and self-evident reasons, and to avoid those in which the authors whom I praised before have erred. . . . Moreover, just as I have in good faith given credit to all from whom I have learned something regarding this work for that which is theirs, . . . so in material of this kind, in which reason reigns by its own right, no man's authority could seem to me so great that I did not rather embrace that to which weightier reasons were leading. Consequently, I am not at all afraid that learned men who are still among the living, especially my own countrymen, have taken offense because I have not rarely diverged from their opinions; for I have done so modestly and without eagerness to detract from them, and in such a way only as to counter reason with reason. And hence the freedom which I have assumed for myself against others I also readily grant to them against me. For I profess no association with the sort of men who immediately boil over into hatreds and angers if all their statements are not revered as if they had been spoken by an oracle, or who do not hesitate to boast loudly with an intolerable arrogance that they acknowledge no errors.

Still, now that His Royal Majesty has deemed this work worthy of his most kind approval, I should not be afraid to announce that I am not frightened by the authority of any other censor. And it would be most appropriate to pipe back to those whom arrogance conjoined with ignorance, or some pert busybodiness [*polupragmosunē*] impels to pass judgment on such things: "Let the cobbler stick to his last."[1] If any others should wish to begin carping at those things, let them know that they must deal with me solely with reasons. For if any of those who have been enjoined to expound the Divine Scriptures have taken upon themselves the definition of some questions that properly pertain to this discipline, these could not for this reason become articles of faith, and their ultimate determination should not be removed from sound reason; nor is it appropriate here for such persons to arrogate to themselves a greater authority than those whose profession it is to deal with these matters. Nor, indeed, ought we in these matters—so long as sound reason has given its assent—to flee or fear the reproach of novelty more than those who have in this age, to their own immortal glory, illumined medicine, natural science, and mathematics by discovering things that were previously unknown. . . .

Furthermore, it also seemed appropriate to point out that I have posited the sociality of man as the foundation of universal natural law because I could discover no other principle which all men could at the recommendation of their mortal condition itself be brought to admit, whatever conviction they ultimately had about the divine. Nor indeed, with this foundation laid down, are the limits of this discipline seen to be any narrower than what is just. . . .

It is said, to be sure, that "the natural law is more ancient than society." But besides the fact that there is nothing opposed to the existence of an obligation in another before the existence of the object toward which it can be exercised, there is also the Deity's utterance, as soon as the first man had been fashioned, that it is not good for man to be alone. There are of course also duties or "virtues toward God, and of each person toward himself." But since religion, insofar as it pertains to the discipline of the natural law, is confined within the sphere of this life, it can in consideration of the fact that it provides the most effective bond for societies of men, also be referred to sociality. And those things which a man ought to observe toward himself surely render him more fit for society.

But what that "uprightness and innocence of mores" is, "which is everywhere to be preserved, even outside of society" or without reflection on other men, I have not yet been able to discern. The further statement that "the formation of society and the application of means thereto have been left to the decision of nature; therefore, if the natural law were of society only it would be completely voluntary, arbitrary, and mutable," is without substance. For the nature of man has always been determined to sociality in general by the Creator, but the establishment of and entry into particular societies were left to men to decide according to the guidance of reason, and the natural law is in no way rendered arbitrary through this. Moreover, what is more obvious than this, that the nature of man, insofar as it has been made social by the Creator, is the rule and foundation of that law which is to be followed in both universal and particular society?

Nor, indeed, do those who commend this foundation as follows bring more firmness or light to this discipline: "The final proof of everything that is naturally just is nature itself, which makes its own law. The guidance of nature is to be followed,

---

[1] Pliny, *Natural History*, 35, 10, 36, #85.

and one must diligently consider what it leads to of itself in moral matters, and what it keeps us from. Therefore, the natural law is to be sought in the agreement or disagreement with nature. However, nature is to be understood here not as it is now, depraved by its corrupt offspring and their degenerate mores, but whole and uncorrupted as it was first created." For besides the fact that most of the things said here may seem to beg the question and to explain the obscure by that which is equally obscure, even the claim that man's nature was at first created whole by God and afterward depraved by man's sin is a question of fact whose truth cannot be established except on the authority of the Divine Scriptures. And consequently that foundation is admitted only by those Christians who together with our church acknowledge original sin. But since this discipline concerns not Christians alone but the race of all mortals, it would obviously be more appropriate to establish a principle which no one, provided he is in possession of reason, can deny. But let those who are of sound mind judge about this matter themselves.

As for what remains, just as I do not despair that good and sensible men will dignify this labor of mine with their approval, so if perchance my mind has wandered anywhere, I ask with all my might that they ascribe it to the imperfection of the human condition, since it would plainly be inhuman, and a folly bordering on insanity, to set fire to a whole field on account of one or two useless plants, . . . Indeed, I am neither so haughty, nor do my gray hairs make me so stubborn yet, that I shall think I must blush at having learned something from or having been corrected by the advice of those who are wiser. Instead, I will be ready both to rebut without stubbornness and to be rebutted without anger. . . . Farewell.

BOOK I

Chapter 1

ON THE ORIGIN AND VARIETY
OF MORAL ENTITIES

1. The task of first philosophy, insofar as it has lived up to its own true nature, has been to define things in the broadest possible manner and to arrange them consistently into certain categories, and also to provide a general description of the nature and condition of each kind of thing. But those who have heretofore undertaken to cultivate this discipline, and who seem to have accomplished its task so well in the class of natural entities, have—the matter speaks for itself—not given moral entities the attention they deserve. Many people have not even thought about these things; others have dealt with them, but only lightly, as if they were worthless or unimportant fictions. This despite the fact that it greatly behooves man to know the nature of such entities, which he has received the faculty to produce, and whose power deeply suffuses itself throughout his life. This consideration makes it necessary to provide a preliminary account of this generally neglected doctrine that will at least suffice for our own undertaking. For we do not want the obscurity or novelty of our definitions of moral entities to obstruct a reader who has perhaps seldom encountered these sorts of things in the common treatises. . . .

2. And so we see that all things which collectively make up this universe, consisting as they do of principles assigned and fitted to each of them by the Great and Good Creator Who constituted their respective essences, have their own particular characteristics. These issue from the arrangement and aptitude of their substance and express themselves in certain actions according to the measure of strength imparted to them by their Creator. We usually call them 'natural,' since the term 'nature' has customarily designated not only the entirety of created things as such, but also the modes and activities flowing from their innate strength, which produces the infinitely varied motions whereby we see everything in this universe to be stirred.

Those things which operate either entirely without sensation, or with only a direct or minimally reflective sense, are driven by natural instinct alone and do not know how to moderate their actions by any self-discovered standards. But man has been given a special light of the mind in addition to his remarkable physical aptitude. By means of this light he can more accurately comprehend and compare matters, infer the unknown from the known, and judge of the proper arrangements among things, so that he is not compelled to act always in the same manner but can exert, suspend, or moderate his actions as seems fit. It has also been granted him to invent or apply certain aids by means of which his faculties may be specially assisted and directed.

Let others give a more careful account of those notions invented to aid the intellect, so that it is not confounded by the infinite variety of things. Our present task is to examine how things and their natural motions have had superimposed on them, chiefly for the direction of voluntary acts, a certain kind of attribute that gives a peculiar consistency to human actions and adorns man's life with a remarkable grace and order. These attributes are called *moral* entities because the human mores and actions directed and moderated by them assume thereby a character and aspect different from the unrefined simplicity of brutes.

3. It seems that moral entities can be most conveniently defined as certain modes superadded by intelligent beings to physical things and motions for the special purpose of directing and regulating man's free, voluntary actions, and for giving human life a certain order and grace. We call them 'modes,' since Being in its broadest sense seems more appropriately divided into substance and mode than into substance and accident. This distinction between mode and substance makes it abundantly clear that moral entities are not self-subsistent but depend on substances and their motions, which they only affect in a certain manner. Moreover, some modes flow naturally from things themselves, as it were, while others are superadded to physical things and their modes by an intelligent power. For a being endowed with understanding can, by reflectively considering and comparing things, form notions whereby a faculty may be consistently guided. And this is the sort of thing moral entities are.

Their primary author, you may justifiably say, is the Great and Good God, who surely did not wish mortals to pass through this life without culture and mores, in the fashion of brutes, but wanted men's life and actions to be tempered by certain principles—something that could not happen without moral entities. Yet most were superadded later by the will of men themselves, being introduced according to their apparent conduciveness to the cultivation and, as it were, the ordering of human life. This also reveals their end, which is not as in the case of physical entities the perfection of this universe, but the distinctive perfection of human life, insofar as it exceeds the life of brutes in its capacity for a certain beautiful order, and the production of a finely wrought harmony in so highly variable a thing as the motion of the human mind.

4. Now, as the original manner of producing physical entities is creation, there is hardly a better way to describe the production of moral entities than by the word 'imposition.' For moral entities do not arise from the intrinsic substantial principles of things but are superadded to things already existent and physically complete,

and to their natural effects, by the will of intelligent beings who alone determine their existence. They are also assigned certain effects by these same causes, at whose pleasure they can be destroyed again without any physical alteration in the thing to which they were superadded. Hence, their operative power consists not in directly producing some physical motion or change in things by means of their own internal efficacy, but partly in showing men how they ought to regulate their free actions, and partly in making men specially fit to receive some benefit or harm, or to have their actions toward others be accompanied by a particular effect. The efficacy of the moral entities instituted by God flows from the fact that He has, by right of creation, circumscribed the free will it pleased Him to grant men within certain limits, and that by threatening some evil He turns the recalcitrant in whatever direction He wishes. But men too have been able to enforce the moral entities invented by themselves by threatening anyone who refuses to conform himself thereto with some evil which they have the strength to inflict.

5. Therefore, since moral entities have been instituted to order men's lives (an end requiring those who must live according to that norm to treat each other in a certain fashion, to rule their actions in a certain manner, and finally to conduct themselves in a certain way toward the things useful for human life), they are understood to inhere chiefly in *men* and their *actions*, and to some extent in the *things* produced by nature, either alone or with the aid of human industry. Although it would have made sense to divide moral entities according to these three heads, it nonetheless seems more fitting to categorize them according to the patterns of physical entities. This is partly because philosophers have more carefully inquired into these, allowing moral entities to be greatly illuminated by comparison with them, and partly because our intellect is so immersed in considerations of physical entities that it can conceive moral entities in hardly any other way than by analogy with them.

6. Even though moral entities are not self-subsistent and must generally be classed as modes and not as substances, we nonetheless find that some of them are conceived like substances. This is because other moral entities seem to be immediately grounded in them in nearly the same manner that quantity and quality inhere in corporeal substances. Indeed, just as physical substances presuppose the space in which they naturally exist and move, so, analogously, are moral persons in particular said and understood to be in a *state* [*status*] that likewise supports and, as it were, underlies them as the medium of their actions and effects. Hence, a state can on account of its analogy with space be consistently described as a sub-posed entity, for it also seems to be not a primary entity but one intended to underlie and in a certain manner sustain other things. Thus, certain states have been established not for their own sake but so that moral persons may be understood to exist in them.

Yet space differs from a state in being an immobile kind of substance essentially extended from the first, and also able to exist after natural things have been removed. But a state—like the rest of moral entities considered formally and as such—is no more than a mode or attribute: Remove the persons understood to be in it and it seems itself scarcely able to exist any longer.

7. Moreover, we find that this state is of two kinds, corresponding to two kinds

of space, according to which things are said to be either *somewhere* or in a place (for example, here or there), or *when* or in time (for example, today, yesterday, or tomorrow). One of these indicates a moral *where* and is somewhat analogous to place; the other concerns time insofar as it has a moral effect on those said to be in it. The former state, which is analogous to place, can be considered either *indeterminately* or *determinately*, depending on whether it results only from moral qualities or also involves a moral quantity or comparison.

Considered indeterminately, man's state is either *natural* or *adventitious*. We call it natural not because it flows from the physical principles of the human essence without any imposition, but because it is imposed by the Deity (not men's will) and accompanies man immediately from birth. However, we are accustomed to consider man's natural state either *absolutely* or *in relation to other men*. Lacking a more suitable term, we shall refer to it in the former sense as man's 'humanity,' namely that condition in which we understand him to have been constituted by his Creator, Who wished him to excel all other animals. . . . It follows from this state—to which the life and condition of beasts are opposed—that man should be a creature who acknowledges and worships his Author, and admires His works, and that he should lead a life that is utterly different from that of brutes.

Now, since that state of being a man gives rise to certain obligations and also has connected with it certain rights, it will not be irrelevant here to say when it begins in particular individuals. This, it seems correct to say, is at the point when someone can truly be said to be a man, namely when he begins to live and feel as a unique substance while still in his mother's womb, even though the perfections a man acquires only after some time are still lacking. But since obligations require for their fulfillment an awareness of one's self and what one does, they do not become effective until a person knows how to direct his actions according to some norm and to distinguish them from one another. Rights, however, which obligate already rational beings, can benefit even those who are unaware of what is happening, and exhibit their power as soon as someone begins to be a man.

Therefore, since all men have a right not to be hurt by others, harming the body of someone still in the womb clearly injures not only his parents but also the fetus itself; and we think that he can afterwards seek restitution for the injury in his own name, when as an adult he has come to understand it. But if anyone destroys or aborts the content of a mother's womb before it has coalesced into the form of a man, he cannot be said to have injured that unformed object. Even so, he sins against the law of nature by cutting off a member from human society, and injures the state and the parents by depriving them respectively of a hoped-for citizen and offspring.

Considered *in relation to other men*, however, that state is said to be natural insofar as men are understood to conduct themselves toward one another according to that bare and universal kinship resulting from their similar nature, before any human deed or pact has made them specially answerable to each other. In this sense those who have no common master and are not subject to one another, and who do not know each other by means of benefit or injury, are said to live together in a natural state.

There is in addition a third way to consider the *natural state*, namely, as one bereft of all human inventions and institutions by means of which this life has been rendered beautiful and useful, be they divinely inspired or not.

Adventitious states are superadded to men at or after their birth by means of some human deed. It will be easier to introduce their divisions later on. . . .

8. Although every state involves a certain regard for and bearing toward other men on the part of one who is said to be in it (since the rights or obligations that always accompany it are unintelligible without an object revealing their effect), some states nonetheless indicate their other-regardingness more distinctly by also describing men's manner of dealing with one another. Chief among these are the states of *peace* and *war*. . . . For peace is that state in which men live quietly without doing violent injuries to one another, freely paying their mutual debts from a sense of obligation, as it were. War, by contrast, is a state where men mutually inflict or repel injuries, and where they strive to extract what others owe them by means of force.

Peace can be divided into the *common* peace observed toward all men solely on the basis of duties flowing from the simple law of nature, and *particular* peace, which depends on formal treaties and definite guarantees. The latter is once more divided into *internal* peace among members of the same commonwealth and *external* peace with those outside it, be they common friends or special friends and allies. There is no such thing among men as a *common* or universal *war* of all against all, since that follows upon the state of beasts. A *particular* war waged only against certain men is either *internal* or civil, or *external*. The former is waged among members of the same commonwealth, the latter among those who are not contained in the same state. The suspension of hostile acts during an ongoing state of war is called a *truce*.

12. Moral entities which are conceived analogously to substances are called moral *persons*. These are either single individuals or those joined together into one system by a moral bond, considered with their status or function in communal life. Now moral persons are either *simple* or *composite*. Simple persons are either *public* or *private*, depending on whether the different statuses or offices they occupy look directly to the welfare of civil society or toward each individual's own advantage. Public persons, as Christians have traditionally divided them, are either *political* or *ecclesiastical*. The former are either *of greater importance* or *of lesser importance*. Of these, some of the former rule the commonwealth with supreme sovereignty; others (whom ordinary usage appropriately calls magistrates) execute some part of the sovereignty with an authority delegated by the supreme sovereignty, or offer advice on how the commonwealth ought rightly to be governed. *Lesser political persons* render a less noble service to the commonwealth and the magistrates as such. In wartime, for instance, the common soldiers subservient to higher and lower officers, who are as magistrates to them, may also be considered public persons in view of the fact that they are directly or indirectly authorized by the highest civil authority to bear arms for the commonwealth.

There is also a special type of political persons who may be called *representatives* because they assume the personae of others. Though the authority vested in

them is clearly another's, they negotiate matters in his place just as effectively as if
he himself had disposed of them. Such are legates, deputies, syndics, and the like.

A distinction has recently been drawn, however, between ministers having a *representative character*—namely, ambassadors in the strict sense—and second-
order ministers like envoys or residents, who represent less fully than the former
the eminence of those who sent them. . . . The former bear a certain resemblance
to private tutors and guardians insofar as these manage the affairs and business of
their pupils and wards.

Here Hobbes . . . is incorrect in saying that it is frequent in states for someone
to represent or assume the persona of some inanimate thing that is not itself a person, such as a church, a hospital, a bridge, and so on.[1] For it seems unnecessary to
fictionalize these things as persons when it is so easy to say that the state has
charged certain men with the collection of revenues intended to preserve them,
and with the prosecution or defense of any lawsuits arising in their regard.

It is easy for anyone to know the different ecclesiastical persons, depending on
the particular religion in which he has been brought up. And no educated man can
fail to notice what sorts of persons are produced by the schools.

There is a great diversity of private persons, whose chief distinguishing features are drawn mainly from the following sources: (1) The business, occupation,
or craft in which someone is engaged and from which he makes a living, be it an
employment worthy of free men or something disreputable. (2) The situation or
moral position occupied by someone in the state, where some persons are citizens
with a full or partial right, others resident aliens, and still others foreigners. (3) One's
place in the family, in which respect one is a family-father, who can simultaneously
unite in himself the personae of husband, father, and master; another a wife, another
a son, and another a servant—a circle of ordinary family members occasionally
enlarged by a guest. (4) Lineage, which gives rise to different grades of nobles in
different civil states, and to commoners. (5) Sex and age, the latter being distinguished into childhood, youth, manhood, and old age, and the former into male
and female. For though sex and age do not arise by imposition, they are nonetheless morally significant in the communal life of men insofar as the different sexes
are subject to different standards of propriety and their members fittingly treated
in disparate ways.

13. A *composite* moral person is created when a number of individuals are so
united with one another that whatever they will or do by virtue of that union is
considered one will and one action. This is understood to happen when single
individuals subject their own will to the will of one man or council in such a way
that they are willing to acknowledge whatever the latter decrees or does about those
matters which pertain to the nature of their union as such, and are compatible with
its end, as the will and action of them all, and are willing to have others regard
them in this way as well. Hence it is that although in other instances where several individuals have willed or done something, there are thought to be as many
wills and acts as there are physical persons or human individuals involved, one

---

[1] Leviathan, XVI.

will is attributed to those who have coalesced into a composite person, and an action stemming from them as such is reckoned as one, no matter how many physical individuals have concurred in it. And so this kind of composite person also can and usually does acquire special rights and privileges which that body's single members as such can by no means demand or claim for themselves. . . .

Now composite moral persons, or societies, can be divided in the manner of simple persons into *public* and *private*, with the public being further distinguished into *sacred* and *political*. Some of the sacred, like the Catholic church and the particular churches that are contained within civil states' fixed boundaries, or distinguished by their public confessional formulas, can be called *general*; others, like councils, synods, consistories, presbyteries, and so on can be called *specific*. Political societies are likewise either *general*, like the many kinds of commonwealth (simple, composite, regular, irregular), or *particular*, like a senate, an equestrian order, a tribe, a parliament, and so on. An army divided into legions, squadrons, cohorts, companies, and so forth is called a *military* society.

Private societies include not only families but also the so-called fraternal associations of merchants, craftsmen, and the like that are found in states. It does not seem worth the effort here to make a detailed inventory of all their kinds.

16. It seems unnecessary, however, to classify *things* that are objects of the law as moral entities in the proper sense. . . . Thus, one should not think that a new quality was imposed on certain things when they came under dominion, while the rest were left free of dominion. Rather, once ownership of things had been introduced, a moral quality began somehow to exist among men, who were indeed affected by it, but which things served only to define.

For just as it was right for man under primordial conditions of joint possession to occupy for his personal use the things available to all, once dominion had been established an owner received a special right to dispose of his things, which the rest as non-owners were then obligated to leave alone. The things themselves, as the object of that right and obligation, acquired no more than a certain extrinsic denomination from this. Thus, calling certain things religious or sacred does not mean that a moral quality or sanctity inheres in them as such, but only that men are obligated to treat them in a certain manner; and when this obligation ceases, the things are understood to revert to common use. But if anyone still insists on speaking of certain things as moral, we must take him to be attributing morality to things only objectively, and not formally [or really].

17. So much then for moral entities conceived analogously to substances. Now we must also examine those that both formally are and are conceived as modes. These, it seems, can be most conveniently divided into *affective* and *estimative* modes. By the former, persons are understood to be affected in a certain manner; by the latter persons and things are capable of being evaluated. The former are called *qualities* and the latter *quantities*, in the widest acceptance of each term.

It is sufficient for our present purpose to divide qualities into *formal* and *operative*. Formal qualities—which may also be called simple attributes for this reason—are neither inclined nor directed toward any act or operation, but are suited and joined to their subject like bare forms only. Operative qualities are either *primary* or *derivative.* According to the former, things are thought to be suited for or capable of action; the latter, like acts, come from them. A primary quality is also either *internal* or *external*, and may be called a passive moral quality.

18. Some of the most conspicuous moral attributes are *titles*, which designate the varying importance and status of persons in communal life. They are chiefly of two sorts. Some indicate directly the importance of persons in communal life, or their special qualities, but only more or less obscurely suggest or hint at their status (depending on a particular title's customary assignation to either few or many statuses). Such are the honorary titles commonly adjoined to people's names, like 'most serene,' 'most eminent,' 'most illustrious,' and so on, whose significance grows or diminishes along with the kinds of nouns they modify. Other titles directly indicate a certain status, or a special position within a status, and only indirectly suggest how important that status or office is commonly taken to be. Such are the names of moral persons, at least of those occupying positions of honor. We examine them here not so much in themselves, as notions representing the status and office of one person to the understanding of another, but because they indicate the humanly imposed rights, authority, and function of those to whom they are attributed. And so it is not much ado about nothing if men fight heatedly over titles now and then, for when someone is denied a title we understand that he is also being denied the status, function, authority, and rights commonly expressed or implied thereby. . . .

19. Operative moral qualities are either *active* or *passive.* Among the former, the noblest kinds are *authority, right,* and *obligation. Authority* enables someone to do something legitimately and with a moral effect. This effect refers to someone else's becoming obligated to perform some task, or to permit or not hinder actions undertaken by another; or to the ability to confer on others a previously absent faculty to do or have something. It is a quality that tends to spread itself as widely as possible, as it were. By reason of its effectiveness, authority is either *perfect* or *imperfect.* The former may be exercised even through force against those who attempt illegitimately to obstruct it. (Inside states, however, force is exercised chiefly through legal action; outside of states, through war.) Though anyone illegitimately prevented from exercising imperfect authority is surely being treated inhumanely, this does not grant him a right to legal action or war, unless by chance necessity supplies what is lacking in effectiveness.

Next, in regard to its subject, authority is either *personal* or *communicable.* The former cannot be legitimately transferred from one person to another, though there are a few distinctions here. For certain kinds of authority are so closely linked with a person that they cannot be rightly enacted by another at all. Such is a husband's authority over the body of his wife—which the laws by no means permit him to discharge by proxy. Certain other kinds, however, though we may not transfer them as such to someone else as his possession [*ktēsin*], can have their enactment delegated to others, yet only in such a way that these others derive their entire authorization from the one in whom the authority fundamentally inheres. The authority of kings who have been constituted by the people's will is of this type. For they cannot transfer the right to rule to anyone else, though they may employ the services of ministers in actively exercising it. Communicable authority is that which can be rightly transferred from one person to another, either at one's own discretion or by the authorization or consent of a superior.

Finally, in terms of its object, most authority is reducible to four kinds. For it concerns either *persons* or *things*, and in each case either *one's own* or those *of others*. Authority over one's own person and actions is called *freedom* (though the ambiguities belaboring this term must be presented elsewhere). But this freedom must not be conceived as if it were a principle distinct from the one to whom it is attributed, or as a power of forcing oneself to do something against one's will.... Rather, it is a faculty of disposing of oneself and one's actions according to one's own choice, involving of itself the negation of any impediments arising from some other superior authority. Authority over one's own things is called *dominion*, that over the persons of others *sovereignty* in the proper sense, and that over their things *lordship*.

20. The word *right* is very ambiguous. For besides standing for 'law,' for a complex or system of homogeneous laws, as well as for judicial verdicts, it most often refers to the moral quality by means of which we rightly command persons or possess things, or by virtue of which something is owed us. The difference between the terms 'authority' and 'right' seems to be this. The former better conveys the actual presence of the said quality to things or persons, though it connotes less clearly the manner in which anyone has acquired it. The term 'right,' however, gives clear and proper indication that the quality has been correctly acquired and is now correctly possessed. Most kinds of authority have a special name. But since the quality through which something is understood to be owed us does not, we have decided to distinguish it here with the word 'right'—even though ordinary usage makes us unwilling to avoid the term's other meanings.

We classify right as an active quality in view of the fact that it enables us to demand something from another. But insofar as it enables anyone to be a proper recipient of something, it is also considered to be one of the *passive moral qualities*. For passive qualities are those through which anyone can rightly have, suffer, accept, or receive something.

There seem to be three kinds of these. The first makes it appropriate for us to accept something, but not as if we had any authority to demand or another an obligation to provide it. Such is the ability to receive a purely gratuitous gift. That this kind of quality is not a complete fabrication may be gathered from the fact that, for example, a judge can be forbidden to accept gifts from the parties to a suit under any pretext. The second kind qualifies us to receive something from another, not by force if he be unwilling (unless necessity happens to compel us), but from some moral virtue that binds him to furnish the thing. Grotius calls this an aptitude. The third kind enables us to compel another to furnish something even against his will, and he is fully obligated thereto by some law that assigns a definite penalty.

It must also be noted, however, if we wish to speak accurately, that many things commonly falling into the category of rights are composites of authority and right in the strict sense, and at the same time involve or suppose an obligation, an honor, or the like. Thus, citizenship or the right of citizenship encompasses the faculty of fully exercising the privileges reserved for a state's members, and the right to enjoy their proper benefits, while also supposing an obligation toward the state. And the honors of the learned, for example, encompass the authority to perform certain actions proper to their stature and the right to enjoy the advantages of their rank, which is highly esteemed besides.

21. *Obligation* is that through which a person is bound by a moral necessity to do, or to admit or suffer something; its kinds will be treated in more detail below. There are also 'sensible' moral qualities which are understood to affect men's judgment in a certain manner, just as there are physical qualities by which the sensitive faculty is affected, and which are referred to by that name. Such are honor, disgrace, authority, seriousness, clarity, obscurity, and the like.

22. Now we must also add a few remarks about modes of estimation or *moral quantities*. For it is evident that in common life persons and things are valued not only according to their extension as physical substances, or the degree of their motion and physical qualities—inasmuch as these are considered to spring from natural principles—but also according to another kind of non-physical and non-mathematical quantity arising from imposition and the determination of a rational power. This moral quantity is found in things, where it is called *price*, in persons, where it is called *esteem* (both of these fall under the notion of value), and in actions, where it lacks a special designation. We will treat each of these in its own place. . . .

23. Finally, the imposition to which moral entities owe their origin also determines their stability or changes: When it ceases, as it were, they themselves vanish at the same time, just as a shadow disappears once the light has been extinguished. Entities sprung from divine imposition are eliminated only by divine choice; those constituted by human resolve are also abolished by it, without the least alteration in the actual physical substance of persons or things. For although the nature of things does not allow something once done to be undone (for example, that a former consul not be a former consul), we nonetheless see everyday how people cease to be what they were, and also how the moral entities inhering in someone disappear entirely with no real trace remaining. For a moral entity can never become as strong as a physical quality. Hence, it is very foolish to believe that when a persona is imposed on someone, an indelible character is impressed on him by virtue of that moral imposition alone. Thus, if a commoner becomes a noble he acquires new rights only, without the least change in his substance and physical qualities; and if a noble is expelled from his rank he loses only his rights, all of his natural endowments remaining unimpaired.

Chapter 3

ON THE HUMAN UNDERSTANDING'S
CONTRIBUTION TO MORAL ACTIONS

1. Since the chief task of this discipline which we have undertaken to set forth is to demonstrate the right and wrong, good and bad, and justice and injustice of human actions, we will first have to consider the principles and characteristics of these actions, and then how they are understood to be morally connected with man through imputation.

So, to begin, man's excellence far outshines the brutes in that he is endowed with a most noble soul capable of knowing and judging things by means of a special light, and of seeking or rejecting them with an exquisite rapidity. And human actions are consequently assigned to a much more distinguished class than the movements of brutes, which are elicited by sensory stimuli without any preceding reflection. . . .

Now that power of the human soul which it bears as a kind of light comes with the name of 'understanding.' This is conceived to have two faculties, as it were, which it exerts in the case of actions that are voluntarily undertaken. One is that through which an object is presented to the will as in a mirror, and which simply shows what is appropriate or inappropriate, good or bad, about it. The other is that which weighs and compares the good or bad features that offer themselves on either side in the case of many objects, and which judges what ought finally to be done, and where and how, and at the same time deliberates about the means most suited to the end. Here it must also be noted that voluntary action as a rule begins from man's understanding. . . .

2. We must observe, however, that the former faculty of the understanding is one of those commonly called *natural*, in contradistinction to those faculties called *free*. Thus it is not under man's control to apprehend things otherwise than as their images present themselves to the understanding; nor can the will keep the understanding from assenting to a proposition that appears clear and evident to it. Yet it is under man's control to pay close attention to the thing to be considered and, by carefully reflecting on it, to make a more precise and balanced assessment of its good and evil features, and therefore not to stop at the thing's bare surface but to penetrate to its very entrails, as it were. And when this has been done an accurate judgment about the thing can follow. . . .

Hence we understand in passing the extent to which there is a place for cultivating and legislating about this part of the soul. To be sure, human effort cannot bring it about that the understanding apprehends things otherwise than as they appear. And since assent or belief cannot but respond to the image apprehended by the understanding, a person cannot judge differently about a thing than as he himself has seemed to perceive it. Nor is there any law by which someone rightly demands that he do otherwise—just as no one can be wise from a bare and simple command.

Yet because many things commonly escape a casual observer that spontaneously present themselves, as it were, to those who carefully examine them, and because the will can hinder the understanding in its contemplation of some truth by thrusting other objects before it, a diligent contemplation of things serves greatly to confirm the judgment of the understanding, and those charged with the care of others should see to it that suitable opportunities for this are given. They can also employ the sanction of penalties to induce someone to make meticulous use of those means by which the obscurity of things can be dispelled and their real condition represented.

3. Now, since the understanding precedes our actions like a torch, as it were, and we cannot avoid going astray unless it lights us properly, we must take it as certain that our apprehensive faculty and our judgment both contain a natural rectitude that does not allow us to be deceived about moral matters if we attend to them as we should, and that neither faculty is so depraved that we cannot avoid being deceived about such matters. An imperfect mirror is bound to reflect distorted images, and a tongue coated with bile prohibits correct judgments of taste. And if we were unable clearly to discern good and evil, we could not be faulted for having done something wrong, and it would be very unfair to impute to us errors which we were never able to avoid. Therefore, unless we wish to subvert entirely the morality of actions, we must absolutely maintain that the human understanding is naturally correct, and that upon due investigation it grasps its objects clearly and as they are in themselves. Nor can our practical judgment, at least about the natural law's general precepts, be so depraved that the immorality of actions stemming from it, supposedly because of some invincible error or ignorance, cannot be imputed to it. . . .

We note here that we are not discussing what our understanding is now capable of in regard to things that depend on God's special revelation, without being particularly favored by divine grace. The inquiry into this belongs to another discipline. Nor are we concerned about whether someone can, by being misinformed, so imbibe a false opinion about theoretical truths that must be sought out by means of an exact mental investigation, that he cannot extricate himself from it by any reasoning. Rather, we are dealing with the powers of the understanding insofar as they are needed to adjust actions properly to the natural law. And here we think that no man of a mature age and possessed of reason is so dull as not to be able to comprehend at least the general precepts of the natural law, and those which have the most frequent use in common life, and to discern the agreement they have with the rational and social nature of man. . . .

4. When the understanding is thoroughly acquainted with the laws and therefore accountable to the legislator for what they command and forbid, its judgments concerning the morality of actions are commonly and peculiarly called 'conscience.' We can for the sake of distinction call this an 'antecedent' or a 'consequent' conscience, according to whether it precedes or follows human actions. A consequent

conscience is a reflexive judgment of the understanding concerning things done or omitted, approving those done well and condemning those done badly. It is accompanied by an inner calm or unrest depending on its testimony about a person, and it lets us anticipate whether a legislator will be satisfied or not, and also whether other men will be well or ill disposed toward us. . . . An antecedent conscience really does precede our deeds, telling us repeatedly what is good and evil and therefore to be done or avoided.

But here it must be carefully noted that conscience has a place in the direction of human actions only insofar as it is thoroughly acquainted with the laws, which are the proper guide thereof. And so, if anyone attributes to practical judgment or conscience a special power to direct actions that neither originates in nor depends on the law, he is ascribing the power of laws to men's arbitrary fancies and introducing the utmost confusion into human affairs. . . .

8. But if the judgment of the understanding wavers between two alternatives, being unable to discern whether something is good or evil and consequently to be done or avoided, it is called a 'doubtful conscience.' To it this rule applies: As long as there are no reasons weighty enough to divert the judgment of the understanding from its neutral position the action ought to be suspended, and anyone who acts while his conscience hangs still in equilibrium, as it were, does wrong. For such a person has, inasmuch as he can, violated the law. It is as if he said: "Though it is not clear to me whether this action goes against the law, I will do it anyway, whether it does or not." . . .

9. A doubtful conscience is akin to a 'scrupulous conscience.' This refers to situations where the judgment of the understanding is accompanied by an anxious fear that what one has deemed good is perhaps evil, and vice versa. When such a scruple is based on probable arguments, the action should be suspended until the scruple is removed by reasons or by wise authority, but if it arises from some feeble superstition, it should be disregarded and put out of mind.

Descartes . . . quite correctly prescribes the following remedy for the mental fluctuation and pangs of conscience preceding action: "to accustom oneself to forming certain and determinate judgments concerning all things that one encounters."[2] It must be added, however, that such judgments should be formed from a genuine and reliable moral science, or the discipline of natural law, and from the Christian religion cleansed of men's superstitious additions. For though it may be possible without this to harden the mind in some way so as not to experience mental pangs and fluctuations, such firmness neither lasts a long time nor frees us from sin. And so we cannot approve the continuation of the quoted passage, that "one should always consider one's duty discharged when one does what one judges to be better, even though that judgment may be the worst possible."[3] For this is not to cure the illness but to induce mental insensibility by means of a badly concocted anodyne.

---

[2] *The Passions of the Soul*, 170.

[3] Ibid., 177.

Chapter 4

ON THE HUMAN WILL'S CONTRIBUTION
TO MORAL ACTIONS

1. Since the most wise Creator wished to make man a law-governed animal, He instilled into his soul a will as a sort of internal directress of his actions. This allows him, by means of an internal principle not dependent on any physical necessity, to pursue and select among the familiar objects before him those he judges to be most suited to himself and, on the other hand, to avoid those that seem not to agree with him. Now, there are two faculties, as it were, through which the will is conceived to exert itself concerning human actions: Through one of them it is understood to act *spontaneously*, through the other *freely*. To spontaneity, so to speak, we attribute certain acts or movements of which some are interior and others exterior; the former are customarily called 'elicited' and the latter 'commanded.'

Elicited acts are those that immediately affect the will whereby they are produced. Some of them, like volition, intention, and fruition, concern ends; others, like consent, election, and use, concern means. An act of will is said to be a 'volition' when the will itself proceeds directly toward the end, without regard to its presence or absence, or when it simply approves the end. Others call this a 'will of simple approbation' because it lets us understand a thing's congruence with the nature or inclination of a person who has, however, not actively and effectively begun to produce or obtain it. Intention or choice is a desire capable of obtaining the end, or an act of the will whereby it tends effectively toward an absent end and strives actively to produce or obtain it. Since it involves effort and a hope of obtaining the end, it is easy to gather what sorts of things it is occupied with. . . .

Acts called 'commanded' are those whose execution depends on other faculties moved by the will.

2. Freedom, they say, is a faculty of the will enabling it, when all the requisites of action are given, to select one or more among a number of given objectives and reject the rest, or if but one objective is given, to accept and do it or not. (The so-called requisites of action are generally grouped together under the term 'occasion,' and they are conceived as separate from the final determination of the agent which, when added thereto, is definitely followed by the action. Thus, they are distinguished from a man's own contribution to his actions.) More specifically, however, the faculty of selecting one or more of a number of objectives is called 'freedom of specification or contrariety,' and the faculty concerned with the choice or rejection of only a single objective 'freedom of contradiction or exercise.'

Now freedom, it is supposed, superadds to spontaneity an indifference concerning the exercise of its own actions. This means that the will's acts of choice and refusal are not necessitated, and that it can opt either way in the case of a particular given objective (though it is generally impossible not to be attracted to good and repulsed by evil as such), even if it happens to lean more toward the one than toward the other. It also adds a free determination, so that the will, out of an internal impulse, here and now elicits either one of its acts, that of willing or that of not willing.

It must also be added, however, that even though a person's opinion about a thing's desirability or repulsiveness depends not on the will but the object's condition, namely its appearance as good or evil, the appetite or aversion following this appearance is nonetheless incapable of eliminating the will's freedom to determine its own external action toward that object. This is especially so since an evil can appear attractive only while it is compared with another evil. Hence, in order to refute Hobbes's doctrine . . . that appetite or aversion follows necessarily from one's preconception of the future pleasantness or discomfort of objects, and that therefore no place remains for free will, we must carefully distinguish the volition of simple approbation from effective volition or choice, which is not so necessarily dependent on particular objects.

In what follows, Hobbes introduces an empty subtlety by asserting: "When we say that someone's will is free to do this or that, it must always be understood with the accompanying condition 'if he so wills.' For saying that someone's will is free to do this or that whether or not he wills is absurd."[4] Surely no one is so stupid as not to see that this implies a contradiction. And it is foolish to add to a proposition as a condition the very thing that it asserts. To say that a man can freely will to do something if he wills is like saying "Peter runs, if he runs." Who would call this added clause a condition? . . .

3. Furthermore, the primary affection of the will, and that which seems to flow immediately from its nature, is that it has not been restricted to a certain, fixed, and inflexible mode of action (something we shall for now call its 'indifference'), and that this intrinsic indifference cannot be wholly extinguished through some external means. And this must be all the more firmly maintained because if that indifference were removed the morality of human actions would all at once be fundamentally destroyed. . . .

4. But to understand this indifference of the will rightly we must note certain things about the nature of the *good* in general. Indeed, although certain philosophers go so far as to consider good an absolute, so that every being which really exists is held to be good, we have not paid attention to this meaning, for which we see no use, and consider something good only insofar as it has a bearing on others and is understood to be good for or on behalf of someone. Considered in this way, the nature of the good is seen to consist in that aptitude by which a thing is capable of benefitting, preserving, or perfecting another thing. And since this aptitude depends on the very nature of things and on a capacity that is either inborn or acquired by effort, that *good*, which we can call 'natural,' is firm and uniform and in no way dependent on the erroneous or varying opinions of men.

Now because a good does not excite man's voluntary appetite unless it is known, at least by way of a vague idea, and indeed knowledge that is sensual, as it were, represents the true character of things and what can come from them quite obscurely, and the understanding itself as well is often surprised by errors and drowned out,

[4]*De Homine*, XI,2.

as it were, by impetuous senses and passions, it happens that some people apply the idea of good to certain things that are not so, thereby giving rise to what are called 'imaginary' goods. Moreover, individual men love and seek anything whatever insofar as they understand it to have a relation to their advantage, preservation, and perfection; and vice versa, they likewise oppose it insofar as they conceive it as evil. Yet just as it is not required for the nature of a good and its power to elicit an appetite that it be considered good specifically and solely for the one who seeks it, in abstraction from the advantage of others (especially since the good of others can, on account of the sociality and conjunction of men, also redound on us), so there is among all men a sufficiently harmonious consensus about the general nature of the good and its chief parts and kinds. Consequently, it by no means seems that a general notion of the good, one that is unshaken and uniform, must either be denied on account of disagreements about certain particulars, or else said to depend solely on the opinion of each person in natural freedom, and in the civil state on that of the supreme sovereign, and to be necessarily measured by this alone. . . .

Given these premises, it is evident that it is the nature of the will always to seek the good in general and always to turn away from evil in general. For not to be carried toward that which you see to be in agreement with yourself, and to be carried toward that which you judge to be in disagreement with yourself, obviously implies a contradiction. And no indifference can be supposed in this general inclination of the will, as it were, as though the will might by an appetite of simple approbation seek good and evil alike.

It is true though that the will of individual men, who incline toward different things at special moments, does in the end exert the strength of its indifference with respect to particular goods and evils, and this because most goods and evils do not by any means appear as pure and simple to man, but as mixed with one another: evils with goods, goods with evils. In addition, since there is in individual men a particular inclination toward certain things peculiar to themselves, and not everyone can distinguish solid and lasting goods from the false and momentary, an almost infinite variety commonly arises in the wills and pursuits of men, and all of them go about seeking what is good for themselves, but in a different way. . . .

5. Indeed, the mind does not always bring itself to act or not to act from a position of equilibrium, as it were, without any additional influence. Instead, various causes frequently carry it vehemently in one direction, and sometimes external violence falls so heavily upon it that its own strength seems of no avail. In the same way, a sailor does not always travel the sea with a backwind, but sometimes, when the zephyrs howl, he barely clings to the rudder against the crosswinds, and at others he is completely shaken from the helm and forced to commit his ship to the winds' whim. . . .

6. Frequent repetition also inclines the will powerfully toward certain actions, as does custom, which brings about the free and expeditious undertaking of an action and makes it seem as if the mind is carried toward the object as soon as it presents itself. When such inclinations are joined to a pleasure and ease of acting, they are commonly termed 'habits'; and these, insofar as they concern good and evil moral actions, are respectively called virtues and vices.

Since up to now most of those professing to treat moral philosophy have taken themselves to have expounded the main part of their discipline once they have explicated the names of the eleven virtues, there is no reason to tire ourselves as well by enumerating these. It is sufficient to give only a general indication that virtues are those mental dispositions by which men are inclined toward actions that preserve themselves and human society, and vices on the contrary, those that make them prone to do things tending to their own and to society's destruction.

We must also note here Hobbes's statement . . . that "A common measure of virtues and vices is found only in civil life," and therefore that "such a measure, whereby virtue and vice can be estimated and defined, does not exist in a natural state."[5] For the definition we have proposed surely has a place even in the natural state, and the things that ought to be prescribed as virtues in civil states should conform to it. And if anything with which that definition does not square were prescribed in a civil state, it would have to be considered absurd.

The noticeable variety in the laws of different states does not prevent there being a common and uniform definition of the virtues. For this diversity either concerns things outside the sphere of natural laws; or it arises from the fact that, in one place, some precept of the natural law has acquired the force of civil law, while elsewhere it has not; or, finally, it indicates that some legislators did not have the benefit of sound reason. . . .

7. The will is also impelled toward certain actions in no small way by motions of the mind called 'passions.' Aroused mainly by an object's appearance as good or evil, they also obscure considerably the judgment of the understanding. . . . Their number, the manner in which they are aroused and calmed, and their uses have been artfully presented above all by Descartes[6] . . . and Antoine le Grand[7] . . . , with whom Hobbes[8] . . . can also be grouped. For our own purposes, it suffices to note that however vehement the passions may be, they do not entirely overcome the force of the will. As Descartes . . . has pointed out, "Even those with weaker souls are able to acquire an absolute control over all their passions if they are sufficiently diligent in forming and directing them." . . .

9. Furthermore, it must be noted that the will is sometimes under such immense pressure, when it is threatened by grievous evils judged to exceed the ordinary strength of the human mind, that it consents to undertake things it absolutely avoids when not so necessitated. Such actions are commonly called 'mixed,' since they are partly voluntary and partly involuntary. They are voluntary insofar as their principle lies in an agent aware of the action's details, and also insofar as the will, for now and by necessity, turns toward them as a lesser or a partial evil, since it would otherwise have to undergo a greater or an entire evil. This lesser evil imitates the nature of a good in the present situation, where it is not possible to avoid both evils at the same time. . . .

Such actions have something involuntary about them, however, because the will

---

[5]*De Homine*, XIII,9.

[6]*The Passions of the Soul*, 50.

[7]*Institutes of Cartesian Philosophy*, VII,c.9.

[8]*Leviathan*, VI; *De Homine*, XII,9.

is driven to them against its own inclination and would never undertake them if it could escape the graver evil in some other way. For this reason, they also share with involuntary actions the feature of wholly or at least partly lacking the moral effects which otherwise follow upon purely spontaneous actions. For although sometimes so strict an obligation may be laid on someone that he ought not to depart from it even at the threat of death (which is held to be the most terrible of human evils), it is nonetheless not easy to presume such an obligation, unless it is clearly apparent, since it is too harsh for the human condition; and when it is absent it would be foolish not to wish to be rid of the greater evil. And so, many things that would have merited blame if performed in situations other than this, are praised by fair-minded men if they are undertaken because of such an impending necessity. Others are considered more deserving of pity than of indignation; and others, in which the odium or fault of the action devolves finally upon someone else, are either wholly or partly excused, and the doer of the deed declared innocent. . . .

Chapter 5

ON MORAL ACTIONS IN GENERAL

1. Now that we have carefully considered the understanding and the will as principles from which human actions derive that which allows them to be classed apart from the actions of beasts, the next step is to examine moral actions in general. For it is with the investigation of their rightness or wrongness that our discipline is chiefly concerned. Moral actions, therefore, are voluntary human actions regarded with the imputation of their effects in communal life. We call voluntary those actions that so depend upon the free causality of man's will that without its determination (through acts of its own elicited by a previous knowledge of the understanding) they would not be done; that is, those actions which man has the faculty to do or not do. We consider them here not as motions produced by some natural power, but insofar as they proceed from a decree of the will, a power capable of selecting either member of a contradiction.

For a voluntary action involves two things: one material, as it were, and the other formal. The first is the motion of a naturally existing power or its exercise as such, the other its dependence on the will's decision in such a way that the action is conceived as determined by a free and self-determining cause. The exercise itself, considered apart and as such, is for distinction's sake called an 'action of the will,' or one that stems from man's power of willing, rather than a 'voluntary action.'

A voluntary action is further considered either in itself and absolutely, as a physical motion undertaken by a preceding decision of the will, or reflexively, insofar as its effects can be imputed to someone. Voluntary actions involving this reflexivity are, according to a special usage, called 'human actions.' Moreover, because someone is said to be 'moral' when he performs these actions well or badly, or in accordance with that law which is their norm, and because the inclinations of the mind resulting from repeated actions are called 'morals,' human actions themselves have come to be designated as 'moral actions.'

2. The essence of moral actions considered in the latter way is comprised of two elements, one material as it were, the other formal. The material element is some physical motion of a physical power, such as locomotion, the sensitive appetite, the external and internal senses, and the understanding during the exercise of apprehension (for a judgment is so dependent on the apparent quality of an object that there is no place for the will to direct it, even though there are some elements of choice and effort in its formation). Indeed, it is the act of the will itself considered in its natural being, or insofar as it is regarded strictly as an effect produced through a power that has, as such, been instilled by nature. Moreover, it is the privation of some physical motion which a man could have directly or indirectly produced. . . .

3. The formal aspect of a moral action consists in its imputativity, so to speak. Through this the effect of a voluntary action can be imputed to an agent or regarded as something properly belonging to him, whether he has himself also physically produced it or caused others to do so. By virtue of this formality of action the agent himself also shares in the denomination of morality and is called a 'moral cause.' One can easily understand from this that ultimately considered, the formal principle of a moral cause in the proper and strict sense consists in imputation; in other words, it is nothing other than a voluntary agent to whom an effect is or is to be imputed because he has authored either all or part of it and must be held responsible, and thus answerable, for whatever good or evil comes from it. Thus, someone is the moral cause of another's hurt if he has given him a lump on the head with his hands, broken it with a stick, set dogs upon him, or sent assassins after him. . . .

5. Now a moral action can belong to someone and be imputed to him (in which we have said its formal principle consists) only because he had the authority and ability to do or not do it, to undertake or to omit it. This is so clear that even the most ignorant mortals, when they are accused of having done or omitted something, think that their most effective excuse is to say that the deed's performance or non-performance was not under their control. It must therefore be considered a prime axiom of morals that a man is accountable for those actions whose occurrence or non-occurrence he controls, or—what comes to the same thing—that any action which can be directed according to a moral norm, and which someone has the power to do or not do, can be imputed to him. On the contrary, whatever was not under his control, either in itself or in its cause, cannot be imputed to him as something owed, as it were. And it is no obstacle to this rule that a person is sometimes bound to do something that is surely beyond his ability, for such a case does not occur unless he has so obligated himself of his own accord. But it is surely under a person's control to bind himself to repair the damage stemming from a cause beyond human direction. . . .

8. It is evident that what we are not strong enough to prevent or bring about can also not be imputed to us, unless that weakness has been contracted through our own fault. This is the foundation of the common maxims that there is no obligation to do the impossible; that no one be taken to have issued laws enjoining such things; and consequently, that if any law, agreement, or testament does so, it should be considered unintended and a more favorable interpretation found. . . .

It should be carefully noted, however, that to call a thing *physically impossible* is one thing, and to call it *morally impossible* another. The former impossibility poses obstacles constraining the will itself, so that it either cannot issue in action or else completely wastes itself in trying to do so. Moral impossibility, however, poses no hindrance superior to the will's effective agency but arises entirely from the will itself. Thus we say that it is impossible in this sense for all men willingly to conspire for no good reason to hand down a falsehood to posterity, and likewise for someone to lead so circumspect and holy a life as not to offend in even the smallest way, at least through sudden outbursts of passion. . . .

9. Things that a person is coerced to suffer or do can also not be imputed to him. For they are understood morally to belong to him who brought the force to bear, while the one made to suffer or do these things is like a mere object or physical instrument. . . . Now it is considered coercion not only when a person in whom the principle of motion lies forcibly bends another's struggling and protesting limbs to do or suffer something, but also when, by threat of death or other grave evil, he compels him to commit a crime whose authorship he wishes to have attributed to himself, and which the latter is otherwise strongly disinclined to do. The first case is exemplified when a stronger person violently shoves someone into another or seizes his hand to strike him, or when a woman is violently raped by someone whose lust she has provoked through no fault of her own. Her body is indeed dishonored in this way, but the blemish does not reach her soul. . . . Those women, however, who allow the ring to be drawn from their weakly resisting finger can in no way be excused.

An example of the second sort occurs when a soldier is ordered upon pain of death to kill a man he knows is innocent. Nothing can be imputed to him on this account, for he was ordered only to do the deed; and this is neither incompatible with his persona as a soldier, nor a reason for refusing at the cost of his life, since his own death would in no way save the innocent man. It must nonetheless be admitted that the performance of some acts is so grave or shameful that a noble man, in our opinion, would rather die than lend his limbs to their performance, even though the blame would attach to someone else. . . .

Chapter 6

ON THE NORM OF MORAL ACTIONS,
OR, ON LAW IN GENERAL

1. Next we must examine that moral norm or law [*lex*] by which moral actions are to be measured, and whose consistency or inconsistency with them determines their special qualities. Before all else here, law must be carefully distinguished from *advice, pact*, and *right*, from those things, namely, whose partial resemblance to law leads some people to confuse them with it.

Now advice differs from law in that through it one tries to induce someone to do or omit something by means of considerations drawn from the thing itself. Since one has no authority over the other person, at least as regards the matter at hand, no direct obligation is brought to bear on him, and it remains at his discretion either to follow the advice or not. Still, advice can occasion an obligation insofar as the knowledge it bestows on someone produces a new or magnifies an existing obligation. Thus, a doctor cannot order a patient to take one thing and abstain from others, but when he shows him what is healthy and what hurtful to him, the latter is bound respectively to embrace and avoid them. This is not because the doctor has a right against the patient but because the law of nature orders everyone to care for his own life and health. A law should also have its reasons, to be sure, but these are not properly the ground of obedience to it. This lies rather in the authority of the one prescribing the law who, in announcing a decree of his will, obligates a subject to act in complete accord with his prescription, even if the reasons for it are perhaps not so clearly apparent to him.

Hobbes's comments . . . amount nearly to the same thing: "Advice is a precept where the reason for obedience is derived from the prescribed thing itself." But a law or "mandate is a precept where the reason for obedience is derived from the will of the prescriber. For it is improper to say, 'Thus I will, thus I command' unless one's will takes the place of a reason." And so laws are obeyed principally because of their prescriber's will and not because of their content. It also follows from this that "laws are issued by those with authority over those to whom they prescribe, advice by those with none. Doing what a law prescribes is a duty, heeding advice a matter of discretion. Advice is directed at the end of the one to whom it is prescribed," who is himself able to evaluate and approve that end. The end of a law, however, though it frequently also affects those to whom the law is prescribed, is not theirs to evaluate or approve, but is determined by the one who prescribes the law. "Advice is given only to those who want it but law also to those who do not. Finally, an advisor's right ceases at the pleasure of the one advised, but not a legislator's at the pleasure of those on whom the law is imposed."[9] . . .

---

[9]*De Cive*, XIV,1.

2. Those among the ancients who now and then refer to laws as *koinas
sunthēkas, homologias,* or 'common agreements' are also not sufficiently accurate.
. . . For one, neither divine positive laws nor natural laws have arisen from human
agreement, and this term can therefore refer only to civil laws. But not even these
are pacts or agreements in the proper sense, even though pacts played a role in the
establishment of civil legislative authority. Indeed, it is quite clear here, as in the
Greeks' other political doctrines, that they had in mind their own democratic states
where the laws, being made somewhat in the manner of a bargain (with a magistrate proposing them to the people for their approval and ratification), were called
agreements. But the laws of a democracy cannot properly be called pacts, even
though a majority of the people must consent to them. For that consensus is but
the manner in which the supreme sovereignty residing in the assemblage of all the
citizens expresses itself, that in which the majority concurs being considered the
will and decree of all. Thus, the effect of a vote which individual council members cast when drafting a decree differs greatly from the consent expressed by someone upon entering into a pact. For in the latter instance a person who has not consented is not bound, there being no other way to enter into a pact together; but in
the former the votes of the majority bind even those who have not consented.

The remaining differences between a pact and a law are obvious. To wit, "a
pact is a promise, a law a mandate. In pacts one says 'I will do'; laws say 'Do.' In
pacts," whose origin depends on our will, "what must be done is determined before
we are obligated to do it. In the case of a law, however," which presupposes
another's authority over us, "we are obligated to act before it is determined what
ought actually to be done." Therefore, no one is held fast by a pact unless he has
constrained himself by his own consent, but we are obligated by a law because we
owe a prior obedience to its author. . . .

3. Finally, since the word 'right' [*ius*] often means the same thing as 'law' [*lex*],
especially when it stands for a system of laws, we must beware of taking it for
law itself in cases where it denotes an authority to do something granted or left
unaffected by the laws. For example, when there is said to be a right to do this
or that by divine law, we must not think that divine law commands it, and therefore that we may rightly do it even if it is forbidden by human laws. The common
saying that specific laws grant a right to do whatever they do not explicitly forbid
comes from the fact that a man has the authority to do whatever lies within his
own natural capacity, unless a law prohibits it. But in this sense, at least, 'right'
refers to a freedom while 'law' denotes a bond by which our natural freedom is
constrained.

4. In general, law seems best defined as a decree whereby a superior obligates
someone subject to himself to conform his actions to the superior's prescription.
We call it a 'decree' not because it remains in the mind and will of the person
who decrees it, but because it is instilled into a subject's mind in such a way as to
make him understand the necessity of conforming himself to it. And for this reason we take it here as equivalent to an order.

We also think it matters little whether a law is called a decree or a pronouncement, so long as oral or written promulgation is not considered essential to it. For

it suffices that a lawgiver's will becomes known to his subjects in any way whatever, even through the inward intimation of their natural light. Hence we consider useless Hobbes's subtlety . . . in maintaining that the laws of nature acquire legal force only "to the extent that they have been orally promulgated by God in the Sacred Scriptures, but not insofar as they are mere conclusions of reason concerning things to be done and omitted."[10] For we know clearly by reason not only that the observance of natural laws is beneficial to humankind, but also that God wishes and commands mortals to direct their actions by that norm; and this suffices for the essence of a law. Still, it might be replied that natural laws, even as dictates of reason, can be conceived only as orally delivered.

Concerning the Grotian definition . . . of law as something obligating to "what is right,"[11] we must note that it supposes something just and right is given before any law and norm, so that the law of nature does not create what is right but only points to something right already existing. . . .

5. Furthermore, since we have defined law as coming from a superior and containing in itself the power to obligate, it seems necessary here to show what an obligation is and from where it arises, and also how someone can be obligated by or obligate another. In other words, how is it that one person can enjoin something upon another as a command?

We defined obligation above as an operative moral quality by which someone is bound to do or suffer something. (This is to consider it as inherent in the one being obligated, of course. By contrast, Richard Cumberland . . . defines it as the act whereby a legislator indicates to those to whom his law is given the necessity of conforming their actions thereto).[12] The Roman lawyers called it a bond of law by whose necessity we are constrained to do something. For it throws a kind of moral bridle over our freedom of action, as it were, so that we cannot rightly proceed in any other direction than the one in which it leads. Yet an obligation can in no way so constrain the will that it is in fact, and at its own risk, unable to diverge from it. . . .

Furthermore, though many other things may cause the will to incline in one of two directions, obligation nonetheless has this special advantage over them. While they press upon the will with a sort of natural weight after whose removal it returns of itself to its former indifference, obligation affects the will morally by imbuing it with a special internal sense that compels it to censure its own actions and deem itself blameworthy if it has not conformed itself to the prescribed norm. . . .

It is also understood from this that obligation contains sufficient force to bend the will. For there is nothing capable of imposing on a human mind deliberating about the future the necessity of either doing or omitting something, besides thoughts of the good and evil that will arise for others or ourselves from what we do—if, at least, the will is to retain its freedom and the actions to be performed are such as can be rightly imputed to the agent. And this is the point in which

---

[10]*De Cive*, III [sec. 33—ed.].

[11]*On the Law of War and Peace*, I,1,9.

[12] *A Treatise on the Laws of Nature*, c.5,xxvii.

obligation chiefly differs from coercion, that although each of them ultimately points to some thing to be feared, the latter shakes the will in an external fashion only and impels it to select an unwelcome thing solely through the awareness of an impending evil, while obligation has the result, besides, that someone is himself forced to acknowledge that the evil befalling him, which was proposed for anyone deviating from the announced rule, is not undeserved, since he could have averted it by voluntarily following the rule.

6. One reason, therefore, that man is capable of being obligated consists in the fact that, in contrast to beings which are internally determined to a uniform mode of action, he has a will that can turn toward either of two alternatives and thus conform itself to some moral norm. From this it follows that insofar as he is not necessitated by an external principle, a man is taken to be free and authorized to do anything his natural strength allows him to accomplish. Even after he has made a final determination and firmly committed himself to something, the force of his decision (insofar as it stems from his will) is not so strong as to prevent him from changing or abrogating it at his own pleasure, if it is right to do so—unless, that is, external considerations prohibit him from altering his will once it has been determined and declared. For by signifying a decision of one's will it is possible to create a situation that no longer allows one subsequently to depart from it. . . .

7. It can also be gathered from what we have said why a person cannot be obligated to himself, or why he cannot enter into an agreement with or make a promise to himself regarding something that concerns no one else. For one who acquires a right through an obligation is free to give it up again whenever the act does not defraud a third party. In this case, however, the person who obligates and who acquires the right is the same as the one obligated to secure it. Accordingly, no matter how much he intends to obligate himself it is nonetheless in vain, since he can free himself at his own pleasure without having done anything. The mere ability to do so already makes him free in fact. Note further the uselessness of this kind of obligation, where one either gives or denies oneself something, since its performance or neglect respectively neither gains nor loses one anything. . . .

But when we say, for example, that someone is obligated to preserve himself, it means that the exercise of that inherent human obligation is focused on the person himself as end. The obligation as such, however, goes back to God, Who as author of the natural law has the right to demand its execution and to punish its neglect. It is only as God's servant, therefore, and as a member of human society to which God commands him to be useful, that a man is bound to preserve himself. Just as a master can rightfully punish a servant, and a state a citizen, if the latter have made themselves unfit for the labors and services they owe. . . .

8. Another reason that man's will, which is capable of conforming itself to a norm, can have that norm prescribed to itself with the effect that it is bound to follow it, is that he is not exempt from the authority of a superior. These two reasons make a man capable of obligations coming from an external principle. For when an agent's powers are so tied by nature to a uniform mode of acting that they cannot by an internal motion digress into another mode, they produce not a moral but a physical action, which is said to arise from necessity rather than from obligation. On the other hand, when someone does not acknowledge anyone as a

superior, there is no external principle strong enough to place a bridle on his internal freedom. And even if he should observe a certain restraint in acting and continually refrain from some actions, he is understood to do so not from any obligation but from his own good pleasure. It follows, then, that a person capable of obligation is someone who both can know a prescribed norm and has a will that is intrinsically free and able to turn in different directions, a will that is aware, however, that when a norm has been imposed by a superior it ought not to diverge from it. It is evident that man has been endowed with such a nature.

9. Now an obligation is properly introduced into a man's mind by a superior, that is by someone who not only has the strength to threaten some evil against those who resist him, but also legitimate reasons allowing him to demand that our freedom be restricted at his discretion. For when these two things are found in someone who has expressed his will along with the good and evil awaiting those who respectively obey and resist it, there necessarily arises in the composed faculty of reason a fear mingled with reverence: the former in response to the other person's power and the latter from a reflective consideration of the reasons which, quite apart from fear, should suffice for embracing his will, as when we accept advice.

We therefore believe that the right to lay an obligation on another, or in other words to command and prescribe laws for him, does not arise from strength alone, nor even from a superiority [*huperochē*] or preeminence of nature. It is true that strength alone can set me against my own inclination, so that I prefer temporarily to obey another's will instead of experiencing his power. But once my fear is gone, there is nothing to prevent me from acting more according to my own discretion than according to his. And when someone can adduce nothing but power as the reason I should conform myself to his decision, nothing prohibits me from trying in every way to shake off that power and assert my freedom if I deem it in my own interest. . . .

10. It is worthwhile here to consider carefully Hobbes's statement . . . that "Under the natural reign of God, His right to rule and to punish those who violate His laws comes solely from His irresistible power." Hobbes proceeds to prove this statement in the following manner: "Every right over others comes either from nature or a pact. It is derived from nature insofar as it has not been taken away thereby. For since everyone had by nature a right to all things, each also had a right to rule over all the others that is coeval with nature itself." Men abolished this latter right among themselves, however, because they feared one another's equal strength, which would have led to a war destructive of the human race. "But if anyone had been so much more powerful than the rest that these were unable to resist him even with their combined strength, he would have had no reason at all to give up the right that nature granted him. Because of the exceeding power by which he could have preserved both himself and the rest, he would have retained his right to dominate them. Those, therefore, whose power cannot be resisted, and consequently Almighty God, derive their right to rule from that power itself."[13]

Several things deserve criticism here. First of all, I question the consistency of

---

[13] *De Cive*, XV,5.

the following statements: "The right to command has been granted by nature on account of strength alone," and the same right is derived from nature "because nature has not taken it away." For, in general, one does not automatically grant what one does not take away. And since "not taken away" and "granted" are not one and the same, that right may have been granted by a principle other than nature.

Next, the principle that "Nature has given everyone a right to all things" must be skillfully explicated. A right for Hobbes is the freedom of all to employ their natural faculties according to right reason. The sensible meaning of the stated principle will therefore be this: By nature, that is, in the absence of all laws, each person may use his natural strength against anyone toward whom his reason declares it should be brought to bear, and certainly to preserve himself. But it does not follow that an obligation in the proper sense can be imposed on another by natural strength alone. For compulsion and obligation are different. The former can be produced by natural strength alone, but by no means the latter. For even Hobbes thinks that in the natural state the right to compel others is matched by their right to resist. Yet obligation is incompatible with a right of resistance since it presupposes reasons that inwardly affect a man's conscience and make him rationally conclude that resistance is neither proper nor right. And though it may be unreasonable to invite a greater evil upon oneself by struggling in vain against a superior's strength, . . . one nonetheless retains the right of trying in every way to shake off his power, even by force, or to elude it by subterfuge. This, precisely, is inconsistent with obligation in the proper sense. . . .

Naked force therefore does not abolish the right of resistance as such but merely its exercise. This can be exemplified by using brutes, with whom we humans live in a lawless state. We subjugate and bring into our service whatever brutes our strength can overcome. But if they manage somehow to elude our power, no one complains that he has been injured thereby. Nor can anyone respond that brutes are incapable of obligation and thus restrainable only by force. For Hobbes himself acknowledges . . . that a prisoner of war, who surely is capable of obligation, is not restrained thereby so long as he is held by natural bonds alone and has not made a pact or a promise. He can therefore flee his captor or even rise against him with force at the earliest suitable opportunity. . . .

Needless to say, Hobbes's proposition that "Nature has given a right to all things" is absurd and without meaning when applied to God. For how can nature have given God anything when it is either God Himself or His handiwork? For these reasons, therefore, and also because it seems unworthy of the divine goodness, we think that God's right to rule, or His sovereignty (insofar as it denotes the power to impress an obligation on men's minds) should in no way be derived from His bare omnipotence alone.

And further, the scriptural examples adduced by Hobbes offer no support for his thesis. It does not follow from God's appeal to His power in the case of the calamities sent upon Job that He has no right over His creatures except one based on power alone. In fact, Job himself at first correctly acknowledged God's right to deprive him of his goods and children: "The Lord has given," he said, "the Lord has taken away." That is, why may God not take back at His pleasure what He granted only as a favor? . . . True, when Job's overwhelming grief led him to accuse

God and neglect to consider the other reasons for the divine sovereignty, God rightly asserted His power in order to quell Job's insolent complaints. For this is how we usually deal with other insolent subordinates: When they refuse to listen to our reasons we threaten them with force to make them realize that in daring to point their horns at us they are not only wicked but foolish as well. So if someone complains that bad things happen to good people and good things to bad, and refuses to acknowledge the real reasons for this, he is ultimately silenced by appeals to the divine power. It is just as if we said to him: "Since you are so sure you have been wronged, go and fight against God!"

These same considerations also reveal the error of Hobbes's inference that humans are obligated to obey God because they are weak. For weakness can only persuade someone that it is foolish not to save himself from a greater evil by submitting; it does not eliminate his right to desire and to try in every way to escape from another's power. But such a right is entirely excluded by a genuine obligation. . . .

11. There are others who derive the origin of sovereignty or the authority to obligate another from a superiority [*huperochē*] or eminence of nature, maintaining that this is itself sufficient to bring about an actual obligation. They rest their case on human nature whose most excellent part, the mind, has a ruling [*to hēgemonikon*] or directing power. . . .

But we remain unpersuaded that the right to impose an obligation on someone who has in himself a principle of self-governance arises from a superiority [*huperochē*] of nature alone. For natural preeminence does not always entail an ability to govern someone else less well endowed by nature, nor are diverse grades of perfection among natural substances automatically linked with subordination and the dependence of one on the other. Indeed, since a person on whom an obligation is to be imposed has in himself a principle for regulating his own actions that he can judge to be adequate for himself, there is no clear reason for thinking him immediately convicted by his own conscience if he acts according to his own rather than a natural superior's discretion. And so, despite their impious opinion that the gods enjoy their happiness in supreme peace, being far removed from any concern for human affairs and neither pleased nor angered by men's merits or misdeeds respectively, the Epicureans nonetheless correctly inferred from these assumptions the futility of all religion and fear of the gods. For why should anyone worship someone who is neither able nor willing to help or hinder him? . . .

12. Since these things are so, one must altogether acknowledge that strength alone is not sufficient for an obligation to arise for me from another's will. Instead, he should also have procured some notable goods for me, or else I myself must have consented voluntarily to his direction. . . . A person cannot avoid being well inclined toward another from whom he has received many goods; thus, if the other's good intentions toward and his ability to better provide for me have also been confirmed, and if he claims as well an actual privilege to direct me, there is no clear reason why I should want to oppose his sovereignty. This is even more so if I know that I owe him my very existence. . . . And why does the one who gave man the power to act freely not have the right to restrict some small portion thereof? Alternately, a person who consents to another's sovereignty of his own accord declares by that deed of his that he must abide by the agreement it has pleased him to make.

And yet, for consent to give rise to legitimate sovereignty, that new submission may not infringe on the properly established right of a third party, and it must be permissible for the one party to have such a subject and the other such a sovereign. From these two sources flows, we think, the force of obligations, which are generally understood to lay a sort of inner bond upon the freedom of our will.

But since a moral bond does not destroy the natural freedom of the human will, and also because the superficiality and wickedness of most mortals' minds make them pay no heed to these reasons for sovereignty, something more weighty than shame and a sense of propriety is required to check men's immoderate desires. This is all the more necessary because men's wickedness tends for the most part to harm others; otherwise, if they hurt only themselves by sinning they could more easily be left to themselves. Now we know of nothing having such an effect except the fear of an evil to be inflicted for a violated obligation by someone stronger, who is interested in its observance. Thus the ultimate strength of obligations, as it were, comes in the end from force, and from the fact that he who wishes to secure their observance is furnished with enough personal or delegated power to inflict a grave evil on those who refuse to obey. Among the wicked, certainly, one who can be disregarded with impunity rules only by the indulgence of others. But the rule of a person who has a just title thereto, and who always has readily available a force whereby he can coerce the non-compliant, stands on a solid footing. . . .

What has been said indicates that the overly crude assertion of certain writers that right is what pleases the stronger should be qualified. It is true that laws can hardly attain their external end unless they are equipped with strength capable of prodding even the unwilling. . . . For the happy conscience after the fulfillment of one's duty, and the internal torments and accusations consequent to wrongdoing, all come—we piously acknowledge—from the strength of Almighty God, for Whom it is easy to punish through themselves those who are unimpressed by other men's power. . . . And it is certainly of the greatest importance to the whole human race that no one doubt that even those who have neglected their duty by trusting in strength, cleverness, or collusion must go before the incorruptible divine tribunal. . . . On these foundations, therefore, do those who would prescribe effective laws for others rest their authority.

13. Furthermore, before a law can exercise its directive force in men's minds, both it and its legislator must be known to the one to whom it is propounded. For how can anyone be obedient without knowing what and whom to obey? To have known it at one time is sufficient here, however, for if someone forgets what he once knew he is not at all released from his obligation, since he could well have remembered if he had had the requisite concern for obedience. At any rate, no one can easily avoid being acquainted with the legislator. For anyone who has acquired the use of reason will know that the author of natural laws is the same as the author of the whole universe. Much less can the maker of civil laws be unknown to citizens, since in somehow subjecting themselves to him they constitute him as such by their express or tacit consent. . . .

Civil laws become known to subjects through clear and public promulgation, wherein two things should always be evident: first, that the laws come from the one who has supreme sovereignty in the state, and second, the meaning of the laws. The former becomes known when the supreme sovereign promulgates a law either by his own voice or through his delegates. There is no reason to doubt that these delegates are authorized to do so by the supreme sovereign if it is well known that he commonly employs them to declare his will, if the laws come to be used in judicial proceedings, and if they contain nothing derogatory to the sovereign's supreme authority. For it is implausible that a minister would publicize as a permanent decree of his prince something that is not such, or recklessly arrogate to himself an office of that kind, since he could not hope to hide his attempt or avoid punishment for such brazen presumption.

In order that the meaning of a law may be correctly understood, those who promulgate it must do so as clearly as possible—in contrast to Caligula, who used to propound his laws by writing them in tiny print high above the ground. . . . If anything in the laws should seem obscure, one must request a clarification from the legislator or from those who have been publicly appointed to pass judgment according to the laws. For it is the latter's role to apply laws to individual cases by means of a correct interpretation, that is, to declare, when particular deeds have been proposed, what the legislator has ordained concerning them. . . .

Moreover, we must caution here that the claim of those who assert that the consent of the people is required for laws to obligate the conscience of subordinates is true neither of natural laws nor of civil laws under monarchies or aristocracies—except where rulers and citizens have formally agreed to this, or when someone who has consented to another's sovereignty is understood thereby to have implicitly consented to all acts flowing from it. Still, it would certainly be very useful for eliciting the voluntary obedience of subordinates if the laws were made with their consent and approbation, especially those laws that are to become customary among them. . . .

14. Someone who is going to direct another's actions through laws requires two things: first, an understanding of what it is appropriate to prescribe to the other, and second, the strength to threaten some evil if the one for whom the law is made (and whom we presume capable and desirous of opposing the mandate) fails to conform himself thereto. Similarly, every law is taken to consist of two parts, one specifying what must be done or omitted, the other indicating the punishment proposed for one who neglects the precept or does what is forbidden. The latter is usually called the 'sanction.' . . .

A law has two parts, therefore, one to define it and one to provide its punitive sanction. Two parts of the same law, I say, not two kinds of laws. For it is as vacuous to say "Do this" if nothing else follows, as it is absurd to say "You will be punished" if the reason that punishment is merited has not been made known. It must be well noted, therefore, that the entire force of a law properly consists in indicating what a superior wishes us to do or not do, and what penalty awaits its violators.

We also understand from this the sense in which a law has the power to obligate. For the power to obligate, that is, the faculty to bring an inner necessity to bear in order that something be done, is properly in the one who has sovereignty.

The law is but an instrument whereby he makes his will known to a subject in whom his power produces an obligation once his will is understood.

From this it also appears that the common distinction between a law's directive and coercive force is not correct, unless by coercive force you understand its penal clause. For a law's effectiveness in directing depends on how well it displays the sovereign's will and threatens the subjects. Its coercive force, however, that is its authority to demand of subjects that they conform their actions to the norm prescribed to them, and to threaten and actually inflict punishments on them, belongs properly to the maker or executor of the laws. . . .

18. With respect to its origin, law is most conveniently divided into *divine* and *human*, the former having God as its author and the latter man. But if law is considered according to the necessary agreement it has with its subjects, it is divided by a different rationale into *natural* and *positive*. The former is so attuned to the rational and social nature of man that there can be no moral and peaceful society for humankind without it; or—if you prefer—it has a sort of natural goodness, that is, a utility which from its own native orderliness affects humankind in general. Although there is yet another reason for that denomination, in that natural law can be discovered and known from men's own innate mental powers and from a consideration of human nature in general. The latter does not flow in any way from the general condition of human nature but proceeds solely from a legislator's decision. Even so, it should also not lack its own rationale and utility, at least for a particular society of men. . . .

Chapter 7

ON THE QUALITIES OF MORAL ACTIONS

1. Next we must examine the qualities of moral actions. Now according to these, actions are said to be necessary or not necessary, licit or illicit, good or evil, just or unjust; and so the moral qualities of moral actions will be necessity, license, and the qualities opposed to these (which lack a proper name), goodness and badness, justice and injustice.

2. A necessary action is one which someone to whom a superior has given a law or command is altogether bound to do by virtue of that law or command. For this necessity of moral actions consists in the fact that they should not be omitted or done differently, even though they can in fact be omitted or done differently by

virtue of one's natural strength. . . . Opposed to necessary action, however, is not only forbidden action, whose performance is prohibited by laws or the interdict of a superior, but also permitted action, which the laws neither prescribe nor forbid, but which has been left to each person's choice to undertake or omit. . . .

3. . . . The formal principle of the goodness and badness of actions consists, of course, in their bearing or determinative relation to a directive norm which we call law. (This we always understand here as necessitating, not permitting, and, if human, as not contrary to divine law.) For an intentional action which proceeds from and is undertaken in accordance with what a norm prescribes, so that it agrees exactly with the norm, is said to be good. Insofar as it is undertaken against what the norm prescribes, or is discrepant with it, it is declared evil or, in a word, a sin.

Now just as any directive norm, such as a nautical compass for example, is said to be the cause of a journey's rectitude, and of a ship's arrival in port, not so much because the ship cuts a course that coincides exactly with the direction in which it points as because the captain steers the course prescribed by it, so a law is said to be the cause of rectitude in an action not so much because the action—whatever the intention with which it was undertaken—squares with the law, but mainly because the action proceeds from the dictate of and from dependency on the law, that is, with the intention of rendering obedience to it. Hence if anyone by chance, or without any thought of rendering obedience to the law, does what the law prescribes, he is, to be sure, said to have acted correctly (more in a negative than in an affirmative sense: that is, not badly), but not morally well; just as someone who has downed a bird with a chance discharge of a gun cannot be said to have fired in an expert and skillful manner.

4. Now since a law determines the quality or disposition of the agent, or the object, the end or, finally, the particular circumstances of an action, a certain action is morally good or evil either because the agent is or is not disposed as the law requires, or else because the action is or is not directed toward the object, with the end, and in the circumstances ordained by the law. It must be noted here, however, that for an action to be good it is necessary both that it agree with the law regarding all its material requisites, so to speak, and that as far as its formal aspect is concerned it be performed not out of ignorance or from some other cause, but in order to render to the law the obedience owed to it. Hence an action that is otherwise materially good, as it were, is imputed to an agent as evil on account of his evil intention. . . .

In contrast, however, an action that is otherwise materially evil, as it were, by no means becomes good on account of an agent's good intention. That is why no one can use his own sins as means, as it were, for the attainment of a good end, and evils are not to be done so that goods may come of them. For to render an action evil it suffices if even a single material or formal requisite thereof does not agree with the law. And so an action immediately becomes evil if either the quality of the agent, or the object, or the end, or any of the circumstances, or the intention should differ from the law. And it is vain to say, as some do, that an action can be good as far as its substance as an activity is concerned, even if the agent does not intend a legitimate end. For the end of a moral action also belongs very much to its essence, as it is connected with the intention, which is the principle that most affects an action's quality. Hence it is a sin not only to direct an action toward an evil end, but also to direct it toward a different end than that prescribed by the laws. . . .

6. Now let us also examine justice. Here we must above all observe that justice means something very different when attributed to persons and to things. For in relation to persons, being just means to delight in acting justly, to strive after justice, and to try in all things to do what is just. To be unjust, on the other hand, is to neglect justice or to think that it should be measured not by what we owe but by our present advantage. Thus, a just man may perform more than a few unjust actions, and an unjust man just ones. For a man should be called just if he does just things because the law requires them and unjust things only because he is weak; and he should be called unjust if he does just things because of the penalty attached to the law, and unjust things either from a perverse mind or to gain glory or some other advantage. . . .

It is clear from this that the Roman lawyers' familiar definition of justice as a constant and abiding will to give every person his own regards only the justice of persons and not that of actions. And this seems quite inappropriate to me. Since jurisprudence has been occupied mainly with the justice of actions, its interest in the justice of persons is merely incidental and focused on a few particulars.

7. The main difference between the justice and the goodness of actions is that goodness simply denotes an action's agreement with the law while justice also regards those toward whom it is performed. And so we call an action just if it is intentionally directed toward the person to whom it is owed—justice in this sense being the correct application of actions to a person. We have chosen to divide it mainly according to the matter that is owed another or, as it were, extended to him like the payment of a debt.

We note in advance here that some actions can be called pure and others mixed. Pure actions are completed when a motion of some power touches an object in a certain manner, as in honoring, deferring, loving, shunning, comforting, praising, censuring, and so on, and the object is as a result somehow affected or thought to be affected by either pleasure or displeasure. Mixed actions, however, involve the transfer of some advantage or disadvantage to the person toward whom they are said to be performed, and so their effect consists mainly in some activity that actually helps or hurts another person or his things. Then there are also actions that enter into men's business dealings and are valued at a certain price, as well as others whose value men do not usually determine by price. . . .

Finally, we must also note that some things are owed us by a perfect right and some by an imperfect right. In the former case, if another does not render what he owes us on his own initiative, those who live in natural freedom with him are permitted to make him do so by either force or war; or if they live with him in the same civil state, they may take legal action against him. But in the latter case we cannot claim our debts by war or extort them by threatening legal action. Writers often add the word *suus* [his own] to express a perfect right, as in "he demands this by his own right [*suo jure*]."

The reason that some things are owed us perfectly and others imperfectly is (at least among those living in natural freedom with respect to one another) the diversity of the natural law's precepts, some of which contribute to the being of society but others only to its well-being. Since it is not as necessary to observe the latter as it is to observe the former, it also stands to reason that they cannot be as strictly demanded as the others; for it is foolish to prescribe a remedy that is far more elaborate and troublesome than the disease. Moreover, perfect rights nearly always involve a pact, but not imperfect rights. Since imperfect rights are left to each person's sense of decency and conscience, it would be inconsistent to extort them from another by force except when a grave necessity compels it. In states, the distinction between perfect and imperfect rights arises through civil laws that either allow or forbid certain actions-at-law. Yet states have for the most part followed in the natural law's footsteps here, unless they were persuaded otherwise by special considerations of their own.

8. Therefore, when the actions or things extended to another are owed him only by an imperfect right, or when the actions affecting him are unrelated to business matters (for example, as when a person provides another with the counsel, goods, or help he needs, and performs the duties of piety, respect, gratitude, humanity, and beneficence toward those he ought), it is commonly said that universal justice is being observed. This justice is concerned only with furnishing another what he is owed and does not consider whether that which is furnished is equal or not to that on account of which something is owed. Thus it is satisfied if a grateful person dutifully repays his debt to the extent his faculties allow, even if the benefit was perhaps far greater. But when the actions performed toward someone involve business matters or the transfer to another of something to which he had a perfect right, it is said to be particular justice.

9. Now this perfect right arises either for individuals when they make a tacit or express pact with a certain society in order to become its members; or for a society that seeks by such a pact to make individuals members of itself; or, finally, it arises from the pacts of various individuals concerning commercial goods and transactions.

The performance of actions owed because of the mutual pacts between a society and its members, entered into for the purposes just mentioned, is called distributive justice. For when someone is received into a society, it and its member-to-be tacitly or expressly agree that the society, for its part, undertakes to allot him his proportionate share of the goods that belong to it as such. The member, on the other hand, promises to bear his proportionate share of the burdens conducing to the society's preservation. Now the proportionate share of goods to be allotted to a member is determined by estimating the work or resources he spends to preserve the society as such, considered in relation to the work or expenses of the society's other members. The proportionate share of burdens to be imposed on him, on the other hand, is determined through a comparative estimate of the advantages he and other members receive from the society.

Since one member usually contributes more to a society's preservation or derives more advantage from it than another, it is easy to see the reason that, among many unequal persons, distributive justice must observe a comparative equality. This consists in adjusting two persons' respective rewards to their respective worth and merit. . . . It is not required that a person's reward be strictly equal to his merit; instead, it suffices that the proportion of one person's worth to another's matches their respective shares of the common good. The same rule should also be applied when imposing burdens.

But what Hobbes alleges . . . in order to overturn the relative equality observed in this kind of justice—namely that I can distribute more of what is mine to one who deserves less and give less to one who deserves more, so long as I have given what was agreed upon (alleging our Savior's pronouncement in Matthew 20:13)—[this] really does not affect the matter.[14] For the statement cited shows that one who generously gives some people a higher wage than they deserve, or out of generosity (which is contained under universal justice) adds something to the wage owed them according to commutative justice, does not sin against commutative justice (which governs contracts of employment) so long as the rest are not denied their agreed-upon wage. But what does this have to do with our distributive justice, which must assign to many people a fixed share of something to which they have a perfect but, as it were, a quantitatively unequal right? For the word 'distribute' which occurs in this example does not at all imply that the deed pertains to distributive justice, but that there were many employees, each of whom had—according to commutative justice, at any rate—to be given their own wage.

With respect to the difficulties advanced by Grotius . . . , it is to be observed that his expletive and attributive justice by no means coincide exactly with commutative and distributive justice, and that his division does not rest on the same foundation as ours. For ours is drawn chiefly from the matter owed itself, and from the origin of the debt, but his from the manner and, as it were, the degree to which it is owed. From this appears the reason that the distribution of gain in a partnership contract belongs in Grotius's case to expletive justice, and to distributive justice in ours. Even if a geometrical proportion is observed in such a contract it is accidental, since the partners' contributions are not necessarily unequal. Rather, they can also be equal, in which case there will be a simple equality in the parts of the gain.

As for the [Grotius's] example that "if only one person is found suited for a public office it will be allotted by none but a simple [arithmetical] proportion,"[15] we must inquire further whether that person has a perfect or an imperfect right to that office. If the latter, then the example will pertain to universal justice; but if the former, then we agree with Grotius's caution about proportion, that geometrical proportion usually but not always has a place in distributive justice.

Indeed, we have not drawn the distinguishing feature of each kind of justice from the use of a different proportion. Thus, the assignment of legacies also looks not to distributive but to universal justice. And when a state repays some citizens from the common stock what they have spent upon the public welfare, there is an exercise of commutative and not distributive justice, because the reason for the

[14] *De Cive*, III,6.

[15] *On the Law of War and Peace*, I,1,8.

debt does not arise from the pact by which the state received a citizen, but from a special and quite different contract.

10. But to extend to anyone what he is owed on the basis of a reciprocal pact involving commercial goods and services is called commutative justice. Since the aim of such pacts is to make the commercial goods and services I receive from another equivalent to my own, at least in my estimation, it is easy to see why this kind of justice requires the strict equality popularly called an arithmetical proportion. . . . The moral value of a commercial good or transaction should therefore correspond exactly to that given or offered in return. . . .

13. Hobbes . . . seems to reduce justice to but one kind, namely keeping faith and fulfilling one's agreements. . . . Commutative justice, he says, is involved in contracts of exchange, in buying and selling, hiring and letting for hire, lending and repaying, and the like; while distributive justice—though improperly so-called —comes into play when an arbiter assigns each of the parties who have agreed to come before him what he is owed. And the only equality observed in justice is this: Since all of us are by nature equal, one person should not demand more of a right for himself than he concedes to another, unless he has acquired it through pacts.[16]

Now since Hobbes thinks an injury, or an unjust action or omission, is the same as the violation of a pact, he concludes that no one can be injured unless he has entered into a pact with someone. The reason for this view of his comes from his famous doctrine that nature has granted a right to all things. But he has stretched this right beyond its proper limits by imagining that when there is no pact whereby someone has resigned his right and transferred it to someone else, anyone has a right to do whatever he wishes to another, and that one who so exercises his right does no injury. . . . But we will show in more detail below that this "right to all things" can extend no farther than this: that nature allows a man the use of every means which right reason deems conducive to his firm and lasting preservation. Hobbes himself says as much . . . by referring to the use of 'reason' in his definition of 'right.'

Now sound reason will never tell us to inflict upon another, simply because we so desire, such things as cannot fail to incite him to war and a reciprocal desire to hurt us. Moreover, it certainly implies a contradiction to say that many men who are equal with respect to their right have each a right to all things and against everyone, since one man's right to all things—if it is to be effective—must surely absorb those of the rest. And it is no less absurd to concoct a right that is totally ineffective against others. For in moral matters, 'not to be' and 'to have no effect' are nearly the same.

But what sort of right is it that another can oppose with an equal right? Who would say "I have a right to command another" if the other has an equal right to disregard my commands? Or that I have a right to beat whomever I please if my blows can by an equal right be returned to me, and with interest? It is certain, therefore, that there is by no means a right to do such things to another, and that one who does them, since he acts *without a right*, inflicts an *injury*. On the con-

---

[16] *De Cive*, III,6; *Leviathan*, XV.

trary: The other person has a right not to have such things inflicted on him by another, and he is surely injured when they are. Hence, that right upon whose violation an injury is said to have occurred was not obtained only from a pact with others, but was also bestowed by nature itself without any intervening human deed. And so it is false to say that no one can be injured unless he has become a party to a pact or received a gift.

We will show elsewhere the falsity of Hobbes's other claim . . . , that justice, no less than dominion over things, owes its ultimate origin to states. Indeed, it is so far from being true that justice can be entirely reduced to keeping one's pacts that, on the contrary, before one can know whether some pact ought to be fulfilled, one must be certain that it was entered into at the command or at least by the permission of natural laws. . . .

14. Now that we know what justice is, it is easy to form a notion of injustice and its kinds. An action is unjust, therefore, when it is intentionally misdirected toward a person whom we owed a different action, or when it denies someone what he is owed. That is, it is unjust either to inflict upon another an evil we were not authorized to inflict, or to deny or seize from him some good that he was owed. For the nature of a good is such that it can be bestowed on anyone without a reason, provided a third party is not deprived of anything thereby; and the non-infliction of evils upon someone who deserves them involves no injury if it does no harm to others. And so an unjust action either inflicts on someone what it should not have inflicted, takes away from him what it should not have taken away, or denies him what it should have given. For even the denial or omission of an action that is owed counts morally as an action.

15. Now an unjust action which has been undertaken by choice, and which infringes the perfect right of another, is commonly referred to by one word as an 'injury.' To understand this accurately we must know that someone can be hurt in a threefold manner: by being denied what he should have; . . . by having something of his own, which he now has, taken away from him; or by the infliction of some evil which another did not have the authority to inflict.

About the first of these we must observe that something is owed to someone either from a pure right of nature—in such a way, however, that he does not have a perfect right to it—as are the duties of humanity, beneficence, and gratitude; or from a pact, and this either a special pact or that contained in our obligation toward civil laws, by means of which we bind ourselves to render the things which those laws order us to furnish to another. If the latter are denied to anyone there is properly said to be an injury; but not if the former are denied, even if the law of nature is sinned against. Indeed, the law of nature itself also does not permit one to compel another to furnish those things by force—at least when one does not have sovereignty over him—unless perchance necessity urges one to, since the character of those duties requires them to be rendered voluntarily and without fear of punishment. . . .

16. Moreover, it is required for an injury properly speaking that it proceed from choice and from a firm resolve to harm or vex another. Hence, the name 'injury' does not accompany those hurts which are accidentally done by someone who is

ignorant or unwilling; for example, if a soldier practicing with javelins in the usual place strikes a passer-by, or if someone pruning trees in the middle of a field throws down a branch on an unexpected person who has no right to be there. . . .

17. Finally, that which is to be called an injury should also be done to someone against his will. For the saying "No injury is done to someone who is willing" is a commonplace even in ordinary speech. . . .

BOOK II

Chapter 1

IT DOES NOT SUIT MAN'S NATURE
TO LIVE WITHOUT LAW

1. Now that we have given a general account of moral matters in the previous book, and of the most frequently used terms (whose random insertion into our system would have interrupted its flow), we must focus more directly on our intended object by asking, first of all, whether it was appropriate for man to pass through this life without any law. This will make it clear why the Good and Great Creator did not bestow on man the freedom to do whatever pleases him, or to act according to the vagaries of impulse, without being accountable to any law, rule, or necessity. For since God gave man a will, namely, a faculty of turning himself by a sort of internal impulse toward those things that seem to suit him, and away from those that displease him (a will, moreover, which cannot be compelled), one may certainly wonder whether it did not befit God's goodness to allow man an undiminished and unimpeded use of that flexible faculty. For why did He give man a flexible will if He then demanded that it follow definite rules? Just as fetters render useless the mobility of our limbs, so it seems that the freedom of our will also amounts to nothing if we can will many things that we ought necessarily to omit and reject many that we ought necessarily to undertake.

2. And so—to repeat what we said just above—it seems that before all else it must be shown that complete freedom is useless to and destructive of human nature, and that its restriction by laws conduces to man's welfare. From this it will also be evident how loose his reins can rightly be made.

Here we must know, then, that freedom is generally conceived as an internal faculty of doing or omitting what one has oneself decided on. To call it a 'faculty' implies that the one to whom it is attributed not only has the strength to do something and the power to move himself, but also the power to impart motion to or somehow affect other things. To call it 'internal' signifies that this motion and power arise from an internal principle and not from a violent, external impulse, in the manner that a log, too, is sometimes able to move by means of efforts not its own. Finally, we add the phrase "what one has oneself decided on" in order to imply that the motion is not excited by accident or a blind impulse, but presupposes that the agent is at least somehow familiar with the object and determines himself to act after deliberation of some sort, and therefore, that the immediate reason for his acting is the fact that it seemed good to him. At the same time, however, we also understand that no other impediments capable of inhibiting the motion or diverting it in another direction may be present where an undiminished freedom is thought to be involved.

3. Once these things have been established it appears that anyone surveying the entire universe will find many things with no freedom at all, such as all those without soul and sensation. Others enjoy freedom, but in different degrees. Freedom that is in every way complete and knows no impediment or defect belongs to the Good and Great God alone; it is considered one of the noblest attributes of His most perfect essence and, being connected with His omnipotence, cannot be circumscribed. Hence the reason that God does not do some things, or not all things always, is not because His freedom is deficient but because it so pleases Him. . . . His purported inability to do certain things comes not from any external impediment, be it natural or moral, but from His own good pleasure which we mortals conceive to be adjusted to His greatness and excellence. This is the sense in which the common saying "God is a law unto Himself" must be interpreted. . . .

4. We see that brute animals whose condition is below our own also enjoy a certain degree of freedom. It is of a very low sort, however, in that their strength and blunted senses are confined within narrow bounds, and their abject appetite is directed only toward a few objects (and rather superficially at that), being stirred by nothing but those very gross and everywhere obvious things that serve the belly. In addition, they observe no custom, law, or right among themselves or toward humans. Some rudiments of marriage exist among a few of them, but it is limited to acts of merely bodily conjunction and to a slight show of affection without any bond of fidelity. And in most of them, no trace of love remains when they have satisfied their lust, nor any concern for modesty or kinship. It is true that many of them fervently love their offspring, but this love lasts only until the latter are able to nourish themselves. Parents do not care for their progeny after that, having thoroughly forgotten their former love, and the latter do not feel they ought to pay back any debt of gratitude, as it were, or to render any other service. Thus, carnivores do not scruple to tear apart and devour whatever pleases their palate, and many of them destroy one another out of uncontrollable anger. Moreover, knowing no laws of dominion, when hunger drives them they often fight fiercely over the things available to all and are not ashamed to seize what others have already gathered for their own use. There is, indeed, no esteem, no honor, no sovereignty, and no prerogative among them beside that bestowed by superior strength alone. . . .

5. Now there are many evident reasons drawn from either the original or the subsequent condition of human nature why the Creator was unwilling to grant men a lawless license of this sort, and why it is entirely unsuitable for them. The dignity of human nature and its preeminence over other living things required that

men's actions conform to a certain norm, one apart from which their order, decorum, or beauty is surely inconceivable. Man owes his supreme rank to the fact that he has an immortal soul endowed with the light of understanding and a faculty of judging, choosing and, as well, becoming highly skilled in many arts. Because of this, he is said to be "an animal more sacred than the others, one with a deeper mental capacity and the ability to dominate them." . . .

That the soul was destined by its Creator for a far nobler end than to keep this paltry body fresh may also be gathered from its special distinction by such faculties as seem to contribute little or nothing to the preservation of the body, which can be maintained by means of a much humbler equipment, as it were. For the power of the human soul exerts itself mainly about things that concern the worship of the Deity and social and civil life. These are served primarily by its ability to infer the unknown from the known, and to determine what agrees with itself and what not; by its ability to abstract universal ideas from particulars, to invent signs through which the ideas inhering in the mind can be communicated to others, to understand the number, weight, and measure of things and compare them with one another, to understand and observe order and its effects; and by its ability spontaneously to rouse, repress, and moderate the passions, to remember many things and recall them again as if they were present, to scrutinize itself and, recollecting its own dictates, to compare them with its actions—from which the force of conscience flows. All these abilities would be of little or no use in a lawless, brutish, and unsociable life. . . .

Now the more splendid the gifts with which man was equipped by his Creator, and the more numerous his intellectual abilities, the more shameful it was to let them atrophy through lack of cultivation or to squander them for nothing, as it were, without order and decorum. Nor, indeed, did God lack a purpose in giving man a mind that discerns decorum and order, to which he can therefore adjust himself. Instead, He no doubt intended man to use the faculties granted him in such a way as to manifest the Creator's glory and to amplify his own happiness. . . .

6. Another reason that made it inadvisable to grant man the same license as brutes is his greater depravity—an attribution that will come as no surprise to anyone who has thoroughly examined the natural inclinations and pursuits of us mortals. Brutes are stirred by hunger and by lust, and the latter, at least, rouses them only at certain times during which they indulge it not for a superfluous titillation but to generate offspring. When this aim has been achieved their lust rests quietly, as if asleep. . . . But the blaze of man's carnal desire is by no means limited to certain seasons only, and it arouses him far more often than seems necessary for the preservation of his kind. Similarly, the hunger of brutes is very easily satisfied by the food that nature sets out here and there, craving no additional preparation or seasonings; once quieted, it stirs up no further trouble. And without hunger and lust, brutes are not prone to anger or eager to hurt one another unless they themselves are hurt.

Man, however, wishes not only to satisfy his belly but also to tickle his palate. Nature has seen to it that brutes need no clothes, but man seizes upon the tenderness of his naked body as an opportunity for vain and haughty display. In addition, he is bloated with a great tide of passions and desires unknown to brutes. A craving for superfluities, ambition, a desire for glory and to outshine others, envy, jealous emulation and a spirit of contention, superstition, anxiety about the future, curiosity: all these (to which brutes are not at all sensitive) constantly disturb him. . . . Hence, anyone who considers the matter will find that the various conflicts and wars by which men are every day disturbed are for the most part initiated by desires unknown to brutes. . . .

Therefore, given such fierce and varied human passions, what would men's life have been like without a law to compose them? A pack of wolves, lions, or dogs fighting to the finish, that is what you would see. Indeed, everyone would have been a lion, wolf, or dog to his neighbor, or something even more savage, because no living thing is able and willing to harm man more than man himself. Since men inflict so many evils upon one another even now, when law and punishment are threatened, what would be the case if everything were done with impunity and no inner bridle restrained man's desires? . . .

7. In addition, man's natural abilities are far more diverse and varied than those of any class of brutes, whose members have nearly similar inclinations and are directed by the same passion and appetite. Anyone who knows one of these knows them all. But among men there are as many senses as heads, each with its own idea of beauty. . . . Nor are they all stirred by a simple and a uniform desire, but by many and in various combinations. Indeed, the same man often differs from himself, greatly desiring at one time what later on he strenuously abhors. . . . Their interests, institutions, and inclinations toward mental exertion are no less varied, as can be seen today in their nearly infinite modes of life. . . . And just as voices sound more repugnant and displeasing to the ears as they increase in number, unless they harmonize properly together, so would the greatest confusion have occurred among men if laws had not composed their variety into a seemly order.

From another point of view, however, this same variety of natural abilities and inclinations bestows a remarkable ornament and advantage on humankind. For by being properly arranged it has allowed the emergence of a marvellous order and beauty which perfect similarity could in no way have produced. Moreover, there were bound to be fewer clashes among that great multitude of men if they were naturally inclined toward different interests. Thus, nature seems also to have been most wise in fashioning men's faces with such wonderfully various features. For as different people have different duties, and as we ought to behave differently toward different individuals, the utmost confusion would result if all men resembled one another so exactly that one person could not be distinguished from the others except by certain externally derived signs which, being dependent on human decision, would provide opportunities for countless deceptions. . . . One other secret lies hidden beneath this diversity, as it were: Since its different aspects please different individuals, it becomes possible for everyone to find the form most beautiful and satisfying to himself.

8. Finally, man's weakness has also required that he not live without law. A few days are sufficient for a brute to reach a point of maturity when it can provide for its own maintenance, and it seldom needs the society of others for this task. But man is weak for a long time after his life begins. . . . How many years are required, and how great an educational effort, before someone is able to produce

food and clothing on his own? Imagine a man raised by someone without ever having been spoken to: He can walk where he wishes, but being otherwise deprived of all education and discipline, he has no knowledge except that generated by his own natural abilities. Imagine him abandoned to himself without the assistance and society of any other man. What a pitiable animal you would see! A dumb and ignoble creature reduced to pulling up plants and roots or gathering naturally growing fruits, slaking its thirst at any spring, river, or ditch it happens to come upon; avoiding inclement weather by crawling into caves or covering its body with moss and grass; passing its life in the most tedious boredom but trembling at the sound or approach of any other living thing; and, finally, dying of hunger, cold, or in the jaws of some wild beast.

Thus, it is man's association and society with those similar to himself that keeps his life from being the most miserable among all living things. The saying "It is not good for man to live alone" pertains not only to marriage but also to society with other men in general. Yet a society of men can be neither established nor remain peaceful and firm without law. And so, unless man was meant to be the most degraded and miserable of all living things, it in no way suited him to live without law. . . .

It appears from all of this that man's natural freedom—that, indeed, which really belongs to him and is not conceived through abstraction—must always be understood with some bond, namely that of sound reason and of the natural law.

Chapter 2

ON THE NATURAL STATE OF MEN

1. We understand here by man's natural state not that most perfect condition ultimately intended by nature as most suited for him, but one into which we conceive him placed by the mere fact of his birth, and from which all human or divinely inspired inventions and institutions that now give the life of mortals a rather different aspect, as it were, have been removed. These include not only the various arts and the general culture of human life, but also and especially the civil societies at whose origin humankind was arranged into a well-defined order.

To become better acquainted with this state we will therefore consider it both *in itself*, noting especially the disadvantages and rights by which it is attended (that is, what the condition of individual men would have been without the invention of the arts and of culture, and without the introduction of civil states), and *in relation to other men*, [where we want to know] whether it has the appearance of war or of peace. That is, should men who live mutually in natural freedom and are subject neither to one another nor to a common master be considered enemies or friends?

Moreover, the natural state is either *pure*, or absolute, or *limited* and restricted, depending on whether it is concerned with all men equally or focused only on a certain number of them. For it is possible to consider humankind in two ways, either conceiving all men to live by themselves in natural freedom, or understanding them to have united with certain others into civil society, being joined to the rest by no bond but their common humanity.

2. To enable us to form a mental picture of the natural state as it would have been without any human or divinely inspired supports and inventions, we must imagine a man as somehow thrown into this world and left entirely to himself, without any human assistance coming to him after his birth. We must imagine him, moreover, to be equipped with no greater physical and mental gifts than those now found in men before the advent of culture, nor favored by any special care of the Deity. Such a person's condition can only be conceived as extremely wretched, whether we suppose him to have emerged thus from somewhere as an infant, or as someone already endowed with his full stature and strength.

As an infant he would certainly have come to a very miserable end unless some brute animal had miraculously offered to suckle him—an association with brute beasts that would, however, have given the unfortunate nursling a considerable share of their ferocity. But if fully grown already, he will surely have to be conceived as naked, capable of emitting only inarticulate sounds, lacking all instruction and improvement, and amazed and "dumbfounded at the changing light of the world," as Manilius . . . puts it.[1] When pinched by hunger he would grab and taste whatever is in front of him, stilling his thirst with any liquid he came upon; caves or dense foliage would offer him a kind of refuge against inclement weather. Even many men like this, if we conceive them left to themselves on a still wholly uncultivated earth, would in our opinion have led a very wretched and almost bestial life until, either by their own experience and ingenuity or by opportunities derived from the cleverness of certain animals, they advanced gradually toward a certain standard of living and "devised the various arts by reflecting on their own practice." This will be readily admitted if someone is willing to consider all the things we now use in our lives, and how difficult it would have been for anyone to discover all of them on his own if other men's guidance and labor had not preceded; indeed, how most of them would never have entered most men's minds. No wonder, therefore, that pagan writers who knew nothing of the true origins of humankind from Sacred Scripture handed down such shocking accounts of men's primeval state. . . .

3. Now the rights accompanying man's natural state can be easily gathered, first of all, from that inclination common to all living things whereby they necessarily seek in every way to preserve their body and their life, and to repel whatever appears destructive thereto; and secondly, from the fact that those who live in that state are subject to no man's sovereignty. For it follows from the former that those placed into a natural state may use and enjoy any item of the common stock, and employ

---

[1] *Astronomica*, Bk.I [sec. 68—ed.].

or do whatever contributes to their own preservation, so long as the right of others is not hurt thereby; and from the latter, that they may defend and preserve themselves by using not only their own strength but also their own judgment and choice, provided these are formed according to the natural law. And in this respect that state also comes with the name of natural freedom, since apart from a preceding human deed anyone is understood to be within his own right and authority, and not subject to the authority of any other man. And by virtue of this anyone is considered equal to anyone else whom he himself is not subject to, and whom he does not have subject to himself.

And it is along these lines that we must correct and interpret Hobbes's assertions . . . that "the primary foundation of natural right is that everyone may guard his life and limbs to the extent he can, and make every effort to defend and preserve his own body and limbs from death and pain." From which it follows that "since a right to an end is useless if one is denied the right to the means, everyone has a right to use all means and to perform every act without which he is unable to preserve himself."[2]

But since no one in a natural state has another man as a superior to whose decision he has submitted his own will and judgment, it follows that "everyone is by natural right a judge." That is, everyone determines on the basis of his own judgment "whether the means to be employed and the action to be done are necessary or not for preserving his own life and limbs." For if anyone should undertake to advise someone else about such matters, even in the strongest terms, the latter, since he has not subjected his will and judgment to him, will still be permitted to decide whether the advice suits him or not. And so he will do what the other has urged not insofar as the advice was given as an order but insofar as it is pleasing to him, and will consequently act as his own judgment determines him to.

Hobbes finally concludes from all this that "nature has given everyone a right to all things; that is, in a pure natural state, before men had mutually bound themselves with pacts, everyone was permitted to do anything to anyone as he pleased, and to possess, use, and enjoy whatever he would and could. From which it is understood, as well, that in a state of nature the measure of right is usefulness."

However paradoxical these things may at first appear, one will by no means admit that a license to do anything to anyone should be derived from them if one keeps in mind that, according to Hobbes, a man in that state is surely subject to the rule of natural laws and sound reason. Since such license is a worthless thing that no sane man can consider an adequate means for his lasting preservation, we must not think that nature granted it in any way. And if anyone should go so far as to put it into practice, he would discover to his own great misfortune its ability to harm him. Thus, the ultimate meaning of Hobbes's statement is this: Before men divided them among themselves through pacts, nature had made the things conducing to man's preservation available to everyone; and someone who has no superior can act according to the dictate of his own sound reason and do whatever makes for his own lasting preservation. Yet if Hobbes's opinion of the matter was as crass as his words apparently seem to indicate, and if it is wholly opposed to

[2] *De Cive*, I,7.

this benign interpretation, let him find out on his own how to deflect the criticism launched deservedly against him. . . .

4. We maintain, however, that the human race as a whole has never at one and the same time existed in a pure natural state. Nor could it have, since the authority of Sacred Scripture has persuaded us to believe that all mortals originated from one conjugal pair. According to Genesis . . . , Adam's Eve was surely subject to his marital sovereignty, and those born of them placed immediately under paternal authority and the sovereignty of the family. But the entire race of mortals could have been in such a state at that time if, as some pagans believed, it emerged initially from the earth like frogs or sprouted from scattered seed like the brothers in Cadmus's tale. This fable may for all I know represent Hobbes's natural state, which he depicts distortedly as a war of all against all where "complete confusion rages, and brothers of an hour fall from wounds inflicted mutually by and on one another."[3] . . .

So there never actually was a natural state except in a tempered and, as it were, a partial sense, as happened when separate individuals united together with certain others into a civil state or something analogous, but retained their natural freedom toward the rest. Yet as the bands into which humankind was divided became more numerous and smaller, the closer it came to that pure natural state. Both formerly, when humankind separated into distinct family groups, as well as now, when it has been divided into civil states, those who do not obey one another and have no common master among men live mutually in a natural state. Thus, brothers who in ancient times left their father's family and founded their own independent families began mutually to live in freedom and a natural state. It was not the first mortals, therefore, but those coming after them who began actually to exist in that state.

When tempered in this fashion, the natural state lacks at least those disadvantages which attend its pure version, especially among those who have come together into civil states. Furthermore, it is considered the height of mortal achievement to rely on the strength of an entire state and acknowledge no one on this earth as one's superior. Thus civil states and their rulers, who are equipped with the strength to exercise their natural freedom securely, can extol their own condition by describing it in terms of this freedom. But those who live alone in a pure natural state, and whose safety is always suspended in uncertainty on account of their meager strength, find little appeal or utility in having no superior.

They are mistaken, however, who contend either that this natural freedom does not exist, or that it is not correctly said to be natural, arguing that since nature seeks an ordered society, but order cannot be understood without sovereignty (since there is no society without it), sovereignty should instead be said to be the truly natural thing. . . .

Hence Hobbes is accused of having designated and imagined as purely natural a state that is not worthy of man, or naturally human, but more fit for beasts, whose nature is ignorant of reason and speech. For there is no reason, no nature that judges in a right and upright manner, which dictates that everyone be permitted to do, to

---

[3] Ovid, *Metamorphoses*, III,122-23.

seek, or to possess all things. These kinds of impulses, they say, can be from our depraved nature, but they cannot be dictates of right reason which, in seeking society, also seeks a social order that precludes all license for such disorderly motions. For what order can there be, unless it aims at something that is first? This first thing is both supreme and capable of regulating all things; that is, it is sovereignty or the supreme authority in the state, without regard to which no society is sought by any living thing that enjoys the use of reason and speech. Nature goes so far, they say, as to show that sovereignty is natural in every society, but that freedom, which shuns all sovereignty, conflicts with nature. . . .

Now what we ought to think about these things can be easily determined from those that have preceded them. Man's condition is said to be a purely natural state insofar as it abstracts from those things which have been superadded to it by human institution, not because nature destined man to live in that state. Similarly, ignorance of all things can be said to be natural, or congenital to man, but not because it is repugnant to nature for him to acquire a knowledge of many things.

Furthermore, we do not attribute to man a natural freedom that is exempt from the obligation of natural law and divine sovereignty. However, a freedom that shuns all human sovereignty no more conflicts with nature than it admits of an infinite increase. Indeed, sovereignty is natural; that is, it was nature's intention that men establish sovereignties among themselves. But it is no less natural for one who wields that supreme sovereignty over other men to be himself exempt from human sovereignty, and so to enjoy natural freedom in this regard (unless we wish to admit something superior to what is supreme in the same order), just as it is natural, in general, for someone who has no master to govern himself and his actions according to the dictate of his own reason.

5. It is a question of greater importance whether the natural state in relation to other men is characterized by war or by peace, or—what comes to the same thing—whether those who live in such a state by virtue of neither having a common master nor commanding one another's obedience should be considered mutual enemies or peaceable friends. Here the opinion most deserving of careful examination is that of Hobbes, who calls the pure natural state a war (not a simple one, but of all against all) and maintains that those who have come together into the same civil state put aside their hostile stance toward one another while continuing to confront the rest as enemies. . . .

7. . . . But there is an opposite point of view based chiefly on the origins of humankind as taught us by the infallible authority of Sacred Scripture, which represents men's natural state as peaceful rather than warlike, and men themselves as friends instead of enemies. Accordingly, when the first man had been divinely brought forth from the earth, there was joined to him a companion whose matter was taken from himself, so that he might immediately embrace her with a tender love as someone taken from his own flesh and bones. In addition, God joined her to him by a most holy bond. Since all mortals are descended from this pair, the human race is understood to be associated not only by an ordinary friendship that can spring from natural similarity . . . , but also by another which (involving the tender affection that is usual among those who are somewhat close to one another) is brought about by a common lineage and blood relationship. Though awareness

of it has nearly faded among those farther from the common stock, anyone who puts it aside and adopts a hostile attitude toward others must be deemed to have fallen away from his primeval and natural state.

It is futile to object here that it follows from our account that men's natural state is one of war, by maintaining that if the reason societies are as old as humankind is that men might live in peace, then it follows, contrarily, that they would not have lived peaceably without them, and therefore that societies and men had to come into being together so that men would live in peace. To this we respond that here we are investigating the natural state as it really is, not as it may be conceived in the abstract. Accordingly, since the first men existed in a state that was by no means hostile but suffused by genuine friendship, and since the rest of men have also come from such a state, it is evident that men, if they are willing to be mindful of their first origin, are to regard one another as friends instead of enemies. Indeed, societies were introduced into the human race at the very beginning not in order to prevent a natural state from existing, but because humankind could otherwise not be increased and preserved. But when men had multiplied and could no longer be contained in one society, from this a natural state emerged. Therefore, unless one wishes to assume from the very start a multitude of men not linked to one another by any procreative ties, it makes no sense to say that when things first began, men without a social state would have lived in enmity with one another. . . .

8. We are also at no loss for replies to Hobbes's reasons. Those whom distance separates cannot directly hurt one another, for whoever hurts me while he is absent does so through someone present. Nor can my things be destroyed except by such a one. Therefore, since those who have been scattered far apart from one another can do each other no hurt so long as they have no closer ties, it is unclear why they should not be regarded as friends instead of enemies. For anyone who prefers to call them 'neutrals' should know that an unwillingness and inability to hurt can also be regarded as friendship.

Next, that very equality of strength offered by Hobbes in support of his position is better suited for restraining than inciting the will to hurt. For no sane man likes to begin a fight with an equal unless he is driven to it by necessity or encouraged by an opportunity of success. Otherwise, to engage in an unnecessary fight where the blows one gives must be returned with equal force, and where the combatants' strength makes the outcome merely uncertain, is a mark of foolishness and reckless savagery. For when one enters a fight with an equal and both lives are exposed to danger, surely neither gains as much from victory as is lost by the one who is killed. Nor is having killed another worth the risk of one's own life. For endangering my own life deprives me of more good than can accrue to me from the fact that my enemy's life is equally endangered, and his security is not increased on account of the uncertainty of mine. Rather, what each of us loses in the process is to neither's advantage. . . .

As for the causes adduced by Hobbes for men's desire to hurt one another, they are only particular and therefore by no means sufficient for stirring up a necessary war of all against all among humankind, but only of some against some. Nor is it always the case that aggressive and wicked individuals live intermingled with more modest ones, or that they have a great desire to provoke them. And a spirit of contention is seldom found in any but those who rank above the common crowd: Most mortals are either untouched by that illness or only slightly afflicted thereby. Finally, the Creator was not so grudging in providing for the necessities of mortals that they are always bound to clash in laying claim to the same thing. The general wickedness of men can certainly give one cause for not rashly trusting just anyone and exposing one's bare flank, as it were, especially if one does not know him very well. . . . But no sane man will admit such suspicion and distrust as a valid pretext for seizing and oppressing another who exhibits no specific intention to hurt him. . . .

Hobbes's opinion is even less acceptable insofar as he is prepared to have his natural state eliminated only by submission to the sovereignty of another and by uniting into the same civil state. For it makes no sense to anyone that even those civil states linked by treaties and by friendship should be in a mutual state of war. An insufficiently trustworthy peace is not immediately equivalent to no peace at all, just as the mutability of human affections and wills does not immediately mean that no one enjoys another man's favor.

9. Now it should also be well noted that we are not dealing here with the natural state of an animal ruled solely by impulse and the inclinations of a sensitive soul, but with that of an animal whose chief part is reason, by which the other faculties are ruled. This reason has even in the natural state a common, firm, and uniform measure, namely the nature of things, which very readily avails itself as a guide, at least to the general precepts of living and to the natural law. And anyone who would depict man's natural state correctly must by no means exclude the proper use of this reason but link it, rather, with the operation of the other faculties.

Therefore, since a man can hear not only the craving of his passions but also his reason (which certainly does not measure itself solely by its own advantages), he is rationally dissuaded from the wars into which his base passions drive him (including that imagined war of all against all) by two main arguments. These make him recognize, of course, that starting an unprovoked war against another is both improper and unprofitable.

For it is surely easy for a man to gather that he did not begin to exist of himself but was produced by some superior being who consequently has authority over him. And when he feels himself impelled by two principles, as it were, one of which inclines only toward the present and instinctually impels him toward dangers, doubts, and disorders, while the other considers also what is future and not present, leading him toward things that are safe and seemly, he may conclude with certainty that the Creator wishes him to submit to the latter's guidance and not the former's. When we add to this consideration the obvious utility of the peace recommended by reason, then a man can but naturally incline toward it. This is especially so since, afterward, whenever he has neglected reason and obeyed his passions, he discovers from the outcome that he has chosen the worse alternative and usually wishes that what he did against reason could be undone.

We conclude from all these things that the natural state of men, even when they are considered outside of civil states, is not war but peace. This peace depends almost entirely on the following laws: That a person do no hurt to another who has offered no provocation and allow all others to enjoy their own goods, that he faithfully abide by any agreements he has made, and that he willingly promote others' advantage to the extent permitted by his stricter obligations. For since man's natural state includes the use of reason we cannot, or should not, separate from it any obligation pointed out thereby. And since anyone at all can appreciate the fact that it is good for him to conduct himself in a manner that will allow him to enjoy others' benevolence instead of their enmity, he can easily presume from the similarity of others' nature that they feel this way as well. It is wrong, therefore, to suppose in one's description of that state that men, or most of them at least, neglect the guidance of reason which nature has established as the supreme directress of human actions, and wrong as well to call that a natural state which is produced by the neglect or abuse of a principle that is to the highest degree natural. . . .

11. Furthermore, by claiming that the peace which is to be observed toward all men as such is man's natural state, we imply that it has been instituted and sanctioned by nature itself apart from any human deed, and therefore that it rests solely on that obligation of the natural law by which all men as rational beings are bound, and that its first introduction was not due to any human agreement. Consequently, it also seems useless to fortify that universal peace alone with pacts and treaties. For such a treaty adds nothing to the obligation of the natural law, as there is no agreement about the performance of anything to which men were not already bound before by the natural law itself; nor does it make that obligation any stricter.

For we suppose that each of them remains the natural equal of the other, so that they are held to the observance of the pact by no further bond than reverence for God and a fear of the evil that can redound on them from its violation. (Though it seems more wicked and foul not to do what one has expressly promised.) Thus, one who has been hurt has the same license to proceed against a violator of the natural law when there has been a previous pact as when there has not. And so more cultivated men are customarily averse to entering into pacts whose articles and conditions merely state that someone will not directly violate a precept already expressly given by nature. It also seems insufficiently reverential toward the Divinity to act as if we were not sufficiently necessitated by His command unless we freely consented to it ourselves, or as if this obligation depended on our free choice.

Hence, every pact must lay down something which another otherwise cannot demand of me by virtue of the law of nature itself, or which I did not previously owe him in a perfect way on the basis of that law; but something which I shall fully owe him once I have expressed and he has accepted my consent. Therefore, just as someone who lends his services to another does not expressly and directly stipulate as articles of his pact that he will not act dishonestly toward him or secretly despoil him, so ought one to be ashamed of an agreement in which one binds oneself to no other performance toward another than not to violate the universal peace against him; that is, not to employ against him the right we commonly invoke against beasts.

But if some barbarous nations are used to preying on each other in these ways, restoration of the universal peace requires a pact in which they all agree to treat one another according to the natural law. This also happens when two peoples heretofore at war lay down their arms: If there is no agreement about specific guarantees, nothing but that common peace is restored. Indeed, there are many examples of civil states reduced to such dire straits that they were forced to procure that universal peace and a cessation of injuries not by pacts only, but also by paying tribute to those who deemed it right to live by plunder. . . .

12. Yet it must be admitted that this natural peace is rather weak and untrustworthy, and therefore something that by itself, without other safeguards, provides very scanty protection for men's welfare. . . . The cause of this is men's wickedness, their unbridled lust to augment their own power, and their avarice, which threatens the possessions of others. . . . Accordingly, just as it is characteristic of an upright man to be content with his own things and not provoke others, and not to seek others' things, so it is characteristic of a cautious man, and of one who loves his own welfare, to trust all men as friends, yet in such a way that they could soon become enemies, and to have with all of them a peace that could soon erupt into war. . . .

Chapter 3

ON THE LAW OF NATURE IN GENERAL

1. Seeing that man's condition did not allow him to live without law and to act by a vague impulse, as it were, without regard to any norm, it follows that we should inquire about the most common rule of human actions to which all men as rational animals must conform themselves. This rule, which has customarily been designated the right [*ius*] or law [*lex*] of nature, may also be called the universal and everlasting law because it binds the entire race of mortals and, unlike positive laws, is not subject to change. What sort of law it is, how it comes to be known, the proofs on which it rests, and what ought to be referred to it and what to positive law, must all be more carefully investigated, because if this foundation is not correctly laid everything built thereon will necessarily collapse of itself. . . .

4. Some lay down as the object of the natural law those acts which are morally necessary or base of themselves, and which are therefore in their own nature either owed or illicit, and for this reason understood as necessarily prescribed or forbidden by God. This feature, they maintain, distances natural law not only from human law but also from divine voluntary or positive law, which does not prescribe or forbid things that are of themselves and by their own nature owed or illicit, but makes things illicit or owed by forbidding or prescribing them. For the things forbidden by the natural law are not base because God has forbidden them, they say,

but God forbade them because they were base in themselves. Similarly, those which are prescribed by that same law are not made honorable or necessary because they are prescribed by God, but they are prescribed because they are honorable in themselves. . . .

Now besides the fact that it would remain obscure, if this opinion were admitted, just what those acts are which are in themselves illicit, and by what sign they may be clearly known apart from other acts, and likewise what the most obvious reason is that they are such, it has also been shown above . . . that no acts are owed or illicit in themselves before being made so through law. Nor can anyone be moved to wonder: If all morality of human actions depends on law, could God not have formed the law of nature in such a way that it would prescribe the opposites of the things now prescribed; so that, for example, killing, stealing, adultery, and false accusation would be among the mutual duties of man, while exhibiting gratitude, keeping pacts, repaying loans, and the like would be among those that are forbidden?

It may seem vain and impudent here to ask what God could have done, since it is well known what He has done. Nonetheless, if anyone takes pleasure in the uprooting even of vanities, one can easily reply that such wondering plainly involves a contradiction. For even if no necessity compelled God to create man at all, . . . still, once He had determined to create him as a rational and social animal the natural law could not but accord with him, not from an absolute necessity but a hypothetical one. For if man had been bound to the opposite duties, no social animal would have been produced, but another, wild and rude kind of living thing.

Despite this fact, it nonetheless remains firm that all acts whatsoever are indifferent previous to any law. For God, in the very act of deciding to create man, that is an animal for whom not all acts should be indifferent, also established a law for him at the same time. But it does not follow either, from our assertion that all acts are in themselves indifferent previous to law, that God could if He had wished have ordained that He be worshipped by blasphemies or disregard. . . . For a rational creature, that is one into whom God has placed the faculty to apprehend things as they are, cannot conceive God in any other way than as endowed not only with a certain infinite superiority, but also with supreme sovereignty over himself. For otherwise he would conceive a lifeless idol, or anything whatever, rather than God. . . .

13. Most men agree that the natural law is to be derived from man's reason itself, and therefore that it flows from the injunctions of this faculty when it is functioning correctly. . . . Thus, even the Sacred Scriptures declare that the law has been inscribed on men's hearts. It is evident here, in our judgment, that even though the Divine Scriptures shed additional light to make the natural law more clearly known, it can nonetheless be investigated and firmly demonstrated even without that assistance, through the rational powers which the Creator has granted to and still preserves in us. But we hardly think it necessary, in this respect, to insist that the general precepts of the natural law, at least, have been produced or, so to speak, impressed upon men's minds at birth itself, in the form of distinct and actual propositions which a man can articulate upon acquiring the use of speech without any further education or reflection. For anyone so curious as to observe

with any care the gradual emergence of children from their infantile ignorance will easily recognize this as a baseless fiction. Nor should we overlook the fact that the Sacred Scriptures commonly describe infancy as a time of ignorance about the upright and the base, and our riper age as one of knowledge thereof. . . .

Therefore, the sense in which we maintain that the natural law is a dictate of right reason is this: The human understanding has a faculty that enables it to see clearly from a contemplation of the human condition that it ought necessarily to live according to the norm of this law, and that enables it at the same time to discover the principle from which the law's precepts can be firmly and plainly demonstrated. . . . The fact that most men have no knowledge or grasp of how the natural law's precepts may be formally demonstrated, and that most of them usually learn and observe the natural law from custom or the course of ordinary life, poses no obstacle to this. For we also see artisans doing many things by imitation every day, or with the aid of instruments which they themselves do not know how to explain; yet the things they thus devise can nonetheless be called scientific and rationally grounded.

These things also clarify how we are to gauge whether reason's derivation of the natural law is correct, or how it is determined whether a certain dictate proceeds from right or depraved reason. As everyone knows, the dictates of right reason are true principles in agreement with the properly observed and examined nature of things, and derived from true first principles by valid deduction. A dictate of depraved reason, on the other hand, occurs when someone either posits false principles or, through syllogistic error [*asullogistian*], formulates false conclusions. For in saying that the natural law is impressed on us by the nature of things, we imply that it is true. This is because nature indicates only what exists and is never the cause of anything containing falsehood—something that arises, as we know, from the error of men, who disjoin ideas connected by nature or conjoin those it has disjoined. . . .

After noting this, we need no longer fear anyone's ability to pass off the ravings of his sick brain or his mind's disorderly desire as natural law. For someone who cannot demonstrate his assertions by means of legitimate principles consistent with the nature of things appeals in vain to reason, since truth and rectitude surely consist in the agreement of concepts and propositions with the things to be expressed through them. And someone so dull-witted as not to know how to devise demonstrations is exceedingly impudent if he demands any regard for deliverances of his brain that diverge from the received opinions. It is readily apparent, moreover, even to those who do understand the character of a demonstration, that principles should not only be necessarily true and fundamental but also appropriate to and, as it were, at home in the discipline under investigation; so clear, as well, that a mind seeing in them the reason for an assertion will give its quiet assent and seek no further proofs. . . .

Furthermore, although not everyone has the skill to deduce the natural law from its first principle, there is sufficient ground for claiming that it is nonetheless known by all men who enjoy the use of reason, in that average minds, at least, are able to grasp its demonstration when presented to them by others, and can clearly see its truth when they compare it with their own natural condition. The common crowd, however, which usually derives the law from popular notions and public practice, should be sufficiently assured of the law by the authority of the superiors charged with its implementation in civil states, both because it has no plausible reasons capable of shaking or undermining the law's truth, and because it observes the law's immediate utility on a daily basis. By this also is the natural law understood to have been sufficiently promulgated, so that no adult of sound mind can plead invincible ignorance of it. . . .

14. It seems to us that there is no more direct and appropriate way of discovering the natural law than to contemplate carefully man's nature, condition, and inclinations, though this consideration must necessarily include as well a reflection on other things external to man, especially those capable of benefitting or harming him in some way. For whether the law has been imposed on man to promote his happiness or to check his wickedness (which would lead to his own destruction), there is no more fruitful way to learn the law than by examining the kinds of assistance and restraint he needs.

The first thing, therefore, that man has in common with all living things which are aware of themselves is that he loves himself to the highest degree, is eager to preserve himself in every way, and strives to acquire those things that seem good to him and to repel those that seem evil. . . .

Besides this love of and eagerness to preserve himself by all means, we also find in man an extreme weakness and a natural neediness. Hence, if we were to conceive him as abandoned to himself in this world without any assistance from other men, his life could seem to have been given him as a punishment. It is evident as well that, after the Divinity, no greater help and relief can come to a man than from other men. For even though we find the strength of individuals to preserve themselves so slight that they need the help of many things and men in order to live well and comfortably (since individuals would lack both the strength and the time to produce most of the things that are most useful and supremely necessary for men, if many men had not joined their efforts together), they can, on the other hand, still provide many things for the uses of others which they themselves do not need, and which would therefore be of no use to themselves if they were not dispensed to other men. . . .

It must also be noted here, however, that in setting forth man's condition we have given priority to self-love not because one should always prefer oneself to everyone else or assess everything in terms of one's own interest, proposing this to oneself (insofar as it has been separated from others' advantage) as one's highest goal; but because man, being naturally aware of his own existence before that of others, naturally loves himself before he cares for them. Besides, the task of caring for myself belongs more properly to me than to anyone else. For even if we set our sights upon the common good, since I too am a part of humankind whose preservation should be of some concern, the distinct and special care of myself can surely rest on no one else as much as it does on me.

15. Once these things have been established, it is easy to discover the foundation of the natural law. Man, it is clearly apparent, is an animal most eager to preserve himself, essentially in need, ill-equipped to maintain himself without the aid of those who are like him, and very well suited for the mutual promotion of

advantages. All the same, he is often malicious, insolent, easily annoyed, and both ready and able to inflict harm. For this kind of animal to be safe and enjoy the goods that befall his worldly condition, it is necessary that he be sociable. That is, he must will to be united with those who are similar to himself and conduct himself toward them in such a way that they are provided with no cause to hurt him, but instead have reason to maintain or promote his advantage. . . .

And so the fundamental law of nature will be this: "Any man must, inasmuch as he can, cultivate and maintain toward others a peaceable sociality that is consistent with the native character and end of humankind in general." For sociality, as we understand it here, is not merely a tendency to form particular societies, whose purpose and manner of formation can also be evil, like an association of thieves— as if just any intention for joining oneself to another would do. Rather, we mean by it a kind of disposition whereby a man is understood to be joined to every other man by ties of benevolence, peace, and charity, and therefore by a mutual obligation. And so it is utterly false to claim that the sociality we are introducing is indifferent as to whether a society is good or evil.

Now we have said that sociality is to be cultivated and actually practiced by any man "inasmuch as he can." The reason is that, since it is not under our control to bring it about that all others conduct themselves toward us as they should, we have therefore sufficiently done our duty if we have omitted none of the things in our capacity which were able to induce them to be sociable toward us in turn. . . .

Moreover, our fundamental law is not different from that of Richard Cumberland . . . , on striving after the common good and displaying toward everyone the greatest possible benevolence.[4] For in maintaining that man should be sociable we too imply that he ought not to aim at his own good as something separate from that of others, but also at theirs; and that no one should seek to benefit himself by oppressing or neglecting others, or hope to achieve his own happiness if he neglects or provokes them with injuries.

Further, this sociality of man, and the fact that everyone has been born not for himself alone but for humankind, is the basis of certain excellent conclusions deduced by Bacon of Verulam. . . . These include, for instance, that an active life is to be preferred to a contemplative one, that man's happiness is to be sought in virtue and not in pleasure, that we ought not to withdraw from public affairs or quit the company of others because there are events we cannot foresee, and finally, that we should not retire from civil life because we are too tender-minded and unskilled at ingratiating ourselves.[5] Bacon also points out here that no philosophy, religion, law, or other discipline has ever been found to exalt the good of the community, and to deemphasize that of the individual, as much as the Christian faith.

16. . . . [I]t must be noted . . . that self-love and sociality should by no means be opposed to one another. Instead, these inclinations should be moderated in such a way that the latter is not disturbed or overturned by the former. . . . When that balance has been disrupted by inordinate desire and each person sets out to seek his own advantage to the detriment of others, there arise all the various disturbances

---

[4] *A Treatise on the Laws of Nature*, I,iv.

[5] *The Advancement of Learning*, II,xx.

that set the race of mortals at odds with one another. For these to be averted, the care for our own welfare itself orders us to observe the laws of sociality, since our welfare cannot remain secure without this.

As for Hobbes's rather clever deduction of natural laws solely from the care for one's own welfare, it must be noted at the start, concerning that demonstration, that it does indeed clearly establish that it is conducive to men's welfare that they lead their lives according to those dictates of reason. Yet it cannot be immediately concluded that man has a right to apply them as a means toward his own preservation, and that he is therefore bound to observe them as by some law. Hence those dictates of reason must, in order to receive the force of law, be deduced from an altogether different principle.

Next we must also take great precautions lest anyone conclude from this that when a person appears to himself to have secured his own welfare, there is no reason [for him] to consider that of others, or that I can as I please insult someone who contributes nothing to my welfare, or does not have enough strength to harm it. For the reason we said that man is a sociable animal is also that men are more suited to promote their mutual advantages than any other living being, just as on the contrary, no animal can experience more harm from man than man himself. Indeed, the excellence and perfection of any man is the more resplendent insofar as he contributes more to the advantage of the rest; and these very deeds are considered the noblest and to demand the highest wisdom, since on the contrary, even a man of little worth and a fool can bother and hurt others. . . .

Indeed, reason is also quite insistent that one who has his own welfare and preservation at heart cannot renounce the care of others. For since our safety and happiness depend for a large part on the benevolence and help of others, and indeed men's nature is such that they wish to be repaid in kind for their good deeds, and when this does not happen they put aside the spirit of beneficence, surely no sane person can set his own preservation as a goal for himself in such a way as to divest himself of all regard for others. But rather, the more rationally a person loves himself the more he will see to it, by means of his services, that others love him. For no one can with any reason expect that men will be ready and willing to devote their efforts to making happy those whom they have found to be malevolent, untrustworthy, ungrateful, and inhumane toward themselves; but it must rather be believed that other men will lie in wait in order to restrain and eradicate such individuals.

17. Next, though individual men unite with certain [other] men into a particular society or group in order to reap some special advantage for themselves, it does not follow that human nature in general is not meant for sociality, or I myself not bound to be social toward one from whom I anticipate receiving no particular benefit. For it is surely obvious that the uniting together of certain men into a certain kind of society comes either from a special harmony of minds or other qualities, or from the fact that they think it more possible for themselves to obtain a particular end among these than among those. Still, besides the fact that as a rule it does not befit any man not to live in any particular society, those connected by no other bond than their humanity must also willingly cultivate among themselves that common sociality and peace. This consists almost entirely in refraining from unjust

harms and, to the extent that one's stricter obligations allow, in the mutual promotion and sharing of advantages and goods.

18. It readily appears from this what response should be made to the following objection: "If men loved one another naturally, that is, as men, no reason could be given why everyone does not love everyone equally, as they are equally men, or why they frequent the society of those who honor or profit them more than the rest." This objection confuses that common sociality with special, narrower kinds of societies, and common love with that which stems from special causes. For that common love really does require no other reason than the fact of being a man, since nature has, indeed, for the reasons mentioned above, established a general sort of friendship among men, from which no one is to be excluded unless he has made himself unworthy of it through monstrous crimes.

Although the law of nature has through the Creator's wisdom been adapted to human nature in such a way that its observance is always linked with men's utility and advantage, and that common love is therefore conducive to their highest good, still, in assigning a reason for this love one usually appeals not to the advantage that comes from it but to men's common nature. For example, if a reason must be given why a man should not hurt another man, one usually says not that it is useful (even though it may in fact be so to the highest degree), but that the other is also a man, that is, an animal related to us by nature whom it is wrong to hurt. . . .

To be sure, there are many things in addition to that common friendship, on account of which someone loves one person to a greater degree than another. For instance, there may be a greater agreement between their characters with respect to certain inclinations; the one may be more suited or prone than the other to promote his advantage; or their origins may make them closer to one another. Moreover, a man more readily frequents those in whose company honor and utility are conferred on himself rather than on another, because each person cannot but naturally love the things that are to his own advantage, at least if he knows how to estimate them correctly.

This is by no means repugnant to the sociable nature of men, provided that the harmony of society is not disturbed through that love. For nature did not order us to be sociable so that we might neglect the care of ourselves. Rather, men cultivate sociability so that we can, through a mutual sharing of assistance and goods, more adequately provide for our own goods. And although someone primarily has his own advantage before his eyes when he joins himself to some particular society, and only secondarily that of his fellows (insofar as the former cannot be obtained without these), this does not prevent him from being bound to strive after his own advantage in such a way that the advantage of society is not hurt or injury inflicted on its individual members, or, now and then, to care for the good of society by considering his own advantage as less important.

19. Furthermore, this principle for deducing the natural law is not only true and evident, in our opinion, but also so sufficient and adequate that there is no precept of the natural law regarding other men whose reason is not ultimately derived from it. Yet, as we shall soon show, for such dictates of reason to have the force of law it must be presupposed that God exists and that His providence governs all things, especially humankind. For we cannot support Grotius's claim, in the *Prolegomena*,

that natural laws "would have a certain validity even if we should grant what cannot be granted without the greatest impiety: that there is no God, or that He does not care about human affairs." For if anyone went so far as to assume that impious and absurd hypothesis and conceived the human race to have sprung from itself, then those dictates of reason could in no way have the force of law, as this necessarily supposes a superior. . . .

20. . . . Finally, it seems that not even human sovereignty can, by itself, bestow the power to obligate on these dictates. For since sovereignty cannot arise without the intervention of pacts, and these, indeed, borrow their force from law, it is unclear how human sovereignty capable of conferring obligatory force can come into being if the dictates of reason have not acquired legal force before that. Or, to speculate completely, if human sovereignty depended on men's consent alone and the observance of reason's dictates as laws were enjoined through it, these dictates would still have no greater force than positive laws, which depend on a legislator's will for their origin and duration. . . .

And so it must absolutely be maintained that the obligation of the natural law is from God Himself, the Creator and supreme governor of the human race, Who by virtue of His sovereignty over men, His creatures, has bound them to its observance. And this can be demonstrated by the light of reason. We are supposing now that God is the maker and ruler of the universe, since wise men have for a long time clearly shown this to be so and no pious person will dispute it. Since He formed the nature of things and of man in such a way that the latter cannot be preserved without a sociable life (and for this reason placed into him a mind capable of grasping ideas conducive to that end, instilling these into men's minds through the motion of natural things, which derives from Himself as prime mover, and clearly manifesting their necessary connection and truth), it is no doubt understood that He also wished man to adjust his actions to that native character, as it were, which He is seen to have specially assigned to the life of men over that of brutes. But since this may be obtained in no other way than by observing the natural law, the Creator has understandably obligated men to observe it, not as a means they have chosen to invent and can change as they desire, but as one expressly ordained by Himself for procuring this end. For someone who enjoins an end upon another by virtue of his sovereignty is thought also to have obligated him to employ the means without which that end cannot be obtained. . . .

That the Deity has by virtue of His sovereignty enjoined a social life on men is apparent not only from the fact that men cannot be secure in their present condition unless they remain firmly convinced of this, and that, as First Cause, He has effectively willed that happiness and unhappiness issue by a natural consequence from acts respectively prescribed and forbidden by the natural law; but also from the fact that a sense of religion or fear of the Deity is found in no other living thing besides man. There is in addition the very delicate conscience in the minds of uncorrupted men, by which they are convinced that by sinning against the law of nature they offend the one who has sovereignty over men's minds, and who is to be feared even when there is no impending fear of other men. . . .

But laws of nature that have been brought to light by reasoning cannot be conceived except in the manner of propositions, and in this respect they are rightly called propositions. However, just as it does not matter in the case of civil laws whether they are promulgated in writing or orally, so divine law will be equally obligatory whether it has become known through God Himself in a visible appearance, imitating the sound of a human voice, through most holy men who have been moved by a special divine inspiration, or, finally, whether it is brought to light through natural reason from a contemplation of the human condition. For reason is not properly speaking the law of nature itself but the means by whose correct employment it may be found out. But the manner of promulgating a law does not pertain to its inner substance. . . .

22. As for the matter of the law, Grotius . . . observes that many things are commonly said to belong to the natural law not in a proper but a *reductive* sense of not being incompatible with it, as when we term 'just' not only those things owed out of justice but also those not in conflict with it (though one would do better to call these 'permitted').[6] But perhaps it would be more appropriate to apply this distinction to the institutions that reason has been persuaded to introduce into a certain state of humankind for the sake of peace and tranquillity, and to the actions undertaken or carried out in accord with them. For you may also hear lawyers debating questions like these: Is dominion over things in accord with the natural law? What of acquisition by use, making a will, and buying and selling? It is impossible to give a suitable answer to these questions unless one distinguishes matters of which the natural law disposes by direct precept or prohibition from those that reason has persuaded men to institute on account of sociality, or that may be undertaken by virtue of a license flowing directly from these institutions— in which case they are said to have a reductive relation to the natural law.

Thus, dominion over things is not immediately from nature, and one cannot allege an express and definite precept for its introduction; yet it is attributed to the natural law insofar as the condition and peace of humankind, when multiplied, have made the continuation of a primitive communion of goods unfeasible. Likewise, there is no distinct precept of the natural law regarding acquisition by use; but given separate dominions over things, the tranquillity of humankind has tended to favor it, lest dominions be always uncertain. Finally, nature orders no one to make his last wishes known, or to engage in buying or selling; but once dominion has been established it follows naturally that one about to die may dispose of his own goods, and that anyone may alienate the things that belong to him or, through a contract, acquire those of others. . . .

24. The most convenient division of the natural law, it seems to us, is that which first of all considers how a person under its command should conduct himself toward *himself*, and then how he should conduct himself toward *other men*. The precepts of the natural law regarding other men can be once more divided into *absolute* and *hypothetical*. The former obligate all men in any sort of state or condition, even apart from humanly introduced or formed institutions, while the latter presuppose a certain state or institution formed or received by men. . . .

And so, although dominion over things, such as it is now, has been constituted by the human will, once it has been established the natural law itself declares it a

---

[6] *On the Law of War and Peace*, I,1,10.

crime to take what belongs to another without the owner's consent. . . . To be sure, there are many things which are arbitrary as far as the exercise of an act is concerned, or where it has been left up to men to decide whether they wish to act or not. But once that act has been undertaken it is followed by a moral necessity or obligation from some precept of the natural law, or its manner and circumstances are determined thereby. Thus, for example, though the law of nature does not order me to buy from another, it commands that I not seek my own gain at his loss nor cheat him in the bargain, once I have freely decided to do so. Likewise, there are very many precepts of the natural law which are not understood, and have no place, unless a separate dominion over things, and civil sovereignty, are supposed.

It does not follow from this, however, that all positive laws belong to the natural law, in that we submit ourselves through our own consent to the supreme sovereignty of another whose commands the law of nature itself orders us to obey. It is certain, of course, that on account of that intervening pact, those who violate civil laws sin indirectly against the natural law itself as well. But there is still a vast difference between hypothetical natural laws and positive civil laws, in that the reason for the former is derived from the condition of humankind considered in general, while the reason for the latter is taken from the special interest of a certain civil state, or from the bare decision of a legislator. And so, positive civil laws are not hypothetical precepts of the natural law but borrow the power to obligate in a human forum from a hypothetical precept.

Among the institutions on which hypothetical precepts are based, the chief three, we find, are *speech, dominion over things, and their price,* and *human sovereignty.* And from here on we will treat this discipline according to this division.

BOOK III

Chapter 1

THAT NO ONE BE HURT,

AND THAT ANY DAMAGE DONE BE REPAIRED

1. Thus far we have set forth what the natural law enjoins a man to do with respect to himself, and how much license or partiality it allows him concerning the preservation of his own self and things.[1] Now we must pass on to those precepts containing the duties that are to be performed toward other men. These we have divided above into *absolute* and *hypothetical*.

In the class of *absolute duties*, which obligate all men apart from any antecedent human institution, we deservedly award the principal place to this: "Let no one hurt another; and if he has done some harm to another, let him repair it." For this is the broadest duty of all, encompassing all men as such, and likewise the easiest, since it consists in the bare refraining from an action—except when desires that struggle against reason (among which the inordinate love of our own interest does not occupy the last place) must be subdued. Indeed, it is also supremely necessary, because without it the social life of men could in no way be sustained. For I can still live quietly with someone who bestows no sort of good on me, and who does not enter with me into an exchange of even ordinary services, provided he does not hurt me in any way. Indeed, we desire nothing more than this from the greatest part of mortals: The reciprocal sharing of goods is almost always among a few. But how could I live peacefully with one who hurts me, since nature has instilled into each person such tender love of his own self and things that he cannot but in every way repel someone who undertakes to harm them? ...

This precept protects and orders us to hold sacrosanct, as it were, not only those things that nature itself has immediately granted us, such as life, body, limbs, chastity, simple esteem, and freedom; but its force is also understood to diffuse itself throughout all the institutions and agreements by means of which a man acquires something, as if they would be plainly useless without it. Thus this precept for-

---

[1] The reference is to the material in the omitted chapters 4, 5, and 6 in Book II—ed.

bids that what is ours, by whatever title, be taken away, destroyed, damaged, or in whole or part withdrawn from our use. . . .

2. Now it follows from this precept that "If someone has inflicted a hurt upon a person, or in any way done harm that can be rightly imputed to him, he must make up for it as much as he can." For the precept that another should not be hurt would otherwise be empty if, when he has in fact been hurt, he would have to swallow the harm done to himself without recompense, and the one who did the hurt could enjoy the fruit of his injury securely and without refunding it. For without the necessity of restitution, corrupt mortals will never refrain from hurting one another, nor will one who has suffered a harm easily compose his mind so as to make peace with the other, so long as he has not obtained reparation from him.

Chapter 2

THAT ALL MEN BE CONSIDERED NATURALLY EQUAL

1. In addition to that love which man has for his own life, body, and things, and because of which he cannot avoid repelling or fleeing everything tending to their destruction, we also find embedded in his mind a very delicate self-esteem. And if anyone detracts from this in any way, he is usually no less, but in fact often more upset than if some harm is done to his body or things. Although this esteem is heightened by various causes, its primary basis seems to be human nature itself. Indeed, the very word 'man' is thought to contain a certain dignity, and the ultimate as well as the most effective argument for deflecting others' rude insults is taken to be: "Surely I am not a dog or a beast, but as much a man as you." . . .

Now since human nature belongs equally to all men, and since one cannot lead a social life with someone by whom one is not esteemed at least as a man, it follows as a precept of the natural law that "Everyone must esteem and treat other men as his natural equals, or as men in the same sense as he."

2. To understand better this equality among men, we must observe that Hobbes . . . restricts it to a parity of strength and other natural faculties with which mature men are equipped, and wishes to show from this that men have a natural reason to fear one another.[2] For someone whose strength is not extensive enough to hurt me can strike no fear into me. But among men even someone who is slightly inferior to another in strength can still kill even the strongest person, at least by deceit or with the aid of skill and a familiarity with weapons. . . . But since the greatest natural evil that can come from a man, and that any adult can inflict on another, is

---

[2] *De Cive*, I,3.

death, and since those who can inflict equal things on one another are equal, and those capable of the maximum—namely killing—can inflict equal things, it follows that men are by nature equal to one another. . . .

Yet Hobbes seems to us to have been sleeping when he added that "the inequality that now exists has been introduced by civil law." For he spoke earlier of a natural equality of human strength, which it is improper to contrast with the inequalities introduced by civil law, which affect not men's strength but their status and condition. Civil law does not make one man stronger than another, but more dignified.

Furthermore, Hobbes's statement . . . that he finds in other faculties of the soul an even greater equality than that of strength, seems not so clear. For he says that "all prudence is from experience, and that in equal time nature grants it equally to all in the case of things to which they equally apply themselves."[3] Yet we see one man anticipating the consequences of things more accurately than another, and more skillfully applying his previous observations and ascertaining the similarities and dissimilarities among cases. Hence it often happens that among those occupied with the same affairs for an equal length of time, one person's skill becomes preeminent while another's dullness is little remedied by experience.

Nor, indeed, does the apparent disparity of prudence among men stem merely "from the opinion of those who esteem themselves too highly, and from the fact that everyone believes himself to be far wiser than any member of the common crowd, barring a few whom he tends to admire for their fame or because they concur with him." For this disparity appears not only when someone compares himself to others but also when he compares them with one another—in which case it does not matter to him who excels whom. Nor do we always favor a person who agrees with us over someone recommended by his work and accomplishment. Although the characteristic desire of humans for esteem makes anyone indignant at being reproached for dullness and imprudence, and extremely hostile toward those who brag of their own prudence before others, it does not follow that no one concedes others to be more prudent than himself. For if one person has skillfully extricated himself from some danger out of which another has emerged badly wounded, will the latter not acknowledge him to have been more prudent?

Because of their equal freedom, however, a more prudent person cannot claim for himself a right to rule a more imprudent one without the latter's consent, especially if the latter professes himself content with whatever skill he has. For, indeed, though equality of strength can also prevent a man from brashly insulting another (since it is risky to contend with an equal, and foolish to wish upon another an evil that is equally destructive to oneself), the equality we are dealing with here, and which is of the highest importance for humankind to keep intact, is nonetheless of a different kind. Indeed, nature has revealed here the cleverness that she also exhibits in other matters, by measuring out her physical and mental goods to mortals in different proportions, amid whose variety the equality of which we are treating maintains a proper harmony. Thus, just as in well-founded commonwealths citizens exceed one another in dignity or wealth, while freedom belongs equally to

[3] Leviathan, XIII.

all, so also, no matter how greatly someone excels others in mental or physical endowments, he is no less bound to exercise toward them the same duties of the natural law that he expects of them, and his endowments do not give him more of a license to afflict them with injuries. Nor does stingy nature or slender fortune as such condemn anyone to a worse position than others in regard to the enjoyment of a common right [*ius*]. Rather, that which one person can demand or expect of another can—other things being equal—be demanded or expected of him by others as well; and whatever law [*ius*] someone has set up for another is quite appropriately followed by himself. . . .

Much less, however, are we able to approve the statement of that American from New France who during the time of Charles IX, when asked what in France seemed to him most remarkable, mentioned among other things the fact that although some people were surrounded by complete abundance while, on the contrary, others tormented by severe want went begging from door to door, the latter did not attack the former and take their goods from them. . . . For just as those who are more richly endowed with the goods of the mind, the body, or fortune ought not to insult those with more meager allotments, so should the latter also not envy them or undertake to destroy their goods.

And we can call this an *equality of law [ius],* since it arises from the fact that the obligation to cultivate a social life, which accompanies human nature as such, binds all men equally.

Here we must also observe that obligations enjoined by a superior seem, in other respects at least, to differ from those that arise from a mutual agreement. The latter cease immediately to bind a person once the other party has deviated from them, while the former can still bind one to do something even though the other person has stopped performing his reciprocal duty. This is because any lack of justice can be made up by the author of the obligation. Nonetheless, the obligation to exercise toward others the duties of the natural law, even though they are regarded as injunctions of the supreme Deity, has this much in common with the obligation stemming from any kind of agreement: When one person departs from it, he can no longer demand those duties of another, and the latter acquires, besides, the right to make him render satisfaction by force—though the character of civil society has made it necessary that this license inherent in the natural state be tempered in civil states.

3. There are other reasons as well, highly plausible to the multitude, that help us greatly to reflect on and illustrate that equality. Not least among them is the fact that every mortal comes from the same stock. . . .

Likewise, there is the fact that our bodies, which are fragile and subject to accidental destruction in numberless ways, are composed of the same matter. And we are all propagated in the same manner, and in the same manner formed in the hidden recesses of our mother's womb; nor do noblemen enter into the divine light of day by any other gate than commoners. . . . We grow and are nourished in the same manner, and our food is transformed into the same foul remainder in all our cases. Finally, we all come to the same end. . . . and everyone's body dissolves into the same corruption or dust. . . . Also, wise men constantly press upon us our common exposure to various accidents and the play of fortune; or the fact, rather, that God has guaranteed no one a stable, unshaken happiness and the continuation of his present state, but sweeps different people along by different kinds of events according to the secret counsels of His providence. . . .

4. From this equality which we have posited flow certain precepts whose observance has the greatest impact on the preservation of peace and friendship among mortals. Here it is evident, right at the beginning, that he who wishes to avail himself of the labors of others for his own advantage should also make himself useful to them in turn. As the proverb says, "Hand washes hand." For one who demands that others be of service to him but desires always to be exempt surely deems them inferior to himself. And one who exhibits such an attitude cannot avoid seriously offending others and giving them a pretext to break the peace. . . .

And surely, just as opposite judgments about things that agree with one another imply a contradiction, so also does the laying down of different rules for two entirely similar cases, namely mine and someone else's. Indeed, since everyone knows his own nature perfectly well, and that of other men (at least their general inclinations) no less than that, it follows that someone who decides differently about another's right than about his own, despite their similarity, contradicts himself in a most familiar matter and gives proof of a seriously ill mind. For no good reason can be given why something I consider right for myself should, if all other things are equal, be considered wrong for another.

Thus, just as those who readily allow everyone the same things as themselves are most fit for society, . . . those are plainly unsociable who deem themselves superior to others and wish that they alone be free to do all things, who forgive themselves everything but others nothing, and who claim honor for themselves before the rest, as well as the best part of the common stock, even though they have no stronger claim to it than others because of a special right. For just as in constructing a building, a stone whose rough and angular shape takes from others more than its share of space, and whose hard material does not easily allow it to be cut and pressed into place, nor the building to be sealed, is rejected as useless; so, greedy men [*pleonektikoi*] whose harsh character leads them to deprive others of necessities by retaining superfluities for themselves, and whose stubborn passions make them incorrigible, are an intolerable burden to the rest. Hence, the natural law is understood to enjoin "that anyone who has not obtained a special right not claim more for himself than for the rest, but allow others to enjoy a right equal to his own." . . .

5. The same equality also indicates how one ought to go about distributing a right among several persons; namely, in such a way "that one treats them as equals and grants neither of them something ahead of the other, except insofar as he has acquired a special right to it." For someone who pays no heed to natural equality, and favors one person over another, both insults and injures the one being less esteemed by not granting him his due and disparaging the dignity given him by nature. . . .

Consequently, if the thing which is to be distributed among several persons cannot be divided, those who have an equal right to it should, if possible, use it in common—as much as each of them wishes, if the thing's size permits. If it does not, however, they ought to restrict its use in proportion to the number of users.

For it is not possible here to devise another way of observing equality. But if the thing can be neither divided nor possessed in common, it should be used by them in turns; . . . or, if even this is unsuccessful and the initial user cannot leave the rest an object of equivalent value, it will have to be awarded to one person by lot. For in such cases one cannot find a more convenient solution than the lot, since it eliminates the impression of disdain and does not diminish the dignity of those not favored by it. . . .

See Hobbes . . . , where he distinguishes between *arbitrary* and *natural* lot.[4] The former comes about by the consent of contenders who agree to abide by a thing's result or outcome, which they cannot control or foresee by any art. Thus, in respect to man, it depends on sheer chance or fortune. Natural lot, he says, includes *first occupancy*, whereby a thing that can be neither divided nor held in common goes to the one who first laid hands on it with the intent to keep it; and *primogeniture*, whereby paternal goods that can be neither divided nor held in common by several children go to the firstborn.

If we want to consider the matter accurately, however, there is no lot in the proper sense but an arbitrary one. For there is no apparent reason why a result of this kind, which no one can bring about by his own industry, should give anyone a right valid against his equals, unless this right was connected with the result by an arbitrary agreement of men. Hence, a thing that belongs to no one goes to the person who occupies it, because when men introduced separate dominions over things we understand them to have tacitly agreed that things not specifically assigned to anyone, and which it would not be in humankind's interest to leave always in common, would properly belong to the one who first occupied them. Similarly, the right of primogeniture also owes its birth to a human agreement or decision. For why, otherwise, should the remaining brothers born of the same parents be in a worse condition on account of something for which they could not be responsible? . . .

8. We also conclude from what has been said that the opinion derived from the ancient Greeks, according to which some men are by nature slaves, deserves to be rejected. For if accepted in such crudely stated terms it clashes head on with the natural equality of men. . . .

It is evident, of course, that some men are blessed with such an abundance of natural ability that they are able not only to look out for themselves but also, indeed, to govern others. Some, however, are too dull-witted to be able to govern themselves, except badly, or they do nothing at all unless they are directed or impelled by others, even though nature has often endowed them with a strong body by means of which they can shower many advantages upon the rest. When these are subject to the sovereignty of someone more prudent, they have no doubt reached a state that agrees with their native character. Hence, if these two types of men establish a sovereignty of their own accord, it is surely congruent with nature that the authority to command be conferred upon the former and the necessity to obey laid upon the latter, for in this way both their interests will be served. . . .

It would be most absurd, however, to believe that nature herself has actually

---

[4] *De Cive*, III,18.

and directly given the more prudent sovereignty over the more dull, or such a right, at least, that the former can force the latter to serve them even against their will. For the actual establishment of sovereignty requires some antecedent human deed, and a natural ability to rule by no means gives anyone sovereignty over those whom nature has given a character fit for servitude. Nor does the fact that something is useful to another immediately allow me to impose it on him by force. For men enjoy natural freedom to an equal degree, and they cannot allow it to be diminished without their express, tacit, or interpretive consent, or without some other deed of theirs by which others have acquired a right to seize it from them even against their will. . . .

This could also have been expressed as follows: Since nature has made all men equal, and since slavery cannot be understood apart from inequality (for to be a slave surely implies acknowledging a superior; freedom, however, does not require one to have an inferior, as it suffices not to be subject to a superior), it is understood that naturally, or apart from any antecedent deed, all men are free. A natural aptitude or the presence of qualities required for a certain state does not immediately place someone into that state. Thus, someone who is worthy to rule or fit to lead an army is not right away a king or a general. . . .

There are other considerations as well by which this crude conception of natural slavery is overturned. For there is hardly anyone so stupid as not to think that he can live more correctly or comfortably by his own wits than by conforming himself to another's decisions. This is even more so in the case of whole nations, none of which is so mean-spirited as to prefer being subject to others to being ruled by a domestic sovereign. Finally, since sovereignty is in fact not constituted by nature, and those whom Aristotle calls natural slaves are for the most part endowed with a robust body, there will no doubt be an uncertain conflict between them and those who are prudent—a conflict in which the latter cannot promise themselves certain victory. . . .

Chapter 3

ON THE GENERAL DUTIES OF HUMANITY

1. It is not enough, however, not to have hurt another, or not to have deprived him of the esteem he is owed: These only remove the just cause for hatred. Something good must also be conferred on the other, at least if the minds of men are to be conjoined by a still closer bond. Someone who has not driven me away from himself by some hostile or ungrateful deed has not discharged the debt of social-

ity; rather, he should furnish something beneficial so that I am glad that others who share my nature also live upon this earth. And, as well, the affinity and kinship established among men by nature must be exercised by means of mutual duties. . . .

2. Now other men's advantages are promoted by us either indefinitely or definitely, and this so that we either do or do not forgo something thereby. The former happens if someone carefully cultivates his mind or body so as to render it fit to produce advantages for others, or if through clever ingenuity he discovers things that make human life better equipped. . . . In these and similar ways, therefore, are the advantages of others generally and indefinitely promoted; that is, by our proposing to benefit not this or that person, but by making goods that we have produced for the public, as it were, available to anyone. One could ask here, however, whether someone who had discovered a way to make gold or silver, for example, without much labor and out of a common material that is encountered anywhere, would be bound to make this art public. The answer to this must be "No," it seems, since such a secret, if divulged, would thoroughly disturb commerce, patrimonies, wealth, and almost the entire order of civil life.

3. A person is useful to others in a more definite way if he bestows on certain men something that can bring them some kind of profit. This can often be done without any loss, or bother and labor, to ourselves. To have denied or begrudged another such a thing is considered a detestable malice and inhumanity. For a faculty of this sort, by which we can furnish a benefit to others while forgoing nothing ourselves, is useless and becomes a reproach to its owner if we do not exercise it when an opportunity is given. . . . Thus, what inhumanity it would be, if in a case where I no longer wished to possess some thing on account of an excessive supply, or because keeping it was bothersome to me, I did not instead of destroying it rather leave it whole, so that it might furnish some use for others! Although often, in war, things that cannot be kept are destroyed lest they equip the enemy against us. . . .

Chapter 4

ON KEEPING FAITH, AND ON
THE DIVISIONS OF OBLIGATIONS

1. The duties expounded thus far are mutually owed by reason of that common kinship which nature established among all men, despite there having been no preceding act among them. But to circumscribe the duties that are to be mutually

exercised among men by means of this boundary alone is insufficient. For, first of all, not just anyone has such goodness of character as to be willing to do all the things by which he can benefit others out of humanity or charity alone, without a well-founded hope of receiving an equivalent return. And the things that can come to us from others are frequently such that we cannot without losing face ask that they be furnished to us for free. Often, too, it does not befit our person or fortune to owe such a benefit to another; and so, quite commonly, the other is unable to give, or we do not wish to receive, unless he receives an equivalent from us. It is not rare, moreover, for the manner in which others can serve our advantage to be concealed from them. Finally, since man's power, which is surely finite, cannot extend itself in the same way to all at the same time, it surely agrees with reason that such actions as have not yet been claimed by prior obligations be awarded to those who have through pacts sought a prior right to them for themselves. Therefore, in order that mutual duties among men—which are the fruit of sociality— might be exercised more frequently and according to certain rules, as it were, it was necessary for men themselves to agree with one another about such things as they would have to furnish each other, which someone could not always promise himself for certain from the law of humanity alone. And so it had to be determined in advance what someone should furnish another, and what he should in turn expect and demand by his own right.

It is understood from these things how the duties of humanity or charity differ from those that are required because of a right properly speaking, and which are therefore regulated by justice in the strict sense. Namely, the former are owed not from express or implicit pacts, but solely from the obligation enjoined on all men whatever by nature itself. But the things which I owe another from pacts and agreements, these I owe for the reason that he has acquired a new right against me from my own consent. There is also the fact that whatever I have settled upon in my agreements with another, I did not so much on account of his advantage as my own, while in duties of humanity the opposite is the case. For although the exercise of these duties is necessary in general so that men can live profitably with one another and, therefore, advantage redounds also on the one who exercises them (in that he can promise himself the same from others); still, a person exercises humanity in a particular instance not on account of himself but for the sake of the one who receives the benefit. For whenever private advantage is sought from a benefit it immediately loses its name and character.

Thus the law of humanity or charity, and pacts, together supply the duties and guarantees men have toward one another, as it were, in that the things that either commonly do not, or that cannot, proceed from charity are secured through pacts, and where these have no place charity enters in. And although it is up to each person to decide which pacts, and what kind, are entered into by individual men, the law of nature has nonetheless generally and indefinitely prescribed that they somehow exist among men, insofar as sociality and peace cannot be preserved among men without them. . . .

2. Now if any pacts are entered into among men, the sociable nature of man requires that they be religiously observed. For if it required less than this the greatest part of the utility arising for humankind from the reciprocal exchange of duties

would be lost. . . . Also, unless it were necessary to keep promises, one could by no means count firmly on other men's assistance. And indeed, the most just causes of quarrels and of war appropriately spring from trust betrayed. For when I have furnished something because of a pact, and the other fails to keep faith, my thing or deed has been lost to me in vain. On the other hand, if I have not yet actually furnished anything, it is nonetheless bothersome to have my plans and intentions disturbed, since I could have looked after my things in another way if the other had not made himself available to me. Also, I do not deserve to be considered a laughingstock because I believed another to be a sensible and a good man. Therefore, it is a most sacred precept of the natural law, and one that regulates the grace, the measure, and the order of human life in general, that "Everyone should keep his given word, or fulfill his promises and pacts." . . .

3. Moreover, since we acquire through pacts, especially express ones, an additional obligation that we otherwise did not have through nature itself—at least so definitely—it seems appropriate at this point to set out the chief distinctions between obligations. Thus, some obligations are *connate*, others *adventitious*. . . . The former are those that inhere in all men by virtue of the fact that they are animals endowed with reason, or that accompany rational nature itself, as such. . . . *Adventitious obligations are* those placed upon men, with their express or presumed consent, because of an antecedent human deed.

4. *Among congenital* obligations the chief one is that which lies on all men with respect to God, the supreme ruler of this universe; by its power we are bound to venerate Him and to be submissive to His sovereignty and laws. If anyone violates this obligation in its entirety he is guilty of the shameful sin of atheism. This happens if someone either denies that God Himself exists, or does not admit that He cares for human affairs. . . .

But it is most false that all sovereignty is constituted by the consent of those who are subject to it. For this is actually true only of human sovereignty, where our faculty to resist another who is naturally our equal is not extinguished except by our consent and by a pact. But who would say that God does not have the right to command His own creature unless it has of itself consented to His sovereignty? . . .

Chapter 5

ON THE NATURE OF PROMISES
AND PACTS IN GENERAL

1. We must examine further now the manner in which obligations not congenital to man arise for him thereafter from some act of his, and how, by virtue of this act, there also springs up in others a certain right which they were formerly lacking. For these two things follow one another in such a way that whenever an obligation arises in one person a corresponding right springs up in another, since it is impossible to understand how I can be obligated to furnish something unless someone is able to demand it or, at least, properly to receive it from me. Yet the reverse, that a right in one person is immediately followed by an obligation in another, is not always the case (as, for example, while there is in rulers a right to exact punishment, the guilty are not obligated to submit to it), unless we are willing to say the following: A right, if taken narrowly as a faculty and competence to have something, always corresponds to an obligation in another; not always, however, if it denotes a faculty to do something. It is certain, therefore, that adventitious obligations arise either from a unilateral [*monopleurō*]or a bilateral [*dipleurō*] act, the former being a gratuitous promise and the latter a pact.

2. Now since everyone grants that rights are transferred to others through promises and pacts, we will first examine Hobbes's opinion . . . regarding the transfer of a right.[5] Having inferred from the natural state posited by him that everyone naturally has a right to everything, and having shown, besides, that the exercise of this right would lead to a war of all against all (a state very little suited for men's preservation), Hobbes concludes that reason, by ordering men to leave that state for one of peace (which is incompatible with everyone's right to all things), likewise orders them to give up a certain part of that right to all things. But according to Hobbes, a person gives up his right either by simply "renouncing" it or by "transferring" it to another. The former occurs when he declares with suitable signs his willingness that it be no longer licit for him to do a certain thing which he formerly had a right to do; and the latter when, with suitable signs, he declares to another willing to receive that right from him, his willingness that it be no longer licit for him to resist the other in the doing of a certain thing which he formerly had as much of a right to resist. Hobbes concludes from this that "the transference of a right consists solely in non-resistance," or that one who transfers a right to another in a natural state does not give the other a new right which he did not have before, but only renounces his own right to resist the other in the voluntary exercise of his.

Hobbes proves this from his hypothesis as follows. Since the one to whom the

---

[5] De Cive, II,3.

right is said to be transferred already had before its transfer a right to all things, it was not possible to give him a new right; rather, the just resistance of the one transferring the right, on account of which the other could not enjoy his right, is eliminated. Therefore, for someone in a natural state to acquire a right means only that he can enjoy his primitive right securely and without justified interference. For example, if someone in a natural state has sold his farm to another, or given it to him as a gift, he takes away the right to that farm from himself alone and not also from others; in other words, he declares his own intention not to resist or impede the other in his plans to enjoy the farm, but does no prejudice thereby to any of the rest, who retain their original right to that farm.

3. But insofar as we have shown above that this Hobbesian state is not at all natural to man (who is destined for a social life), so do we also not acknowledge its consequent, namely, a kind of right to all things, which man had or could have had, and which has a certain effect upon other men. To understand this point more thoroughly one must know that a right in the proper sense is not just any natural faculty of doing something, but only such as involves a certain moral effect on others who are of the same nature as I. Thus, in Aesop's fable, the horse had a natural faculty of grazing in the meadow, and the stag the same, but because these faculties of theirs had no effect upon the other, neither of them had a right. So also a man, when he puts insensate things or brutes to his own use, exercises only a purely natural faculty, at least if it is considered strictly in reference to the things and animals he uses, without regard to other men. But this faculty acquires the nature of a right, properly speaking, only at the point when it morally affects the rest of men in such a way that they ought not to hinder him or use these things against his will. For it is surely inept to wish to distinguish that faculty by calling it a right if everyone else can by virtue of an equal right hinder the one who wants to exercise it.

We admit, therefore, that man naturally has the faculty to employ for his own use whatever insensate things and brutes he wishes. But this faculty, considered precisely as such, cannot properly be called a right, both because these things are not obligated to avail themselves for man's use, and also because, on account of men's natural equality vis-à-vis one another, one person cannot rightly exclude the rest from such things unless he has secured a special privilege for himself from the express or presumed consent of others. Only when this has been done can he say correctly that he has a right to them. To put it more concisely: A right to all things previous to any human deed must be understood not exclusively but only indefinitely. We must imagine, that is, not that one person can acquire all things for himself by excluding the rest, but that before men have agreed among themselves about the division and assignment of things, it remains naturally indefinite what portion belongs to one of them and what to another. This same equality of men allows even less, however, that one person allege for himself by nature a right over any other. Instead, as will be shown at greater length in its proper place, no one has a right to rule another unless he has specially received it from that person's consent or some other antecedent deed.

4. It will become clearer in what the transfer and acquisition of a right properly consist, if we say in advance that some rights regard men and others things,

and that this latter right over things is either original or derivative. One acquires a right over men if someone either expressly or tacitly consents to my being able to prescribe to him what he ought to do, suffer, or omit, thereby obligating himself to strive on his own to fulfill my will, and at the same time, granting me the authority to compel him with a fear of evil if he proves to be reluctant. One acquires an original right over a thing when all others either expressly or tacitly renounce their faculty (which was formerly the equal of his) to make use of it. But once an original right has been established and, thereby, the primitive faculty over things taken away, the transfer of a right takes away something which I had and gives it to someone else who did not have it before. Hence, it appears incongruent to say that the transfer of a right consists solely in non-resistance. For even though non-resistance is a consequence of performing one's obligation, this negative term by no means expresses the force of obligation springing from the transfer of a right, a force that properly contains an internal inclination to carry out one's agreements.

The example attached to this by Hobbes does not square with the matter. For besides the fact that it would be absurd to call it a sale when I alone have given up my claim to some thing, while everyone else retains his unimpaired, even Hobbes himself thinks that the ownership of things began with civil sovereignty and after the elimination of the natural state. Accordingly, in the natural state no one could call a farm his own, nor, as a result, sell it. Indeed, Hobbes should have said something like this: Since in the pure natural state things belonged no more to one man than to another, if anyone wished to enjoy some thing alone it was necessary for the others to renounce their use of it. If they did this without recompense then the transaction amounted to a gift, but if it involved some burden it was called a contract. But say that only one person had renounced his own faculty over that thing, this would in no way have prejudiced the rest, and so he alone, but not the others, could thereafter have been excluded from its use.

Chapter 6

ON THE CONSENT REQUIRED
IN PROMISES AND PACTS

1. Since promises and pacts as a rule restrict our freedom and impose on us a burden of necessarily doing something we were formerly free to do or not do, there is no more appropriate reason that someone cannot rightly complain about having

to carry such a burden than the fact that he himself has previously consented to it and willingly taken upon himself what he was formerly able to refuse.

2. This consent, though as a rule expressed through spoken, written, and gestured signs, is sometimes inferred without them from the business itself and from other circumstances. Even the absence of signs, or silence, when considered in the context of certain circumstances, can sometimes take the place of a sign expressing consent. . . . But here it is necessary for the present condition of things to be arranged in such a way that every element thereof conspires, as it were, toward the presumption of consent, and no plausible conjecture leads to a different conclusion. For it would be quite brazen, otherwise, to impose an obligation on someone on the basis of any sort of evidence whatsoever.

We understand from these things in what the nature of a *tacit pact* properly consists. Such a pact occurs when consent is expressed not by such signs as are regularly accepted in human transactions, but when it is clearly inferred from the nature of the affair and other circumstances. Quite frequently, when a principal pact has been entered into by express consent, we understand from the nature of the affair itself that a tacit pact has been added to and flows from it. Similarly, it is very common to understand pacts to contain certain tacit exceptions and conditions. Yet no more of these should be allowed than the general character of human intercourse can bear, lest they render pacts too slippery and uncertain.

The following can be examples of a tacit pact. Suppose a foreigner comes as a friend to some state that commonly treats outsiders in a friendly manner. He is thought to have promised tacitly, and by his very act of coming, to conform himself to that state's laws as they pertain to his status as soon as he has come to know that such laws apply generally to all who desire to go about in that state's territory, even though he has never given an express promise to that effect. And for this reason he is in turn tacitly promised by the state that it will temporarily defend him and administer justice on his behalf.

Also, when a person's affairs are conducted in his absence without an express order from him, there is a tacit pact to the effect that, after someone has devoted his own efforts to improving another's things, the latter is bound to consider them as self-incurred expenses. For it is surely presumed that, had he known of this, he would have expressly consented to it.

Likewise, one who sits down at a table in an inn is understood from his act to have consented to pay for the food, even though he has not spoken about its price with the host. For it is well known that no one is given food there free of charge. In the same way, the obligation between a guardian and his ward also originates in a tacit contract. . . .

Accessory pacts can be exemplified by the following. For instance, if someone strikes a bargain with another person about safe entry to some place, he is thought to have agreed as well about his exit (even though there was never any express mention of this), because otherwise the former pact could not be acted upon. Similarly, one who consents by means of a pact to the use of his state's marketplaces by foreigners is understood also to have consented to their taking out with them whatever goods they have purchased there; just as it would be absurd, for instance, to sell someone a field but be unwilling to let him possess it in that place, demanding, instead, that he take it somewhere else. Also, a person who leases someone a room in his house is deemed to have granted him the use of those parts he cannot do without, such as the doors and hallways leading to the room, at least to the point of being able to go in and out.

Examples of tacit conditions and exceptions occur in a wide variety of places. In general, however, we must observe that all of them should be interpreted strictly, and that they are valid only insofar as they can be clearly inferred from the agreement. . . . For otherwise it would be easy to impose a bothersome obligation on someone against his will, and most pacts could be either subverted or eluded by indulging excessively in tacit exceptions and conditions. . . .

3. For someone to be able seriously and clearly to consent to something, it is above all required that he have the use of reason to such an extent that he understands the present affair, whether it is to his advantage, and whether he can do what is required of him; and, having weighed these things, can express his consent with sufficient signs. From this it follows that the promises of infants, as well as those of madmen and the demented, amount to nothing. However, it must be observed about madmen in particular that their actions are thought to have no moral effect only while their madness lasts. So long as their madness is punctuated by intervals of lucidity, nothing prevents them from being able validly to obligate themselves until the time when they are left without the use of reason because of their illness. For the recurring madness suspends their obligation to do or furnish something of themselves until they can again consider their actions their own. And so the common saying of lawyers that "the coming on of madness does not negate any affair properly conducted earlier on" must be understood to refer to affairs that have been concluded all together and at once, such as a Will and Testament which, once it has been properly drafted, stands until it is withdrawn by a sufficient declaration of a contrary will—something that cannot happen during madness. . . .

Chapter 7

ON THE MATTER OF PROMISES AND PACTS

1. Next we must see about the subject matter of promises and pacts, that is, the things to which we can voluntarily obligate ourselves by promising and making pacts. This requires that we have both a physical and a moral faculty to produce the thing or action, that is, that it not be beyond our strength to produce it and that we not be prohibited from accomplishing it by some law. For when some-

thing has been placed within my strength and I am left with the faculty to make a decision about it, nothing at all prevents me from voluntarily laying upon myself the necessity of furnishing it to another, when it would have a use for human life. On the other hand, it is pointless to contract an obligation with respect to things that either exceed our strength or cannot be done without violating a stronger obligation, since it would lack any direct and legitimate effect.

6. Furthermore, for an obligation to arise from a promise or a pact, it is required that there be in us a moral faculty to perform the thing agreed upon. It is because of the lack of such a faculty that we cannot obligate ourselves to a thing in itself illicit. For a promise receives its force from the authority of the promisor, and extends no farther; that is, no one is able to bind himself validly beyond the range of his authority. But someone who prohibits an action by law clearly takes away the authority to undertake it, and to accept for oneself an obligation to perform it. For it implies a contradiction that one should, by virtue of an obligation fixed by laws, necessarily do something that is to be omitted on account of the same laws. And our will, which is subject to laws, cannot by its own act alone evade their force. Hence someone who promises things that are illicit sins, and one who does them sins twice. . . .

BOOK IV

Chapter 3

ON HUMANKIND'S FACULTY OVER THINGS

1. The constitution of the human body is such that it cannot be preserved out of its own internal substance but requires certain things taken from outside itself for its nourishment, and to fortify it against things which are destructive of its frame. Most things, indeed, are useful to man by enabling him to live a fuller and more pleasant life. . . . Accordingly, many reciprocal transactions take place among men, providing opportunities for many controversies and disputes. And these, lest they disturb the tranquillity of the human race, are both the focus of the natural law's cautions and, we find, the main object of concern in most peoples' civil laws.

To develop all these matters in the proper order we must first examine the right by which the race of mortals disposes of animals and other things for its own use, or for its advantage and pleasure, and in particular the foundation on which this faculty rests in relation to both the Creator and the things themselves, which man not only uses but often also wastes and consumes.

2. Therefore, the Great and Good God, since He is the creator and preserver of this universe, without a doubt also has, as it were, supreme dominion over all things, and these belong to Him so strictly that no one can pretend any sort of right to them without His will. . . . Yet because He Himself has no need of any thing outside Himself, and His happiness cannot be increased through other things, His goodness made Him ready to allow His creatures to derive advantages from one another. . . .

But however this may be, it is quite certain that man makes use of other creatures with the Deity's consent. This is understood from the fact that he cannot preserve his life without doing so, and that some of them seem spontaneously, as it were, to offer themselves to him. For since it pleased God to bestow life on man, He is also understood to have granted him the use of those things without which His gift cannot be preserved. . . . Besides, there is also the authority of the Sacred Scriptures, which expressly declare that God bestowed on man a faculty not over plants only, but also over animate things born in the heavens, on the earth, and in the sea. . . .

This grant has no prescriptive force, however, but is merely a gracious privilege that one is able to use as much as one pleases without being bound to exercise it in all respects. For otherwise a man would sin against the divine law by setting an animal free or neglecting an opportunity to reassert his authority over it. And this no sane man will admit. Yet this faculty of man over brutes is characteristically different from the sovereignty exercised over men, because brutes do not obey it, on their part, as if obligated to, and it is also far more absolute than sovereignty over men. . . .

3. But if we consider that faculty of humankind in relation to things and animals themselves, it is clearly possible to argue from both man's nature and the Creator's grant that man's use and consumption of them involves no injury. For it seems improbable that the most good and most wise Creator has placed man, who is the first among earthly creatures, under the necessity of being unable to preserve himself unless he injures another—something that can surely not be dissociated from sin. Add to this God's express grant, and all scruples are removed, especially those that can arise from the slaughter of animals. The impression that this practice is somewhat barbarous is sufficiently removed by the simple realization that the Creator has assigned animals to such a condition, and that He has given the tribe of mortals a faculty in the exercise of which (whether it be delegated or granted by Him) they do no injury. . . .

Chapter 4

ON THE ORIGIN OF DOMINION

1. It was due to another principle, however, that this faculty of humankind over things began to have an effect in relation to other men (for no ownership of men should be opposed to the most eminent right of God . . .), or that dominion (through which a thing belongs to one person and not to another) came about from this indefinite right. We must, before dealing with it, preface that ownership and communion are moral qualities that do not physically and intrinsically affect things themselves but produce only a moral effect in relation to other men, and that these qualities—like the rest of this sort—refer their birth back to imposition. Hence it is foolish to ask whether ownership of things is by nature or, indeed, the result of institution. For it is obvious that it arises from the imposition of men, and that whether ownership is added to or withdrawn from things, their physical substance experiences no change.

2. Next, we must carefully consider what communion is, as well as ownership or dominion. The word 'communion' is taken either *negatively* or *positively*. Things are said to be common in the former manner insofar as they are considered previous to any human deed which declares them to belong more especially to this person than to that. They are also, in the same sense, said to be *no one's*, that is, in the negative sense of not yet having been assigned to anyone in particular rather than the privative sense of being incapable of such assignation. And they are referred to as common stock available to all. Things common in the other sense, however, differ from those that are one's own in this point only, that they belong to several persons in the same manner while the latter belong only to one.

Now ownership or dominion is the right by which a thing's substance, as it were, belongs to someone in such a way that it does not belong wholly to another man in the same manner. For dominion and ownership are to us one and the same, even though some people call this right 'ownership' when it is disjoined and separated from usufruct, and 'dominion' when joined thereto—a distinction not always observed, however. Similarly, others are overly subtle in understanding ownership as the thing itself under the quality whereby it belongs to me and not to another, and dominion as a right of free disposition over the thing which issues from ownership as a kind of effect, so that dominion is lodged in the person while ownership seems rather to be lodged in the thing. . . .

Here it is false that dominion is, as it were, the effect of ownership, since if one wishes to distinguish them in such a way at all things are rather the reverse. For the right from which things themselves are also assigned some kind of extrinsic denomination properly inheres in man. And this is well enough understood from the fact that once that right has been extinguished together with man, the things cease to be anyone's own, without any change in their substance or physical qualities.

Now the force of dominion is such that we can dispose at our discretion of the things that belong to us as our own and prevent any others from using them unless they have obtained from us a specific right for themselves through pacts; and such, indeed, that while the things are ours they cannot belong wholly to someone else in the same manner. I say "in the same manner," for there is nothing to prevent the same thing from being held differently by different people—as is in fact quite customary. Thus, the state has an eminent, the field-owner a direct, and the tenant [*emphuteuta*] a useful dominion over the same field. I also add "wholly," for several people can hold the same thing in the same way, albeit not in its entirety but each according to a certain proportion. This happens in the case of goods that are possessed in an undivided fashion by several persons, each of whom has the same kind of dominion with respect to them. . . .

3. It is clear from this that positive communion implies the exclusion of others from things said to be common, just as ownership implies their exclusion from things said to be one's own; and, therefore, that it presupposes the existence of more than one man in the world. Hence, just as if there had been only one man in the world, things could in no way have been said to be his own, so too, things from whose use no man is excluded, or that do not belong more to one man than to any other, should be called common in the former [negative] and not in the latter [positive] sense.

This makes plain the extent to which dominion over things can be attributed to Adam while he was alone on the earth. Even though the vastness of the earth and his own modest needs made it necessary for him to use but a small portion of things, no one else's right prevented him from taking for his own use whatever things were available if he wished and could easily do so. His right over things was therefore different from the kind of dominion now established among men. One could call it an indefinite dominion, not formal but concessive, not actual but potential. It had the same effect that dominion does now, namely, of using things as one pleases. Yet it was not dominion, properly speaking, because there was no one else then against whom to exert that effect—though it could change into dominion after more men were born. And so things were neither his own nor common to Adam so long as he alone existed. For community involves a sharer of one's possessions, while ownership connotes the exclusion of another's right to the same thing. This means that neither of them can be understood before more men than one had begun to exist.

4. Now it must also be carefully observed that the grant whereby God bestowed on men the use of earthly things is not the direct cause of dominion, insofar as this has an effect on other men (something also proven by the fact that brute animals use and consume things—surely with God's consent—even though there is no dominion among them), but that dominion absolutely presupposes a human deed and some tacit or express pact. God did, indeed, allow man to take the earth, its products, and animals for his own use and advantage, giving him an indefinite right to these things. Yet the manner, degree, and extent of this authority were left to men's discretion and disposition. That is, it was left to them whether to confine it within certain limits or none; likewise, whether they wanted everyone to have authority over all things or only over a certain part of them; or whether to assign everyone his own portion so that, content therewith, he could pretend no right to anything else. . . .

Hence it is pointless to argue over whether God gave dominion over things to the first men as representatives of humankind's collective persona, or whether He assigned it to them specifically as individuals so that they would be lords of the entire world by virtue of their own proper right, with the rest of mortals owing them their own dominions. For that divine grant merely rendered men more certain of the Deity's bounty toward them, and of the fact that their disposal of other creatures for their own use and service was according to His will. But the specific provisions to prevent the use of this right from giving rise to discord among men were left to men themselves to determine according to the guidance of sound reason. God Himself by no means prescribed some universal manner of possessing things that all men were bound to observe. And so things were made neither proper nor common (in a positive communion) by an express mandate of God, but were constituted as such by men later on as the tranquillity of human society required. . . .

There is no precept of the natural law commanding men to appropriate all things in such a way that each person is assigned his own separate portion. Even though the natural law clearly indicated that such an assignation of things to individuals be introduced by human agreement, insofar as this would be useful to human society, it nonetheless left it up to men's judgment whether to make all things proper or only certain ones, and whether to possess some things in common while leaving the rest available to all, yet in such a way that no one could claim them for himself alone. And so the law of nature is understood to approve all agreements men have introduced concerning things, provided they do not involve a contradiction or disturb society.

Therefore the ownership of things flows directly from a tacit or express agreement of men. For even though nothing remained after God's grant than for a man to occupy things, still, for such an occupation or seizure to be understood to exclude the right of others to the same thing, an agreement was surely required. The fact that sound reason has recommended the introduction of separate dominions does not prevent their being originally derived from a human pact.

5. Given such premises as these, it is plain that before all human agreements there was a communion of all things. Not a positive communion, of course, but a negative one; that is, all things were available to all and belonged no more to one person than to another. But since things are not useful to men unless at least their fruits are laid hold of, and indeed, since this is done in vain if others are in turn allowed to seize what we have already actively intended for our own use, the first agreement among mortals concerning things is understood to have been this: Whatever anyone had taken from the common stock or its fruits, with the intention of using it for himself, would not be seized from him by another. . . . This can be shown by the example of wild beasts, among which, it is certain, none can allege a special right to anything before the others. Whatever any of them encounters first it immediately snatches up and eats, and if any of them has set aside certain things for its future use, the rest are not prohibited from seizing them, because there is no agreement among wild beasts giving the one who first lays hold of a thing a special right to it. . . .

6. Now men left this negative or primeval communion of things and, by pacts, established separate dominions; not all at once, of course, but gradually and as the condition of things or the character and number of men seemed to require. For example, formerly among the Scythians, flocks and household goods could pass into ownership while fields remained in the primeval communion. . . . Indeed, the peace and tranquillity of humankind, with which the law of nature is chiefly concerned, has suggested in no obscure terms what arrangements would be most suitable for men to establish in this regard. For the peace of humankind (at least after men had multiplied and improved their life by cultivation) did not admit that everyone should retain an equal authority over everything, or that all things should be accessible to all and indiscriminately available for anyone to use. . . . This is because the striving of many persons after the same thing, which did not suffice for all of them at the same time, would certainly have given rise to countless conflicts, and because the character of most things is such that they can serve only one person at a time.

The order in which and the reasons that things came to be owned can, I think, be understood as follows. Most things that offer men an immediate use by serving as food or clothing for the body are not everywhere produced in such abundance by nature, apart from culture, that there is enough for everyone. Therefore, if two or more persons had need of some thing that did not suffice for them all and each wished to acquire it for himself, a perfect opportunity was given for quarrels and wars. . . . Moreover, most things require human labor and improvement to produce them or to make them fit for use. But here it was inappropriate that someone who had contributed no work should have as much of a right to these things as the one by whose industry they were either produced or suitably fashioned. Therefore, in the interest of human peace, ownership of movable things, especially those requiring human labor and cultivation, and among immovable things those (like houses) that offer men an immediate use, was introduced as soon as men had multiplied, so that they would either belong separately to individual persons or, in the case of many individuals, to those who had entered together into a positive communion with respect to them by means of a special agreement. Furthermore, even though there appears to be some reason in the case of these things why it is more appropriate for them to belong to some persons than to others, still the former's dominion (which excludes the rest) had surely to be confirmed by at least a tacit pact also containing a tacit renunciation by the rest that they would pretend no further right to the things assigned to one person, on the pretext that the earth, as men's common abode, had furnished these things with their substance or their sustenance.

As for the immovable things produced by nature apart from human industry (that is, fields), since their great spaciousness more than sufficed for the first few men, only so much of them was occupied at the beginning as men judged suitable for their current uses. The rest were left in a state of primeval or negative communion, so that anyone who pleased could occupy them in the future. Here, then, a pact is understood to have intervened, according to which fields that had been assigned to anyone by the express agreement of other men, or that other men were deemed to have tacitly yielded by quietly allowing one person to enjoy them while they laid similar claims to other fields, would belong to those who cultivated them. And the remaining fields would go to those who occupied them thereafter. . . .

9. Let us now carefully consider the opinion of Grotius . . . , setting aside, however, those things which he mixes in against the received decrees of our churches, which have already been sufficiently criticized by others. "God," he says, "conferred a right to the things of this inferior nature on humankind in general as soon as the world was fashioned, and again when it was repaired after the flood."[1] This we admit in the following sense, that God allowed the race of men to use these earthly things *in general*; that is, He did not at the same time determine whether they should possess all things or some of them, in a divided or an undivided fashion, but left it up to men to decide, so that they themselves might dispose of the matter as seemed to conduce to peace. It should by no means be believed, however, that some positive communion was from the beginning instituted by God, from which men later on withdrew at their own discretion; but rather that, as far as God was concerned, those things were made available for all men to use. So long as the very bodies of things had not yet been assigned to certain ones among them, there was a tacit agreement that each man could seize for his own uses, especially from the fruits of things, what he wanted, and consume those which could

---

[1] *On the Law of War and Peace*, II,2,2.

be consumed. And such universal use of things somehow served in place of ownership; and what someone had seized in this way could not be taken from him by another except through injury. . . .

Grotius says rightly, however, that if that negative communion is to persist without disturbing the common peace, men must live in great simplicity, content to eat things that grow by themselves, to live in caves, and to go about with their bodies either naked or covered with the bark of trees or the hides of beasts. If they prefer a more discriminating kind of life, whose advantages must be procured through industry, there is surely need for ownership of things. But when he adds that communion could have lasted "if men had lived among themselves with a certain mutual and exceptional charity," he confuses negative with positive communion. . . . For this cannot be established and preserved except among a few, and those endowed with an exceptional modesty of mind. It is foolish labor, when men have dispersed into distant places, to gather fruits into one place and distribute them from a common mass. And in a great multitude of men one necessarily finds many who, on account of a lack of justice, and greediness [*pleonexian*], do not wish to preserve the requisite equality in either labor or the consumption of fruits. . . . But it is foolish to believe that men ever instituted or wished to institute such a communion after they had dispersed into more than one family. . . .

Finally, Grotius is right to say that "at the beginning things did not enter into ownership by an act of the mind alone," or by thinking.[2] For others were not able to know what someone wished to be his own, so that they might abstain from it, and many persons were able to wish the same thing. Therefore, there was need for an external act or apprehension which, in order to produce a moral effect (that is, an obligation on the part of others to abstain from a thing that has been seized by another), required an antecedent pact; and an express one at that, when several persons divided the things available to all among themselves at the same time. But a tacit pact sufficed when things that were left vacant by the first dividers of things were occupied. For it is understood to have been agreed among these that whatever things had not be assigned to a certain person in the first division of things, they would concede to the one who had first occupied them.

10. Most of the more recent authors differ with us concerning the origin of dominion. Let us see what strength there is in their arguments. They acknowledge that communion is spoken of in two senses, either as something owned undividedly by many which furnishes individuals with a common use, or as something to which ownership is altogether unknown, and which is available for the indiscriminate use of all. But then they withdraw not only the first kind of communion from things at the beginning, as we do too, but also the second, therefore denying that at the beginning, when ownership was entirely excluded, all things lay open to the use of anyone without distinction, and—what follows from this—that separate dominions arose originally from division and occupation. The reason they give is this: "Whatever kind and amount of right the first mortal had over created things he received entirely from the Creator. Now if he had acquired the bare faculty of using things, without ownership thereof, his posterity could not have assumed his own-

---

[2] *On the Law of War and Peace*, II,2,2.

ership without being guilty of greediness [*pleonexian*] and arrogating to themselves something which the Creator had forbidden mortals to use."

To this it is easy to respond from what we have said above. No doubt, the Deity granted man a right over things, but an indefinite, general, and indifferent right, one restricted neither to ownership nor communion, and one that men could convert into a particular form, as it were, according to the recommendations of reason and necessity. Hence, also, primeval communion does not denote some bare usufruct, to the exclusion of ownership, but something that men can agree to leave as much for ownership as for positive communion.

Nor does it follow that because the first man did not receive or assume a right over things under a formal principle of ownership, his posterity could not exercise it under that formality. Moreover, the divine grant described in the Sacred Scriptures does not designate some definite manner of dominion but an indefinite right to use things in accord with reason and necessity, a right that can be exercised as much in negative communion as in ownership. It is a bad inference to say: Men received a right over things by a divine grant; therefore, ownership did not arise from occupation and division. For the divine grant merely assured man that when he consumed the things created by the Deity to satisfy his necessities, it was in accordance with the Deity's will.

But dominion properly speaking had to produce an effect on other men, so that no one seized the things that were already assigned to one person. And here a human deed was undoubtedly required to make known to others what belonged to someone else, so that they could leave it alone. A theater is made available by a state for all its citizens to use. Yet, for this or that person to obtain at showtime a certain place from which he should not be expelled by another requires a bodily act, or occupancy; in fact, it is also possible for individual citizens to acquire a permanent place for themselves by consent of the state. Thus all things are understood to be available to everyone before the occurrence of a human deed capable of introducing dominion, to be negatively common to all in the sense of belonging no more to one person than to another. But when a division has been instituted by an express pact, or occupancy granted by a tacit one, they pass from negative communion into ownership.

But if some wish to stretch this to the point of saying, "The dominion which God Himself conferred on men before any antecedent human deed is understood as potential dominion only, or as the authority to occupy and possess, and therefore as dominion of the first actuality through which one passes into possession and, from possession, into dominion as such, which is of the second actuality," then their opinion differs only verbally and not substantially from ours. Yet they are not accurate enough in calling the authority to occupy things dominion of the first actuality, and dominion preceded by possession that of the second actuality. For the authority to acquire a right for oneself, and the right itself as something already inherent as a habit, even apart from its operation or exercise, are different, just as there is a difference between being a potential musician and not singing after one has been trained in the habit of music.

Nor, since the two are not a close enough match, can that potential dominion be clarified by the example of an inheritance, "dominion over which passes right after the testator's death, from habit or potency, to an heir, who receives it directly and immediately without [actually] seizing it." For besides the fact that "from habit" and "from potency" are different, a certain fiction of the civil law also comes into play here. The transfer of dominion from one person to another naturally requires not only that the former give it up, but also that the latter accept it. However, since it pleases the laws to make the testator's wishes changeable up to his very last breath, and to allow them to remain secret until after his death, it sustains the deceased's wishes concerning the transfer of his goods to the heir up to the point when the heir has signified his acceptance thereof. Or, if one so prefers, it extends the heir's acceptance all the way back to the testator's final breath, by which his wishes are confirmed, so that the goods are understood to be transferred immediately, from hand to hand, to the heir. This fiction produces the effect of dominion in the heir to the extent that he can claim the inherited thing even before he has actually come to possess it; and without it, an heir would have no more dominion over an inheritance before his accession to it than the recipient of a grant before his acceptance thereof. Hence, also, those who concern themselves with the natural law, from which the fictions of the civil law are generally excluded, will in no way admit any potential possession opposed to an actual one; nor will they call the bare right and power of acquiring possession for oneself possession. . . .

11. Many writers think it good here to appeal to the authority of sacred history, which supposedly establishes that this kind of [negative] communion never existed. . . .

Now it is evident from the above what replies can be made to these things. Namely, the divine grant conferred on man only the right to apply creatures to his own uses, a right that is indifferent toward positive communion and ownership, which are rights having an effect against other men. Hence when others add that "Common dominion over things was conferred on humankind by God Himself upon the condition that they would establish and divide it up as private dominion, and that it therefore neither can nor should be conceived without a relation to private dominion, which was to be established so as to be consistent with rational and social nature," we can without inconvenience interpret it in support of our own opinion. God's grant undoubtedly established things in a negative communion from the beginning. But since this would have been unsuited for the preservation of a peaceful society after humankind had multiplied and life had begun to be cultivated through industry, men easily understood it to please the Deity that distinct dominions over things be introduced. For these to be actually established, there surely had to be an antecedent human deed and agreement. For these two things are not to be opposed to one another: Something has been established by the divine will, and an agreement of men has preceded so as to introduce it into act; just as there is no conflict between these two things: God wishes humankind to be propagated through marriages and not through random lying together, and an antecedent pact is required so that marriages actually exist among certain men.

Furthermore, since positive community and ownership involve a relation to other men, it is not at all accurate to say that all created things were Adam's own, but only this, that he was owner of all things in a concessive but not a formal sense, that is insofar as there was no one's right to hinder him from being able to convert all things to his own uses if there was need. After a dear companion had been joined to him by God, they began to make joint use of that indefinite right over things, since they were linked by the closest of bonds—which is why, even today, the merging of goods among spouses is an accepted practice among many nations.

Nor was there need for distinct dominions so long as Adam's offspring, being of a tender age, had to be nurtured by a parent or still remained within his family. For the fact that an offspring may have found it necessary at that time to conform himself to his father's will in the use of things was due not to the force of dominion but that of paternal sovereignty. Therefore, distinct dominions began only when, with the father's consent, children set about establishing separate families for themselves—a thing brought about, without doubt, by the ancient rivalry of brothers, and in order that each should enjoy the fruit of his own industry and bear the burden of his own idleness.

Still, it is also not to be believed that the whole sphere of the earth was immediately divided among those very few mortals, and that all things passed under ownership all at once. Rather it was sufficient at the beginning that those things became owned which either furnish an immediate use that cannot be divided among many, such as clothes, dwellings, and fruits gathered for nourishment; or which require some industry or cultivation, such as tools or utensils, flocks, and fields. The remaining things came under ownership little by little, as men's desires or numbers recommended. Thus pastures remained in the primeval communion for a long time until, with the multiplication of flocks and the rise of quarrels, it was in the interest of peace that they too be divided.

Moreover, the argument alleging that "there is no place for occupation where things somehow belong in their entirety to a whole group" is valid against those who pass off as the primeval state of things some positive communion in which it is of course not possible for some thing to be occupied by individuals with the exclusion of the entire group. But our primeval state of things is as different from positive communion as it is from ownership strictly speaking, and we assert that there is need for an antecedent pact, at least a tacit one, in order that occupation produce dominion.

12. Others derive the following account about the origin of dominion from the Sacred Scriptures: "God gave men's common dominion to the first humans as an undivided possession, insofar as they bore the persona of humankind; and in this sense it is still rightly said that dominion over the sphere of the earth and its things (insofar as they are suited to pass into ownership) belongs to humankind. But private dominion is not excluded through that common dominion, since the latter neither can nor should be conceived without a relation to private dominion, which was to be set up so as to agree with rational and social nature. But in Adam common dominion also went along with private dominion which, in the absence of any previous cession, excluded his own children." . . .

We will not enter into a quarrel with anyone here, at least over words, since what is for us the right to make use of created things, belonging to men by reason of a divine grant, may certainly be called common dominion so long as this common dominion, when considered in itself, is understood to have no effect on men in relation to one another. It has already been said above, concerning this, that men were able to be content with that right of using the things available to all; nor was it immediately necessary for divided dominions to be introduced so long as humankind consisted of some few and tolerated a simple and uncultivated life. Once it had multiplied and life's conveniences had been promoted by human industry, the necessity of preserving sociality recommended that dominions be introduced— in such a way, however, that things would not enter into ownership all at the same time, but successively as considerations of concord seemed to require. . . .

13. Let us also weigh the arguments of those who contend that primeval communion was impossible. . . . They say that "there neither should nor could have been such a communion in the state of innocence because, just as all order is consistent with right reason, so that most beautiful order of possessing the things whose dominion had been handed over to humankind by God was most agreeable to that state, in which abstention from another's things was deservedly allotted an illustrious name. Hence everyone's certain and separate possession of his own things was, like abstinence, sanctioned in the Decalogue, but the latter law was engraved upon men's minds even before the Fall."

Our response is, first, that it is not so clearly established what sort of life men would have led, as far as those externals are concerned, if they had remained in the primeval state free from sins, and therefore, whether a communion of things would have suited that life more than ownership. Next, we can also raise the question whether there is not a greater perfection of virtue in calmly enjoying with others the things available to all, and not seeking something for oneself in particular before the rest, than in abstaining from that which is another's. Finally, however things may be with the eternity of the natural law, it is obviously not necessary for all objects of this law, many of which arise later on from human agreements and institutions, to have always existed. Thus the law concerning homicide found no object while Adam alone existed; nor the law on adultery when there was no adult male beside himself; nor the law about theft before the division of things, and the law about false testimony before the institution of courts; nor the law about coveting houses when these were still caves, or about male and female slaves before slavery had been instituted; nor the law about honoring parents before Eve had given birth. . . .

They continue: "That communion was also not possible in the postlapsarian state; first of all, because it cannot even be conceived by the mind. For the laws of that communion are described by Grotius to be such that each man could immediately take for his own uses whatever things he wished, and consume whatever could be consumed. And such a use of a universal right then took the place of ownership, for what each person had thus taken could not be seized from him by another except by way of injury. But in this way ownership is set up in communion," and so a contradiction is involved, since it is the effect of ownership alone that a thing cannot be seized from someone by another.

But they needlessly create a difficulty where there is none. For primeval communion is one thing before every human deed and the use of any thing, when all things whatever simply belong no more to one person than to another, and thus equally to neither; but it is another when men begin to use the things available to all. For here, by reason of a previous pact, those things that each has taken for his own use become his own, since without this men would have to abstain from the use of all things. Hence in this moderated communion, as it were, the bodies of things themselves belong to no one, but their fruits become owned after being gathered together. Such a mixture of primeval communion with ownership can, I think, be conceived even by those with an average mental discernment: The oak tree was no one's, but the acorns that fell from it became his who had gathered them.

With this laid down, it is also easier to respond to that which they attach below. For they deny that "such a communion could have lasted even the shortest time and [say] that it was contrary to human or rational nature, bestial, and unsociable; and that it therefore furnishes no other use than to show from itself, as from an imagined hypothesis, the necessity of distinct dominion in a civil state." Now that communion, considered in its actual signification, as it were, could not last unless men were willing constantly to be hungry and to go about naked. But nothing prevented it from continuing with some admixture of ownership so long as there were not a very great number of men and they lived a simple life. It is certain, nonetheless, that the more men's numbers were increased and the more cultivated life began to be, the greater the necessity of subjecting more things to ownership. Hence peoples who are still closer to primeval communion, who maintain their life by means of herbs, roots, spontaneously growing fruits, hunting, and fishing, for example, with nothing else to their name except a hut and ordinary furnishings, are quite barbaric and simple.

Moreover, when we assert that all things were by nature negatively common, it is not as if we were saying that the law of nature commands the constant preservation of that state, but that things, considered apart from any antecedent human deed, were such as not to belong more to one person than to another. On the other hand, when we declare that that communion was left behind at the urging of reason, we do not go so far as to say that it was necessary for all things to pass into ownership at one moment, but rather as the disposition of men, things, and place required, and as seemed most convenient for preventing occasions for disputes. And so neither have we sinned against the law of nature by completely banishing primeval communion, nor have barbarians by still retaining many of its traces. . . .

14. It is clear from these things in what sense we are to take some people's assertion that "ownership and dominion belong to the natural law, properly speaking, which is inscribed on men's minds." Here it must be observed that the expression "this or that belongs to the natural law" has a different sense depending on whether it is uttered about some precept, properly speaking, or about some institution introduced into human life. Uttered in the former manner, it indicates that the law of nature commands something to be done or not done; in the latter, it indicates that sound reason recommends the establishment or reception of an institution among men from a general consideration of the condition of social life. (For institutions introduced on account of the particular advantage of this or that state are said to belong to the civil or positive law.) So when it is asked whether or not dominion refers its origin to the natural law, the focus is on the latter sense and not the former. That is, since the natural law's foundation is a social life, and indeed, since the native character of humanity shows clearly enough that among a multitude of men undertaking the improvement of life by means of various arts, a

peaceful and decorous society cannot exist without separate dominions over things, the introduction of these into human affairs thus in need of them was therefore proper and in accord with the aim of the natural law. When this has been done, the same law commands the observance of whatever things are conducive to the end of the dominion that has been instituted.

It was by no means necessary, however, according to some specific precept of the natural law, that all things everywhere pass under ownership from the very beginning of humankind; rather, ownership was introduced as the peace of mortals seemed to require it. But the precept of the natural law about abstaining from others' things exerted its force only when men had by agreement defined what was 'alien' to each person and what his 'own.' Before that time, it lay virtually hidden, as it were, in that general precept about observing pacts and not infringing on another's right. Nor is it absurd to say that the obligation to observe the law about abstaining from another's things is coeval with humankind, while the distinction between 'one's own' and 'another's' was introduced later on. Thus, we are often obligated to obey before we know what will be enjoined on us, as when we have been generally obligated to obey whatever some certain person will later on order us to do, or when several particular precepts can be subsumed under some general precept.

Chapter 6

ON OCCUPANCY

1. Our next task is to examine the ways in which dominion is acquired. These, following Grotius, are appropriately divided into *original* and *derivative*. The former are those by which ownership is initially introduced into some thing, the latter those by which dominion already established passes from one man to another. The original manner of acquisition is in turn either simply a way of initially acquiring dominion over some thing, or secondarily, a way by which what is already ours is somehow increased.

2. It has been sufficiently shown above that mortals, after resolving to leave their primeval communion, made a pact to assign each person his share of the common stock, either by means of parental authority, consent, lot, or, at times, by individual choice. Whatever things did not come under this primeval division, it was agreed, would go to the one who occupied them, that is, to the first person to apprehend them bodily with the intention of keeping them for himself. Hence, Grotius's statement . . . that "Formerly, when the human race was able to come

together, original acquisition could also take place through division, but now only through acquisition," must be explained as follows.[3] When the race of mortals first began to be divided into several families, separate dominions over things came from division; after that division, a vacant thing is originally acquired by whoever has occupied it, that is, by the one who has apprehended it before the rest or laid claim to it before them. . . .

3. Regarding the occupancy of immovable things, and especially of lands, we must consider separately the case where this is done by one person and that where it is done by several at once. A single person is taken to have occupied land when he cultivates it or marks it with certain boundaries. Yet these should not encompass more than a single family, even after multiplying significantly, can in all likelihood maintain. For if one man, for example, had been conveyed with his spouse to a vacant island sufficient for supporting myriads of people, it would be impudent for him to claim the whole thing for himself by virtue of his title of occupancy, and to try to expel those who may have landed on a different part of the island. . . .

4. Now it must be observed concerning occupancy by a whole that it establishes the dominion of the entire group as such over everything contained in that tract, not over immovable things only but also those that are movable and self-moving. In the latter case, it establishes at least a right to lay hold of them to the exclusion of others. This universal dominion is so very different from the dominion of private individuals that while the latter can pass even to an outsider, the former is retained within the same state. . . .

But it is not necessary for all things occupied in this universal manner to be ascribed to individual and private owners. Therefore, if anything in such a region is found without a private owner, it should not immediately be considered vacant, so that anyone can occupy it as his own, but it will be understood to belong to the people as a whole. And this way of thinking ought, in our opinion, to be extended to desert islands situated in the sea over which a certain state has dominion, or to such as newly arise there. . . .

The people as a whole tend to dispose of such things in various ways. Sometimes the fruits produced from them revert to the public treasury to be disbursed, in turn, for public uses; sometimes their use and enjoyment is granted even to outsiders; and sometimes only to citizens, either all of them or those of a certain rank. Yet it is always up to the people as a whole to determine how much of a right over such things belongs to individuals.

But here we detect some distinction between immovable and movable things. The former, since they lie open and cannot be moved from their place, are understood, so far as concerns their bodies as it were, to belong directly to the people by virtue of that universal occupancy. Some movable things, however, are so situated that, while indeed resting in that region, they still need either to be found and gathered (such as metals embedded in the earth's bowels, gems, pearls, and similar things dispersed on shores and elsewhere) or to be specially caught and confined, lest they escape again from our authority (such as wild beasts, fish, and birds).

[3]*On the Law of War and Peace*, II,3,1.

Since such things which have not yet been acquired or captured are not under men's authority, so that they can use them as they please, a people has not properly acquired dominion over them when it collectively occupies their resting place, but only the right to obtain dominion through a particular act of apprehension.

So it is not correct to say, for example, that wild animals which still roam about in their natural freedom are owned by a prince. Rather, the prince has the right to capture them because he has dominion over the land on which they roam, and because he may prescribe to individuals the extent to which they are permitted to assume that right. And so one who has sovereignty over lands and waters will be able to grant the right of seizing and appropriating those things either to anyone without distinction, to all his citizens or those of a certain rank, or to reserve it for himself alone. For although those things are not yet properly under dominion, still, since the establishment of ownership over them necessarily requires the use of something already subject to dominion, such as earth or water, it follows that the one to whom sovereignty over these latter things belongs will be able, by legislation, to make it illicit for another to use them in order to acquire the former. . . .

8. We are said to have occupied a thing only when we take possession of it—something that commences with the junction of body to body, either directly or through a suitable instrument. Therefore, as a rule, movable things are occupied with the hands and land with the feet—along with the intention to cultivate it and the establishment of exact or rough boundaries thereto. But to have seen a thing only, or to know where it is, is judged to be not yet sufficient for possession. . . .

12. Things in which the dominion to which they were formerly subject has been clearly extinguished are also acquired by occupancy. This happens if a person either openly throws a thing aside with a sufficient sign that he no longer wishes it to be his own but to be available for anyone to occupy, with no intention of thereby doing another a favor, or if he later on abandons it either because he despairs of recovering it or because its recovery is not worth the effort, even though he was initially unwilling to lose possession of it. For otherwise no one loses dominion over what is his against his will, even though he has lost possession of it (unless it is taken away from him by way of punishment, or in war); instead, he retains the right to recover it so long as he has not laid aside his intention to do so, or is not thought to have done so. Hence, it will not be possible to acquire dominion over such things through occupancy while the right of the former owner is still in force. . . .

It is evident that if we lose possession of some other thing against our will, as when, for instance, we have dropped something on the road, its dominion does not pass from us or accrue to the finder unless it is later on determined that we had given the thing up as lost—something usually understood from one's failure to search for it. Therefore, if someone has found something that its owner probably did not throw away on purpose, he should openly say so, so that the owner can have it back. But if the owner does not appear the found object can rightly be kept by the finder. . . .

Chapter 9

ON THE TRANSFER OF DOMINION IN GENERAL

1. Next we must see about *derivative ways of acquisition*, by which an already established dominion passes from one person to another. Before we give a particular account of these, it will be appropriate to preface some things about the transfer of dominion in general. Accordingly, someone's ability to alienate a thing of his, or transfer it to another, results as such from the nature of full dominion. For since this gives an owner the faculty to dispose over a thing as he decides, the chief part of this faculty seems surely to be the ability to transfer the thing to another if it so pleases him, so that in this manner he may either acquire a thing more suited to himself, or at least have the opportunity to obligate another toward himself by means of a benefit.

2. Moreover, just as the transfer of rights and things involves two persons, the one who transfers and the one to whom they are transferred, so in those ways of acquisition that flow from the force of dominion a sort of concurrence of two wills is required, the giver's, of course, and the receiver's. For alienation implies above all that a thing passes from a willing owner and is not seized from him against his will through mere violence. And for a thing to receive another owner than before, it is necessary that he too consent, since it is inappropriate that a thing separate from me in its own physical substance be adjoined to me, as it were, unless I have embraced it with my will and consent. But where by virtue of a right itself—of inheritance, for example—dominion is said to pass even to one who is ignorant, there the law is understood to make an acceptance, as it were, through a legal fiction, in favor of the heir. A proof of this is that the heir could refuse the inheritance, and unless he has actually entered into it, through himself or through another, he is not bound by the obligations that arise from the inherited thing itself.

7. By possession, then, we understand not just any retention of a thing, such as a guardian, for example, an administrator, a borrower, or a usufructuary has with respect to another's thing, but one conjoined with a disposition and intention to have the thing for oneself. It is divided into *natural* and *civil*, a division that is in turn accepted either with respect to the manner of possessing or retaining, or with respect to the form of possession itself.

Possession is said to be natural in the former manner when we lay claim to a thing, once it has been apprehended by us, not with the mind only but also, as it were, with the body, and by means of the act itself. But when someone has already lost bodily control over that thing civil possession is, in this sense, retained only in the mind, in that the civil law in certain cases still allows the gains following upon possession even to those who have lost bodily possession or retention of their own thing. Possession is natural in the latter manner when there are, indeed, an intention and a disposition to have the thing for oneself, yet without a just persuasion of dominion derived from a legitimate title. Civil possession, however, includes both the disposition and a probable cause therefor, which is as a rule understood when some favor is granted to possession in the civil laws. . . .

Now possessions in the proper sense are corporeal things, both movable and immovable. Incorporeal things or rights (which we possess by use and the faculty of using), as also documents on the basis of which action in support of a certain claim can be instituted, are possessed in an analogous sense. But to establish possession it is altogether required that someone physically apprehend some thing, or its symbol or instrument of custody, either through himself or through another in his name, as the nature of the thing allows, so that the thing is brought under his authority in such a way that he can actually dispose of it. . . . (In the case of negative rights, however, there is something like possession if I have prohibited something to another, or refused it to him, and he acquiesces in my prohibition or refusal.) Now this kind of apprehension or exercise is necessarily required to obtain any sort of possession, even though civil laws can, so far as the right itself goes, bring about the passage of dominion to someone, so that he can as effectively institute an action to claim the thing from one who holds it back as if he had taken bodily possession of it. . . .

Furthermore, just as the acquisition of dominion through occupancy requires that a thing be vacant, so, if a thing is to pass to me from another with the effect that I can actually dispose of it thereafter, it is surely necessary that he renounce its possession and remove it from his own custody, as it were, so that I can immediately apprehend it. And this suffices for it to be said that the other has handed the thing over. Nor is it necessary that he lay the thing into my hand; just as it is not required for someone to be said to have provided food to another, that he thrust it into his mouth pre-chewed, but it suffices to have put it out in such a place that the other can himself conveniently lay a hand upon it. . . .

BOOK V

Chapter 1

ON PRICE

1. Since the things subjected to ownership differed in their nature and did not provide the same use for human necessities, and indeed, since frequently it happened either that the same thing (whose parts were not in all respects alike) began to belong to several persons, or that things diverse in nature had to be mutually exchanged, it became necessary that by human agreement some evaluation be imposed on things, according to which those of a disparate nature could be compared and made equal to one another. But since things are compared and made equal to one another by means of a quantitative principle, that is, since equality is a coincidence of quantities, we must now examine the quantity of things and actions insofar as they are useful in human life, as well as this quantity's foundations and common measure.

2. We find, then, that things are said to be equal to one another in ordinary life not only because they coincide according to the three dimensions, but also in a certain other respect. Thus, honors, labors, and wages are said to be equal or unequal to one another on account of considerations other than the coincidence of their dimensions. So there must be some quantity beyond the physical and mathematical, which philosophers seem thus far to have been exclusively concerned about. This will be more clear if we attend to the fact that the formal principle of quantity in general consists not in a substance's extension but, so to speak, its susceptibility to evaluation. In other words, the prime reason things are said to be quantified is that they can be evaluated and, consequently, compared with one another as to their equality or inequality. But since things can be evaluated not only according to their physical substance but also a certain moral consideration, it follows that there is a moral quantity in addition to the physical, according to which they are of course morally evaluated. Physical quantity itself does enter into the evaluation of things of the same nature and goodness (for example, other things being equal, a large diamond is worth more than a small one); yet it is not always

considered in the evaluation of things differing in kind or goodness. Thus, a bigger dog is not always worth more than a smaller one, nor a large mass of lead more valuable than a smaller mass of gold.

How persons are morally evaluated according to their esteem, and moral actions according to their power to produce merit and demerit, are discussed in their own place. Here we must deal specifically with the moral quantity of things and actions insofar as they are understood to have a certain use in ordinary life and are compared with one another, and thereby suited for entering into commerce. This quantity, namely the moral quantity or value according to which things and actions entering into commerce are usually compared with one another, is called *price*.

3. Price can be divided into *vulgar* price and *eminent* price. The former is found in things, and in actions or labors, that enter into commerce, insofar as they afford men some use or pleasure. The latter is found in money and whatever serves in its stead, insofar as it is understood to contain virtually the prices of all things and labors, and to furnish a common measure thereof.

4. A correct understanding of the nature of vulgar price is especially fostered by a separate consideration of both its foundation in itself and the reasons that it is raised or lowered. The foundation of price in itself is the aptitude of a thing or action to contribute directly or indirectly to the necessities of human life, or to render it easier and more pleasant. Hence it is frequent in ordinary discourse to refer to useless things as things of no worth, just as we commonly say as well that men who are useless burdens to the earth are worthless. Thus the cock in the fable considered the pearl he had found to be of no worth, at least to himself, because it was useless to him. . . .

5. Yet it must be observed that some things highly useful to human life are understood to have no price imposed on them. This is either because they are and ought to be exempt from dominion, because they are excluded from human commerce, or finally, when they do enter into commerce, they are never considered otherwise than as an appendage of something else. Also, the law, by placing many actions beyond the commercial sphere, is understood thereby to have withheld all price from them. Thus, since the higher regions of the air, the ether, the celestial bodies, and the vast ocean have been exempted from human dominion, no one has rightly put a price on them however useful they may be for human life. Similarly, Roman law withheld all price from sacred and religious things by excluding them from commerce, even though many of them otherwise lacked nothing in themselves for the determination of a price. And there is no price upon the head of a free man, because to be free and to be subject to commercial exchange implies a contradiction; for as soon as someone is put up for sale he ceases to be free. So freedom is said to be invaluable from this perspective as well, and not only because its advantages are so great that they seem to exceed all valuation. . . .

Many things are also thought to lack a price because they cannot be held separately. Yet they significantly increase the price of that to which they are added, just as their absence or their bad qualities considerably diminish it. Thus, there is no price for direct sunlight, air that is clear and pure, the pleasant appearance of the earth (only insofar as it delights the eyes), wind, shade, and similar things considered in and by themselves, since mortals cannot enjoy such things without making use of the earth. Yet everyone knows how important they are to the price of regions, farms, and estates. . . .

6. Now there are various reasons that the price of one and the same thing is raised or lowered, and therefore that one thing is preferred to another even though the latter seems to have an equal or a greater use in human life. For here a thing's necessity or the excellence of its use is so far from being always the primary consideration that we find, instead, those things being cheapest which human life is least able to do without. This is because nature, by the particular providence of God, pours forth an abundant supply of them. . . .

Accordingly, the main factor in a price increase is rarity, whose intentional procurement is considered by some to be among the secrets of the trade. . . . Also, men in general consider hardly anything a good unless it provides its possessor with something more excellent and rare than what others possess, or enables him to exalt himself over them by reference to it. For this reason even honors are recommended especially by their rarity. . . .

But this evaluation of genuine goods according to their rarity or the number of people who possess them is in fact due to the wickedness and meanness of the human character. For a good in my possession is surely not made worse by the fact that others have it too, or more excellent if they lack it. Thus, for example, my health is not less valuable because others are also healthy, or more valuable because they are ill. Similarly, a knowledge of the truth is not less valuable because others also have it, and the value of wisdom in itself does not grow because others are fools. Therefore, one who prides himself on the fact that others lack a good which he enjoys seems in fact to be enjoying their misfortunes, while one who values one of his own goods less because others also have it is moved by envy toward them.

It comes as no surprise, however, that here too, as in many other things, the common inclination of men departs from right reason. . . . Hence, their ambition for luxury has imposed enormous prices on many things that human life could very easily have done without. (Some think this was done so that great and enormous riches could have a use.) . . . But things that are used on a daily basis and that mainly concern food, clothing, and weapons experience their greatest rise in price when they become as rare as they are necessary. This commonly happens during food shortages and sieges, or on long sea voyages, when hunger and thirst demand to be satisfied and life to be preserved at any price. . . .

The reason that artificial things are usually priced as high as possible is, besides their rarity, the subtlety and elegance of the art which they exhibit. . . . Some things are highly regarded because of the fame of the artisan; some are greatly valued on account of their former possessor's excellence. . . . Other contributing factors are the difficulty of the work, the abundance and rarity of artisans or laborers, and similar things. . . . Finally, the price of labors and actions is raised by their difficulty, skill, usefulness, and necessity; and by their agents' rarity, their preeminence or stature, their freedom to interrupt the action, and other such things. . . . The most important factor, however, in the evaluation of a work is the state of the art. . . .

7. But it commonly happens as well that certain things not highly valued in general are valued by individuals because of some particular feeling. This is usu-

ally called the 'fancy price.' . . . Many people also place great value on things because they see them valued by great personages whom they wish especially to please. . . . Sometimes, finally, the prices of things or labors are markedly increased because of some fault of mind like vainglory, cruelty, and the like. . . .

8. These kinds of factors tend in general to raise the prices of things, just as their opposites lower them. But in determining the prices of particular things here and now, and adjusting them to a fair standard, other factors are usually considered as well.

It is to be observed at the outset that among those who live in natural freedom each person may set the price of his own things as he pleases, since everyone in that state has the final say over his own things and actions. For however much another wants then to put a price upon a thing of mine, it will still be up to me to accept or reject his valuation, and so I will in fact be evaluating the thing myself. And even if I place an infinite price upon a thing of mine, no one can complain about it, since it is no one's business how great I imagine my riches to be, and nothing is easier for others to whom that price seems excessive than to let me keep the thing. Accordingly, if someone really wishes to have a thing of mine he must offer whatever price I find appropriate; just as, on the contrary, if I wish to sell my wares I must accept whatever price it pleases a fastidious buyer to give. There is therefore no just cause for complaint unless, through inhumanity or from hatred and envy, someone either simply refuses to sell things he has in abundance to someone who needs them, or is willing to sell them only upon the harshest terms. It follows from this that in the natural state the prices of all things are determined by an agreement between contracting parties, and that a person cannot be accused of having sinned against the rules of commerce for seeing to his own gain when an opportunity was given, provided he has not been inhumane toward those in need. . . .

In civil states, however, prices are determined in two ways: first, through the decree of superiors or by law, and second, through the common valuation and judgment of men, together with the consent of the contracting parties. The former is commonly referred to by some as the legal price, and the latter as the common or natural price.

The legal price is regularly assumed to agree with justice and equity, unless the opposite is plainly apparent. (For here too, apathetic ignorance or, more often, hatred or favor toward buyers or sellers, some other corruption, or even love of one's own gain, can occasionally intervene.) It stands at a precise point [*stigmē*] and has no latitude, with the smallest excess giving rise to injustice. When it is fixed in favor of the buyer, as is most often the case, the seller is not permitted to demand more. Yet the buyer is permitted to give less with the seller's consent, so long as he attains at least the lowest level of the natural price; and the seller is permitted to accept less, provided it does not defraud other merchants. But if the price is fixed in favor of the seller the buyer cannot rightly urge him to accept less, even though the seller can do so when he wishes, since anyone is permitted to give up his own advantages. Yet the seller can rightly accept more, provided he does not exceed the highest level of the natural price. Admittedly, the price of labor seems more frequently to be fixed in favor of those hired to do it, than the price of wares in favor of sellers. Still it must be noted here that rather subtle precautions are taken in some places to prevent an excessive rise in the price of certain things. Thus, in the city-states of Greece it was agreed that fish sellers should not sit but stand, so that worn out by the tedium and fatigue of standing they might sell their fish as fresh as possible, and at a fair price.

9. But the common [or natural] price, which is not fixed through laws, has a certain range within which more or less may be demanded and given. . . . Moreover, on account of this range, it is commonly divided into three levels, as it were: a lowest or generous price, a middle or moderate price, and a highest or stiff price. A thing can be bought or sold either more dearly or more cheaply if it remains within this range, whose extent, however, cannot in general be that accurately defined. There is no better way of putting it than to say that a just price is that which those sufficiently acquainted with both merchandise and market are commonly accustomed to give. . . .

10. Further, the setting of that common price usually takes into account the labor and expense incurred by merchants in transporting and handling their wares. For this is the main reason that a merchant can sell his wares more dearly than he has bought them. But these expenses must be understood only in reference to common occurrences; extraordinary events are deemed to have no effect on them. Hence, a merchant will get no hearing if he wishes to put a greater value on his wares because he broke his foot or was struck with a serious illness while bringing them to market, or because he lost a portion of them to shipwreck or thieves, unless these accidents have also made them rare. This is even more so if he wishes to charge buyers also for the needless expenses incurred by him outside the laws of prudent commerce. But merchants can definitely figure in the time, thought, and care they spend in acquiring, preserving, and distributing their wares, as well as the necessarily procured services of servants. And it would be quite inhumane, and likely to discourage human industry, to allow a person no more profit from his business, or from any other kind of life, than suffices for the bare and difficult relief of his necessities.

The difficulty, length, and dangerousness of a journey can also enter into the evaluation, as well as the differing value of money and merchandise in different places. In addition, the common value tends to vary according to the manner of buying and selling. Those who sell their wares one at a time or in relatively small amounts can demand a somewhat larger price for them than those who distribute them all at once in bulk. For the former experience more bother, and it is more profitable to receive large sums of money all at once than to collect small sums little by little. But it is also well known how suddenly and often markets change on account of the abundance or scarcity of buyers, money, and merchandise. For a scarcity of buyers and money that is due to a particular cause, along with an abundance of merchandise, reduces the price. . . .

Finally, if a seller experiences any consequent damage or loss of profit through a sale, it can also be added to the common price, especially when a buyer makes an offer on his own initiative. For it would be foolish to part with something of mine except on condition that I at least suffer no damage thereby. But the loss or increase of profit that most of all can, and usually does, get included in the price is that which stems from late or early payment. For surely the time of payment also affects the price, and something is worth more when given immediately than after an interval, since one can make other profit from it in the meantime. . . .

11. Now most nations easily discovered, upon leaving their primeval simplicity, that vulgar price alone did not sufficiently further men's daily increasing business and commercial affairs. For commerce used to consist only of barter, and the labors of others could be secured in no other way than by mutual labor or handing a thing over. But after our desires made us need so many things, and we, not content with goods produced at home, had tasted the delights of lands with a different climate, it was by no means easy for anyone to possess such things as another might wish to exchange for things of his that we desired, or that were equivalent to these. And cultured states, where citizens are distinguished by various ranks, require many sorts of men who could either not maintain their lives at all, or only with difficulty, if that simple exchange of things and labors prevailed. Also, it is well known that nations unacquainted with the use of money do not have a very elaborate standard of living. . . .

12. Hence most nations enjoying a more highly cultivated life deemed it good to impose upon a certain thing, by some agreement, an *eminent* price by which the vulgar prices of other things would be measured, and in which they would be eminently contained, so that by means of it a person could obtain for himself anything offered for sale and easily execute whatever commercial transactions and contracts he wished. . . .

13. Now the majority of nations deemed it most convenient to employ the nobler and less frequent metals for this purpose, such as gold, . . . silver, and bronze. For just as no one accepts a guarantor unless he be a man of proven reliability, and rich, while an ordinary person is thought to offer little surety, so no one would have exchanged a thing which he had secured for himself by great labor and industry for something encountered everywhere, such as a handful of soil or sand. It was necessary, therefore, that money consist of a material that is conveniently stored and into which, on account of its rarity, the prices of many things could, as it were, be compressed. Add to this the fact that metals have a very compact substance, so that they are not easily worn out by use, and are capable of being split into small pieces, qualities that are both very appropriate for something entering into men's commercial transactions as a common measure.

Yet since money has this function not from some necessity of nature but from the imposition and agreement of men, . . . it is evident that because of either necessity or choice, other materials can and at times have been employed as well. Thus, leather, paper, or something similar stamped with a certain sign has during situations of great necessity more than once taken the place of coin. Yet once these situations were overcome these materials were exchanged again for ordinary currency. . . .

Chapter 2

ON CONTRACTS (WHICH PRESUPPOSE THE PRICE OF THINGS) IN GENERAL

1. We should now look at contracts, which cannot be understood apart from dominion over and the price of things. Here we must first inquire into the distinction thought to exist between simple pacts and contracts. Hobbes . . . calls a contract "an action of two or more persons engaged in the mutual transfer of their rights."[1] But since "in every contract, either each person immediately furnishes that which has been agreed upon, so that neither trusts the other"; or "one person does so, while the other is trusted; or, finally, neither furnishes anything on the spot but each has a reciprocal faith in the other"; Hobbes insists that only contracts of the former class be included under the name of this category. Those, however, where one or both parties are trusted, and where the trusted party promises that he will furnish his part later on, ought according to Hobbes to be designated pacts. Yet this difference does not concern the intrinsic character of contracts and pacts itself, but only their execution. And it goes against common usage to call a purchase concluded by means of cash, for example, a contract, but one where the merchandise is furnished immediately while the payment is promised for later a pact.

4. To us it seems best to derive the essential distinction between pacts and contracts from the object. Thus, agreements concerning commercial things and activities, and therefore presupposing dominions and prices of things, are called contracts; while agreements entered into regarding other matters are generally referred to as pacts. In this way, pacts in the strict sense will be all negative agreements by which we agree not to do or seek something that we were able to do or seek. Likewise, they will be those agreements that have as their object the motions of our natural faculties insofar as they tend only toward mutual profit or advantage, and as they are considered separately by themselves without being compared or evaluated by reference to other such motions. In a word, they are agreements about the provision of non-commercial services. And yet there are many agreements not involving things to which the name 'pact' or 'contract' is indiscriminately applied, such as that whereby marriage is entered into.

---

[1] *De Cive*, II,9.

BOOK VI

Chapter 1

ON MARRIAGE

1. Next, we must investigate the origin and nature of human sovereignty, as well as those precepts of the natural law and the law of nations that presuppose it. But since sovereignty can be understood only among many persons, and indeed, since it is well established by the authority of the Sacred Scriptures that at the beginning God produced only one human pair to which all mortals refer their origin, we must, before treating civil sovereignty, examine matrimony, which gives rise to families and furnishes the material, as it were, out of which sovereignties and states are constituted. For just as the human body is composed of different members which, considered in themselves, also appear to be bodies, so are civil states made up of lesser societies. Some of these are called simple and primary while others, being slightly more composite, usually come with the name of associations. Of the former there are three: *marital, paternal*, and *master/slave* societies, which are said to be simple and primary because they are not composed of other lesser societies, not because they contain no more than two persons. . . . For what prevents a father from having several children or a master several slaves, and thereby constituting among themselves a society that is no less simple than if he had but one son or one slave? . . .

2. Now the most wise Creator, in order to avoid having always to supply new offspring by means of creation, once humankind had become vulnerable to death, or else allow such a noble species to be extinguished within the space of one lifetime, provided it with different sexes and endowed it with a natural faculty to propagate itself by a commingling of bodies. And lest mortals should fail to do this, through lack of care perhaps, or because of the bother of having or rearing children, He implanted in the sexes a mutual propensity and strong impulses toward one another, as well as a most ardent affection for their offspring, so that they would willingly and gladly undertake that without which the race of mortals could not survive. . . .

3. Concerning marriage, we must first inquire whether men who are otherwise fit for it are bound by any obligation to enter it and to generate offspring. For some people doubt whether this, no less than the other things toward which man is carried by a natural appetite (such as his own preservation and the love and rearing of offspring), is ordained by natural law. Such ordination was not needed, they say, since instinct and sensitive appetite already drive us strongly enough toward such things. Yet it hardly follows from the fact that we are carried toward these things by natural instinct, that the law of nature does not command them. Instead, since they are directly responsible for preserving the integrity of humankind, it appears that nature wished them to be observed as closely as possible; and lacking confidence, as it were, in the dictate of reason alone, she ordered it to be reinforced by an instinct so vehement that a man can struggle against it only with difficulty. . . .

5. . . . Finally, since families cannot be understood without marital laws, and states without families (on which all seemly order that is to be established in human life therefore depends), it is evident that without marriage men would have led an isolated and almost bestial life. . . . Add to this the fact that without marriages there can also be no patrimonies, upon whose elimination a great part of the advantages by which human life is either sustained or adorned would disappear. . . .

9. Next we must inquire about the terms of a marriage pact concluded purely according to natural law, and about the rights arising for both parties. We suppose here from the beginning that all men naturally partake of equal right, and that no one has sovereignty over another unless he has acquired it by his own or the other's act. For although the masculine sex is generally superior to the feminine in strength of body and mind, this excellence by itself is in no way suited to give the former sovereignty over the latter. Therefore, whatever right a male has over a female, as over someone equal to himself, must be acquired from her consent or through a just war. Yet since it is most natural for marriages to be formed through good will, the former manner of acquisition is more apt for wives and the latter for female slaves. And if some men have been willing to marry women captured in war and reduced to slavery, they have usually relaxed the severity of the sovereignty they have over them as masters. . . .

So if we conceive men to be constituted in natural equality and freedom, it can happen that a female, no less than a male, desires to acquire for herself in particular offspring over which she has a right. It is necessary for this end that the male and female enter into a pact about furnishing their bodies for each other's use. If this pact is but a simple one regarding the procreation of offspring alone and not linked to an agreement about continued cohabitation, then it will also not confer on one party any sovereignty over the other. Nor will either of them have any right over the other beyond that of furnishing his or her body for the procreation of offspring, offspring that will be under the mother's authority if it was expressed in the pact that she is seeking progeny for herself and not for the man. . . .

11. We must further investigate whether, according to the natural law alone, the principal pact of a completed marriage necessarily gives rise to sovereignty, properly speaking, of the husband over the wife. It is true that in the Divine Scriptures the wife is ordered to subject her will to the husband, and he is expressly constituted her master. Yet because this is said to have been imposed on the female

as a punishment it can be regarded as a mere provision of [divine] positive law. As for determining the natural law on this point, we must first observe here that one who is bound to follow the will of another in certain matters is not immediately subject to the other's sovereignty, since that bond can also arise from a simple pact. For there are pacts where, at least at the beginning, both parties are equally free to choose whether they wish to enter them or not (such as those, especially, where "I give in order that you do," and "I do in order that you do"). Yet once the pact has been initiated it is necessary for one party to follow the will of the other in the matter agreed upon, and not vice versa. Hence, in whatever way a wife is bound to conform herself to the will of the husband in matters pertaining specifically to the marriage, it does not follow directly from this that he necessarily has sovereignty over her in regard to other actions as well. . . .

It seems, however, that the special end of marriage can likewise be attained easily enough even if one spouse does not have sovereignty properly speaking (which encompasses the right of life and death, and a rather harsh constraint) over the other, but they are held together only by friendship and a pact. Yet this pact, in favoring the position of the husband (who has, in addition, the excellence of his sex), imitates the nature of an unequal treaty in which the main things that wife and husband respectively owe each other are obedience and protection. . . . Yet the natural law also poses no obstacle even to the wife's passing under the husband's sovereignty properly speaking. For a fear of sovereignty and conjugal friendship no more destroy each other than a prince's sovereignty by itself extinguishes the love of citizens. . . .

Chapter 2

ON PATERNAL AUTHORITY

1. Marriage gives rise to offspring over whom paternal authority is established. This is at once the most ancient and most holy sort of sovereignty, and children are bound by it to honor the commands of their parents and to acknowledge them as their superiors. Grotius . . . and most others refer its origin to the act of generation whereby parents, by bringing into being someone not yet in existence, somehow resemble God.[1] Since both parents contribute equally to generation, they say, each of them originally acquires an equal right over the offspring. Yet if they contend among themselves over sovereignty and cannot both be satisfied at the same time, the sovereignty of the father is to be preferred, not only because of the excellence of his sex but also because he has sovereignty over the mother.

[1] *On the Law of War and Peace*, III, 5, 1.

4. . . . Having said these things, it seems that we must first put beyond doubt the fact that generation furnishes an occasion to acquire over offspring a right that is not only valid against others who are not the parents (just as the owner of a thing is owner of its fruits, so the owner of the body from which an offspring was generated is the one best situated to acquire sovereignty over it), but that also has force against the offspring itself. I say *an occasion*, since generation alone does not seem sufficient to us to establish a title of sovereignty over human offspring. For even though our offspring is made up of our substance, still, because it turns into a person similar to us, one equal as concerns the rights belonging naturally to men, another title seems surely required for it to become unequal to us or subject to our sovereignty. This is especially so because offspring is produced by an act which we usually undertake for the sake of our own pleasure, and for which we therefore cannot impose so high a charge that the offspring is bound to be subject to us whether it wishes or not. . . .

The right of parents over children is therefore based on a twofold title. First, the law of nature itself, in commanding man to be sociable, has enjoined on parents the care of their children and—lest they neglect it—also implanted in them a most tender affection for their offspring. For social life is plainly unintelligible apart from the supposition that parents rear their offspring. This care cannot be rightly exercised, however, unless parents have the authority to direct the actions of their children toward the latter's welfare, which these do not yet understand on account of their lack of judgment. . . . For this reason, therefore, nature surely commands parents to exercise over their children a sovereignty that is sufficient for that end. For whoever obligates someone to an end is thought also to have conferred on him, at the same time, the authority to employ the means without which the end cannot be obtained. In turn, the authority of parents resulting from the injunction to care for their children necessarily imposes on these the obligation to submit themselves to their parents' direction, since without it such direction would be in vain.

Second, the sovereignty of parents seems also to rest on their children's presumed consent, and therefore on a tacit pact. For just as a parent declares by his acceptance of an infant that he will fulfill the obligation enjoined by nature and rear the infant as well as he can, so the infant, on the other hand, even though he cannot expressly promise the reciprocal duties directly corresponding to his parents' obligation, on account of his still undeveloped use of reason, contracts from his parents' labor no less of an obligation toward them than if he had expressly consented to it. . . . This obligation will exert itself as soon as he can understand what his parents have done for him. For it is presumed that had he had the use of reason at the time he was accepted, and seen that without his parents' care and the sovereignty over him connected with it he could not preserve his life, he would gladly have consented to it in return for their promise to provide him with the benefits of rearing. This reasonably presumed consent is equivalent to express consent. . . . In the same way, someone whose affairs another person has conducted in his absence, and without his knowledge, is understood to have contracted an obligation from a tacit contract, as it were, to repay the other what he has spent in his interest. It is clear from this that a parent's sovereignty over offspring is established by his act of accepting and nurturing him, and by his undertaking to do what he can to form him into a useful member of human society. . . .

BOOK VII

Chapter 1

ON THE CAUSE IMPELLING MEN
TO ESTABLISH THE STATE

1. After the so-called primary societies we must now treat of the state, which is considered the most perfect society, and that by which the safety and integrity of humankind (now that it has multiplied) is most of all maintained. It will be clearly apparent why men who were formerly dispersed in separate families established the state, if we inquire somewhat more carefully into both the nature of civil society and the inclinations of human character. The elucidation of this matter will, in turn, be considerably advanced by a prior examination of what is ordinarily said about it.

2. Thus, most authors take refuge here in man's nature, which supposedly carries him so strongly toward civil society that he is neither willing nor able to live without it. They allege, in support of this claim, the arguments adduced above (in Bk. II, Ch. 4)[1] on behalf of man's social nature, which were drawn mainly from the miseries of a solitary life, from the tedium of solitude, from speech (which would have been given man in vain apart from society), from the appetite to associate with men, from the utility that comes of being joined with others, and from other like considerations. Hobbes . . . , on the contrary, tries to show that man is really an animal who principally loves himself and his own profit to the highest degree, . . . but loves society and others only in a secondary manner and insofar as some pleasure or profit can redound on him from them.[2] This he shows by noting that one is not sufficiently induced to seek another's society simply because he is a man, but because one hopes to obtain honor or profit in his company instead of

---

[1]The reference is Pufendorf's, but it seems to be in error. The material referred to is in Bk. II, Ch. 3—ed.

[2]*De Cive*, I,2.

someone else's, illustrating the point by means of inductions derived from particular societies.

Those who come together for commercial reasons are looking out for their own gain, which they hope to obtain better by taking on partners than by conducting their own separate affairs. If this hope deceives them they are considered mad if they do not withdraw from that harmful society as quickly as possible. Those joined by reason of a public office enter into a sort of legal friendship that contains more mutual fear than love and involves the deceitful trappings of external signs rather than a genuine union of minds. Thus, such men sometimes form a faction in order to pursue their private advantage by means of their combined strength, but there is hardly ever any pure benevolence among them. And whoever has confidence in his own resources is not very anxious to acquire associates.

When people come together for the sake of enjoyment or to while away the time, each is most pleased with himself if he can raise a laugh for others or himself. But he usually gets nowhere with this unless he discloses something shameful or indecent about others, since one cannot rightly laugh at something in another that one finds in oneself. . . . Therefore, those who laugh at others cannot but disdain them as lower than themselves and seek a bit of glory by comparison with their dullness. And even though laughter is sometimes sought without offense and through jokes that have no bite, it is evident that here, too, a person is led more by his own pleasure than by fellowship. Indeed, those who profess to amuse others through laughter are chiefly interested in securing some favor or advantage through their display of a merry disposition. Besides, most men have had implanted in them by nature a very great itch to examine, judge, condemn, and criticize the words and deeds of others, and they consider the ability to scratch it abundantly the sweetest spice of their life. And it is difficult to repress or extinguish this itch through either discipline or reprimands. . . .

The same thing is demonstrated by another argument taken from the very definitions of 'will,' 'good,' 'honor,' and 'utility.' Men enter voluntarily into societies. Wherever there is a will, however, there is also its object, the good. But toward what good is the appetite of individuals carried except that which each of them has judged good for himself? For no matter how good a thing may be by nature, we are usually slow to seek or value it unless it affects us. If things go as well as possible for the king of the Persians, I still do not consider it good for myself. Now a good is always accompanied by some pleasantness that pertains either to the mind alone or also to the body. All pleasure of the mind is either glory or something ultimately traced back to glory; those which affect the body are called advantages. Therefore, every society is contracted for the sake of advantage or glory; one's own, that is, not that of one's fellows. . . .

3. Although we have shown above . . . that it by no means follows from these considerations that man is not a sociable animal, or that he is not destined by nature to live in society with those similar to himself, it does not follow immediately from the appetite for society which we have posited in man that he is carried by nature to civil society—no more than it follows from the fact that man desires some occupation that he is carried by nature to scholarly pursuits. This is because that

appetite can be satisfied through the primary societies and by the friendship whereby he is joined to his equals. . . .

Hobbes . . . , on the other hand, proves what we have said as follows, saying that civil societies are not mere gatherings but alliances, entry into which requires faithfulness and pacts. The force of these pacts is unknown to infants and the uneducated, and the utility of such societies unknown to those who have not experienced the harms arising from their absence. Hence it is that the former are unable to enter civil society because they do not understand what it is; the latter, not knowing its benefits, either do not care to enter it, or at least live in it in such a way that they do not value its excellence. Accordingly all men, being born as infants, are born unfit for civil society, and most of them remain so throughout their entire life. For it is by instruction, not by nature, that a man becomes fit for that society. . . .

4. The matter will become clearer if we consider what condition arises among men from the establishment of states, what is required for someone to be able truly to be called a political animal (that is, a good citizen), and finally, what there is in the nature of man that resists this 'civility,' so to speak.

One who enters into the state sacrifices his natural freedom and subjects himself to sovereignty. This embraces, besides other things, a right of life and death over oneself. And by its command many things ought to be done that one would otherwise abhor, and many omitted that one would otherwise vigorously seek, so that most actions are to be referred to the good of society, which seems often to differ from the good of individuals. . . .

Next we say that a truly political animal, that is, a good citizen, is one who promptly obeys the commands of sovereigns; one who strives with all his strength toward the public good and gladly places it before his private good, considering nothing good for himself, indeed, unless it is so for the public as well; and finally, one who contributes to the advantage of the other citizens. . . . But no one is so inexperienced as not to understand how poorly the characters of most men have been fitted to this end. Few have been able to meet all the requirements of a good citizen; most of them are somehow restrained by fear of punishment; most remain bad citizens and non-political animals throughout their whole life.

Indeed, there is no animal more fierce and unrestrained than man, and none inclined toward more faults able to disrupt the peace of society. Most brute animals scramble after their natural food, the appetite for which sometimes sets them against each other. If there is enough of it, they will not start to quarrel without any reason. Some of them are also carried away by lust, yet they commonly burn with it only at a certain part of the year. . . . But men are brought into conflict with one another not only by the desire for food and drink, and by prods of lust to which they are exposed at any time of the year, but also by other vices that are unknown to brutes and often at odds with one another.

The first place among these is occupied by an insatiable desire for superfluous things, and by that most immoderate of evils, ambition. To this, man, who alone seems to have a sense for it, is also most sensitive, since brutes, by contrast, are stirred by nothing except that which brings some harm to their body. . . . There is in addition a most lively memory of injuries and a burning desire for vengeance, evils that are found to be more rare and sluggish among brutes. And—worst of all—man enjoys raging against his own kind with such fury that the greatest part of the evils to which the human condition is exposed come from man himself. It would not be absurd to say that man, through the Creator's providence, and unlike brutes, grows into maturity so slowly that, through long delays, the ferocity and harshness of his human character can somehow be broken and reduced to harmony with other disparate characters. For an adult man brought suddenly to his full strength would have been more unmanageable than any beast. . . .

Moreover, in any class of brutes there is usually a similarity of inclinations and appetites; but among men there are as many perceptions and feelings as heads, and in most of them a great resolve to extol their own concerns. This fact, even by itself alone, can suffice to disrupt a multitude of men who are to be joined together into one group. . . .

Accordingly, man is so far from being by nature a political animal, or from being fitted immediately through birth to play the part of a good citizen, that instead, barely a few of them are by long discipline somehow brought to that point. . . .

It is therefore plain enough from these things in what sense man can ultimately be said to be by nature a political animal. Namely, it is not that all individuals as such have through nature an inner aptitude to play the role of a good citizen, but that at least some men can be molded through discipline to play the part; and that the welfare and safety of humankind (now that it has multiplied) cannot be preserved except through civil societies. Nature, which is most eager to preserve itself, surely impels men to enter these societies, whose chief fruit is, in turn, that men become accustomed in them to live a decent civil life.

6. Many think that neediness moved men to enter civil states and to improve and enrich their life, which could only be both primitive and destitute so long as it was solitary. Here it is certain, at any rate, that there would hardly be a more miserable animal than man if individuals were left to themselves alone without any assistance derived from other men. Nor can it be denied that human life began to be refined to the point of luxury after men had come together into states. . . .

Nonetheless, it seems certain to us that neediness was by no means the sole or the chief cause of the establishment of states. . . . For even before, when men still lived dispersed into separate families, they provided adequately for the necessities of life by inventing agriculture and herding, viniculture, weaving, and other arts. . . . Indeed, let us suppose a family-father amply supplied with land, livestock, and slaves: what can he lack for the support of this life? Or, if something is lacking, he can make up for it through commerce . . . , just as there are many states today which seek the merchandise that satisfies their need or pleasure from outsiders, and which nonetheless do not consider it necessary on that account to coalesce into one state with them. On the other hand, there are quite a few peoples who, for many ages now, have been living a civil life by no means more refined or abundant than that which once sustained the ancient family-fathers. . . .

Thus, the luxuries with which the life of many peoples now teems owe their origin not so much to states as to large cities. For the urban masses, deriving nothing from field and flock, devoted themselves to the cultivation of various arts in order to sustain themselves. Moreover, there was among city dwellers a cultural emulation leading to extravagance, something that, in many places, is served by no fewer trades than those that serve necessity. Yet civil life could easily have done without these.

7. The true and chief reason, therefore, why family-fathers gave up their natural freedom and resorted to the establishment of civil states was to surround themselves with defenses against the evils threatening man from man. For just as man can render the greatest *help* to man (after the Great and Good God), so also and no less can he *hinder* him. . . .

Although the race of mortals is molested by various evils, its cleverness has devised a remedy against each one. Against the power of illnesses the arts of physicians have been invented; the harshness of climate and weather is resisted by means of dwellings, clothes, and fire; hunger is driven off by men's industrious cultivation of the earth; the ferocity of beasts is restrained by weapons or traps. But against those evils which humans, on account of their depraved character, enjoy directing against one another, the most effective remedy had to be sought from man himself, from men joined together into states and from the establishment of sovereignty. . . . And after men were so organized that they could be secure from mutual injuries, it easily followed that they had that much richer an enjoyment of the advantages that can come to men specifically from men.

Those who conclude that the cause of civil states is *fear* are in accord with us, since fear as they understand it is by no means the disturbance of a trembling and unsettled mind, but any sort of precaution against future evil. . . . By this [definition] we elude the argument of some who have objected that fear is so far from having provided the cause of the establishment of states that, instead, if men had feared one another, they could not even have stood the sight of each other and, with one person rushing off in this direction and another in that, would have remained constantly apart, as though it were true that fearing meant flight alone, and not also distrust, suspicion, and caution. On the contrary, this too is characteristic of one who fears: to take precautions so that you do not have a probable cause for fear.

Hence, those going to sleep close the doors because they fear thieves; when the doors have been closed they fear no longer. Those who go on a journey take a weapon because they fear bandits; being well-armed, they fear them no longer. . . . States secure their borders with garrisons and their cities with fortifications, filling their armories with the apparatus of war even during the profoundest peace— all of which would be useless unless they feared the neighboring states. Yet when they have been well equipped they fear no longer. Thus fear commonly contrives the means by which it may be expelled. By a similar rationale men have, on account of their fear of one another, derived defenses from themselves by the establishment of civil society, whose power has, after all, been thoroughly understood by those who say: "Unless there were courts of justice, one man would devour another." . . .

8. Nor, as someone may believe, could reverence for the law of nature alone (which surely prohibits all injuries) have brought it about that mortals might live mutually secure in natural freedom. There certainly are men who care very much about honor, morality, innocence, and faithfulness, and who would not wish to

violate them even if they could do so with impunity. . . . If everyone were naturally so disposed, it seems there would not have been a need for states. But how great, on the other hand, is the crowd of those to whom all sacred things are cheap whenever they are enticed by the hope of gain and by confidence in their own strength or cleverness, by means of which they hope to be able to repel or elude those whom they have injured! Not to distrust these is to expose oneself voluntarily to their malice and sport. . . . Indeed, there is in most people such a perversity that, whenever it seems that they will gain a greater good from a violation of the laws than from their observance, they readily violate them. . . .

Yet to convict the whole of humankind of this perversity would be excessive. Nay, Hobbes himself admits that there are also certain modest characters who do not demand more for themselves than they leave for others, and so have before their eyes the maxim: "That which you do not wish to have done to you, do not do to another." How anyone can rush to oppress these persons on the pretext of his own security, I myself do not see. Nor will sound reason ever approve my undertaking the oppression of another whose will and effort to destroy me is not specifically established, since there are far more suitable remedies for securing peace with him. For that common wickedness of men alone, which surely has its degrees, does not immediately make man a professed enemy of man.

Therefore, while we admit that in the state of nature the guarantee that others will exercise toward me the duties of the natural law is not as great as it is in civil states, it nonetheless does not shrink to nothing, so that one must act in a hostile manner toward everyone. For, certainly, when I see that my strength is equal to or greater than that of another, when the other has announced with words and pacts his willingness to live peaceably with me, and confirmed it through certain actual proofs, why should I consider him an enemy? Or, how does the sole suspicion that he may be feigning friendship toward me, or that he may change his mind, give me a justifiable reason to attack him?

This point is seen much more clearly in the case of entire states, which live in a natural state with respect to one another. For here no doubt everyone confesses it a crime if one state undertakes by force or treachery to attack another from which it has known neither benefit nor injury (not to mention friendship, as demonstrated by a treaty or deed); and this simply because it does not have a common master with the other state, by whom the latter can be restrained and punished if it has somehow injured the former.

It is clear from these things that "the natural laws are" by no means "silent" in the natural state, as Hobbes claims, even though one is far more secure in following them in civil states where, by means of the magistrate, I can compel anyone who does not respond to me with the duties of peace. Nonetheless, despite all these things, prudence surely dictates that we not only fortify ourselves betimes against the professed malice of lawbreakers, but that we also keep in mind the mutability of the moral rectitude in evidence among the rest. But here it is impossible to find a generally more appropriate safeguard than civil society.

10. There is yet another reason that the law of nature alone cannot maintain the peace of humankind. Namely, it is characteristic of natural freedom that everyone, just as he defends his own welfare with his own strength, also uses his own

judgment about attaining that end and in governing his actions. And who does not know how greatly this judgment varies among different individuals? Very few are blessed with the kind of natural disposition that enables them to perceive on their own what is permanently advantageous to humankind and individuals, and that makes them willing constantly to abide by this realization. Many are deceived by shameful error posing as reason, on account of their natural dullness, and most are carried along by the rash impulse of their passions in whatever direction their lust or the appearance of a false utility drives them. What reliable peace or harmony can there be amid so great a discrepancy of opinions and desires, when both the dullard and the sage deem their own opinion the most attractive, and the former no more deigns to follow the lead of the latter than the latter that of the former? But since reason alone, as found in single men, is unable to settle so great a disagreement, some kind of harmony of opinions must be obtained in another way.

Chapter 2

ON THE INTERNAL STRUCTURE OF STATES

1. It is appropriate now to examine more carefully the inner structure of states. Thus, men were able to think of no other way to make themselves secure against the wickedness of other men (as secure, at least, as their condition allows) than for each to surround himself with suitable aids by means of which one person's attack on another would be rendered so dangerous that he would think it better for himself to restrain his hands and keep the peace than to raise them and provoke the other with war. For nothing can more effectively repress the wickedness of the human character and its inclination to hurt others than reference to an immediate evil that awaits anyone who has attacked another, and the elimination of any hope of impunity.

Now a place is by no means able to provide such assistance, be it fortified by nature or by art. For to stay there alone is like being in prison, nor could a single person easily defend it. But if one admits companions, danger threatens from these themselves, unless you fortify yourself against them by means of some other defense. It is true that weapons can provide some assistance, but not so much that one man is able to promise himself a lasting security from them even against many. Similarly, the protection that can be derived from brute animals is also slight, or uncertain, and not suitable for repelling those dangers. . . . It was therefore not possible to find a more appropriate remedy against the dangers threatened by man than that which comes from man himself—from men's joining their strength together, mutually intertwining their safety and conspiring in common to repel dangers. . . .

2. It is obvious, however, that a consensus of two or three people can hardly provide so great a security, on account of the fact that the addition of one or a few men to the party about to attack them assures a certain and indubitable victory, and gives the adversaries confidence in their undertaking by promising success and impunity. Therefore, to obtain the security we are seeking, it is necessary that the number of those who conspire to assist one another be so great that the addition of a few men to the enemy does not conspicuously enhance his chances of victory, and thus, that a significant number of men join themselves together. . . .

Another conclusion from these things is that the right size of a state must be gauged by the strength of its neighbors. Hence states which formerly were large, when the race of mortals was divided into a great multitude of states, are less than the right size now that great empires have arisen. . . .

3. Next, it is necessary that among the many who come together for this end there be a consensus about the application of means that are suited to it. For however great their number may be, if they do not agree about the best way to arrange for their common defense but each of them wishes to use his own strength according to his own judgment, nothing will be accomplished. For their divided and differently inclined opinions will be an obstacle to one another. Even if a hope of victory, booty, or revenge, derived from impulse or deliberation, sometimes makes them sufficiently agreed about one action (something that is also seen, sometimes, in an infuriated mob . . .), they are afterwards so torn apart by the diversity of their characters and deliberations, by the emulation or the envy that makes men naturally contend among themselves, or by their lack of seriousness and their inconstancy, that they are neither willing to aid each other nor to have peace among themselves. . . . And so such bandings together of many men are hardly going to last for a long time unless men are restrained by some common fear, so that they cannot afterwards depart again at will from something it once pleased them to agree to.

It follows from this that the bare consensus of many men, even if confirmed by a pact, does not provide the security we are seeking. That is, it is not sufficient for many to enter a society of mutual assistance, promising one another that they will direct their actions and strength toward the same end and the common good. Rather, something more must be added, so that those who have once consented to peace and mutual assistance for the sake of the common good are prevented by fear from dissenting again later on, when their private good seems to clash with the common good.

5. Now what that is, which is fitted to maintain a consensus among many men for a long time, will be readily apparent to anyone who probes deeply into the nature of the human character. Here one encounters two main faults that prevent a number of men from being able to aspire together for long toward some common end. One is the diversity of inclinations and judgments concerning the determination of what most conduces to a common end; conjoined with the fact that many people are slow to see which of many means is the most useful, and obstinately persist in defending what has once pleased them in some way. The other is a slug-

gishness and aversion to doing what is useful on one's own, when no sort of necessity compels those who are reluctant to do their duty, whether they wish to or not. The remedy for the former evil lies in permanently uniting everyone's wills, or in so arranging things that henceforth there is one will of all concerning those things which contribute to the end of society. The latter is remedied by the establishment of some authority able to inflict a present, sensible evil on those who oppose the common interest. . . .

A union of wills can certainly not be brought about in the following ways: by naturally commingling all people's wills into one; by having only one person begin to will, while all the rest cease to do so; or by wholly eliminating in some way the natural discrepancy and diverse inclinations of wills, and combining them into a lasting harmony. Rather, the way in which many wills are ultimately understood to be united is this: if each person subjects his own will to the will of one man or one council, so that whatever the latter has decided about matters necessary for the common security is considered as the will of each and all. For each person is also thought to will that which another, on whom he has conferred the prerogative, may will. . . .

By the same reasoning, a power so great that all must fear it cannot be constituted by naturally transfusing into one person the strength of each and all, who would afterwards be completely enervated. Rather, the only way in which one person is understood to possess the strength of all is this: if each and all of them have obligated themselves to bring their strength to bear in the manner that he wills. From this union of wills and strength, when it has been brought about, there finally emerges the state, the strongest of societies and moral persons.

These things will be understood more precisely if we consider that the submission of wills on the part of subjects does not extinguish the natural freedom of the will through which they can, as it were, actually retract what they once gave and refuse the obedience they have promised. Moreover, the strength and faculties of subjects are not transfused into a sovereign in such a way that, for example, the strength which was in all their shoulders passes over into his. Therefore, the wills and strengths of subjects are drawn into conformity with sovereigns' wills by two weights, as it were. The first of these is based on the very pact by means of which subjects have submitted themselves to sovereigns. This pact's force is much increased by the precept of the Divinity and by the sacredness of oaths, which are more effective in bending men's minds insofar as the latter happen to have been well disciplined since childhood and have thoroughly examined the necessity and utility of civil sovereignty. Those, however, who resist the pressure of this weight through a wicked mind, who are either stupid in thinking that sovereignty is something invented for the pleasure of a few and the annoyance of the rest, or sluggish and averse to doing that which duty requires on their own, are driven to perform the commands of sovereigns by another weight, namely by a fear of punishment and by external compulsion.

Now, since one who would compel another should be stronger than he, and indeed, since the strength by which sovereigns exceed the strength of individual men comes from the fact that citizens employ their own strength as the former direct them to, it follows that the ability of sovereigns to compel and coerce bad citizens is from the obedience of good citizens. Furthermore, it is easy for one who has acquired his sovereignty lawfully and demonstrates even a moderate effort to do his duty, to bring it about that the greater part of the strength in a state is in his hand. For he can always expect the majority of citizens to be mindful of the divine precept and their given promise and oath; and it will never fail to be in the interest of the greater and better part of the people that the state be calm and safe, and that the authority of lawful sovereigns be well established. But there are also a number of other devices, as it were, by means of which the power of sovereigns is significantly increased, such as well-fortified places and a standing army bound to the sovereign by special bonds (through which a multitude of any size can be coerced, especially if it is unarmed and dispersed throughout a wide territory), and a cautious foresight on the part of sovereigns lest their citizens join together into factions.

6. For a more thorough understanding of this union one must know that so long as a number of physical persons have not coalesced into one moral person, whatever they do or whatever obligations they contract, they do and contract as individuals, so that there are as many actions and obligations as there are physical persons. Although many men are often referred to as a 'multitude' (which seems to denote a unity), still, if one were to consider the matter more accurately, 'multitude' is not a collective word, or one that denotes a one consisting of many, such as, for example, 'army,' 'fleet,' 'assembly,' 'senate,' and so on; rather, it actually denotes nothing but many things, abstracting from the question of whether they are of the same or different kinds, gathered together or dispersed. And so a multitude of men is really not some one thing but many men, each of whom has his own will and his own judgment concerning all things proposed for his consideration. Accordingly, a multitude, insofar as it is distinguished from individuals, cannot have attributed to it a single action separate from those of individuals, or a special right. Hence, even if someone were part of some multitude or surrounded by many men not conjoined into one body, if most or all the rest of these did or contracted something that he himself had not consented to or otherwise actually participated in, that act would in no way pertain to him. Indeed, for a multitude, or many men, to become one person to whom (insofar as it is opposed to individuals) one action can be attributed, and to whom certain rights belong which single individuals cannot attribute to themselves, they must have united their wills and strength by means of intervening pacts, without which a conjunction of many natural equals cannot be understood.

7. The number and the kinds of pacts by whose intervention a state is formed are discovered in the following manner. If we conceive in our minds a multitude of men enjoying natural freedom and equality, who are about to establish a new state on their own initiative, it is necessary that all the future citizens first enter into a pact with one another as individuals, expressing their desire to come together into a single, lasting group, and to deal with the considerations of their own welfare and security by means of a common counsel and leadership. (In most such pacts, however, individuals reserve for themselves a license to emigrate.)

This pact is entered into either absolutely or conditionally. The former occurs when someone binds himself to remain with that group, whatever form of government finally pleases the majority; the latter, when he attaches this condition: "if a form of government approved by me is introduced." Furthermore, when this pact is entered into, it is necessary that each and everyone consent to it. One who has not consented, even though he may go about with the rest in the same place for some time, remains outside the future state. He is not bound in any way by the consensus of the rest to join himself to that group, no matter how numerous they are, but remains in his natural freedom, in which he will be permitted to make his own judgments about his welfare.

Now, after this kind of group exhibiting the rudiments and beginnings of a state has formed by means of the pact just described, it is necessary, in addition, that there be a decree concerning the form of government to be introduced. For before this matter has been settled, nothing contributing to the common welfare can be undertaken on a regular basis. Here, those who have joined themselves absolutely to that group will, if they wish to remain in the place it has settled, be bound by the consensus of the majority to acquiesce in the form of government pleasing to it, even if they themselves would have preferred another. For by not taking exception to anything in the pact, they are understood to have submitted themselves—in this respect at least—to the will of the majority, since they cannot reasonably demand that all the rest prefer the judgment of a few to their own. But someone who has joined himself to that group upon a condition will not become a member of the future state, or be obligated by the consensus of the majority, unless he has expressly consented to the form of government to be introduced.

8. After the decree concerning the form of government, a new pact will be needed to constitute the person or persons on whom the government of the group is conferred. By means of it, these persons bind themselves to care for the common security and welfare, while the rest bind themselves to obey them. This pact also contains that subjection and union of wills through which the state is understood as one person, and from it there finally results a perfect state.

Now this pact does not appear so clearly later on where a democracy has been established, since those who command and those who obey are, in different respects, the same. But a pact requires two distinct persons, and different respects do not seem to suffice. For example, one and the same Titius can in different respects be father, son, husband, son-in-law, father-in-law, merchant, and so forth; in which case there will be no pact if Titius as merchant has promised anything to the same Titius as father. But one should know that in a popular commonwealth the citizens and the council (in which the highest power resides) do not differ in a mere respect but are really different persons (although of a different kind) to whom a distinct will, actions, and rights belong. For that which individual citizens will is not immediately willed by the people, and that which individual citizens do is not immediately considered an action of the people, and vice versa. Individuals do not have supreme sovereignty, or some part of it, but the people does. For it is one thing to have a part of the sovereignty, and another to have the right to cast a ballot in a council in which the supreme sovereignty resides. Hence, nothing so far seems to prevent the existence of a pact between a council of the people and individual citizens.

It could perhaps be urged, not inappropriately, that such a pact between a sovereign people and obedient citizens would be useless, because each person, in consenting to a democratic form [of government], is also understood to have subjected his own will to the will of the majority; and, at the same time, each person seems already sufficiently necessitated by the love of himself and his own things to watch out as much as he can for the public good, to which his own welfare is also connected. Nonetheless, even if it is perhaps not as necessary in democracies as in other forms of the commonwealth that that pact, or a mutual promise concerning the exercise of the duties of ruler and subject, be expressly made, it is absolutely necessary to understand it to have intervened, at least tacitly. For whether that decree concerning the introduction of a democracy is conceived merely as an agreement of many wills conspiring together, or as a pact among individuals (in the form "I will submit my own will to the council of the whole, if you will do the same"), no other obligation results from it, upon close consideration, than that individuals are bound to acquiesce in that form of commonwealth so long as it has not been altered by everyone together.

But one surely finds more of an obligation in the citizens of democracies. For they are both bound as individuals to abide by the decrees and commands arising from the council of the whole, and, at the same time, individually obligated to assume the care of the commonwealth as much as they can, and to consider their private advantage less important than the public good. For on what pretext could a citizen otherwise be censured and punished for being infrequently seen at the council? Now, as the obligation is apparent, it is also necessary that it have an origin, and this is nothing other than the pact we have referred to. . . .

But this latter pact is far more clearly discerned where it has pleased men to establish an aristocracy or a monarchy. For once nobles or a king has been designated, there is surely a mutual offer and acceptance of promises, giving rise to mutual performances on each side. That is, once sovereignty has been conferred and accepted, the king and nobles are no less bound than the citizens to perform tasks that were previously not owed. Before that pact, the citizens were no more bound to obey one man, or a few, than he or they to care for the welfare of the state. But from where can this mutual promise and the obligation to perform previously unowed tasks have originated, except from a pact? . . .

It must be well noted that this manner of generating the state by means of two intervening pacts and one decree is most natural, and common to all forms of the commonwealth. Nonetheless, it is possible for a monarchy to be constituted through a single pact only, as when many people, either at the same or different times, and apart from an antecedent pact among themselves, have subjected themselves to one person, much in the fashion of standing armies that are assembled out of volunteers and mercenaries. Similarly, those who are later added to an already constituted state need only a single agreement whereby they themselves ask to be received into the state, and those who embody the persona of the state receive them after exacting their obedience.

Moreover, it is not possible for anyone to think that we are making up these things about the pacts generating the state on the ground that the first origins of most states are unknown, or, at least, that it is not so clearly established that they have been formed in this manner. For it is certain that every state had its origin at some time. It was necessary, however, before the constitution of a state, that those of whom it consists not be connected among themselves by the same sort of bond as connected them after it was established, and that they not yet subject themselves to those whose subjects they afterward were. But since that conjunction and subjection cannot be understood to have been brought about apart from the compacts mentioned earlier, these must have at least tacitly intervened in the formation of states. Nothing prevents our being able to conduct a rational investigation of a thing's origins, even though no literary accounts thereof are extant.

11. . . . Indeed, those who have agreed among themselves about conferring sovereignty on someone are understood also to have consented that all of them will subject their own wills to that person, or that in the conduct of public affairs his will shall represent the will of all. Nor is it infrequent for such a consensus about the conferral of sovereignty on someone, as also about the conditions under which sovereignty is bestowed on the person, to be confirmed by a people's mutual pacts and oaths. Still, to agree with one another about conferring sovereignty on Gaius, and to bestow sovereignty on Gaius by means of an exchange of promises, are surely distinct.

Now there is nothing opposed to citizens' also giving each other mutual assurance about rendering obedience to a king, just as there are pacts where all obligate themselves for one, and one for all. Yet it is not at all necessary for this to be done, nor is it all that frequent in practice. One who is newly received into a state gives a promise to the king himself: nowhere, as far as we know, is it required that he make a pact with the remaining citizens about rendering obedience to the king. . . .

But we assert that the legitimate authority of a king and the duty of citizens correspond exactly with one another, and so we completely deny that a king can by right command something that a subject can by right refuse. For a king cannot by right order more things than are consistent with, or are judged to be consistent with, the end for which civil society was instituted. If by malice or through madness he has ordered anything contrary to this end, he will by no means be thought to do this by right. But whether subjects may resist these kinds of orders is another question which we shall examine in another place. . . .

13. Through these pacts, therefore, a unified multitude of men constitutes a state, which is conceived in the manner of a single person who understands and wills, and performs other, peculiar actions distinct from the actions of single individuals. It is distinguished and known apart from all particular men by means of a name; . . . and it has rights and things of its own that are no less peculiar, and that neither single, several, nor even all individuals together can claim apart from the one who has the supreme sovereignty. Similarly, there proceed from it peculiar actions that individuals can in no way attribute to or claim for themselves. . . . Hence, it seems most suitable to define the state as a composite moral person whose will, a single strand woven out of many people's pacts, is considered as the will of all, so that it can use the strength and faculties of individuals for the common peace and security. . . .

14. Furthermore, the will of the state exerts itself either through one single person or through one council, depending on whether supreme control has been con-

ferred on the former or the latter. When sovereignty resides in one man, the state is understood to will whatever pleases that man (assuming his reason remains sound)—at least in the case of matters concerning the end of states, but not those that concern other things. Thus, for example, if a king declares war, if he makes peace, if he enters into an alliance, the state is said to have willed and done these things; but not so if he eats or drinks, if he sleeps, if he takes a wife, if he indulges in vices. . . . And so one can also distinguish between a monarch's public will, which represents the will of the state, and his private will, by means of which he disposes of non-public affairs like any other man.

Here the question arises: What if he in whom the will of the state resides wills otherwise than he ought, and therefore sins in exercising the public will; must an action that proceeds from his depraved will be considered an action of the state? For a person who has submitted his will to the will of his prince is understood to have done so in the expectation that the latter shall will nothing except what is to the advantage of the state, and just.

Here it seems we must say that an action which proceeds from the abuse and corruption of the public will is, in itself at any rate, a public action and an action of the state, because it is undertaken by the sovereign as such. Thus, if a monarch or a senate proposes bad laws, renders bad judicial decisions, appoints unfit magistrates, or undertakes unjust wars, the monarch or senate is surely performing public actions. (If a charioteer overturns the chariot, it is still the action of a charioteer, but of an inexperienced or a negligent one.) Yet in the divine forum no one is held accountable for such an action unless he has contributed to it by his own positive and effective consent. Hence subjects, as well as those who have dissented from a ruling council and have been defeated by the majority, are not guilty of a public transgression. But the disadvantages that redound on innocent citizens from such public transgressions must be placed in the class of those evils to which the human condition is exposed in this mortal state, and therefore endured like drought or excessive rains and other natural evils. Although basic laws, good discipline, and especially religion are found to be quite effective in preventing such disadvantages. . . .

15. But when supreme control has been conferred on a council consisting of many men, each of whom retains his own will, it must first be determined how many of them agreeing together represent the will of the whole council, and therefore of the state. For otherwise, even though a person has entered a society with others in order to deliberate in common about conducting their affairs, if he has done so with the express reservation that he wishes to be bound to nothing which he himself has not consented to, he is in no way bound by the decrees of the majority; just as no one is bound to follow the opinion of another rather than his own unless he has subjected his will to that of the latter. Thus there are associations where the dissent of one person can render the consensus of all the rest ineffective. Though when someone is unwilling to listen to the plain voice of reason and opposes the correct sentiments of the rest through stubbornness alone, he can be expelled from the society as unfit, or sometimes even be coerced by means of an evil. For although he is not bound here by his own consent to follow the opinion of the majority, he is nonetheless bound by the general law that he should make

himself serviceable to the rest and, as a part, conform himself to the good of the whole.... Hence the votes of the majority regularly have, in all councils, the force of all, not because it is naturally necessary that it happen so, but because there is hardly another way to accomplish business there....

20. Finally, once a state has been constituted in this way, the one on whom the sovereignty has been conferred is called either a monarch, a senate, or a people, depending on whether it is one man or one council, composed of either a few or of all; the rest are known as subjects.

Here it must be observed that someone becomes a member of any state in two ways, namely by an express or by a tacit pact. For those who constituted states at the beginning are certainly not thought to have done this so that states might be extinguished at the same time as the individuals who initially constituted them, but rather, they expected to obtain through the state long and lasting advantages which even their children and all posterity would enjoy. Therefore, they must also be thought to have made the following arrangement: Their children and posterity would, as soon as they were born, enjoy the common benefits and advantages of the state. But since these cannot be obtained without sovereignty, by which the state is, as it were, animated, all who are born in a state are also understood thereby to have subjected themselves to that sovereignty. Hence it is that he who has once accepted the sovereignty in some state does not find it necessary to demand anew the express subjection of a recently born offspring, even though all those who initially conferred the sovereignty on him may have died.

Next, since every state occupies a certain part of the earth where its citizens have settled themselves and their fortunes in safety, and since the security of these fortunes would be easily endangered if anyone who did not acknowledge the sovereignty of the state were permitted to go about there, it is understood to be a common law of all states that one who has entered the territory of a particular state—and especially if he wishes to enjoy its advantages—is deemed to have renounced his natural freedom and subjected himself to that state's sovereignty, at least so long as it pleases him to remain there. But if he is unwilling to make this acknowledgment, let him be considered an enemy, at least to the point where he can rightly be driven outside the state's borders. Similarly, it is obvious as well that those who are added to a state after it has been constituted are no less subject to the civil sovereignty than those by whose coming together the state was initially constituted.

Finally, it must also be noted here that certain learned men are insufficiently agreed about the definition of a 'citizen.' ... To me it seems that since a state is constituted by the submission of wills to one man or council, citizens are primarily those by whose pacts the state was initially formed, or those who have taken their place. And since it was family-fathers who did this, I would have thought that the name of 'citizens' belonged chiefly to them; whereas women, children, and slaves, whose wills have been contained under the will of the family-father, to them it belongs only in a consequent sense, insofar as they also enjoy the common protection of the state and some rights by virtue of that relation. Resident aliens, foreigners, and similar temporary inhabitants, however, are not citizens, because they wish to remain only for a time but not to seek lasting security and the seat of their fortunes there....

21. Now we notice that there are two particular bonds, above all, that apply to citizens in most commonwealths. Through one of them, some citizens are formed into particular bodies that are nonetheless still subordinate to the state; through the other, they are admitted by the supreme sovereigns into some part of the public administration. Those bodies which are subordinate to the state, whether they come with the name 'associations,' 'societies,' or something else, can first be divided into those that preceded states and those that sprang up after states were constituted.

Those bodies more ancient than the state are families; we have set forth above the kind of sovereignty and right that belonged in them to family-fathers. These retain of this right whatever has not been taken away from them through the nature of the state, or through civil laws and public mores. Of bodies which arose after states were constituted, some can be called public, some private. Public bodies are those constituted by the authority of the supreme civil sovereignty. Private bodies, however, have been formed either by an agreement of the citizens themselves or depend on some external authority which, in a foreign state, can be considered as nothing but some private right or endeavor. . . .

22. It must be observed about all lawful bodies that whatever right they have, and whatever authority over their own members, is entirely defined by the supreme authority and can in no way be opposed to or prevail against it. For otherwise, if there were a body not subject to limitation by the supreme civil sovereignty, there would be a state within a state. Hence if a state was formed somewhere out of several absolute and independent bodies, it was necessary for these to have given up so much of their former authority as the nature of the state required, since otherwise they would have fallen short of the end which they set for themselves. . . .

Chapter 3

ON THE GENERATION OF SUPREME CIVIL
SOVEREIGNTY OR MAJESTY

1. Let us see now from where the supreme sovereignty that exists in every state and is, as it were, its vivifying and sustaining soul, is directly and immediately produced. We presuppose here at the beginning that sovereignty, in order to achieve its proper effect, requires both the natural strength by which a subject, if he by chance presumes to refuse that which is enjoined, can be compelled by the mani-

festation of some evil, and a title by right of which others, in whom there is a corresponding obligation to obey its commands, can be enjoined to do or not do something. Both of these flow immediately from the pacts through which the state is formed.

For even though no one can naturally transfuse his strength into another, a person is understood to possess the strength of others if these are, at his discretion, so bound to apply it that there is in them no authority to resist or refuse his command. There is indeed no other transfer of strength among men. But since all, in submitting their wills to the will of one man, have bound themselves thereby not to resist, or to obey that person, who seeks to apply their strength and wealth toward the public good, it appears that the strength of one who has the supreme sovereignty is such that he can compel anyone to abide by his commands. . . .

This same pact also provides a clear title by which that sovereignty is understood to be legitimately constituted, not by violence but by the spontaneous subjection and consensus of the citizens. This is therefore the proximate cause from which supreme sovereignty as a moral quality results. For given submission in one person and its acceptance in another, there immediately arises in the latter the right to enjoin something on the former, or sovereignty. And just as a right to our things can be conferred through pacts, so can a right to dispose over our freedom and strength be conferred through submission. Hence, for example, if anyone voluntarily delivers himself into slavery to me by means of a pact, he really confers on me the authority of a master. And it is amateurish to intone against these things the threadbare maxim that one cannot confer on another what one does not have.

But for sovereignty to acquire a peculiar efficacy and sanctity, another principle besides the submission of the subjects must be added. And so one who teaches that sovereignty results immediately from pacts does not by any means detract from the sanctity of supreme civil sovereignty, or maintain that a prince commands by human right only, and not also by divine right.

2. It is beyond doubt, at any rate, that after humankind had multiplied, sound reason was sufficiently insistent that its honor, peace, and safety could not be maintained without the establishment of states, which cannot be understood without supreme sovereignty. And this is the reason that states and supreme sovereignty are thought to come from God as author of the natural law. For not only are those things from God which He has established directly without the intervention of any human deed, but those also which sound reason has led men to undertake, in accordance with temporal and spatial conditions, in order to fulfill the obligation enjoined on them by God. . . . And since, in a great multitude of men, the natural law cannot easily be put into practice apart from civil sovereignty, it is evident that God Who has enjoined it on men also commands them to establish civil societies, insofar as these serve as a sort of means for the cultivation of the natural law.

Hence God expressly approves that sovereignty in the Sacred Scriptures, acknowledging it as something in accordance with His will and confirming its sanctity and veneration by means of the severest laws. But it is not evident whether He distinctly commanded that a state be established at a specific place and time. For the precept of Noah's sons about judicial procedures, which could perhaps be brought to bear on this, does not expressly refer to a time and place when they ought to be established. Thus, it could mean that judicial procedures should be followed where they have been established. . . .

Chapter 4

ON THE PARTS OF SUPREME SOVEREIGNTY

AND THEIR NATURAL CONNECTION

1. Even though supreme civil sovereignty is in itself something one and undivided, it is nonetheless commonly understood to have many parts analogous to those called potential, because it exerts itself through different acts corresponding to the different means it must employ to preserve the state. For supreme sovereignty is by no means a whole consisting of heterogeneous parts that, by being conjoined with one another and held together by some bond, have coalesced into one, yet in such a way that the individual parts can also subsist separately. Rather, just as the soul is a 'one' that dispenses life and vigor to the whole body, and is conceived to have potential parts in accord with its production of different operations corresponding to different objects and organs; so the supreme sovereignty is called a legislative authority when it is occupied with the prescription of general rules of acting, a judicial authority inasmuch as it decides the controversies of the citizens according to these rules, the right of war and peace when it arms the citizens against outsiders or commands them to be peaceful, the right of constituting magistrates inasmuch as it acquires for itself ministers concerned with public affairs, and so on.

2. But what these parts of the supreme sovereignty are is very plainly seen from the nature and the end of states. A state is a moral body understood to have one will. But since it consists of many physical persons, each of whom has his own particular will and inclination, and these wills cannot be naturally commingled into one or tempered into a lasting harmony, the manner in which a single will is produced in a state is for all persons to submit their own will to the will of that man or council on whom the supreme sovereignty has been conferred.

Now since individual citizens ought to conform themselves to the will of the state, it is necessary that this become known to them through clear signs. Hence it is understood to be the role of the supreme sovereignty to indicate and prescribe to all what they ought to do or omit. And because it would be impossible in such a great multitude of men to promulgate special commands for individuals and concerning particular actions, general rules are prescribed from which it is clear to everyone, in perpetuity, what things ought to be done or omitted. Moreover, since we find among men an extreme diversity of judgments and appetites from which an infinite crop of controversies can arise, it is also in the interest of peace that there be a public definition of what each person should count as his own and what another's; what ought to be considered permitted or not permitted in the state, as well as moral or immoral; and again, what remains for each person of his natural freedom, or how he should temper the use of his own rights for the sake of the tranquillity of the state.

3. Now the chief end of states is that men, by means of mutual cooperation and assistance, be safe against the harms and injuries they can and commonly do inflict on one another, or rather, that they enjoy peace or have suitable defenses against those who attack them. But for peace it is above all necessary that everyone be so far protected against the violence of others that he can live securely, that is, that he have no just cause to fear the rest so long as he himself has not provoked them by means of injury. Of course, the human condition does not allow men to be made safe from mutual harms, or to be entirely incapable of being injured. But it is possible to see to it that there is no probable cause for fear. And this security is the end on account of which men subject themselves to others. Did they not consider themselves more secure due to their conjunction with others than if someone is protected by his own strength alone, it would be foolish to renounce the natural freedom in which everyone defends himself as he chooses.

But it does not suffice for this security that each of those about to coalesce into a state make a verbal or written agreement with the rest about not killing, stealing, or inflicting other harms. For the wickedness of the human character is obvious in the case of most men, and we know too well by experience how weakly most of them are kept within the bounds of duty solely by a reverence for their own fidelity and the dictate of sound reason, once you remove the fear of punishment. For this reason, it is not even sufficient that there be someone who prescribes rules about the things that ought to be done, if he has no authority besides this. . . .
Therefore, if men are to observe both the common precepts of the natural law and those especially laid down for the good of a state, a fear of punishment and the faculty to impose it are needed. And for the punishment to suffice for this end, it must be made so great that violating the law is clearly a greater evil than observing it and, thus, the severity of the punishment overcomes the delight or gain derived or expected from the injury. For of two evils men cannot but choose that which seems to them the lesser. Thus the heads of others protect my own. And although rashness or an extreme commotion of the mind may sometimes drive some people to prefer the perpetration of a crime to the omission of an offense, this is nonetheless considered to be among those less frequent occurrences that the human condition does not allow us to avoid. . . .

4. In addition, each of the two powers just mentioned is understood to be reinforced by a judicial authority, because even when the laws that have been framed are most meticulous, controversies over their right application to particular deeds tend to arise on many occasions, and there are often many things to be weighed when something is said to have been done against the laws. It is the task of this judicial authority to hear and decide the disputes of citizens, to examine the deeds

of individuals alleged to be contrary to the laws, and to assign a penalty appropriate to the laws. . . .

5. But even though precautions for the security of citizens against their fellow citizens have been taken in this manner, this is nonetheless not yet sufficient for attaining the end of states. For those who cultivate peace among themselves do so in vain if they cannot protect themselves against outsiders—which those whose strength is not united certainly cannot accomplish. The fact that many persons are more powerful than one comes from their union, for otherwise even a thousand, when they are divided, are not stronger than one. Therefore, it is necessary for everyone's security and welfare that there be in the state an authority whose task it is to gather, to unite, and to arm as many citizens (or those hired in their place) as seem to be needed for the common defense, in light of the uncertain number and strength of the enemies, and then, when it has become expedient, to make peace with the enemies. And since alliances make it possible in times of both peace and war to share better the advantages of different states, and to repel or reduce to order a stronger enemy by means of their combined strength, it will be up to the supreme sovereignty to enter into alliances useful at either time, and to bind all subjects to their observance while deriving from them advantages that redound to the state.

6. Since the affairs of a state, whether they occur in a time of peace or war, can surely not be administered and executed by one man without ministers and subordinate magistrates, a state will also need the authority to constitute men who examine the controversies of citizens . . . , ferret out the plans of neighboring states, govern the military, collect and dispense the state's wealth, and finally, see to the interest of the state in every way whatever. This authority can compel these persons, once they have been constituted, to do their duty, and can demand from them an account of their deeds. . . .

7. Now because it is not possible in a time of either peace or war to conduct the affairs of a state without incurring expenses, there is required in it the authority to reserve for such uses a certain part of the goods or crops of the region inhabited by its people, or to force individual citizens to contribute so much of their own goods as the assumption of those expenses is deemed to require; and, no less, to command and exact the services of citizens if they are required. This is also the concern of that authority which looks about for other licit means by which the wealth of the state may be increased, chief among which is the right to impose taxes on imported or exported merchandise, and also to appropriate a moderate part of the price of things consumed.

8. Finally, even though it is beyond human ability to remove the intrinsic freedom of the will and, at the same time, through some intrinsic means compose men's judgments concerning things into a constant harmony, it is altogether necessary to see to it that these judgments, though they clash, do not disturb the tranquillity of the state. Now since all voluntary actions are initiated by and dependent on the will, but the will to do or not to do something depends on the opinion of the good or evil, reward or punishment, that everyone conceives will follow for himself from his deed or omission (and the actions of all are therefore ruled by each person's own opinion), there will surely be need for external means so that those opinions and judgments do as much as possible agree, or at least so that their discrepancy

does not disturb the state. Hence it is expedient that the state publicly profess, as it were, doctrines that agree with the end and function of states, and also that the minds of the citizens be imbued with them from childhood. For most mortals tend to perceive things as they have been accustomed to, and according to what they see as the common judgment. Very few of them are able to discern what is substantial in human affairs by their own mental acuity.

Indeed, there is almost no doctrine, either about the worship of God or the human sciences, from which dissensions, discords, reproaches and, finally, wars cannot arise. This does not happen because of the falsity of a doctrine or because, if its opposite is allowed, great disadvantages may redound to humankind or states, but because of the disposition of humans who, seeing themselves as wise, want to be seen as such by everyone and are very greatly annoyed at those who feel differently. This will be readily acknowledged by anyone who has paid even random attention to the quarrels of the learned about trivialities, in which they are no less actively engaged than if they were fighting for hearth and home. Although it is true that these kinds of dissensions cannot be prevented from arising, the supreme sovereignty can nonetheless bring it about, by means of punitive sanctions against those who engage in them, that they do not disturb the public peace. . . .

But our discussion is not properly about these kinds of doctrines but about those which—whether forwarded under the guise of religion or in another manner—undermine the natural law and the principles of sound politics, and so are apt to produce fatal diseases in the state. Nor is any true doctrine endangered on this account. For no true doctrine conflicts with peace, and one that does conflict with peace is not true—unless even peace and concord may be said to be contrary to natural laws. Therefore, the examination of at least these kinds of doctrines, and the authority to proscribe and ban them from the state, are rightly attributed to the supreme civil sovereignty. . . .

9. Next, we must show that these parts of the supreme sovereignty are naturally so united and, as it were, interwoven with one another, that if we were to imagine some of them to be independently controlled by one person, and some by others, the regular form of the state would be completely destroyed. To have a solid understanding of this matter, one must observe that there are two bonds, in the main, by which the wills of many men and groups are connected, so that they conspire together as one: namely, pact and sovereignty. Of these the latter binds far more strongly than the former. Those who are restrained by a pact alone are bound by the law of nature to furnish on their own that which was agreed upon, while remaining naturally equal in other respects. As long as both parties keep their agreements, concord and unity can be sufficiently maintained among them in this way. But when someone has deceitfully backed out of a pact, he is of course guilty of violating the natural law; the rest, however, in whose interest it was that the pact be kept, have nothing with which to bring the violator back into line besides violent war, in which he who did the injury predominates as often as the one who received it. Thus there is concord among equal confederates so long as each of them voluntarily furnishes what he has promised; but when the treachery of one of them has intervened the bond is destroyed and a cause for war provided.

It appears from this that pacts alone are not sufficiently strong bonds, at least for keeping many persons collected into one moral body for a long time, especially since it is not always the few and the weak who depart from a pact to the detriment of those more numerous and strong, but also the many to the detriment of the few. And even though we suppose that another pact has been added to the main pact, to the effect that all the rest will, by means of their combined strength, punish anyone who violates it, still (aside from the fact that this would be useless when many people have withdrawn from the pact at the same time), unless a democratic sovereignty has been constituted among the allies, or unless those formerly allied have coalesced into one state, another pact will in turn be needed on how to coerce a person who refuses to abide by this additional pact, and thus to infinity.

But sovereignty is indeed a far stronger bond by which many people can be gathered into one body. For those who are held together by the same sovereignty do not remain equal to the one in whom it resides. Rather, when one man or council has conferred on it the authority to issue prescriptions and to threaten those who neglect to obey them with some evil as a punishment, there is incumbent on everyone a far greater necessity to obey than if they were bound by a pact alone, by which the equality among allies and the right of each to decide about his own things according to his own judgment is not eliminated.

10. It must also be noted that if there are those who wish to maintain that, in one and the same state, the parts of sovereignty called potential belong in a fundamental sense to several distinct persons or councils, they must also admit that one to whom some part of the sovereignty belongs must necessarily be furnished with the authority to compel the citizens to observe the things instituted by virtue of that part, and to defend that right of his if anyone should wish to attack or disturb it, even when the right of war belongs to someone else; and, finally, that he can determine according to his own judgment and by his own right the time and manner in which that part of the sovereignty is to be exercised. For it is anything but sovereignty to have only the right to indicate to others what you wish them to do, and yet to lack the power also to compel those who are reluctant to observe what has been indicated. Our hold on that which we are not permitted to defend against another is precarious, and someone who exercises a right as another decides is but his minister or executor.

11. It will be readily apparent from what has been said that the conjunction among all parts of the supreme sovereignty is such that one part cannot be torn from the other without the regular form of the state being destroyed, resulting in an irregular body held together only by an infirm pact. For if the legislative authority belongs in the end to one part and the punitive power to another, fundamentally and independently to each, either the former will necessarily be without substance or the latter will minister to it. This is because passing laws which you are unable to put into effect is a hollow exercise, and to have the strength by which you may compel others, but only if another decides that it should be brought to bear, is characteristic of a minister or a bare executor. But if you also give the latter the privilege of making an informed judgment about the application of his own strength, you by the same act reduce the legislative authority to nothing. It is necessary, therefore, that both faculties depend on one and the same will.

Now it is obvious that the right of war and peace, and the right to impose taxes, cannot be separated from this right. For no one can rightfully compel citizens to take up arms, or to assume the expenses of war and peace, unless he can rightfully punish those who do not comply. It would be absurd, moreover, to assign the right of making treaties conducive to peace and war to someone other than the one who has the right to decide about peace and war. For in that case either the latter will be a pure minister, or the former will depend on someone else's decision in readying the means useful for the exercise of his own right. Thus, if you wished to entrust a certain matter to someone yet did not at the same time give him the authority to constitute and hold accountable the ministers without whom it cannot be accomplished, you would in fact make him the ministers' equal. Therefore, the authority to constitute magistrates cannot be separated from the remaining parts of the supreme sovereignty. . . .

Finally, the same authority will also be in charge of the critical examination of doctrines, especially those that are somehow concerned with the end of states, and that have an effect on men's consciences by either promoting or impeding their obedience to the supreme sovereignty. For if someone has commanded the citizens to do something on pain of natural death and another persuades them that by doing it they will incur the punishment of eternal death, and each by his own separate and independent right, it not only follows that citizens can by right be punished even though they are innocent, but also that the civil state will be reduced to an irregular status where it has two heads. For no one can serve two masters, and he who we believe must be followed on fear of eternal damnation is no less a master than he who is obeyed on fear of temporal death. And once the right of regulating doctrines has been lost, the fantasies of superstitious citizens will encourage them to rebel. . . .

12. These things will appear more clearly if we examine the various kinds of this sort of division. Accordingly, let the authority of war and peace belong to the prince, the right to pass laws and make judicial decisions to the senate, and the right to impose taxes to the council of the people. Here, if the king calls the citizens to arms and they do not wish to obey him, either he will have the right to compel them himself by means of punishments, or he will have to hand them over to the senate to be judged. If we admit the former, it is not clear how one who does not have the authority to execute the laws will exact punishments from citizens who have not yet been enrolled in the military. If you say that the king has the right to impose punishments on the non-compliant in this case alone, you thereby give him the right to molest all the citizens at his pleasure, and therefore reduce the rights of the rest to nothing. For when he has commanded them to take up arms, he will inflict punishments upon them if they do not obey; when he has led them into a campaign, the rationale of military discipline will give him the right of life and death over them. And nothing is easier for a commander than to destroy a soldier whom he hates. . . .

But if the king finds it necessary to bring those who refuse to take the military oath before the senate, either the senate will pronounce a sentence of condemnation at the king's bare command and follow it up with punishment—which is against the hypothesis—or it will conduct its own investigation into the citizens' alleged crime. This investigation is without substance unless the senate can also inquire whether it is advantageous or not for the commonwealth that the king now undertake a war. In this manner the right of the king will be reduced to nothing.

We will find the same disadvantages if we compare the rights of king and people with one another in such a condition. . . . Thus, if a king does not by virtue of his sovereignty have the authority to compel citizens to pay taxes, his right of war will be nothing other than the bare faculty to persuade them that taking up arms here and now is to the commonwealth's advantage. But if a people does not have the faculty of knowing whether the war for whose undertaking it must contribute a tax is useful or not, what other function will it have but that of laboriously assessing and collecting taxes? And each of these is contrary to the hypothesis. Nor will things go better if we divide the parts of supreme sovereignty in another manner. . . .

These matters can be illustrated by the example of the human soul, to which the supreme sovereignty in a state bears some resemblance. For if we imagine the potential parts of the rational soul, the understanding and the will, to exist separately in different subjects, the understanding alone belonging to one and the will to the other, such a subject could neither be called a man nor human actions be expected from it, since one of them is always in an immovable torpor, as it were, and the other engaged in fruitless activity as though blind. . . .

Hence if anyone should wish to separate entirely the parts of sovereignty, he will by no means constitute a regular state but an irregular body whose members, being in possession of the separated parts of the sovereignty, are held together not by a common sovereignty but only through an agreement. It will be possible somehow to preserve harmony in such a group, as long as individuals' opinions about the public good are in friendly agreement and each person is prepared on his own to supply that which contributes to this end. But when dissension has arisen, nothing remains but to go to arbiters or to decide the matter by war.

Chapter 5

ON THE FORMS OF COMMONWEALTHS

1. Supreme sovereignty, which is found in every state as in a common subject, produces different forms of commonwealths according to its inherence, as in a proper subject, in one man or one council consisting of either a few or all the citizens. (We think here, first of all, that we may still avail ourselves of the word 'form' in order to express that condition of states resulting from the different subjects in which the supreme sovereignty fundamentally inheres.)

It is a well-known fact, of course, that the *actual administration of a common-wealth* often departs from this condition, as when, say, some things in a *democracy* are done *in the fashion of a monarchy* and some *in the fashion of a polyarchy*, when the people entrust the carrying out of certain affairs to one or a few persons. And because it makes a great difference whether the authority exercised by some-one is his own, or an alien authority granted by another who can strip him of it at any time, it is quite unwarranted [*akuros*] to assert the following: "It is in fact a polyarchy when a king allows himself to be led by the nose by a few persons who abuse his patience, or a monarchy when a people allows a demagogue to do so, or when one person, even in a supreme senate, controls the rest by means of his pru-dence, eloquence, or the fear of his power. Nothing remains here except the empty name and external appearance of a monarchy in the first case, of a democracy in the second, of a polyarchy in the third." And in the same way, a sensible person will not believe the form of a commonwealth to have been changed when the persons or number of ministers changes, no more than he believes that an interregnum exists when a successor drives the minister in charge of the adminis-tration of things under the former prince headlong from his court.

The capacity and inclinations of the person or persons who exercise a sover-eignty by their own right, or one that has been delegated, do affect and alter the administration of a commonwealth, to be sure, but by no means its form. Thus, even though the administration of sovereignty may be outstanding in one place and corrupt in another, the different exercise of the same authority, as it were, does not immediately produce a new kind of state. Hence, just as healthy and sick per-sons do not immediately differ in kind, nor badly formed limbs make up different kinds of men, so the faults of rulers or of those who obey them, or corrupt laws, by no means constitute a different kind of commonwealth.

3. There are only three forms of a regular state, resulting from the proper sub-ject of supreme sovereignty, which is either one simple person or a council that consists of either a few or all [the citizens]. For supreme sovereignty is entrusted either to one man or to a council of many men. This council is, in turn, either one of all the citizens or of a smaller but select part. Therefore, the first kind of state exists where supreme sovereignty resides in a council consisting of everyone, and where any citizen has the right to cast a vote; it is called a 'democracy.' The sec-ond exists where supreme sovereignty resides in a council consisting of select citi-zens, and is said to be an 'aristocracy.' The third exists where supreme sovereignty resides in one man, and is called a 'monarchy' or a kingdom. Those in charge of things are called a 'people' in the first, 'nobles' in the second, 'monarch' in the third. . . .

4. We shall first see about democracy, not because we think it surpasses the other forms in dignity or external splendor, or in advantage, . . . but because it is undisputedly the most ancient among most nations, and also because reason shows it to be more likely that a number of men enjoying natural freedom and equality, who decided to come together into one body, chose first to administer their com-mon affairs by common counsel and therefore to establish a democracy. Also, we should not presume that a free family-father who, upon noticing the disadvantages of a life apart, voluntarily came together with others similar to himself into a state,

could in one moment, as it were, have forgotten the former 'state' in which he used to make his own decisions about the arrangement of all things affecting his welfare, so as to be willing right away, with respect to the common affairs to which his own welfare was also connected, to submit himself to the will of one person. On the contrary, it was from the beginning believed to be most advantageous that that which concerns all should be under the care of all, until the majority left that 'state,' either of themselves or through a necessity brought about either by some citizens or by outsiders. . . .

7. Now the things that seem to be most necessary in a democracy are these. First, a certain place and time must be established for assemblies where the public interest is to be deliberated and decided. For the private affairs of individuals will not allow them to be in constant attendance at such an assembly; and if there has not been agreement on a place and time, those who are from the same group can either come together at different places and times (from which factions will arise) or not come together at all—in which case there will not be a people (*dēmos*) but a scattered multitude to which, as to one person, neither action nor right can be said to belong. . . .

Second, the vote of the majority must be valid for all, since it happens only very rarely that a great multitude of men feels the same way about the same thing.

Finally, since some affairs of a commonwealth are of the everyday variety and of lesser importance, others rarer and such as affect the public interest, and indeed, since it is not convenient for the people as a whole to be constantly coming together into council in order to deal with the former matters, or in such short intervals that nothing of this sort can escape their care, it is necessary for certain magistrates to be appointed as delegates authorized by the whole people to deal with everyday matters; to look into serious ones at the proper time and, if anything more important occurs, to refer it to the people when they have been convoked; and also, since a large group is quite unsuited for this, to execute the people's decrees.

8. An aristocracy is constituted when a group that has united itself through the first pact into some rudiment of a state decrees that the public interest is to be entrusted to a council consisting of a few persons. These, after they have been designated by that group (either by their own names, by a general description, or by some other mark by which they can be known apart from the rest) and have accepted that designation, are understood to receive the supreme sovereignty when the rest submit themselves to their will. . . .

9. Finally, a monarchy is constituted when the supreme sovereignty is conferred upon one man. That this is done by means of an intervening pact surely has, against Hobbes, been sufficiently demonstrated. . . .

A monarchy differs from the former kinds [of state] in that these require fixed times and places so that there can be deliberation and decision, that is, so that sovereignty can actually be exercised; while in a monarchy on the other hand (or at least an absolute one), it is possible to deliberate and decide at all times and places. . . . For a people, and nobles, who are not one natural body, must come together, while a monarch, who is also one physical person, always has the power to exercise his sovereignty at hand.

It is also correctly noted by Hobbes that in a people or a council of nobles, if something has been decreed against some natural law, the state itself or the moral person it constitutes does not sin, but rather those citizens by whose votes the decree was made. For a sin follows upon a natural and expressed will, not a moral or political one, which is artificial. Otherwise those whom the decree displeases would sin as well. . . . In a monarchy, however, surely the monarch himself sins if he has decreed something against natural laws, because in him the civil will is the same as the natural.

10. Most writers have customarily added a number of *faulty* or *corrupt* forms to these regular forms of the state. Here it is certain, at least, that there is in many commonwealths a crop of maladies and faults no less abundant than in individual men, so that to be beset by the fewest is considered equivalent to perfection. Now we see that some of the maladies by which states are infested arise from the wickedness of men, others from the defective arrangement of a state itself. Hence, you may hear some of them called 'faults of men,' others 'faults of condition.' Let us touch upon a number of them for the sake of illustration.

It is a fault of men in a kingdom if he whom the lot of birth or the unhappy votes of citizens have brought to the throne is devoid of the arts of ruling and touched by little or no concern for the commonwealth, which he lays open to be torn apart by the ambition and avarice of evil ministers; if he is terribly cruel or angry and does not remember that he is a man or in charge of men; if he enjoys endangering the commonwealth without necessity; if by means of luxury or through ill-advised largess he dissipates the things collected for the support of the commonwealth's expenses; . . . if he extracts and accumulates more money from the citizens than is reasonable; if he is insulting and unjust; . . . and whatever other things there are through which the name of 'prince' is classified as an evil. . . .

The faults of men in an aristocracy are if through cheating and corrupt practices the way to the senate is open to those who are dishonest and unfit, while their betters are excluded; if the nobles are pulled apart by factions; if they set about to employ the common people as their slaves and to misappropriate the goods of the state in order to increase their own fortunes.

It is a fault of men in a democracy if unfit persons commonly maintain their opinions in a turbulent and importunate fashion; if virtues that are uncommon and not too troublesome for the commonwealth are suppressed by envy; if laws are rashly promulgated and revoked through frivolousness, and things that once were pleasing later displease without a reason; if base and unfit men are put in charge of the administration of things. . . .

Finally, a fault of men that can befall any kind of state is if those on whom the administration of sovereignty lies perform their office negligently or dishonestly; and if the citizens, for whom the glory of obedience alone remains, chafe at the bit. . . .

On the other hand, you may speak of faults of condition in general when the laws and institutions of a state are not adjusted to the character of a people or region; when they dispose the citizens toward internal disorders or make them incur the just hatreds of their neighbors; when they render them unfit to assume the functions necessary to preserve the commonwealth (if, for instance, through a state's laws, they cannot avoid being reduced to an unwarlike stagnation or rendered unfit to bring about peace); or, finally, when they clash with the chief tenets of true civil doctrine, in which case they are all the more pernicious if they have put on the appearance of religion. . . .

13. Some more recent authors invent many mixed kinds [of states], yet after rejecting most of them as incongruent, they recommend chiefly two mixed modes. One occurs when the parts of the supreme sovereignty belong separately and independently to different persons and bodies of the same commonwealth, so that individuals hold whatever part they have by their own right and administer it according to their own judgment, whereas they are like subjects in regard to the remaining parts of sovereignty. . . . The other occurs when the supreme sovereignty belongs indivisibly to more than one person, yet in such a way that a majority cannot effectively decide anything, or exercise the parts of sovereignty, without a minority, nor all the rest without a single dissenter. And this is so, again, in two ways: Either all are equal here, or certain select rights belong to one or another person who can exercise them himself without the rest. . . .

It has of course been shown above that the essence of a perfect and regular state requires that there be in it a union of the sort through which all things pertaining to its rule seem, as it were, to proceed from one soul. It is obvious, therefore, that through the former mode of mixture there is constituted a body which is held together not by the bond of a single sovereignty but only by a pact, and which must by no means, therefore, be classed among regular states but among irregular commonwealths, as it is something quite feeble and much exposed to internal upheavals.

As for the other mode of mixture, I would think it ought to be considered whether those in whom the supreme sovereignty so undividedly resides constitute a permanent senate that governs the entire state as a single and, as it were, a continuous body. In this case it will be an aristocracy, though one very unsuited for the dispatch of affairs, since one or a few refractory persons can void the resolutions of the rest. But if the individual parts of a commonwealth belong specifically and in their entirety to individuals who, in other respects, enjoy an equal right, but no one is permitted to exercise the acts of supreme sovereignty unless everyone unanimously consents, it will properly speaking be a system, but one that will also be quite incapable of managing its affairs on account of its excessive and superfluous regard for individual opinions. However, when one person is significantly more endowed with authority and some small parts of the supreme sovereignty than the rest, it will be an irregular commonwealth inserted, as it were, between a monarchy laboring under a mass of important personages, and a system. And the irregularity will be so much greater if the rest are outranked by more than one person.

22. Finally, it is common at this point to argue about the excellence of the forms of the commonwealth, about which of them deserves to be preferred to another, either because the welfare of the state can more easily and certainly be procured through it or because the force of sovereignty is less open to abuse. Here it is evident, at any rate, that no form of commonwealth can be so precisely outfitted with laws that no disadvantage can, through the inattentiveness or wickedness of rulers, redound on the citizens from the very government established for their welfare. The reason for this is that supreme sovereignty was established in order

to repel the evils threatening mortals from each other. But that very sovereignty had to be conferred on men, who are surely not immune from those vices which provoke men to molest one another. . . .

Chapter 6

ON THE CHARACTERISTICS
OF SUPREME SOVEREIGNTY

1. Among the characteristics of sovereignty we encounter, first of all, the fact that it is, and is said to be, *supreme*. The chief reason for this denomination seems to be that one man's authority over another can be no greater than that which binds the latter to apply his strength and means toward the public good as the former chooses, and subjects him to the former's right of life and death. In addition, just as no greater freedom can be understood in the case of individual men (setting the divine sovereignty aside) than their being able to dispose of their own actions, strength, and faculties as they themselves judge, so the highest freedom in a group is to be measured by its ability to decide about the things that seem to affect its advantage and welfare according to its own independent judgment. It also follows from this that because sovereignty is supreme, or not dependent on any superior man on this earth, its acts cannot be nullified by the decision of another human will. For a person's ability to alter the decisions of his own will is, itself, a consequence of his freedom.

2. One who holds the supreme sovereignty will for the same reason be unaccountable [*anupeuthunos*]; that is, he will neither have to give reasons nor be subject to human punishment. For both of these presuppose a superior, something that cannot be understood here without a contradiction, as there cannot be a superior to one who is supreme in the same order. . . .

Yet it should be noted that there are two ways to give a reason: either to a superior who, if I have not made my reason acceptable to him, is able to rescind my acts and inflict a punishment besides; or to an equal whom I want simply to approve of my deeds, for the mere purpose of being considered a good and prudent man by him. Supreme sovereignty is not bound to give a reason to any man in the former manner; but princes who care about their fame often strive to give reasons for their own affairs to the whole world in the latter manner, for the sake of maintaining their reputation, and this does not prove any kind of subjection. Thus, I am permitted to do whatever I please with the money I have earned, and yet I sometimes wish to make my reasons known so that I am not considered a dissolute or foolish family-father.

Similarly, punishment can have no place in one for whom there is no court or judge able to impose and execute a sentence. For courts, which exist in states, are only concerned with subjects and borrow all their force from the supreme sovereignty itself. And if princes let themselves be brought before their own courts in some places, for debts and similar reasons, it is not as if they acknowledge that court as something superior to themselves, and by whose authority they can be compelled; rather they desire only to acquire a clear knowledge of a plaintiff's allegation and are of themselves willing to fulfill their own obligation in that regard when it has been established. Yet this discussion is properly about human punishment, which a human judge inflicts as a superior. For divine punishment commonly exerts itself in different ways against violators of the natural law, who otherwise need have no fear at all of human tribunals. . . .

3. Also, by virtue of the fact that it is considered supreme, civil sovereignty is understood to be unconstrained by, or rather, superior to human laws. (It would be foolish, however, to raise questions about divine and natural laws.) . . . For human laws are nothing else than decrees of the supreme sovereignty about those things which subjects must observe for the welfare of the state. It is obvious that the supreme sovereignty is not directly obligated by them. For it is supreme, and so it cannot accrue an obligation from a superior man, and no one can obligate himself through the mode of law, that is, in the manner of a superior. . . . It is true though, that sometimes a legislator is as it were reflexively obligated by his own law, out of natural equity and for the sake of public decorum, so that in order to rouse his subjects to obedience he devotes himself energetically to that which he demands in the morals of citizens as conducive to the public good, and does not, by forbidding vices in which he himself is immersed, seem to begrudge others the pleasure they provide. . . .

4. To justify the supremacy of this sovereignty, especially in monarchies, we must examine the common distinction of majesty into *real* and *personal*. The application of this distinction to sovereignty in such a way that real and personal majesty are at one and the same time provided a place in a monarchical state, with personal sovereignty in a kingdom being attributed to the king and real sovereignty to the people (insofar as it is distinguished from the king), the latter being equal to or superior to the former on the ground that real rights are almost always considered more noble than personal ones—this is, in our judgment, not only absurd but also pernicious. For it is clear as day that it involves a contradiction and makes states two-headed, which leads to destructive convulsions. Also, it is no more necessary to imagine a double majesty because a people enters into its own right upon the death of a king or ruling family (insofar as it can constitute another king or another form of commonwealth as it pleases), than to imagine in a slave a real sovereignty distinct from the personal sovereignty of his master, on account of the slave's acquisition of a right over himself when his master has died without an heir. . . .

6. . . . Some say that the right of a people which has assumed the yoke of monarchy is equal to the right of someone who has sold himself into slavery to take

himself out of it again. But this no sane person will admit unless it is added that this is done with the indulgence of the master or king, who willingly parts with the right he has obtained. . . .

It is also false that a people whose natural disposition formerly suited it for absolute sovereignty is right in shaking off that sovereignty and reclaiming its freedom as a people when in the course of time it has put aside its servile character. For if such a case arises it will be incumbent on a prince prudently to adjust his rule to the people's altered disposition. It is silly to say that since an owner who makes bad use of his things can be restrained or denied his goods, a prince who abuses his authority can also be brought back into line. For the reason for the former is that a prince has a superior right over his citizens' goods, which it is in the interest of the commonwealth not to have uselessly squandered. But who will say that subjects have some more eminent right against the rights of a prince, that is, that they are masters of their master?

As for the claims of princes, not a few of which are made as boasts, the response is that a prince ought surely to consider the people's welfare in all things. But it does not yet follow from this that citizens can restrain a prince when they have judged him to be employing means that are not suited enough for that end.

It is absurd to declare that since a people does not have the right to destroy itself or to inflict savage cruelties on its own body, such a right cannot be transferred to a king either. For who will claim for a king the right to destroy a people? It will be shown soon that absolute sovereignty is not that formidable a thing, and we must elsewhere examine what a people may do if a king is openly bent on its destruction. . . .

7. Furthermore, it is clear enough that in some states sovereignty, especially that of kings, is free in the exercise of its acts, but that elsewhere it is restricted to a certain mode of acting. From this the distinction of sovereignty into *absolute* and *limited* has arisen.

Here we must first give an accurate account of the proper meaning of the word 'absolute,' which labors under great hatred among those who have been reared in free states. If explained in a sinister way, it can indeed encourage evil princes to vex the commonwealth and perpetrate many crimes, and it is often given a bad name by flatterers who find it easy to nourish the ambition and other vices of princes by means of boastful references to it. "You are absolute," they say, "therefore if something pleases you, it is permitted. So wear down your citizens and neighbors with unnecessary wars so that you may be called a great warrior; abuse whomever you wish with insults; exhaust the citizens with levies and robberies to supply the means for your ambition or luxury." . . . There are those, even, who seek to buttress the absolute right of kings by means of arguments and opinions that make it seem they are measuring it solely by impunity for crimes and a license to vex the people.

Now, just as individual men are understood to be supremely and absolutely free when they can decide about their own things and actions according to their own choice and judgment, and not someone else's (so long as they always observe the natural law), and this same freedom belongs naturally to all men who are not subject to the sovereignty of another man, so it is surely necessary that where many men have coalesced into a perfect state the same freedom, or the faculty to decide according to one's own judgment about the means pertaining to the welfare of society, exists as in a common subject. This freedom is accompanied by supreme sovereignty, or the right to prescribe those means to citizens and compel them to obey them. Hence absolute sovereignty exists in every state properly so-called, at least in principle if not always in practice. For to be accountable to no one, and not to have the right to decide about one's own things according to one's own judgment and choice, implies a contradiction.

It is easy to see from the end for which states were established that absolute sovereignty does not in itself involve anything unjust or intolerable. For we certainly did not establish states so that the natural law might be neglected and all things done out of base desire, but to provide more adequately for the safety and welfare of individuals by joining the resources of many people, and therefore to make room for the safe exercise of the natural law.

8. Furthermore, when we consider supreme sovereignty as it has been conferred, as on a proper subject, on one man or one council consisting of a few or all men, it is not everywhere observed to be so absolute and free, but to be restricted by certain laws in some places. It is true that the distinction between absolute and circumscribed sovereignty does not seem to be so obviously detected in democracies. For although certain institutions established by use or sanctioned by written laws, such as when and by whom the people should be convoked and public business proposed and executed, must exist in any democracy (for without such things a state cannot be understood), still, since the council in which the supreme sovereignty resides consists of all the citizens, and therefore no one outside it has acquired a right from those statutes, there is nothing to prevent them from being abrogated or changed by the people at any time. . . .

In aristocracies and monarchies, however, where some command and others are commanded, and where the latter can therefore acquire a right from the promises and pacts of the former, the difference between absolute and limited sovereignty is clearly apparent. Here that person is absolute who administers sovereignty out of his own judgment, not according to a norm of certain and permanent statutes but as the present condition of things seems to require, and who therefore procures the welfare of the commonwealth out of his own judgment as demanded by the times. Hence the word 'absolute' is so far from hiding something invidious or intolerable to free men that, instead, it enjoins on princes the necessity of a far stricter and more circumspect care (if, at least, they wish to satisfy the demands of their position and their conscience) than is imposed on those who must carry out the public affairs according to a prescribed formula. . . .

9. But because one man's judgment can easily be deceived in discerning that which furthers the public welfare, and not everyone with so much freedom has such firmness of mind as to know how to subdue the desires that struggle against reason, . . . it has seemed advisable to many peoples not to entrust such great authority so absolutely to the fallible judgment and corruptible choice of one man, but rather to prescribe for him a certain manner of conducting the sovereignty. This was especially so after it was noticed that certain institutions and a certain manner of conducting affairs are best suited to the character of a people and the condition of a state.

Also, this limitation of sovereignty does no injury to princes who are elevated to that degree of eminence by a deliberate decision of the people. For if it seemed burdensome to receive a sovereignty which they would not be able to wield as they chose, it was open to them to refuse it. But their regard for the pledge by which they are bound when they accept this kind of sovereignty by no means permits them, later on, to seek to subvert the laws of the kingdom by means of secret machinations or through force, and to make themselves absolute. . . .

It is therefore entirely up to the discretion of free peoples whether they wish to give a king an absolute sovereignty or one under certain laws, so long as those laws contain nothing impious in themselves or do not subvert the very end of sovereignty. For even though men entered freely into civil society at the beginning, they had, of course, since they were surely subject to the natural law, to establish such rules of sovereignty and civil obedience as were consistent with that law and the legitimate end of states.

10. To understand correctly the sort of promise by which a king's sovereignty (the same rationale holds for nobles) ceases to be absolute—for not just any promise has this force—one must know that in accepting a kingdom a king binds himself to administer it well by means of a general or a special promise, which is on most occasions confirmed by an oath.

A general promise can be made either tacitly or expressly. A tacit promise to rule well is understood to be contained in the very act of accepting a kingdom, even if there has been no express statement to that effect. . . . These kinds of promises in no way detract from the absoluteness of sovereignty, and so a king is indeed obligated through them to wield the sovereignty well. But the manner or means he may employ to produce that end is left to his judgment and choice.

A special promise, however, and one in which even the manner and means to be employed in administering the sovereignty are expressed, seems to have a double force. One only binds the conscience of a king, while the other makes the obedience of citizens dependent on its fulfillment as on a condition. The former kind of promise occurs if a king pledges, for example, that he will not assign magistracies to a certain kind of men, that he will give no one privileges that will burden the rest, that he will not make new laws, impose new levies or taxes, make use of external soldiers, and the like. Yet it does not at the same time establish a council which the king is bound to consult if the circumstances of the commonwealth order him to depart from those promises (for these are always understood to contain this tacit exception: unless the welfare of the commonwealth, which is the supreme law among laws of this kind, requires otherwise), a council which could by its own and not a granted right look into those affairs, and without whose consent the citizens would not be obligated to obey the king's commands concerning such things.

The administration of sovereignty is surely restricted to certain laws here, and when a king has done otherwise without necessity he is without doubt guilty of having violated his trust. Yet the citizens do not therefore have the faculty to refuse the orders of the king, or to render those acts ineffectual. For if the king says that the welfare of the people or a significant advantage to the commonwealth demands it—and this presumption always accompanies a king's acts—the citizens have nothing to reply, since they lack the faculty of knowing about those acts whether the necessity of the commonwealth requires them or not.

It also appears from these things that a people is not sufficiently watching out for itself if it is willing to allot a king only a limited sovereignty yet does not establish a council without whose consent those excepted acts cannot be exercised, or does not lay upon the king the necessity to have assemblies where there may be deliberation about the exercise of those acts. For this is better than if it were necessary for the king to consider the advice of only a few citizens, since it could happen that the private advantages of those few differ from the public good, and therefore that, on account of their private interests, they do not agree with the salutary intentions of the king.

The sovereignty of a king is more narrowly constricted, however, if there is an express agreement between king and citizens in the conferral of sovereignty that he will wield it according to certain fundamental laws, and will refer affairs over whose disposal he has not been left absolute authority to a council of the people or leading men, without whose consent he will not decide anything; and if he has done otherwise, will not expect the citizens to be bound by his orders concerning such things. A people that has constituted a king for itself in such a manner is understood to have promised him not an absolute obedience, and in all things, but only insofar as his sovereignty is consistent with the terms of its capitulation and the fundamental laws; acts not consistent with these are by that very right void, and do not have the power to obligate the citizens.

Yet the supreme sovereignty is not crippled through fundamental laws of this kind. For in such a kingdom all acts of sovereignty can be exercised that are exercised in an absolute kingdom, except that here the king employs his own judgment alone, at least ultimately, while there a council has a concomitant oversight, as it were, one on which the power of sovereignty depends not in a fundamental sense but as a condition *sine qua non*. Nor are there two wills in such a state. For surely all things that the state wills, it wills through the will of the king, even if it is with the limitation that unless a certain condition exists, the king cannot will certain things, or wills them in vain.

Nor is it the case, in such a kingdom, that the king ceases to have supreme sovereignty, or that a council is superior to the king himself. For it does not follow that "[because] this person cannot do all things according to his own desire, therefore he does not have supreme sovereignty"; that "[because] I am not bound to obey this person in all things, therefore I am superior or equal to him"; or that "[because] I cannot command this person in any way I please, therefore he himself can lay some positive injunctions upon me." And these two things are far different: "I am bound to abide by what pleases this person because I have obligated myself to this by means of a pact," and "I am bound to follow this person's will because he can impose it on me by virtue of his sovereignty." Supreme and absolute are by no means one and the same. For the former denotes the absence of a superior or equal in the same order; the latter, however, the faculty of exercising any right whatsoever according to one's own judgment and choice. . . .

Chapter 8

ON THE SANCTITY OF SUPREME
CIVIL SOVEREIGNTY

1. Just as supreme civil sovereignty was established for the safety of human-kind and to take away the infinite miseries of the natural state, so it is in human-kind's greatest interest that everyone consider it sacrosanct and inviolable. . . . No sensible person doubts, at any rate, that it is wrong to resist sovereigns so long as they stay within the limits of their authority. For it is apparent from the end and character of sovereignty that there should necessarily be conjoined with it an obligation not to resist, that is, to obey without reluctance by doing or omitting that which it enjoins. On the other hand, it is a subject of the greatest debate whether a supreme sovereign, if he should order a subject to do something beyond what is right, or threaten some kind of injury, would then also be so sacrosanct that the subject could in no way repel that injury by means of force.

2. . . . The subjection of the will of citizens to a state must, once it has taken place, be interpreted and limited by the latter's end. Thus the thing finally comes down to this: Individual citizens have subjected their will to the will of the state in regard to matters affecting the state's preservation; if in these cases a deed of the state should displease a citizen, he is not done an injury. But since a sovereign can enjoin or inflict things on citizens outside these matters, thereby violating a right acquired either from a special pact or the common law of humanity, it is not apparent why a citizen cannot be injured by a state.

3. Yet it must be properly observed that unruly and querulous citizens make out as injuries many deeds of princes that are hardly such. That is, they condemn as wrongdoing whatever differs from their own judgment. Even Jupiter is not pleas-ing to everyone, whether he brings fair weather or foul. And so, as it cannot hap-pen on account of the variety of human characters and the ill-adapted desires of many people, that the administration of a commonwealth is equally pleasing to individual citizens, if anyone wants whatever displeases him to be immediately considered an injury, he is either seeking the dissolution of the state or longs, him-self, to command. And this fact, that they themselves do not rule, is without a doubt the sole reason for many people's complaints. . . .

4. Although these things are so, there is nonetheless no doubt that a citizen can be injured by a state and its ruler, since there surely exists among them a commu-nity of natural right, at least, which suffices to make someone capable of being injured by another. Now it seems that there are two ways in which a prince injures his subjects: if he violates against them either the duty of a *prince* or the duty of a *man*; that is, if he treats the citizens not as citizens or not as men.

The duty of a prince is directed either to everyone together or to separate indi-viduals. A prince owes it to everyone to look after the welfare of the entire state, according to his own judgment if he is absolute, or, if circumscribed by certain laws, according to the manner of government they define. Accordingly, a prince injures the citizens as a whole if he casts aside all care for the commonwealth and does not see to the dispatch of public affairs, even through ministers. Consider, for instance, if he should neither undertake to defend the state against external enemies nor maintain internal tranquillity by executing laws, and nonetheless continue amid such neglect to enjoy the dignity and income of a prince, and measure the fortune of his principate solely by his luxury and the license to satisfy his lusts. . . .

Now a prince owes individual citizens permission to enjoy the same right as others of their rank, as well as defense and the administration of justice on their behalf, insofar as this can be done while the state remains safe. If a prince does not provide these things to individuals when the circumstances of the commonwealth lead them to expect them, he surely does them an injury. . . .

A prince can violate the duty of a man toward single individuals in different ways. Consider, for instance, if he disgraces a good man who does not merit it; if he denies a promised wage or refuses to pay back a loan, or to fulfill other contracts; if he is unwilling to make amends for the harm he has done through his impudence; if he assaults the chastity of honorable virgins or pollutes the bedchambers of others through his adulteries; if he harms another's body, seizes his goods, or ruins him; if, at last, he takes the life of an innocent person through sheer violence, by suborning false accusers, or by getting judges (by means of promises) to hand down an unjust sentence, and other similar things. . . .

5. It is more difficult, however, to sort out the question whether citizens are bound to endure any of these injuries without resisting, or whether in a certain case they can repel them with force. Here the matter seems to us as follows. Since the condition of human life is such that it cannot be without all inconvenience, and since it is not easy to find any man with morals so well elaborated that he satisfies everyone down to the smallest detail, it would be foolish as well as shameless to wish to rise up against a prince on account of any faults whatsoever, especially since we are not so careful in doing our duty toward him either, and it is also common for the laws to pass over lighter failings in the case of private individuals. How much fairer would it therefore be to condone the slight failings of a prince, by whose care the tranquillity of the citizens and the security of their life and fortunes are maintained? This is especially so since experience testifies to the great slaughter of citizens and the great convulsion of the commonwealth that have accompanied the overthrow of even the worst princes. Accordingly, the lighter injuries of princes are to be condoned for the sake of the noble function they serve and the other benefits they provide, and indeed, for the sake of our citizens and the entire commonwealth. . . .

This too is certain: Even when a prince threatens the most dreadful injury with a hostile intent, it is preferable to emigrate, to look out for oneself by fleeing, or to place oneself under the protection of another state.

But what if a prince is about to destroy an innocent citizen with a hostile intent and there remains no place to flee? Certainly many people are unable to conceive how the same person can simultaneously maintain the personae of a prince and an

enemy toward a citizen, and under what guise he demands that he himself be sacrosanct when he longs fervently to sacrifice an innocent citizen to his own desire
as if he were a miserable beast. They say, rather, that if someone owes another his
patronage and for either no reason or an unjust one assumes a hostile attitude toward
him, he also releases the latter from his client's obligation toward him, at least to
the point where the latter is allowed to resort to force in order to protect himself
against the former's most dreadful injuries. This defense is more favorably considered as the number of those whom the prince is going to destroy through his
injury is greater.

But since one hardly finds any examples of princes who openly profess that they
have undertaken to kill innocent citizens simply because they so desire, a greater
difficulty arises. Namely, what is permitted when a prince wishes to vent his rage
under the guise of law, claiming, for example, that the citizens have neglected some
unjust mandate?

Here we suppose that since all authority conferred on someone is understood
with the condition that the right of a superior is preserved, the citizens also, in
establishing supreme civil sovereignty, were neither able nor willing to renounce
God's sovereignty over themselves, and are therefore not bound by commands of
the civil sovereignty known to clash openly with a mandate of God. It is not ours
to define what a citizen is to do here if he is threatened with force on account of
his profession of the Christian religion, since the same scriptures from which that
religion is drawn can make it plain to anyone how important it should be to him
that he not do anything that is or seems to be contrary to his religion. . . .

We will show below that when death is threatened someone can, without sinning in the proper sense, undertake the performance of an action repugnant in itself
to the law of nature. Yet if it is the performance of a kind of action that can in no
way be undertaken without sinning in the proper sense, or that is judged to be more
bitter in itself than death, and no reason is shown or at least pretended as probable, from either my own failing or the public good, why I in particular am under
so great a necessity to do such a thing, which could have been done by another, or
which it is totally absurd to do, then it appears without a doubt that the sovereign
is acting in order to destroy an innocent person solely because of his desire and
hostile attitude toward me. And by this act of assuming the role of enemy instead
of prince, he is also understood to have released the citizen from the obligation by
which the latter was held tied to him. Yet one should flee here, if possible, and
seek the patronage of a third party who has no obligation toward that prince. Indeed,
if there is no way to flee one ought to die rather than kill, not so much because of
the person of the prince himself as because of the whole commonwealth, which
tends nearly always to be involved in grave disorders on such an occasion.

But, indeed, when a sovereign undertakes to punish a citizen for some transgression—even though the latter is not bound to bring the punishment deliberately
upon himself, by giving himself up or voluntarily appearing before him—the reason he may not defend himself through force in this case is that the sovereign is
making use of his own right, and to harm him on whatever pretext would certainly,
for this reason, be to injure him.

It must be observed, on top of this, that even if it were entirely conceded that it is sometimes not wrong for a citizen to defend his own welfare against the most dreadful injuries of a superior by force, the remaining citizens will nonetheless not be permitted, on this account, to put aside their obedience or to protect the innocent person by force. For besides the fact that they are not allowed to inquire into the deeds of a prince which he exercises by virtue of his judicial authority, as it were, and that it often happens that guilty persons proclaim innocence in order to arouse ill will against a prince; even if an injury has been done to a citizen the rest are by no means released from their own obligation toward the prince. This is because each of the citizens negotiates on his own behalf for a prince's care and protection toward himself, and does not suppose as a condition of his own subjection that the prince will treat each and every citizen justly. . . .

6. Furthermore, just as there are not a few who think that these things do not detract from the sanctity of princes, so we ought certainly not to put up with those who so crudely assert that a king can be stripped of his sovereignty by the people and punished when he has degenerated into a tyrant. For since the obscurity of most civil actions is so great that the common people cannot recognize their equity or necessity, or often, because of the welter of their passions, do not wish to; and that most of the time it is also conducive to a commonwealth's interest that the reasons for its counsels not be open to many, it would be extremely difficult to designate precisely those actions for whose performance someone rightly deserved to be called a tyrant, against whom any force of which the citizens avail themselves would be permissible. . . . Hence it is possible that hatred for the term 'tyrant' could also devolve on a good prince, from those whom either he himself or his present status displeases, since men have customarily expressed through words not only things but also their own passions.

It is commonly thought, of course, that private vices do not make a tyrant, nor an administration of the commonwealth that is somewhat too negligent. Are the taxes commanded too heavy? But a subject not admitted to counsels is unable to judge whether the necessity of the commonwealth demands them. Are harsh punishments adopted? But if they are determined according to the laws and because of a preceding transgression, no one can by right complain, even though it would have been more correct to show mercy. What of that which is most hateful to the common crowd: when certain great and innocent men are plucked from its midst on account of private hatreds or because of suspicions? But if transgressions or machinations against the status of the prince are alleged as a pretext, or the ordinary form of trials is observed, even if those removed and a few others besides are perhaps certain of their innocence, how can the rest be clearly convinced of it— especially since the presumption of justice stands always on the side of a prince? Are promises not kept, or previously bestowed privileges reduced? But if an absolute prince alleges either a transgression, a necessity, or a significant advantage to the commonwealth, he will be thought to have acted by right, a matter about which his subjects do not have the faculty to judge clearly. For all privileges have this exception: unless the welfare or necessity of the commonwealth forbids such things to be observed.

A considerable portion of the arguments offered for the other opinion collapse on their own if it is observed that these two statements are by no means the same: "A people has the authority to bring force to bear against kings, and to reduce them to order, if the kings do not command them as they desire"; and "A people, or separate individuals, have a right to defend their own welfare against a prince at the approach of extreme danger, and when the prince has become an enemy." For the reasons that prove the latter statement by no means lead to the former in the same way, though many people confuse them.

Thus, the statement that a people, even though it may have given itself into servitude, has nonetheless not lost all right to reclaim its freedom or security, can be admitted in no other sense than that a people can defend itself against the extreme as well as unjust force of a prince, which defense, when it has succeeded, is also accompanied by freedom. This is because a master, in becoming an enemy, seems himself to absolve a subject from any obligation toward himself, so that the latter is thereafter not bound to return under the yoke even if the former wishes to change his mind.

Apart from this case, a people that has given itself into servitude, or rather subjected itself to the absolute sovereignty of one person, has no more of a right to reclaim its freedom by force than I do to seize again by force a thing that has already been handed over to another by means of a contract. For that civil servitude is not so abhorrent to nature—as some people dream—that although someone has found it necessary at some time to consent to it, in order to avoid a greater evil, he can shake it off again later on as the opportunity arises, with nature itself giving him that right. And even though this state is contrary to the natural disposition of a certain people, either from the beginning or after their minds have changed, it is still by no means permitted, for this reason alone, to seize from a prince by force a right which he has acquired, no more than it is to seize from a buyer a thing handed over to him by contract, even if the seller discovers later on that the contract was not in his own interest.

9. Now there arises the difficult question of what is or is not allowed against illegitimate usurpers of the sovereignty, and this not after they have acquired a true right to rule by means of long possession or a subsequent pact, but so long as the unjust cause of their possession continues and they are seen to be relying on force alone. Here we must first inquire whether the commands of such usurpers have the power to obligate while they are in possession of the sovereignty. And in this regard we must repeat from what we said above that an obligation to obey is not produced unless another has legitimate authority over me. For through violence alone, it is true, one can lay on someone an external necessity to do something, but not an obligation, which is an internal bond that binds the soul in such a way that, unless it has done what has been commanded it is accused of sin. And so if someone stronger threatens force, a person is undoubtedly compelled to do things which he is not bound to do, and which he abhors, in order to avoid a greater evil. Yet no one will fault him for breaking out of that unjust necessity if a way is somehow given.

But what if someone has, at least initially, usurped the sovereignty through force or evil arts, yet wishes to be seen to have it by right, and though trusting in weapons nonetheless does not conduct himself as an enemy but as a true prince? Here it seems to us in general most probable that he who in fact has the supreme sovereignty, though he took possession of it by devious means, is to be regarded as the legitimate prince by individual citizens so long as there is no one who can claim the sovereignty for himself with a better right. For here it is reasonable that the authority of any possessor should be valid so long as he imitates the rule of a legitimate prince, since it is surely in everyone's interest that someone look out for the commonwealth, instead of its being involved in constant turmoils with no certain ruler. Hence, since the citizens are understood to have consented to the sovereignty of these persons, at least tacitly, they will indeed be obligated to obey them. . . .

10. But what is a good citizen to do when someone seizes the sovereignty after expelling a legitimate prince and, though in fact a usurper of another's right, conducts himself as king, since he seems to owe allegiance to the former prince so long as the latter is still alive? Here it seems correct to declare that things can often reach the point where obedience to the sovereignty of one who is in any sort of possession of the kingdom is not only licit but even required (namely, when a legitimate master has been reduced to such a condition that he can no longer exercise the function of a prince toward his citizens). Although his commands do not have the power to obligate because they are devoid of legitimate authority, anyone who is prudent will nonetheless look out for his own affairs, make provisions for the future, and cautiously reflect on his own present condition, lest he rashly expose his own life and fortunes to danger. For this is what would happen if, by his vain reluctance, he persisted in stirring up the possessor's anger against himself, for the benefit of neither his fatherland nor the ejected king. . . .

It appears unlikely, therefore, that anything more probable than the following can be said here: If a legitimate prince has been cast into such a state that he himself cannot furnish his citizens the defense he should, and the strength of the citizens is also not such as to be able to resist a usurper without immediately being destroyed, the expelled prince is presumed to have released the citizens from their obligation toward himself until the fates open to him the way to his kingdom once again, and to the extent at least, that it is necessary to preserve and ward off dangers from the citizens. And the allegiance that the citizens have given to the usurper seems also to bind only up to this point, so that it is temporary, as it were, and expires when the expelled king has the ability to recover his kingdom, since it is maintained not so much by an inner necessity of conscience as by a present fear. . . .

From all these considerations, there scarcely appears to be a case where a private individual can by his own authority rightly impede even an unjust possessor of sovereignty, especially since experience testifies that usurpers are more incited by such conspiracies to oppress the people. . . .

Chapter 9

ON THE DUTY OF SUPREME SOVEREIGNS

1. It remains for us to look at the duty of supreme sovereigns, which we must do all the more diligently insofar as more evils arise for mortals if it is not properly observed, and because it is the proper function of this discipline to give an account of that duty, which goes beyond the limit of civil laws. But because such things are frequently inculcated by others, we can accomplish our task by repeating only the main headings. The precepts by means of which that duty may be fulfilled can be easily gathered if we ponder carefully the end and nature of states, as well as the parts of supreme sovereignty.

3. The general law for supreme sovereigns is this: "Let the people's welfare be the supreme law." . . .

4. It is necessary for the internal tranquillity of states that the wills of citizens be so moderated and directed that it conduces to the welfare of the state. Hence, it is the task of supreme sovereigns not only to prescribe suitable laws for this end, but also to maintain public discipline in such a way that citizens conform themselves to legal prescriptions not so much from fear of punishments as from habit. This is because penalties alone engender not so much a concern for doing the right thing (for this is the task of reason and discipline) as an anxiety not to get caught in one's evildoing. . . .

But the greatest contribution toward the achievement of this end is made, in Christian commonwealths, by that pure Christian religion itself, purged of human fabrications and inculcated by pious and sensible ministers by means of teaching and example; by a religion, that is, which contains, besides doctrines conducive to eternal salvation, most perfect moral precepts by which the minds of mortals are especially disposed to bear well [the burdens of] civil life, but which nonetheless cannot be so conveniently sanctioned by means of civil laws. . . .

The contribution of public schools is also of the greatest moment in this regard, at least if they do not teach empty trifles and the fabrications of idle men (the remains of the kingdom of darkness . . .), but solid learning and knowledge whose use dispenses itself throughout human and civil life. Chief among these is that which teaches solidly about the right of supreme sovereigns and the obligation of citizens corresponding to it. . . .

But the example of sovereigns also contributes great vigor to public discipline. . . . Supreme sovereigns must therefore see to it that all these things are right in a state.

5. This same end is achieved by having clear and simple written laws concerning the affairs in which citizens are most frequently engaged. . . . Moreover, civil laws should not sanction more things than conduce to the good of the citizens and the state. For since men commonly deliberate more often through natural reason

about that which they should or should not do, than through knowledge of the laws, when there are more laws than memory can easily comprehend and they prohibit things which reason in itself does not, men necessarily, through ignorance and without any evil intent, run into laws as into traps. By this means, sovereigns create a pointless inconvenience for the citizens, which is contrary to the end of states. . . . The judicial process must also be so regulated that anyone can secure his own right through a brief and minimally expensive procedure. There is a proverb among the Persians: "A small injustice is better than slow justice."

6. But since laws are passed in vain if supreme sovereigns allow them to be violated with impunity, it is the latter's task to see that they are executed, and to exact penalties according to the circumstance of each deed and the intention and wickedness of the transgressor. In this matter one must proceed in such a way that the severity of the laws is exercised not only against citizens of modest means but also against the rich and powerful, whose wealth and nobility should never give them a license to insult humbler citizens with impunity, especially since the greatest danger to a state threatens usually from the common people who have been infuriated by excessive oppression. . . .

8. Now since men have come together into states with the end of obtaining security against the injuries of others, it is the task of supreme sovereigns to prohibit injuries among the citizens with a severity increasingly proportionate to the easier opportunity for doing harm that is furnished by constant cohabitation. Nor should distinctions of rank and honor have such force that the more powerful can insult the weaker as they desire. . . .

9. Furthermore, although one prince is not sufficient for dealing directly with all the affairs of a larger state, so that ministers must necessarily be called upon to bear a part of the responsibilities, still, since these borrow all of their authority from the supreme sovereign, the imputation of their deeds, both those done well and those done badly, redounds ultimately on him. . . .

11. Although supreme sovereigns are not bound to nourish their subjects (except that charity orders them to have a special care for those who cannot sustain themselves because of some undeserved calamity . . .), they must nonetheless see to it, inasmuch as they can, that the private wealth of citizens increases, not only because the expenses necessary for a state's preservation must be collected from the citizens' goods, but also because the hardiness of a state consists in the virtue and wealth of its citizens, and because "it is burdensome for a master to be served by need." . . . This end is served by disposing citizens to take the richest possible harvest from land and water, to apply their diligence to the materials that arise around them, or not to purchase from others labor which they can conveniently perform themselves—which happens only if the mechanical arts are properly fostered. . . .

Not only must laziness be proscribed, however, but citizens must also be recalled to frugality through sumptuary laws by which superfluous expenses are prohibited, especially those through which the wealth of citizens is transferred to outsiders. . . . Yet if there is anywhere a region that abounds with a multitude of people and money, there it is expedient to tolerate unnecessary and nearly luxurious consumption, so that the common people may have the opportunity to nourish themselves and the great power of money does not lie idle—provided that inordinate luxury is not nourished and materials that should be profitably exported to outsiders are not consumed in vain.

12. Also, because the internal health and strength of states come from the citizens' union, and the force of sovereignty dispenses itself with greater efficacy throughout the entire body of the state the more all-encompassing this union is, it is therefore incumbent on supreme sovereigns to take precautions against the rise of factions in the state. For there is an easy lapse from these into seditions and civil war, which is so much worse than a war waged unanimously against outsiders than war [itself] is worse than peace. . . .

13. Finally, since the situation of states among themselves is sufficiently untrustworthy, supreme sovereigns must take care to maintain the citizens' courage and skill with weapons, and make timely preparations of all the things required to repel force, such as fortified places, weapons, and soldiers. . . . But on the other hand, even if there is a just cause for war, no one is to be attacked unless one is favored with a very safe opportunity and the condition of the state will easily bear it. Also, for the same end, the plans and moves of neighbors are to be carefully sought out and observed (an end served today by permanent legations, among other things . . .), and friendships and alliances prudently contracted. . . .

BOOK VIII

Chapter 1

ON THE RIGHT TO DIRECT
THE ACTIONS OF CITIZENS

1. Now that we have set forth the things that concern the nature of supreme sovereignty in general, we must also explore the chief questions raised about its individual parts. And since we have put the authority to direct the actions of citizens (from which civil laws flow) in first place, we must now add to the things about laws in general, which we set forth above, those that pertain to civil laws and the commands of supreme sovereigns in a special way.

Accordingly, a law is said to be civil either in respect of its *authority* or its *origin*. All laws in relation to which rights are determined in a civil court can be called civil laws in the former sense, from whatever origin they ultimately flow. . . .

Natural and divine laws, we may be sure, obligate all men, for whom they have been enacted, and a penalty to be determined before the divine tribunal awaits those who transgress against them. But for them to have the full force of law in a civil court depends on the civil sovereignty, whose task it is to define those crimes on account of which a penalty is to be exacted in a civil court, and those which are to be left to the Deity to punish; and similarly, to determine which natural obligation gives rise to an action in a civil court and which does not, being dependent on men's shame and probity alone. Hence no one is prosecuted in states, or punished by what is properly speaking a penalty, for violating natural laws that have not been given the authority of civil law. For such sins are undoubtedly accompanied by those evils commonly called natural penalties.

It is also true that those precepts of nature without whose observance there can by no means be lasting internal peace among the citizens have the force of civil law in all states. But some have not had this force attributed to them, either expressly or through judicial practice, not only because the debate about the things said to have been done against them would be too obscure; but also to avoid having the courts resound with an immense number of quarrels; and to leave intact for good men, as it were, the special basis of their praise, which is to have acted rightly out of reverence for the Deity alone, apart from any fear of a penalty to be inflicted by men. For this praise surely ceases when it is not possible to discern whether someone has done something out of fear of a penalty or love of virtue. . . .

Now a law is civil with respect to its *origin* if it proceeds solely from the will of the supreme civil authority and deals with those things which have been left indifferent by natural and divine law, even though they contribute to the special advantage of the state. It is to be no less observed by citizens than other laws, however, since it is evidently more conducive to sociality that the opinion of sovereigns prevail in the case of indifferent things and that subjects consider good that which seems so to a sovereign, than that there continue to be eternal quarrels among them about such a thing—from which wars and slaughter, which are without a doubt evils, would be justifiably expected. . . .

Although the combination of these laws comes ordinarily with the name of 'civil law,' it is to be observed that not all things contained in the bodies and codes of the civil law are properly speaking laws, but that besides the mandates enjoined on citizens by the supreme sovereignty on account of the special good of the state, many things are found inserted regarding the discipline of the natural law. Most of the things that pertain to the discipline of the civil law can be brought chiefly under two heads. For it either prescribes certain formulas or methods that should be observed in dealings which confer a right on another or give rise to an obligation in someone so that they are binding in civil court, or else it propounds the method by means of which someone should pursue his right in court. Thus, if you claimed for the natural law all the things that are its own, and that interpreters of the civil law have so far nearly always treated without discrimination, the civil law would have fairly narrow boundaries. This is not to mention the fact that where civil law is lacking in some respect recourse is always had to natural reason, and therefore that in all states the law of nature supplies what is missing in the civil laws. . . .

2. . . . It should be presupposed here, however, that men were already acquainted with the natural law when they were about to come together into a state, that among the ends of the states to be constituted the chief one was that the natural laws by which the peace of humankind is governed could be securely exercised, and finally that there is nothing in natural laws which conflicts with the nature and the end of states, but on the contrary, that they are in amicable agreement with it. Therefore, those about to come together into a state, who bound themselves by means of a pact to observe the civil laws, must surely be thought to have presupposed that the civil laws would establish nothing contrary to the natural law, and that the particular advantage of states, from which civil laws arise, does not conflict with their common end. Hence a civil law opposed to the natural law could indeed be enacted, but no one but a madman, and one whose heart was set on the destruction of the state, would wish to enact such a law. . . .

6. We must also examine at this point the rather difficult question of whether a subject can ever sin in carrying out the mandates of his prince, particularly if he indicates that he is merely executing the mandate, with all knowledge of and necessary accountability for it having devolved on the one who gave the order. For

the mandates of princes differ from laws in that the latter are general mandates addressed to any subjects whatsoever, while the former are enjoined on certain subjects in regard to a particular matter, though when it comes to producing an obligation in the one to whom they are directed, they have the same effect as laws.

And so it is a widely held opinion that sometimes a sin is committed if some-one obeys the orders of a civil sovereign, and that a citizen therefore can and should measure such orders by his own well-informed conscience. . . . And indeed, it is understood that good men who are convinced that they must render an account of their actions before the divine tribunal, and that every kingdom is beneath a weightier kingdom, should promise their obedience upon this condition: that they are indeed willing to carry out the orders of sovereigns, provided they do not manifestly conflict with natural and divine law. . . .

Hobbes, on the contrary, . . . declares it to be a seditious opinion that "subjects sin whenever they carry out mandates of their princes that seem to them to be unjust."[1] Here it is undoubtedly dangerous, as much for states as for the consciences of private individuals, to believe that if only a scruple or a doubt about the equity of orders should arise, they can rightly be refused. For in this manner citizens must very often fall into sin, acting against their conscience if they obey, and against the pledge they have given their superiors if they do not. For it is surely an acknowledged fact that a conscience wavering between the doubts of the moment best consults its own interest by selecting the side on which there is less danger of sinning. But now the danger of sinning is far more imminent if one neglects an expressly given pledge on account of an uncertain doubt, since the orders of supe-riors are always accompanied by the presumption of justice and often proceed from a rationale which it has by no means been granted to private individuals to judge. . . .

For surely someone can at a sovereign's injunction undertake the mere execu-tion of an action that is imputed as a sin solely to the one by whom it is com-manded, and not to the one by whom it is put into execution. Yet we think that this requires, first, that he be enjoined merely to execute the act; that is, that he make only his members and bodily strength available for it, that he otherwise fur-nish neither opportunity nor pretext for it, nor offer any excuse, and that he go along with it as something completely alien and not his own. Furthermore, he must, as much as he can, also express his aversion to that task and beg to be relieved of it. . . . Finally, it is required that on account of this refusal to execute the act, a present danger to his life, or another grave evil that neither justice nor charity obligates him to undergo for another's sake, be threatened against him by the one by whom the act is mandated, and who has the strength to bring that evil to bear, especially when he would inflict an evil on the other even without our help. Indeed, it is evident that there is no power to obligate, that is, to lay some internal neces-sity on consciences, in the mandates of any men which conflict with the divine law, and that one who fails to obey them is without any fault. . . .

8. It must on these same grounds be determined whether a citizen may rightly take up arms in an unjust war at the order of a prince. Here the opinion of Grotius

---

[1]*De Cive*, XII,2.

. . . is that it is not right for a citizen to be an accomplice to a prince's crimes when it is plain that the latter is unjustly attacking another, and that in case of doubt one must follow the safer course, which is to abstain from war.[2]

But these opinions must be carefully moderated by us, it seems, lest the force of civil sovereignty be destroyed thereby and the obedience of citizens suspended from the judgment of individuals in a matter of such great importance, especially since it is easy for timidity and laziness to pretend to a scruple of conscience here. To be sure, when someone is admitted to deliberations and has the right to cast a ballot, if he is not obligated by the decision of the rest without his own consent, he cannot rightly undertake even that which he doubts, let alone that whose injustice is generally agreed upon. And this can be so even if he is granted the option of either fighting or remaining at peace. But what if he is simply ordered to obey? Here we think that among all nations that have any concern for what is honorable, deliberations about undertaking a war always presuppose a justified cause of war, and that you would argue in vain about conscience among those who neglect to do this.

But the question about which there is most deliberation is this: whether it is expedient for a commonwealth in a particular circumstance to make war on another on the basis of such a pretext. Here the one on whom the care of the commonwealth especially lies, and who has the most thorough view of the state's strength, is no doubt presumed to discern more clearly what is of use than some private individual. But even supposing that a war is just, if someone should doubt whether it is better to neglect or forgive an injury done the commonwealth than to avenge it by means of war, let him know that a citizen's judgment that the civil sovereignty is not observing toward another some virtue containing only the power of an imperfect obligation is in no way considered a sufficient cause for him to refuse obedience to it and incite it to be stern with him. And so it will be safest if the citizen simply obeys here and lets the supreme sovereign account to God concerning the justice of the war. . . .

[2]*On the Law of War and Peace,* II,26,4.

Chapter 3

ON THE SUPREME SOVEREIGNTY'S AUTHORITY
OVER THE LIFE AND GOODS OF CITIZENS
ON ACCOUNT OF THEIR CRIMES

1. There also belongs to supreme civil sovereignty an authority over the body and life, as well as the goods of citizens on account of their crimes. This is commonly called, in short, the right of life and death, and it differs plainly from the right of God over creatures . . . and that of men over brutes. The first scruple that occurs with respect to it is how such an authority could be conferred on a state by individuals through pacts. For since punishment is a thing inflicted on a person against his will, and that which someone inflicts on himself cannot happen to an unwilling person, it can be difficult to explain how someone has a faculty to punish himself and is able to transfer it to another. . . .

Here we must know, therefore, that just as in the case of natural bodies there can arise out of the mixture and proportioning of simple things some composite having qualities found in none of the simple things that enter into the mixture, so also moral bodies consisting of many men can have a right which results from that conjunction itself, having formally belonged to none of the individuals from whose coalescence it, as it were, arose, and which is exercised through the rulers of these bodies. . . . Thus, no one will say that particular men have a faculty to enact laws for themselves, and yet when all subject their will to the will of one person there arises the authority to prescribe laws for all. In the same way, the faculty to coerce individuals by means of penalties can exist in the head of a moral body, even though there was no such faculty in individuals before. . . .

4. Punishment can in general be described as an evil of suffering that is inflicted for an evil of action, or else as a troublesome evil imposed on someone in a coercive way and by virtue of sovereignty in view of an antecedent crime. An "evil of suffering," we say. For although certain labors are often enjoined in place of punishment—as when, for instance, someone is condemned to the mines, to the galleys, to a penal farm, to erect fortifications, to clean the sewers, and so on—these are taken into consideration only insofar as they are laborious and troublesome for the one who does them, and for this reason to be classed as sufferings. Also, because we have said that punishment is imposed "in view of an antecedent crime," it follows that punishments are not properly speaking those disadvantages which someone suffers on account of a contagious disease or a deformed body or some other impurity—many of which are found in Hebraic law, which says, for instance, that lepers are to be kept from associating with the rest, that those deformed in some limb are to be excluded from the priesthood, and so on. . . .

But it must be carefully observed that in most laws the part which, as it were, ordains, and that which threatens, are expressed through two self-contained statements, as in "You shall not do this, and whoever does it will pay the penalty"; but that in some the latter part is, so to speak, a condition of the prior prohibition, as in "You shall not do this unless you wish to pay for it by way of a fine." And in laws of this sort, that which can be seen as the penal sanction is in fact equivalent to a tax, as it is left up to subjects to choose whether they wish to pay the money dictated by the law or to refrain from some act. This occurs chiefly in the case of sumptuary laws, which often have the alternative ends of either inducing the citizens to be frugal or enriching the treasury; for it would be illicit to prostitute natural laws by selling a license to violate them for money. But the remaining laws as a rule intend through punishment only to deter the citizens from sins. . . .

5. Furthermore, since we describe a judge who inflicts a suitable punishment upon a criminal as just, and say that justice is being administered when penalties are rightly determined, there has been a debate among philosophers about the kind of justice to which the imposition of penalties belongs, whether to commutative or distributive justice, or, if one prefers the terms of Grotius, to expletive or attributive justice. Those who have referred the exaction of penalties to distributive justice employ the argument that in the distribution of punishment, just as in the distribution of goods, more should be given to one who deserves more and less to one who deserves less. And since, according to their way of thinking, distributive justice deals with those things that are given by the whole to the parts, or by the state to individual citizens, punishments surely come to individuals from the state.

Our reply to this is that their supposition that distributive justice has a place whenever an equality is established among more than two terms, or as often as something must be proportionately divided among more than one, is false. For in a partnership contract the shares of profit are distributed proportionately among more than one partner, yet they are owed in another manner than either rewards or punishments. It is certainly obvious that punishments are not owed because of a pact; nor does anyone, in subjecting himself to a state, secure a guarantee that punishments will surely be inflicted on him according to his crimes. And so the imposition of punishments by no means squares with distributive justice, which we described above.

Furthermore, the fact that those who do more harm are punished more severely, and those who do less more lightly, is only consequential and accidental, not because it is intended primarily and for its own sake. For in imposing a penalty on someone for a crime it is not necessary that the crime be compared with another crime, and that the proportion between the penalties assigned to each be the same as the proportion between their respective gravity. Instead, each crime has its penalty determined separately, as it were, either heavier or lighter as the public utility requires, even though on most occasions it turns out that a heavier penalty is assigned to a serious crime and a lighter penalty to a less serious crime.

Some of those who have referred punishments to commutative justice have considered this matter thus, as if something were being allocated to a transgressor through punishment, as happens ordinarily in contracts. They have been led into this error by the common expression which says that "One who has committed a crime is owed a punishment." But this expression is obviously unwarranted [*akuros*]. For one who is properly owed something has a right against the debtor, so that he can exact the debt from him. But who would say that a transgressor has a right, so that he is able to demand that punishment be inflicted on him by a magistrate? Therefore, the sense of that expression is this: A magistrate can rightly exact from a criminal the penalty defined by the laws.

Grotius says . . . that it is expletive justice that is primarily and for its own sake considered in the assignment of penalties, and this "because one who punishes should, in order to punish rightly, have a right to punish, which right arises from another's crime."[3] But Grotius was deceived by the ambiguity of the word 'right.' For there is a very great difference between "I have a right to do something" and "I have a right to receive something from another." The former means that I have the authority to perform a certain act, and that no one should hinder me in doing so. The latter's meaning is this: I have a right to have something from another in such a way that he in turn has an obligation to bestow it on me. Now when expletive justice is involved, the word 'right' is taken not in the former but in the latter sense. And this right inheres in the one who receives something, not in the one who bestows it. For example, when I pay a laborer a wage I am said to exercise expletive justice not because I have the faculty to give him something but because he has the right to demand a wage from me. Similarly, I am surely correct in saying that I have a right to order my servant to take off my shoes, but who would conclude from this that when I order him to perform this service I am exercising justice? Yet the inference above, that expletive justice is exercised through punishment because this cannot be rightly inflicted except by one who has a right to inflict it, is on par with this. . . .

Since these things are so, nothing else remains than to say that punishments pertain to neither kind of justice, but that they are regulated by a special kind of justice. Unless you prefer to say that the imposition of penalties, like the distribution of rewards, concerning which there was no antecedent agreement by means of a special pact, is a part of prudence, which is conjoined with the duty to rule others and must for this reason be referred to universal justice.

6. Therefore, all persons of sound mind admit that although all men are by nature equal, and punishment in itself is something harsh and hard, man all the while proceeds of himself to afflict or destroy other men; and also, that although the most wise Creator has so disposed the nature of things and men that wickedness is of itself accompanied by evils which, as it were, wreak vengeance on its author, punishment—even positive human punishment—contains nothing repugnant to natural fairness but is instead supremely necessary for humankind on account of its salutary function. For just as the welfare of humankind required that human equality be eliminated by the establishment of sovereignty, so the force of sovereignty would have perished in the great wickedness of men and their aversion to what is right, if depraved mortals could not be reduced to order by being immediately confronted with some evil. Moreover, since there is prior public proclamation of what ought

---

[3]*On the Law of War and Peace*, II,20,2.

to be done and avoided, as well as of the penalty awaiting those who do otherwise, a person has no one to blame but himself if he voluntarily brings harsh punishments down upon himself by sinning against the laws.

9. In any case, the true end of punishments is precaution against injuries. This comes about either if the one who has sinned is changed for the better, if others are induced by his example not to want to sin thereafter, or if the one who has sinned is so restrained that he cannot sin any longer. . . .

The first kind of punishment aims to correct the sinner's mind and to purge him of the desire to sin through a mode of curing that involves contraries. For since every action, especially when it is deliberate and frequent, gives rise to a certain proclivity of its own that is said to be a habit when it has matured, the incitement to vice must be removed as soon as possible. . . .

11. The second end of punishments is the advantage of the one in whose interest it was that the sin not occur, or who was harmed by the other's sin, so that he does not suffer such a thing thereafter, either from the same person or from others. This can be achieved in three ways: by getting rid of the one who committed the crime; by taking from him his strength to do harm, even though his life is preserved (for instance, by keeping him in custody, by taking away his weapons and instruments for harming, or by banishing him to a remote place); and finally, by having him unlearn his commission of crimes from the evil of his own suffering—something that is linked with the improvement we have just dealt with. But it is not by just any punishment whatsoever that one attains the end of having a person who was harmed not be harmed again by others, but by open and conspicuous punishment, and such as serves as an example. Hence it is that punishments are almost always carried out not in the narrow confines of prisons but in busy places, and with a frightening spectacle that is capable of striking terror into the minds of ordinary people. . . .

12. The third end of punishments is the unspecified advantage of anyone and everyone, in that the severity of a punishment provides for the security of all. . . . This kind of punishment serves either to prevent someone who has harmed a person from also harming others thereafter—something achieved if he is either killed, weakened, or restrained, so that he can do no further harm . . . —or, by means of its bitterness, to get him to put aside his desire to sin. Else it seeks to bring it about that those who may be attracted by the impunity of crimes do not trouble others—something achieved by the conspicuousness of punishments. . . .

We can also include under this end of punishments the advantage of maintaining or restoring to good order the authority of civil sovereignty, which is considerably diminished by transgressions of the laws, especially those that are malicious and excessive. For it is in the interest of the entire state that this authority remain sound, and when unimpaired, it is the strongest possible check to men's lack of moral integrity. . . .

Chapter 4

ON THE SUPREME CIVIL SOVEREIGNTY'S AUTHORITY TO DETERMINE THE VALUE OF CITIZENS

1. There are also certain foundations outside the state, in natural freedom, on the basis of which one person can be deservedly preferred to another. Yet since it depends on a pact or a determination of the civil sovereignty whether these foundations furnish someone with a right, it seems most appropriate at this point to set forth the general substance of the distinctions among men according to their esteem. For esteem is the value of persons in communal life according to which they can be equated or compared with others, and ranked before or after them.

There is evidently no small kinship between the two noblest kinds of moral quantities, esteem and price. The former is taken into consideration in the case of persons and the latter in the case of things, because in communal life persons are evaluated by the former and things by the latter. And just as the chief end of imposing prices on things has been to make it possible for them to be rightly compared with one another, when they are to be mutually exchanged or transferred by one person to another, so esteem has served the end of enabling men to be compared with one another by reason of that value, as it were, so that a seemly order can be established among them when they happen to be joined together, now that it has become sufficiently apparent that equality can by no means be easily preserved in humankind in all respects.

Now esteem can be divided into *simple* and *intensive*. Each of these comes into consideration both among those who live in natural freedom and those who are contained in the same state.

2. *Simple esteem* among those constituted in natural freedom with respect to one another seems to consist chiefly in this: that a person conduct himself as, and be considered as, someone with whom one can deal as with a good man, and one who is bent on accommodating himself to the laws of human sociality; someone, therefore, who is prepared to observe the natural law toward others inasmuch as he can. For just as we say that a thing which has some use in human life is of some worth and call that which is utterly useless a thing of no worth, so you would say that someone who can be dealt with as a sociable animal in some way has at least some value. But if someone openly showed that he is unfit for society by boldly scorning and trampling on the law of nature and the duties owed to others on account of it, you would deservedly judge him to be a man of no value.

3. This esteem can be considered either as *complete*, as *diminished*, or as entirely *squandered*. It is *complete* when someone has not yet knowingly and willingly, with an evil intent, violated the law of nature against another through some malicious and excessive crime. For sins of infirmity are condoned by the human con-

dition and do not immediately extinguish a good man's reputation, provided his mind remains honorable and eager to pursue what is just. And this esteem is presumed to be present in all, to the extent that they themselves do not diminish it through their wickedness. Therefore, it must naturally be said to belong equally to each, and apart from any antecedent evil deed all must be deemed equally honorable. . . . Yet because men *can will* to harm one another, all of them will naturally have to be considered good but capable of becoming evil; and indeed as friends, but such as you may not safely trust in all situations.

4. This esteem is *diminished* through malicious crimes, especially excessive ones, which have been undeservedly inflicted on others against the law of nature, and which make it unsafe for others to trust this kind of deceiver thereafter, and to have any dealings with him without solid precautions. Yet someone's esteem is only diminished through corrupt deeds, not entirely squandered. For even though I can with some probability expect that someone will be toward me the kind of person he has conducted himself as toward others, this is not always so certain that the opposite does not now and then appear. For it is possible that he was driven to deceive others by special reasons not found in me. Also, someone could have been stirred by corrupt passions at one time from which he is free at another. In any case, this stain on one's esteem which has been contracted from one's evil deeds can be removed if one voluntarily repairs the loss one has caused or furnishes some equivalent, and evinces a repentant mind. For these acts, when spontaneously elicited, can sufficiently convince us that a mind has been seriously reformed.

5. But this esteem is in fact entirely *squandered* by a kind and plan of life that aims directly at the indiscriminate harm of others, and at the making of one's fortune from their manifest injuries. . . .

Whatever little esteem such people have is up to the state, which tolerates them, to determine. One who has an official indulgence to exercise a vice should at least enjoy the common right of men. . . . That one's natural esteem is violently prostrated through a kind of life that involves the profession of any sort of vice, is certain; yet unless that vice is conjoined with an injury to others, it does not seem that such persons can be treated as the common enemies of all. But those whose profession has the aim of injuring others, and who indiscriminately employ against any men—or those, at least, who live outside their own company—the same license they employ against beasts, and thus wage war against men and not only enemies, are entirely lacking in that esteem by which we take the measure of any other men. . . .

6. *Simple esteem among those who live within states* is that whereby a person is considered at least an ordinary, and so a full member of a state; or that which belongs to someone who has not been declared a corrupt member of the state according to its laws and mores, and is understood to count for something and to have civil standing.

Now one lacks this esteem in a state either *because of one's mere status* or *because of one's crime*. The former also happens in two ways: Either a status has nothing naturally shameful in itself; else it is connected, or at least thought to be connected, with some vice. Status alone, which has nothing vicious in its own nature, in many states denies simple esteem to slaves, who are not considered civil persons or are understood to have no civil standing and to count for nothing. . . . Status removes or diminishes simple esteem in the second manner when those situated in it are occupied with affairs that cannot be undertaken without vice, or that on account of their baseness are performed only by men of the vilest and meanest disposition. The place assigned to the former sort of men will be evident from the laws and mores of each state. . . .

7. Simple civil esteem is completely lacking *because of a preceding crime* when, in accordance with the laws, someone is marked with infamy because of a certain kind of crime (for civil esteem is not extinguished by all crimes . . .). This happens either when he is expelled from this natural life and, at the same time, his memory is damned; when he is driven from the state in disgrace; or when he is retained in the state, yet not as a complete member, as it were, but an incomplete one who enjoys the benefit of residing in the state and the common protection of its laws, to be sure, but is excluded from public offices and honorable associations, and declared unsuited for or disqualified from performing all legitimate acts that presuppose an unimpaired esteem. But what those crimes are, which bring about such infamy, must be learned from the laws of each state. . . .

9. Furthermore, it is obvious as well that simple natural esteem cannot be taken away from anyone by a sovereign merely because he so decides, except for an antecedent crime that, either because of its own shamefulness or through the express sanction of the laws, is accompanied by infamy. For since such authority can in no way contribute to the preservation or the advantage of a state, it is understood not to have been conferred on sovereigns. Still, just as a sovereign can drive a citizen from the state on account of an injury, he will likewise, on account of an injury, be able to deprive him of civil esteem, at least to the extent of stripping him of those advantages that accompany unimpaired esteem in the state. But a citizen's intrinsic and natural esteem is no more taken away by this than his upright mind. . . .

11. *Intensive* esteem is that according to which persons who are otherwise equal in regard to simple esteem are preferred to one another, insofar as one of them has more of the things by which the minds of others are moved to show honor. For honor, which corresponds to the intensity of esteem, is an indication of our judgment about another's excellence. Hence honor is really not in the one who is honored but in the one who honors. . . .

12. The foundations of intensive esteem in general are thought to be all those things that have . . . or are judged to imply some notable excellence or perfection, such a one, that is, whose effect is consistent with the end of the natural law or of states. . . . In particular, however, these foundations include perspicacity of mind and the capacity to improve the mind by means of a knowledge of various things, especially when this capacity has been actually implemented. They also include appropriate judgment about the conduct of affairs and the resolution of ambiguities . . . ; a firm mind not shaken by external influences, and superior to enticements and terrors; the faculty of giving a seemly and an eloquent account of the contents of the mind; and then, strength, beauty, and notable dexterity of the body, insofar as these are judged to be clear indications or instruments of the mind. . . .

14. Now all these foundations of intensive esteem do not in themselves pro-

duce anything but an imperfect right to be honored and respected by others. And so if someone has denied this right to others, even such as well deserve it, he cannot be said to have done an injury but only to have drawn the stigma of inhumanity or—if it is permitted to speak thus—of incivility upon himself. For it is not apparent how someone among those who live in natural freedom with one another, and thus are surely naturally equal to one another, is able by virtue of his own right to demand honor from someone else, since the latter can judge, on account of the natural love which he has for himself and his own, that there are in him such things as are altogether equal or superior to those which the other prides himself about....

It seems evident from these things that even though it is consistent with natural reason that honor be bestowed on those who are more excellent—indeed, if anyone wishes, and as far as we are concerned, it can also be listed among the precepts of the natural law that those who are more excellent are to be honored—that duty must nonetheless be listed among those which a person cannot demand by his own right, but the praise for which, when they are performed, must be reserved to another's humanity. Indeed, for someone to be able to demand honor or any sign thereof from another by his own right, it is necessary that he either have sovereignty over him, or that he have acquired such a right for himself from a pact or from a law proposed or approved by a common master....

23. Now it is evident that there is in sovereignty a power which bestows on it a preferment valid in the manner of a perfect right against those toward whom it is exercised. For it is surely more excellent to command than to obey, to have another's will be accountable to one's own instead of adjusting oneself to his. And it is necessary that there be in me a deep respect for one to whom I not only owe my protection, but who can also compel me to obey his commands by a fear of punishment. Thus, sovereignty of itself introduces inequality among men. Although besides the respect owed to the office of sovereignty there can also be a special esteem arising from the particular excellence of a sovereign....

But it is also obvious that the more far-reaching sovereignty is, and the more efficacious, the greater the dignity with which it surrounds a sovereign in the eyes of his subjects. Indeed, even the duration of sovereignty, though it does not of itself contribute to its power, nonetheless considerably increases a sovereign's dignity. Yet this does not prevent a subject from surpassing the one who rules him in those foundations of honor that produce only an imperfect right....

Chapter 6

ON THE LAW OF WAR

1. Since nature has granted individuals living in natural freedom no less a faculty than states to defend themselves against force that is unjustly threatened against them, and to claim for themselves by force rights that have been infringed or denied by others, I think it will be appropriate to examine first those things that wars of individuals and wars of states have in common, and then those that are by their own nature, or by the customs of nations, proper to the latter.

2. Now it is to the highest degree in accord with the natural law that someone not inflict a hurt or harm upon another without a right, and that men perform the duties of humanity toward one another and furnish of themselves those things especially, about which there has been a specific agreement. When men observe these things toward one another there is said to be peace, a state most agreeable to human nature and suited to preserve it, and that for whose establishment and preservation the law of nature has above all been implanted in men. . . . Indeed, peace is a state that is proper to human nature as such, arising from a principle that man has in a special way over brutes, while war rushes forth from a principle that is common to them. That is, even brutes strive by natural instinct to defend and preserve themselves by means of force, but man alone understands the nature of peace. For only he can voluntarily furnish something to another and abstain from hurting him, by considering some obligation in himself or some right in the other, which cannot be understood apart from the use of reason. . . .

Nonetheless, war may also be licit for man himself, and sometimes necessary, as when another maliciously threatens to hurt me or refuses to supply what is owed. For then the care for my own safety creates for me the authority to assert and defend myself and my things in any way whatever, even by hurting the one who violates them. . . .

Yet nature permits war in such a way that the one who wages it should set peace as the end for himself. . . . Moreover, even though one who has hurt me immediately provides me—inasmuch as he can—with the authority to undertake a war against him, I must nonetheless consider how much good or evil will probably redound on myself or on others who have not hurt me. For I should not seek to requite by war injuries that do not completely subvert my welfare, if the disadvantages that will arise from this for me and mine are greater than the advantages, or if others with whom I am still maintaining peace may, upon the occasion of my war, encounter great harms that I should on account of the law of humanity have averted by tolerating, without vengeance or recompense, the sort of injury that has been inflicted on me. And so it is right and praiseworthy for anyone to decline to requite by war an injury inflicted on himself from whose vindication more evil than good is judged to arise.

3. The reasons for just wars can be brought under these headings: to preserve

and protect ourselves and our things against others who are trying to hurt us or to take away or destroy these things; to assert ourselves when others, by whom we are owed anything from a perfect right, refuse to furnish it of themselves; and finally, to obtain reparation for harms by whose infliction we have been injured, and to wrest from one who has previously hurt us a guarantee that he will not attack us in the future. From these results the division between just offensive and defensive wars, the latter of which we take to be those by which we defend and strive to retain the things that are ours, and the former those by which we extort debts that are denied us or proceed to recover things that have been unjustly seized from us, and seek guarantees for the future. . . .

4. In general, however, the causes of wars, especially offensive ones, should be clear and not contain any doubt. For it is common for doubts to arise here in many instances, partly from ignorance of fact, when it is not clearly established whether something was done or not, or with what intent; partly from an obscure comparison of strict right with the law of charity; and partly from an unclear apportionment of the advantages apt to result from either undertaking or omitting the war. Therefore, one ought neither to cast about here so boldly with pretensions that are still unclear, nor to fly immediately to arms. Rather one should try in three ways, especially, to prevent a thing from erupting into war: by initiating a discussion among the parties or those commissioned by them, by appealing to arbiters, or finally by lot. . . .

5. The unjust reasons for war are reviewed by Grotius.[4] . . . Some of them are plainly unacceptable; others have some plausibility, though a rather slight one. Those which are referred to the former class are avarice and the craving to have superfluous things, ambition and the longing to dominate, and the burning desire to acquire fame from the oppression of others. . . . To the latter class belongs the *fear* contracted from the strength and power of one's neighbor. . . .

Yet this fear alone does not suffice as a just reason for war unless we determine with a morally evident certitude that there is an intention to hurt us. For while an uncertain suspicion of danger can indeed persuade you to surround yourself betimes with defenses, it cannot create a right that you be the first to bring force to bear, not even for the end of getting the other to furnish what is called a real guarantee that he will not attack you. . . . For as long as someone has not hurt another, and is also not found to be obviously preparing to do so (for an incipient injury, no less than a completed one, can sometimes be vindicated by war), it should be presumed that he will also do his duty in the future, especially when he confirms this by means of words and promises. It would be unfair to extort a real guarantee from such a person by force, since he would in this manner be in a worse condition than we, as he is compelled to be satisfied with our bare assurances. But supposing a just cause for waging war, then the excessively swelling power of a neighbor has great influence on one's deliberations about war, since it has been found by experience that in most cases the craving to dominate grows along with the strength to do so. . . .

7. But to understand correctly how far one is permitted to proceed against an

[4]*On the Law of War and Peace*, II,22.

enemy and his things by force, one must observe that the license against an enemy differs depending on whether it arises simply from a state of hostility, or whether it is mitigated by the law of nature, which orders one to temper it. That is, since the exhibition of the duties of peace ought according to the law of nature to be mutual, one who has first infringed them against me has also, inasmuch as he can, absolved me from their performance, and by declaring himself my enemy grants me the license to exert unlimited force against him, or as much as seems appropriate to me. This is especially so because the end of war, be it offensive or defensive, cannot be obtained without this license, that is, if it would be necessary to keep one's force against an enemy within certain bounds and stop short of the extremes. For this reason even formally declared wars have something like a contract of this sort: "Try what you can; I shall likewise resort to all things." And this is the case not only if the enemy himself has undertaken an unlimited assault against me but also if, by chance, he wishes to injure me without going to extremes. For another has no greater right to threaten a moderate injury than a severe one. And so it is permitted to apply force against an enemy not only to the point where I have repelled the danger which he threatens against me, or where I have recovered or wrested from him that which he has unjustly seized from or refused to furnish me; but I can also proceed against him in order to obtain a guarantee for the future. So long as the other allows this to be wrested from him through force, he gives sufficient indication that he still intends to injure me even thereafter.

Nor, indeed, is it always unjust to repay a greater evil for a smaller. For the objection of some, that retribution should be proportional, has a place only in tribunals, where punishments are inflicted by superiors. But evils that are inflicted by right of war do not properly have the rationale of punishments; for they neither proceed from a superior as such nor tend directly to the correction of either the one doing the hurt, or of others, but to the defense and assertion of my safety, my things, and my rights. And for this end it is permitted to apply whatever means seem to be most appropriate against a person who has, by his injury, brought it about that I can inflict no injury upon him, until we have finally come to an agreement about the omission of hurts in the future.

But on the other hand, the law of humanity wishes us to consider not only what an enemy can suffer without injury, but also what is fitting for a humane—add, and generous—victor to do. Hence one must, to the extent that it can be done and our defense and future security allow, take care that the evils which will be inflicted on an enemy be adjusted to the measure customarily followed by a civil court in assessing crimes and other disputes. . . .

14. It is obvious that people wage war not only on their own behalf, but often also on behalf of others. But for this to be done rightly a just cause for warring is required, at least in the one who is being assisted. In the one who is going to render aid to the other, however, there should be some special bond by which he is connected to the chief belligerent, one that makes it appropriate for him, in order to meet his obligation to one man, to treat another who is equally a man in a hostile fashion. . . .

Now among those whom we not only can but also should rightly defend are our subjects. And this is not only because they are, as it were, a part of the rulers, but also because free men have voluntarily established or submitted to sovereign-ties in order to enjoy such a defense. . . . Yet rulers of states rightly take up arms on behalf of individual citizens only if this can be done without a more serious disadvantage to all or the majority of the citizens. This is because their duty is concerned more with the whole than with the parts, and the greater the part is, the nearer it comes to the whole. . . .

Next after subjects, those on whose behalf we are bound to bear arms are allies with whom we have a treaty containing this provision. Yet these give way entirely to our subjects if assistance cannot be rendered to both, and this while the treaty remains intact. For no state is obligated more to anyone than to its own citizens. Therefore, when it promises reinforcements to others it is understood to do so upon this condition: "insofar as it can be done while maintaining one's obligation toward one's own citizens."

Hence a person who trusts in a treaty whose preservation is not in another's interest is even a fool. For just as no one should undertake unjust or rash wars, so no one is bound to aid an ally who initiates such wars. And even though this applies chiefly to offensive wars, it nonetheless pertains in some way to defensive wars as well. For if my ally sees that he is not an enemy's equal, even with my added strength, and nonetheless persists in rushing into certain destruction when he can settle the matter upon tolerable terms, then I would be a fool if I became a party to his madness. . . .

The place after allies is held by friends, or those to whom we are joined by a special benevolence. Even though these persons have not been promised certain and definite assistance by means of an express treaty, it is understood that the mutual joining together of friendship itself contains an assurance that one person will, as much as his stricter obligations allow, be concerned about the other's welfare, and this to a greater degree than is otherwise demanded by the common kinship among men. And this can itself suffice for someone to undertake someone else's defense against the manifest injuries of others, especially since it can very easily be in our own interest as well, and indeed redound to the public good of all, that a person not insult others by means of injuries with impunity. . . .

Yet there must be some restraint in this, so that not just anyone, even one who lives in natural freedom, immediately has a right to compel and castigate another who has inflicted an injury on someone else, on the sole pretext that the public good demands that injuries not be inflicted on the innocent with impunity, and that that which touches one must touch all. For since the one who is attacked in such a manner has not been deprived of the right to repel with equal force the force of the other, whom he himself has surely not injured, humankind will now be disrupted by two wars instead of one. Indeed, it is also contrary to natural equality to thrust oneself forward unasked as the arbiter of human affairs, as it were; not to mention the fact that this would be open to great abuse, since there is hardly anyone against whom war could not be undertaken on such a pretext. Therefore, an injury inflicted on another can provide us with a sufficient reason for war only when the one affected by it calls us to his aid, so that we do whatever we undertake here in the name of the one injured and not our own. . . .

20. Someone can by natural right, and with a good conscience, acquire by a

just war those of his enemies' things that are owed him or equal to those owed, and on whose account, when their payment was refused, there had to be a resort to arms; including at the same time the expenses he has incurred in this violent pursuit of his right, and anything else that he has deemed it necessary to take from the enemy as a guarantee. Hence, if someone has inflicted an injury on others out of confidence in his wealth, it will be right, when he is conquered, to take his superfluous wealth away from him so that he will be more modest in the future. But by the customs of nations, in a formal war someone becomes the unlimited and unrestricted owner of the things that he has taken from the enemy, even if they far exceed the pretext on account of which the war was begun. . . .

It must be properly noted here, however, that through seizure in war one only acquires a right that is valid against some third party with whom one is at peace. For a captor to acquire a dominion valid even against the one from whom a thing was seized, there must be an additional peace making and a negotiated settlement between them. For without this the former owner is understood to retain the right to wrest that thing from his enemy again whenever he has the strength to do so.

Chapter 9

ON TREATIES

1. Next we must see about those kinds of public pacts that come with the special name of 'treaties.' . . . It will be most appropriate if we draw their division from their subject matter, since some of them establish something that has previously belonged to the natural law already, while others add something further to the duties of the natural law, or at least give them a certain determinacy when they seem indefinite.

2. The former class contains those treaties by means of which there is agreement about the simple humanity that is to be exercised on all sides, or about the reciprocal non-infliction of harms. . . . Treaties of this sort were held by the ancients to be especially necessary among those who had previously had no dealings with one another. This is not surprising, because the doctrine of the natural law that there is by nature a certain kinship among men, and that it is therefore wrong to hurt another apart from a preceding offense, had been forgotten among many, so that it was believed that the duties of humanity ought to be conferred on citizens alone, and that any outsiders were as enemies whom it would not be wrong to hurt for the sake of our own profit. . . . They are certainly not necessary among those who profess their observance of the natural law by cultivating morals, except that—

just as among individuals—it may not be improper to make a more extensive declaration of friendship when parties first begin to have dealings with one another. . . .
Otherwise, cultivated men should be almost ashamed to enter a pact whose articles
contain nothing else than that the law of nature not be simply and directly violated—
as if someone would not be sufficiently mindful of his duty apart from that pact. . . .

Those treaties do indeed frequently come with the name of 'friendship,' but the
law of friendship, properly speaking, requires more than that common duty of
humanity. For although the offices of friendship are not definite, like those owed
from a pact, still in general anyone knows that it is characteristic of a friend to
share his goods generously with friends, to care for their welfare, to come to their
assistance by cautioning or advising them, to ward off (according to his strength)
any threatening evils—and to do all these things with a feeling more intense than
in the case of those which others do out of bare humanity alone. . . .

3. Now of the treaties in which something is added to the duties that men owe
each other by the natural law, some are equal and some unequal. The former are
those which are the same on both sides, that is, when both sides not only promise
things that are equal (either simply or in view of their proportionate strength), but
also do so in an equal manner, so that neither party is in an inferior position or be-
holden to the other. We shall soon see about those which are unequal. . . . Now each
of them is commonly entered into chiefly for the sake of contracting some society,
one that is concerned either with commercial affairs, with a community of war (that
is, the mutual rendering of assistance in an offensive or a defensive war), or with
other things. Equal treaties concerning commercial affairs can vary, as when it is
agreed, for example, that the citizens of each confederate who come to the other's
lands or ports shall not pay any tariff, or no more than is paid at that time, or not
above a certain quantity, or no more than that paid by citizens or other allies, and
other similar things. Equal treaties concerning a military partnership are those where
it is agreed that both sides will furnish equal supplies of soldiers, ships, or other
apparatus of war, and this either at both times, when either party is attacked or itself wishes to make war on another, or [only] if either is beset by war. . . .

4. Now from equal treaties it is easy to understand what unequal treaties are;
namely, they obtain when the things promised on each side are unequal or when
either party is in an inferior position. Unequal things are promised either by the
more or by the less worthy confederate. The former happens if a more powerful
party promises assistance to the other and does not demand a counter-guarantee,
or if he promises assistance that is greater than or not proportionate to that of the
other. The latter happens if the inferior confederate is bound to furnish more than
he receives from the other. . . .

6. There is also that well-known distinction of treaties into real and personal.
Of these the latter are those which have been entered into with a king in consideration of his person, and expire along with him; the former those entered into not
so much in consideration of a king himself, or of a people's rulers, but in consideration of a kingdom and a commonwealth itself, and which endure even though
the rulers of the people with whom the administration of the commonwealth lay
at the time the treaty was entered into have died. To which of these two classes
any treaty pertains will be evident from the following.

That is therefore certain: Whatever treaties are entered into with a free people are by their own nature real and endure up to the limit expressed in the treaty itself, even though the magistrates by whose intervention the treaty was struck have died or been replaced. From this it can be inferred that if a treaty has been entered into by a free people, and the status of the commonwealth has afterwards been changed from a democracy to a monarchy, the treaty will remain; the reason being that the people remains the same even though the form of the commonwealth has been altered, and because a king who has been called to the kingship by a people's consent is understood to have undertaken it together with all the obligations that were contracted by that people while it had the supreme sovereignty in itself. In addition, since treaties are entered into by those who enjoy the supreme sovereignty (whose common subject is the state), the supreme sovereignty exercised through the votes of the whole people, and that afterwards wielded by a king who has been constituted through the people's consent, will be considered the same. Yet those treaties which have as their end the preservation of a present status are to be excluded here: for example, if two free peoples have entered into a treaty of mutual assistance against those who undertake to change the status of their commonwealth by force. For if either people freely consents later on to a change of their commonwealth's status, the treaty itself is also understood to expire, in that its rationale ceases. . . .

11. One should also be advised that treaties entered into for a certain time are not understood to be tacitly renewed when it has elapsed, not only because no one may be presumed to bind himself to a new burden without giving it some thought, but also because there could be no definite agreement about its duration in this manner. Hence if any acts are performed after a treaty has come to an end, they are to be considered as indications of benevolence rather than of the treaty's renewal. For simple friendship surely persists even after a treaty has ended.

Finally, according to the common nature of pacts, when one party has not stood by a treaty the other is also permitted to depart from it. Yet confederates can agree that although a treaty has not been satisfied in one article, the remaining, unviolated articles will nonetheless be observed. Still, this must be taken in the sense that the other party is not bound to furnish that which used to correspond to the article neglected by the one, and that some positive hurt will not be inflicted on it as soon as it fails to do so.

Chapter 11

THE WAYS IN WHICH SOMEONE
MAY CEASE TO BE A CITIZEN

1. Among the ways in which someone ceases to be a citizen, some people reckon, is if a king should die without any heir and successor, or if he has begun to consider his kingdom as abandoned; for then, they say, individuals return to their natural freedom. But since it is plain that a kingdom is not completely dissolved in a case of this sort but falls back into the form of an interregnum, the obligation of citizens toward the king, who no longer exists, does indeed end at that time, yet in such a way that the citizens still remain conjoined with one another by that primeval pact whereby states have come about.

2. What happens most frequently is that someone voluntarily, and with the permission of his own state, withdraws into another state to fix the seat of his fortunes there. The extent to which citizens have been permitted this voluntary change of residence is gathered from the ways in which someone has been received into the state. For some people pass into the jurisdiction of a certain state when they have been conquered in a just war or compelled by extreme necessity, and the amount of freedom they enjoy here must be found out from the laws of the state. But if some free man, who like the ancient family-fathers was either not subject to anyone's sovereignty before, or has now been released from that to which he was formerly bound, has voluntarily joined himself to some state, it will likewise have to be determined from the statutes of this state what sort of freedom concerning change of residence has been left him. For there are states from which one is not permitted to emigrate without their express consent. In other places this license must be purchased by means of a certain burden, such as, for instance, a sum of money or a portion of one's goods....

But where there are no laws concerning the matter one must gather what is allowed from custom, or from the nature of civil subjection. Any citizen is thought to have a license to do the things that custom admits. If this sheds no light either, and the pact of subjection made no mention of the matter in one way or another, it is preferable that a free man be understood to have reserved for himself a license to emigrate at his discretion, and so wishes to conduct himself, along with Socrates, as a *citizen of the world* rather than as someone assigned to a certain lump of soil. . . . For someone who joins himself to a state by no means renounces the care of himself and his things, but rather does so in order to surround himself with a special support. Yet because it often happens that the public administration is not very conducive to someone's private concerns, or that these can be more easily provided for elsewhere, and indeed, because one cannot demand that a commonwealth be altered to please one or a few persons, the next best thing will be that they be allowed to look out for their own affairs by changing their residence. . . .

4. Yet Grotius . . . asserts that people cannot leave together as a group, the reason being that if this were conceded civil society could not continue to exist.[5] But in moral matters, he says, that without which some end cannot be obtained is judged to be necessary, and that which interferes with or destroys this end cannot be done. . . . Yet this opinion is not without doubt. For if single individuals are permitted to emigrate as they choose, why may the same not be permitted to more, for whom it is advantageous to transfer the seat of their fortunes at the same time, so long as none of the things we pointed out above stands in the way?

It makes no difference either that a state may be weakened in this manner, for one who does not have a right to retain me against my will is done no injury if, by my departure, he is cut off from some future advantage which is not yet owed. . . . For although this or that state may be significantly weakened by the emigration of its citizens in groups, or at last completely abandoned, civil society among men is not for that reason entirely destroyed. Rather, the breakup of one state is the generation of another; one's decreases yield an increase to the other. . . .

Yet if some people should wish to depart as a group, they too, just like individuals, must leave the territory of the state. For otherwise there would be a supreme confusion of sovereignties, if whole cities or regions were permitted to withdraw themselves from the sovereignty of their own state at their pleasure and either subject themselves to another sovereignty or establish their own special commonwealth thereafter.

7. Those ejected from a state on account of a crime which they have either really committed or been falsely accused of cease to be citizens against their will. For when a state is no longer willing to acknowledge someone as its member and expels him from its borders, it remits to him the obligation by which he was formerly bound as a citizen. By this act he acquires the faculty of establishing a new residence for himself wherever he can; and the state retains no jurisdiction over exiles of this sort. . . .

8. Another way in which someone unwillingly changes states occurs when he is compelled by hostile force to subject himself to the sovereignty of another as citizen and subject, whether or not he changes his residence at the same time. This, it is generally admitted, is licit not only for individual citizens—at least those bound by no other bond than the common bond of citizens—but also for whole cities and provinces, when there appears to be no other way of promoting their welfare. . . .

---

[5]*On the Law of War and Peace*, II,5,24.

Chapter 12

ON THE CHANGE AND PERISHING OF STATES

1. Changes in a state take place in a threefold manner, so that the state either remains the same, is no longer the same, or ceases entirely to be a state. The first kind of change occurs when the form of a state is changed, if a kingdom turns into an aristocracy, for instance, or if a democracy or an aristocracy is made into a kingdom. For here the essential form of a state remains; only the form resulting from the proper subject of supreme sovereignty is changed. Hence a people is also the same, whether it is ruled by a king, by nobles, or in a democratic manner. Indeed, even if it should happen that a formerly free people comes under the power of some king by war, so that it is thereafter in his patrimony, it does not on that account cease to be the same people, provided that the victorious king is willing to rule the subject people as a distinct kingdom in the future and not annex it to another people as a province. For since a people is that which contains supreme sovereignty within its confines, it makes no difference, as far as the nature of a people is concerned, whether a king has his sovereignty by a full right or one that is less than full, for either way he is the head of one and the same body.

5. Changes which bring it about that a state is no longer seen as the same take place chiefly in a twofold manner: Either two or more states are made out of one, or several states are conjoined into one. The former comes about either by mutual consent or by force of war.

Several states are made out of one by mutual consent when colonies are sent out according to the custom once found among the Greeks. For the Romans (whom European peoples usually follow even today) used afterwards to send forth colonies in such a way that they would remain a part of the mother state or of the greater fatherland. But colonies which were sent forth in the former manner constituted a proper state thereafter; in such a way, however, that they were bound to show the greater fatherland the honor befitting it, and to practice toward it a certain piety, as it were. . . . Furthermore, unless it has been expressly agreed upon in its establishment, a colony sent out in this manner will not be bound to pay the debts contracted by its mother state; for these ultimately affect the latter's goods—in which, it is supposed, the colony has no share. And although some advantages did perhaps redound from those debts to the colonists' persons at the time when they were still attached to their old fatherland, their old state declares that it will not exact anything from them on that account when it sends them forth from itself as free.

Yet if we carefully consider the matter, a state is not changed in itself when it has sent out a colony, nor does it cease to be seen as the same; rather (just as in natural generation) the effect is that two states exist thereafter in place of one. But if some kingdom should be divided by common consent into what are then two or more distinct states, it would be fair for its public patrimony, as well as the debts inhering in the whole, to be divided equally. Though when a division of this sort is voluntarily instituted, it can hardly happen that there is no express disposition over cases of this sort.

6. This kind of change, by which some state ceases to be the same, also includes the case where two peoples are united, not in the manner of a federation, or through a common king, but so that one state is really made out of two. Grotius . . . thinks in this case that when something different has not been agreed upon, the rights had by the individual states that are to be united, as also their burdens and debts, are not lost but shared.[6] . . .

It must be carefully considered, however, whether two or more peoples are joining themselves together so as to constitute some new state wherein all will have an equal right, something that happens, for instance, if two different democratic peoples coalesce into one people and kingdom after abolishing their previous government, or if two kingdoms found a new kingdom after getting rid of their respective fundamental laws and removing their ancient ruling families. It is obvious that the prior states are destroyed by means of such a union, and that a new state springs up. But when one state is so conjoined with another that one of them retains its constitution and abode, while the other's citizens, having left their own abode, are taken up into the rights and abode of the other state, it is certain that at least one of them perishes. The one that remains does not cease to be the same, however, even though it receives a significant increase by such an accession. Otherwise, different states cannot be united so that each of them remains what it was, except by way of a rather strict treaty that is capable of producing some system but not, properly speaking, a state.

7. Finally, a change by which a state altogether ceases to be takes place when a people itself has been dissolved or extinguished. There is, to be sure, the commonly vaunted saying that "Kings are mortal, commonwealths eternal." But the reason this is said is not that peoples cannot also be extinguished or dispersed by some violent occurrence, but that they do not, like individual men, die by nature when a certain span of time has gone by; rather, even though individuals depart, others continually succeed them, and this either by the substitution of outsiders in place of those who die or by the propagation of offspring. By means of this continuous succession a people is always seen to be the same, and enjoys the same rights, however often individual citizens may have changed. . . .

8. Although these things are so, it can surely happen that a certain people perishes altogether, and this either if the material component of the people, that is the multitude of its citizens, all perishes at the same time, or if the moral bond by which the people is held together is ruptured. The material component or body of a people perishes either when all the parts without which the body cannot subsist have been destroyed at the same time, or when the body's rationale has been destroyed. . . . Also, the multitude of men out of which a people consists perishes not only when the individual citizens are killed, but also when they voluntarily disperse on account of plague or sedition, or are so torn apart by force that they cannot associate with one another any more. . . .

9. The formal component or specific character of a people perishes if either

---

[6] *On the Law of War and Peace*, II,9,8.

the entire or the established community of right is destroyed. A community of right and of sovereignty is entirely destroyed if the individual citizens, who have been scattered here and there, are added to different states, whether they retain their personal freedom or are also reduced to a condition of slavery. . . . An established community of right among members of the same people is destroyed if individuals retain their personal freedom and are left in their towns and fields, in such a way, however, that they come under the sovereignty of another state. Such peoples are said to be reduced to the form of a province. Yet a mere change of place and towns, or the pulling down of fortifications, does not bring it about that a people ceases to be the same.

THE END.

Glory to God Alone

Selected Bibliography

I. Pufendorf's Main Works

Elementorum jurisprudentiae universalis libri duo. (*Elements of Universal Jurisprudence in Two Books*), 1660.

De statu imperii Germanici. (*On the Constitution of the German Empire*), 1667. Published under the pseudonym Severinus de Monzambano.

De jure naturae et gentium libri octo. (*On the Law of Nature and Nations in Eight Books*), 1672.

De officio hominis et civis juxta legem naturalem libri duo. (*On the Duty of Man and Citizen According to Natural Law in Two Books*), 1673.

Dissertationes academicae selectiores. (*Select Scholarly Essays*), 1675.

Specimen controversiarum. (*A Sample of Controversies*), 1677.

Eris Scandica, qua adversus libros de jure naturali et gentium objecta diluunter. (*Scandinavian Polemics, in which the Objections against the Book On the Law of Nature and of Nations are Dissolved*), 1686.

Einleitung zu der Historie der vornehmsten Reiche und Staaten so itziger Zeit in Europa sich befinden. (*Introduction to the Principal Empires and States Presently Existing in Europe*), 1682–1686.

Commentariorum de rebus Suecicis libri XXVI ab expeditione Gustavi Adolphi in Germaniam ad abdicationem usque Christinae. (*Commentaries on Swedish Affairs in Twenty-six Books from the Expedition of Gustavus Adolphus into Germany to the Abdication of Christina*), 1686.

De habitu religionis christianae ad vitam civilem. (*On the Relation of the Christian Religion to Civil Life*), 1687.

De rebus Friderici Wilhelmi Magni Electoris Brandenburgici commentariorum, libri XIX. (*On the Affairs of the Great Elector Frederick William of Brandenburg in Nineteen Books*), 1692.

Jus feciale divinum sive de consensu et dissensu protestantium. (*The Divine Law of Covenants, or On the Consensus and Dissensus among Protestants*), 1695.

De rebus a Carolo Gustavo Sueciae rege gestis commentariorum libri VII. (*Commentaries on the Affairs of King Charles Gustavus of Sweden in Seven Books*), 1696.

De rebus gestis Friderici III, Electoris Brandenburgici. (*On the Affairs of Frederick III, Elector of Brandenburg*), 1784.

II. Translations

Pufendorf, S., *Elements of Universal Jurisprudence*. Translated by William Abbott Oldfather. Oxford: The Clarendon Press, 1931. (Carnegie Endowment for International Peace, The Classics of International Law, series editor, James Brown Scott. Washington, D.C., No. 15.)

———, *The Law of Nature and Nations, Eight Books*. Translated by Basil Kennet. 4th ed. London: J. Walthoe et al., 1729. (Includes Jean Barbeyrac's notes and preface, "An Historical and Critical Account of the Science of Morality," that accompany his 1706 French translation of *De Jure Naturae et Gentium*.)

———, *On the Law of Nature and Nations, Eight Books*. Translated by C. W. and W. A. Oldfather. Oxford: The Clarendon Press, 1934. (Carnegie Endowment for International Peace, The Classics of International Law, series editor, James Brown Scott. Washington, D.C., No. 17.)

———, *The Two Books, On the Duty of Man and Citizen According to the Natural Law*. Translated by Frank Gardner Moore. New York: Oxford University Press, 1927. (Carnegie Endowment for International Peace, The Classics of International Law, series editor, James Brown Scott. Washington, D.C., No. 10.)

———, *On the Duty of Man and Citizen According to Natural Law*. Edited by James Tully, translated by Michael Silverthorne. Cambridge: Cambridge University Press, 1991.

———, *Die Verfassung des deutschen Reiches*. Translated and annotated by Horst Denzer. Stuttgart: Reclam, 1976.

Seidler, Michael, trans. *Samuel Pufendorf's "On the Natural State of Men."* Lewiston, NY: The Edwin Mellen Press, 1990.

III. Further Reading

Bodenheimer, Edgar. *Jurisprudence: The Philosophy and Method of the Law*. Cambridge, MA: Harvard University Press, 1967.

De Jouvenel, Bertrand. *Sovereignty: An Inquiry into the Political Good*. Translated by J. F. Huntington. Chicago: University of Chicago Press, 1957.

Denzer, Horst. *Moralphilosophie und Naturrecht bei Samuel Pufendorf: Eine geistes- und wissenschaftsgeschichtliche Untersuchung*. Aalen: Scientia Verlag, 1972.

———. "Pufendorf." In *Klassiker des politischen Denkens*, 2 vols., edited by Hans Maier, Heinz Rausch, and Horst Denzer, vol. 1, 27–52. Munich: C. H. Beck, 1968.

Döring, Detlef. *Pufendorf-Studien. Beiträge zur Biographie Samuel von Pufendorfs und zu seiner Entwicklung als Historiker und theologischer Schriftsteller.* Berlin: Duncker and Humblot, 1992.

Dufour, Alfred. "Pufendorf." In *The Cambridge History of Political Thought, 1450–1700*, edited by J. H. Burns and Mark Goldie, 561–588. New York: Cambridge University Press, 1991.

Finnis, John. *Natural Law and Natural Rights*. Oxford: The Clarendon Press, 1980.

Gierke, Otto. *Natural Law and the Theory of Society, 1500 to 1800*. Translated with an introduction by Ernest Barker. Boston: Beacon Press, 1957.

Goyard-Fabré, Simone. "Pufendorf, adversaire de Hobbes." *Hobbes Studies* 2 (1989): 65–86.

Haakonssen, Knud. "Hugo Grotius and the History of Political Thought." *Political Theory* 13 (May 1985): 239–265.

———. "Natural Law and Moral Realism: The Scottish Synthesis." In *Studies in the Philosophy of the Scottish Enlightenment*, edited by M. A. Stewart, 61–85. Oxford: The Clarendon Press, 1990.

Hochstrasser, Timothy. "The Foundations of the History of Morality: Samuel von Pufendorf and the Invention of a Tradition." Written for the Workshop on Modern Natural Law, convened by Istvan Hont and Hans Erich Bodeker, Max Planck Institute for History, Göttingen, Germany, June 26–30, 1989.

Hont, Istvan. "The Language of Sociability and Commerce: Samuel Pufendorf and the Theoretical Foundations of the 'Four Stages' Theory." In *The Language of Political Theory in Early-Modern Europe*, edited by Anthony Pagden, 253–276. Cambridge: Cambridge University Press, 1987.

Kirk, Linda. *Richard Cumberland and Natural Law: Secularization of Thought in 17th-Century England*. Cambridge: James Clarke & Co., 1987.

Krieger, Leonard. "History and Law in the Seventeenth Century: Pufendorf." *Journal of the History of Ideas* 21 (1960): 198–210.

———. *The Politics of Discretion: Pufendorf and the Acceptance of Natural Law*. Chicago: University of Chicago Press, 1965.

Larmore, Charles "Political Liberalism." *Political Theory* 18 (August 1990): 339–360.

Meinecke, Friedrich. *Die Idee der Staatsräson in der neueren Geschichte*. 2nd ed. Munich: R. Oldenbourg, 1925.

Nutkiewic, Michael. "Samuel Pufendorf: Obligation as the Basis of the State." *Journal of the History of Philosophy* 21 (1983): 15–29.

Palladini, Fiammetta. *Discussioni seicentesche su Samuel Pufendorf: scritti latini 1663–1700*. Bologna: Il Mulino, 1978.

———. *Samuel Pufendorf discepolo di Hobbes: Per una reinterpretazione del giusnaturalismo moderno*. Bologna: Il Mulino, 1990.

Rabe, Horst. *Naturrecht und Kirche bei Samuel von Pufendorf*. Köln: Böhlau, 1958.

Schneewind, J. B., ed. "The Misfortunes of Virtue." *Ethics* 101 (October 1990): 42–63.

———. *Moral Philosophy from Montaigne to Kant*, vol. 1. Cambridge: Cambridge University Press, 1990.

———. "Pufendorf's Place in the History of Ethics." *Synthese* 72 (1987): 123–155.

Seidler, Michael J. "Pufendorf, Samuel, Freiherr von (1632–1694)." In *The Garland Encyclopedia of Ethics*. 2 vols., edited by Lawrence Becker and Charlotte Becker, vol. 2, 1051–52. New York & London: Garland Publishing, Inc., 1992.

———. "Religion, Populism, and Patriarchy: Political Authority from Luther to Pufendorf." *Ethics* 103 (April 1993): 551–69 .

Tuck, Richard. "Grotius and Pufendorf." Written for the Workshop on Modern Natural Law, convened by Istvan Hont and Hans Erich Bodeker, Max Planck Institute for History, Göttingen, Germany, June 26–30, 1989.

———. "The Modern Theory of Natural Law." In *The Languages of Political Theory in Early Modern Europe*, edited by Anthony Pagden, 99–119. Cambridge: Cambridge University Press, 1987.

———. *Natural Rights Theories: Their Origin and Development*. Cambridge: Cambridge University Press, 1979.

Welzel, Hans. *Die Naturrechtslehre Samuel Pufendorfs: Ein Beitrag zur Ideengeschichte des 17. und 18. Jahrhunderts*. Berlin: Walter de Gruyter, 1958.

———. *Die Socialitas als oberstes Prinzip der Naturrechtslehre Samuel Pufendorfs*. Heidelberg: Hermann Meister, 1930.

Wolf, Erik. *Grosse Rechtsdenker der deutschen Geistesgeschichte*. 4th ed. Tübingen: J. C. B. Mohr, 1963.

———. *Grotius, Pufendorf, Thomasius*. Tübingen: J. C. B. Mohr, 1927.

Zurbuchen, Simone. *Naturrecht und natürliche Religion: Zur Geschichte des Toleranzbegriffs von Samuel Pufendorf bis Jean-Jacques Rousseau*. Würzburg: Königshausen & Neumann, 1991.

Index